Teach Yourself®
Microsoft®
Excel 2000

Teach Yourself®
Microsoft®
Excel 2000

Dennis P. Taylor

IDG Books Worldwide, Inc.
An International Data Group Company

IDG BOOKS

Foster City, CA • Chicago, IL • Indianapolis, IN • New York, NY

Teach Yourself® Microsoft® Excel 2000

Published by

IDG Books Worldwide, Inc.

An International Data Group Company

919 E. Hillsdale Blvd., Suite 400

Foster City, CA 94404

www.idgbooks.com (IDG Books Worldwide Web site)

ISBN: 0-7645-3285-5

Printed in the United States of America

10 9 8 7 6 5 4 3 2 1

1P/SY/QU/ZZ/IN

Distributed in the United States by IDG Books Worldwide, Inc.

Norma de Panama S.A. for Panama; by American Bookshops for Finland. Authorized Sales Agent: Anthony Rudkin Associates for the Middle East and North Africa.

For general information on IDG Books Worldwide's books in the U.S., please call our Consumer Customer Service department at 800-762-2974. For reseller information, including discounts and premium sales, please call our Reseller Customer Service department at 800-434-3422.

For information on where to purchase IDG Books Worldwide's books outside the U.S., please contact our International Sales department at 317-596-5530 or fax 317-596-5692.

For consumer information on foreign language translations, please contact our Customer Service department at 800-434-3422, fax 317-596-5692, or e-mail rights@idgbooks.com.

For information on licensing foreign or domestic rights, please phone +1-650-655-3109.

For sales inquiries and special prices for bulk quantities, please contact our Sales department at 650-655-3200 or write to the address above.

For information on using IDG Books Worldwide's books in the classroom or for ordering examination copies, please contact our Educational Sales department at 800-434-2086 or fax 317-596-5499.

For press review copies, author interviews, or other publicity information, please contact our Public Relations department at 650-655-3000 or fax 650-655-3299.

For authorization to photocopy items for corporate, personal, or educational use, please contact Copyright Clearance Center, 222 Rosewood Drive, Danvers, MA 01923, or fax 978-750-4470.

Distributed by CDG Books Canada Inc. for Canada; by Transworld Publishers Limited in the United Kingdom; by IDG Norge Books for Norway; by IDG Sweden Books for Sweden; by IDG Books Australia Publishing Corporation Pty. Ltd. for Australia and New Zealand; by TransQuest Publishers Pte Ltd. for Singapore, Malaysia, Thailand, Indonesia, and Hong Kong; by Gotop Information Inc. for Taiwan; by ICG Muse, Inc. for Japan; by Norma Comunicaciones S.A. for Colombia; by Intersoft for South Africa; by Le Monde en Tique for France; by International Thomson Publishing for Germany, Austria and Switzerland; by Distribuidora Cuspide for Argentina; by Livraria Cultura for Brazil; by Ediciones ZETA S.C.R. Ltda. for Peru; by WS Computer Publishing Corporation, Inc., for the Philippines; by Contemporanea de Ediciones for Venezuela; by Express Computer Distributors for the Caribbean and West Indies; by Micronesia Media Distributor, Inc. for Micronesia; by Grupo Editorial Norma S.A. for Guatemala; by Chips Computadoras S.A. de C.V. for Mexico; by Editorial Norma de Panama S.A. for Panama; by American Bookshops for Finland. Authorized Sales Agent: Anthony Rudkin Associates for the Middle East and North Africa.

Library of Congress Cataloging-in-Publication Data

Taylor, Dennis P.

Teach Yourself Microsoft Excel 2000 / Dennis P. Taylor.

p.   cm.

Includes index.

ISBN 0-7645-3285-5 (alk. paper)

1. Microsoft Excel for Windows.   2. Business—Computer Programs.

3. Electronic spreadsheets   I. Title.

HF5548.4.M523W456 1999

005.369--dc21   99–10979

                                                                            CIP

is a registered trademark or trademark under exclusive license to IDG Books Worldwide, Inc., from International Data Group, Inc. in the United States and/or other countries.

ABOUT IDG BOOKS WORLDWIDE

Welcome to the world of IDG Books Worldwide.

IDG Books Worldwide, Inc., is a subsidiary of International Data Group, the world's largest publisher of computer-related information and the leading global provider of information services on information technology. IDG was founded more than 30 years ago by Patrick J. McGovern and now employs more than 9,000 people worldwide. IDG publishes more than 290 computer publications in over 75 countries. More than 90 million people read one or more IDG publications each month.

Launched in 1990, IDG Books Worldwide is today the #1 publisher of best-selling computer books in the United States. We are proud to have received eight awards from the Computer Press Association in recognition of editorial excellence and three from Computer Currents' First Annual Readers' Choice Awards. Our best-selling ...*For Dummies*® series has more than 50 million copies in print with translations in 31 languages. IDG Books Worldwide, through a joint venture with IDG's Hi-Tech Beijing, became the first U.S. publisher to publish a computer book in the People's Republic of China. In record time, IDG Books Worldwide has become the first choice for millions of readers around the world who want to learn how to better manage their businesses.

Our mission is simple: Every one of our books is designed to bring extra value and skill-building instructions to the reader. Our books are written by experts who understand and care about our readers. The knowledge base of our editorial staff comes from years of experience in publishing, education, and journalism — experience we use to produce books to carry us into the new millennium. In short, we care about books, so we attract the best people. We devote special attention to details such as audience, interior design, use of icons, and illustrations. And because we use an efficient process of authoring, editing, and desktop publishing our books electronically, we can spend more time ensuring superior content and less time on the technicalities of making books.

You can count on our commitment to deliver high-quality books at competitive prices on topics you want to read about. At IDG Books Worldwide, we continue in the IDG tradition of delivering quality for more than 30 years. You'll find no better book on a subject than one from IDG Books Worldwide.

John Kilcullen
Chairman and CEO
IDG Books Worldwide, Inc.

Steven Berkowitz
President and Publisher
IDG Books Worldwide, Inc.

Eighth Annual
Computer Press
Awards ⪴1992

Ninth Annual
Computer Press
Awards ⪴1993

Tenth Annual
Computer Press
Awards ⪴1994

Eleventh Annual
Computer Press
Awards ⪴1995

Credits

Acquisitions Editor
Andy Cummings

Development Editors
Valerie Perry
Philip Wescott

Technical Editor
Dennis R. Cohen

Copy Editor
Zoe Brymer

Project Coordinator
E. Shawn Aylsworth

Book Designers
Daniel Ziegler Design
Cátálin Dulfu
Kurt Krames

Graphics and Production Specialists
Brent Savage
Janet Seib
Michael A. Sullivan
Brian Torwelle

Proofreaders
Christine Berman, Robert Springer,
Janet M. Withers, York Graphic
Services

Indexer
York Graphic Services

About the Author

Dennis P. Taylor has been involved in various forms of computer education for nearly 20 years. Initially teaching programming languages COBOL and BASIC, he branched into presenting orientation classes to early users of personal computers. As a consultant and teacher focused on business users, he has presented over 2,000 seminars and classes in a variety of computer topics, primarily in the area of desktop software.

His clients have included Amoco Oil, IBM, Amgen, US West, Lexmark, Levi Strauss, Texaco, StorageTek, the federal government, and the state of Colorado. Specializing in spreadsheet software, Dennis coauthored five books on Lotus 1-2-3 in the late 1980s and early 1990s. He has written and presented over a dozen videos and CDs on various versions of Microsoft Excel, including Excel 2000, for Keystone Learning Systems.

Dennis lives in Boulder, Colorado, and is an avid listener of classical music, especially opera, and spends far too much time reading maps and almanacs, solving math and crossword puzzles, and playing word games. He welcomes comments and suggestions at *dennistaylor@msn.com*.

To MA, L, & L

Welcome to
Teach Yourself

Welcome to Teach Yourself, a series read and trusted by millions for nearly a decade. Although you may have seen the Teach Yourself name on other books, ours is the original. In addition, no Teach Yourself series has ever delivered more on the promise of its name than this series. That's because IDG Books Worldwide recently transformed Teach Yourself into a new cutting-edge format that gives you all the information you need to learn quickly and easily.

Readers told us that they want to learn by doing and that they want to learn as much as they can in as short a time as possible. We listened to you and believe that our new task-by-task format and suite of learning tools deliver the book you need to successfully teach yourself any technology topic. Features such as our Personal Workbook, which lets you practice and reinforce the skills you've just learned, help ensure that you get full value out of the time you invest in your learning. Handy cross-references to related topics and online sites broaden your knowledge and give you control over the kind of information you want, when you want it.

More Answers ...

In designing the latest incarnation of this series, we started with the premise that people like you, who are beginning to intermediate computer users, want to take control of your own learning. To do this, you need the proper tools to find answers to questions so you can solve problems now.

In designing a series of books that provide such tools, we created a unique and concise visual format. The added bonus: Teach Yourself books pack more information into their pages than other books written on the same subjects. Skill for skill, you typically get much more information in a Teach Yourself book. In fact, Teach Yourself books, on average, cover twice the skills covered by other computer books — as many as 125 skills per book — so they're more likely to address your specific needs.

...In Less Time

We know you don't want to spend twice the time to get all this great information, so we provide lots of time-saving features:

▶ A modular task-by-task organization of information: Any task you want to perform is easy to find and includes simple-to-follow steps.

▶ A larger size than standard makes the book easy to read and convenient to use at a computer workstation. The large format also enables us to include many more illustrations — 500 screen illustrations show you how to get everything done!

▶ A Personal Workbook at the end of each chapter reinforces learning with extra practice, real-world applications for your learning, and questions and answers to test your knowledge.

▶ Cross-references appearing at the bottom of each task page refer you to related information, providing a path through the book for learning particular aspects of the software thoroughly.

▶ A Find It Online feature offers valuable ideas on where to go on the Internet to get more information or to download useful files.

▶ Take Note sidebars provide added-value information from our expert authors for more in-depth learning.

▶ An attractive, consistent organization of information helps you quickly find and learn the skills you need.

These Teach Yourself features are designed to help you learn the essential skills about a technology in the least amount of time, with the most benefit. We've placed these features consistently throughout the book, so you quickly learn where to go to find just the information you need — whether you work through the book from cover to cover or use it later to solve a new problem.

You will find a Teach Yourself book on almost any technology subject — from the Internet to Windows to Microsoft Office. Take control of your learning today, with IDG Books Worldwide's Teach Yourself series.

Teach Yourself
More Answers in Less Time

Go to this area if you want special tips, cautions, and notes that provide added insight into the current task.

Search through the task headings to find the topic you want right away. To learn a new skill, search the contents, chapter opener, or the extensive index to find what you need. Then find — at a glance — the clear task heading that matches it.

Editing Cells

You're probably not error-prone, but you will often need to change the contents of cells, whether they contain text, numbers, formulas, or functions. Usually, the process isn't very complicated. If a cell entry isn't very long, but you want to change part of it, there's no need to do any editing. Simply select the cell, type the correct entry and press Enter. The process of editing, whereby you alter just part of a cell, is straightforward and something you can achieve in a number of different ways in Excel. Normally, you edit one cell at a time, but you can select a number of different cells, edit the active cell, and, upon completion, effectively change all those selected cells at once.

You can start editing in at least three different ways, but the results are all the same. While editing a cell, a red X and a green check appear on the left side of the formula bar; these not only remind you that you're in "edit mode" but give you mouse methods for escaping from, or completing, editing. Also, while you're editing, the word Edit appears in the status bar at the bottom of the screen.

Don't forget those keystroke shortcuts that seem to work nearly everywhere in the Windows environment — use Ctrl+C to copy, Ctrl+X to cut, and Ctrl+V to paste. They're particularly handy during editing because you can copy or cut information from the cell that you're editing and later paste it into another cell.

Learn the concepts behind the task at hand and, more important, learn how the task is relevant in the real world. Time-saving suggestions and advice show you how to make the most of each skill.

If you'd like to edit a group of cells at once so that they will all have the same content, select the cells and then either press the F2 key or click in the formula bar. After making all of the changes you want to make, press Ctrl+Enter.

TAKE NOTE

MOVING THE EDITING CURSOR
Press the Home or End key to move the editing cursor to the beginning or the end of the cell. Use the Ctrl key along with the left or right arrow key to move the editing cursor a word at a time in text cells.

SELECTION WHILE EDITING
Press Shift+Ctrl+Home to select all text from the editing cursor to the beginning of the cell. Press Shift+Ctrl+End to select all text from the editing cursor to the end of the cell. Double-click a word to select it.

DELETING WHILE EDITING
Press the Backspace key to delete a character to the left of the editing cursor, or the Delete key to delete a character to the right of the editing cursor. Press Ctrl+Delete to delete all text from the editing cursor to the end of the cell.

After you learn the task at hand, you may have more questions, or you may want to read about other tasks related to the topic. Use the cross-references to find different tasks to make your learning more efficient.

CROSS-REFERENCE
See Chapter 3 for more details on how you can use formatting tools on portions of selected text.

FIND IT ONLINE
If you're interested in editing, look into The Electric Editors homepage at www.ikingston.demon.co.uk/ee/home.htm.

Use the Find It Online element to locate Internet resources that provide more background, take you on interesting side trips, and offer additional tools for mastering and using the skills you need. (Occasionally you'll find a handy shortcut here.)

WELCOME TO TEACH YOURSELF

The current chapter name and number always appear in the top right-hand corner of every task spread, so you always know exactly where you are in the book.

BASIC WORKSHEET CREATION
Editing Cells

CHAPTER 2

① To alter a cell with a short entry, select the cell, type the new content, and then press Enter. There is no need to erase the cell.

② To start editing a cell at a specific point, double-click the cell at that point in the cell.

③ Click in the formula bar to activate editing for a selected cell.

④ When editing a cell, select a word by double-clicking it.
⑤ Apply formats using the formatting buttons or the Format ⇨ Cells command.

35

Who This Book Is For

This book is written for you, a beginning to intermediate PC user who isn't afraid to take charge of his or her own learning experience. You don't want a lot of technical jargon; you *do* want to learn as much about PC technology as you can in a limited amount of time. You need a book that is straightforward, easy to follow, and logically organized, so you can find answers to your questions easily. And, you appreciate simple-to-use tools such as handy cross-references and visual step-by-step procedures that help you make the most of your learning. We have created the unique Teach Yourself format specifically to meet your needs.

Ultimately, people learn by doing. Follow the clear, illustrated steps on the right-hand page of every task to complete a procedure. The detailed callouts for each step show you exactly where to go and what to do to complete the task.

Personal Workbook

It's a well-known fact that much of what we learn is lost soon after we learn it if we don't reinforce our newly acquired skills with practice and repetition. That's why each Teach Yourself chapter ends with your own Personal Workbook. Here's where you can get extra practice, test your knowledge, and discover ideas for using what you've learned in the real world. There's even a Visual Quiz to help you remember your way around the topic's software environment.

Feedback

Please let us know what you think about this book, and whether you have any suggestions for improvements. You can send questions and comments to the Teach Yourself editors on the IDG Books Worldwide Web site at **www.idgbooks.com**.

> ## Personal Workbook
>
> **Q&A**
>
> ❶ Will a date entry typed as 11/31/99 appear left- or right-aligned in a cell?
>
> _____
> _____
> _____
>
> ❷ Describe three ways in which to select a range of cells.
>
> _____
> _____
> _____
>
> ❸ How would you create a series of text entries for each month in the second half of the year?
>
> _____
> _____
> _____
>
> ❹ What keystroke combination can you use to make a cell entry when you want to select from a list of previous entries?
>
> _____
> _____
> _____
>
> ❺ True or False: When you use the AutoSum tool, you can't edit the function it creates.
>
> _____
> _____
> _____
>
> ❻ True or False: When you write a formula without parentheses, Excel performs all calculations from left to right.
>
> _____
> _____
> _____
>
> ❼ What keystroke combination can you use to display the range names you need when writing a formula?
>
> _____
> _____
> _____
>
> ❽ True or False: You can edit a cell that contains text, a number, a formula, a date, or a function.
>
> _____
> _____
> _____
>
> ANSWERS: 322
>
> 38

After working through the tasks in each chapter, you can test your progress and reinforce your learning by answering the questions in the Q&A section. Then check your answers in the Personal Workbook Answers appendix at the back of the book.

Another practical way to reinforce your skills is to do additional exercises on the same skills you just learned without the benefit of the chapter's visual steps. If you struggle with any of these exercises, it's a good idea to refer to the chapter's tasks to be sure you've mastered them.

BASIC WORKSHEET CREATION
Personal Workbook

CHAPTER
2

Read the list of Real-World Applications to get ideas on how you can use the skills you've just learned in your everyday life. Understanding a process can be simple; knowing how to use that process to make you more productive is the key to successful learning.

EXTRA PRACTICE

❶ A cell contains the text Fiscal Year 98 Expenses. Edit it to change 98 to 99.

❷ There are sales figures in six consecutive cells in a row. Using AutoSum, put a total in the cell just to the right of these entries.

❸ Put the word TOTAL in three separate locations on your worksheet but type it only once.

❹ After entering three different department names down a column, you realize the next few entries will simply be using these names again. Use the Alt+Enter keystroke combination to make these entries without typing.

❺ Write a formula that calculates a 10% increase over a 1998 salary amount located in cell B7.

REAL-WORLD APPLICATIONS

✔ In one of your large worksheets, you frequently need to jump to the summary totals in cell A95. You make cell A95 the active cell, press Ctrl+F3, type the name SUMMARY and press Enter. Thereafter, to go to cell A95, you press the F5 function key and double-click the word SUMMARY.

✔ Column B in you personnel worksheet contains division names. There are only five possible divisions. After at least one occurrence of each exists in Column B, future entries are easy. You press Alt+down arrow to activate the list of previous entries, use the arrow keys to select the appropriate entry and press Enter.

Visual Quiz

In the screen image to the right, you're trying to get a total in cell F5 that sums the cells B5 through E5, but after you clicked the AutoSum tool the function displayed added the cells F2 through F4. What can you do with the mouse to make AutoSum do what you want?

_____

_____

_____

_____

Take the Visual Quiz to see how well you're learning your way around the technology. Learning about computers is often as much about how to find a button or menu as it is about memorizing definitions. Our Visual Quiz helps you find your way.

Acknowledgments

Thanks to Andy Cummings at IDG Books Worldwide for perseverance and guidance in the early stages of this book, to Chip Wescott of IDG Books Worldwide for technical assistance and advice, and to technical editor Dennis Cohen for insightful comments, suggestions, and unusual attention to detail. Thanks also go to my literary agent Matt Wagner at Waterside Press and to others behind the scenes at IDG Books Worldwide who made this book a reality.

A special thanks to development editor Valerie Perry whose patience, advice, understanding, and calm assurance kept this book on an even keel and made this writer's task a simpler one.

Contents

CONTENTS

Contents

CONTENTS

CONTENTS

CONTENTS

PART

I

Getting Started with Excel 2000

As you approach using Excel for the first time, you will be concerned with getting comfortable with the look and feel of the software. You will want to learn some of the terminology used for standard Excel features so that using this book and the built-in help system will proceed more smoothly.

At first, your central objective may be simple and direct. To learn how to create a small worksheet that you can format in the way that you prefer. To be clear on how to preserve what you've created and to learn how to share your creations.

As you learn how to perform these tasks, you will appreciate how easy to use Excel actually is, and anticipate calling on it for greater capability.

With these building blocks in place, you can move on and expand your use of Excel to include more powerful features.

CHAPTER 1

MASTER
THESE
SKILLS

▶ **Starting Excel**

▶ **Identifying Screen Elements**

▶ **Using the Shortcut Menu**

▶ **Navigating Worksheets and Workbooks**

▶ **Using the Help Menu**

▶ **Exiting Excel**

Getting Familiar with Excel

As you start to use Microsoft Excel 2000 for the first time, it's worth noting that some of the basic features of this software package are very similar to those that you will find in other Office 2000 packages, such as Word, Power-Point, and Access. If you are familiar with any of those software packages, your path into Excel is eased by the fact that you will find similar menu commands, toolbar buttons, and shortcut keys. If you are unfamiliar with those packages, much of what you will learn about Excel will put you in good shape if you ever do need to learn any of the other Office 2000 components.

Excel 2000 comes with a coherent set of menu commands, an easy to use (and alter) group of toolbar buttons that makes it faster to get things done without menus, and an expanded Help menu.

In this section, you learn how to enter and exit Excel 2000 and to identify its major components. In addition to getting familiar with the structure of an Excel worksheet — its columns, rows, and cells — you learn about using multiple worksheets in a single Excel workbook. An Excel worksheet (often just called a sheet) is the basic building block of an Excel file. Initially, you might only need a single sheet to track your data, but later you may see the need for additional sheets to store data for different regions or different periods of time. You learn the simple steps of navigating not only around a single worksheet, but also from sheet to sheet within a workbook.

A wealth of options exists for navigating both with the mouse and the keyboard. You get a brief look at Excel's menu and learn how to get an abbreviated list of commands quickly with the handy shortcut menu. The shortcut menu serves a valuable purpose in providing you with a faster way to get to commands, and as a way to alert you to commands that you are not aware of or have forgotten about. As you learn some of Excel's navigation techniques, you will be able to move to any part of a worksheet or workbook more efficiently.

Starting Excel

If you have installed Excel 2000 on your computer from a CD or from diskettes, you will be able to start the software in a number of different ways. In Windows, the traditional way to start any application program is from the Windows Start button, on the left side of the taskbar when it's in the usual position at the bottom of your screen. If you have moved the taskbar to the left or right side of the screen, the Start button will be at the top of the taskbar.

Most of your applications, if installed according to the software publisher's directions, will be found in the Program category, selectable from the Start button. Installation options vary widely, so the name you're looking for could be Excel 2000, Excel, Microsoft Excel, Excel.exe, and so on.

If you are familiar with creating shortcuts in Windows 95/98, you may have created a shortcut to Excel so that it appears on the Windows desktop. This is handy much of the time, but if you're using another application and want to start Excel, you may need to minimize the application in order to see the Windows desktop. There's an easy way to see to it that Excel appears on the initial set of selections that you see when you click the Start button. If you set up a shortcut to Excel this way, you won't need to slide the mouse onto various submenus in order to find Excel.

TAKE NOTE

WHAT IF I CAN'T FIND THE START BUTTON?

If the Start button isn't visible on your screen, you probably turned on the taskbar's Auto Hide property. Press Ctrl+Esc to activate the taskbar and the Start button.

WHAT IF I CAN'T FIND EXCEL FROM THE START BUTTON?

If you're unable to find Excel from the Start button, you can use the Windows Find feature to locate the startup Excel file, which is named Excel.exe. Click the Start button, choose Find ➪ Files or Folders. In the Find dialog box, type Excel.exe and click the Find Now button. If Excel.exe is not found, Excel is not installed on your computer. If you find more than one of these files, those with older dates refer to previous versions of Excel. You want to use the one with the latest date. Double-click it to activate Excel 2000.

HOW DO I GET EXCEL TO APPEAR ON THE START BUTTON MENU?

If you'd like Excel to feature on the initial menu that appears when you click the Start button, use Windows Explorer or the Find procedure described in the previous note to locate the Excel.exe file. Next, simply drag the file directly to the Start button. The next time you click the Start button, Excel will be there.

CROSS-REFERENCE

See Chapter 17 for information on starting Excel from within other applications.

FIND IT ONLINE

For some tips about the taskbar, check out
http://www.geocities.com/~the_taskbar/.

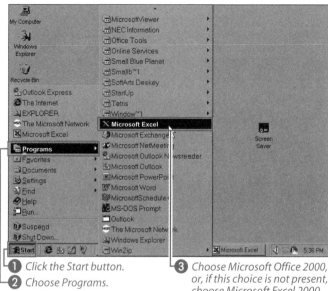

1 Click the Start button.

2 Choose Programs.

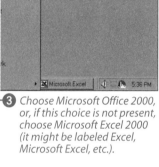

3 Choose Microsoft Office 2000, or, if this choice is not present, choose Microsoft Excel 2000 (it might be labeled Excel, Microsoft Excel, etc.).

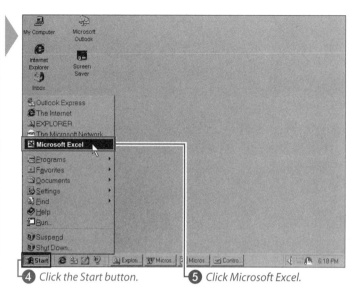

4 Click the Start button.

5 Click Microsoft Excel.

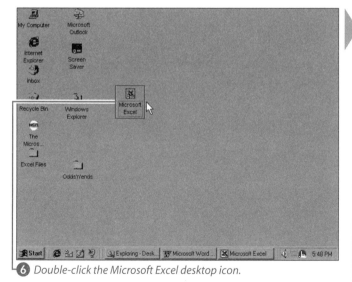

6 Double-click the Microsoft Excel desktop icon.

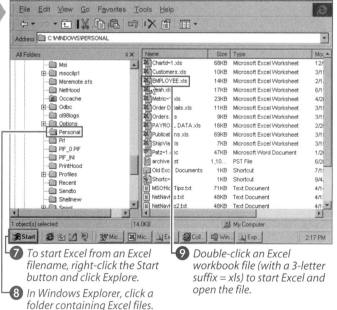

7 To start Excel from an Excel filename, right-click the Start button and click Explore.

8 In Windows Explorer, click a folder containing Excel files.

9 Double-click an Excel workbook file (with a 3-letter suffix = xls) to start Excel and open the file.

Identifying Screen Elements

As soon as you open Excel, you see an empty workbook, identified by the temporary name Book1 at the top of your screen in the title bar. The menu bar is just below the title bar. Click the menus such as File, Edit, View, and so on and you will see a series of drop-down menus. There are many commands in Excel, but most users don't use all of the commands on a regular basis. Different commands may have some of these features:

▶ **Grayed out text** means a command is not usable at this time.

▶ **Icons** located to the left of some commands are like those available on toolbars. You're being alerted to the fact that when you click one of these icons in a toolbar, it's like using the menu command sequence.

▶ **Keystroke shortcuts** to the right of commands are faster ways to activate those commands.

▶ **Triangular arrows** to the right of commands lead you to submenus.

▶ **Ellipses** (...) to the right of commands mean that the commands lead you to further choices in the form of a pop-up window called a dialog box.

Beneath the menu bar, you'll find the Standard toolbar, which contains a number of file-related buttons. The Formatting toolbar contains tools related to the visual aspects of a worksheet — font selection, alignment, numerical formats, indenting, border styles, color background, and text color. In general, each button gives you a faster way of using one of the commands.

In the center of your screen is a worksheet that's composed of 256 columns and 65,536 rows. Each rectangular position in this grid is a cell and is identified by an address — a combination of its column letter(s) and row number. Although there can be many sheets in a workbook, when you create a new workbook, there are seven worksheets in it.

Worksheet tabs, initially labeled Sheet1, Sheet2, and so on, are at the bottom of the worksheet. You can click a sheet name to make that sheet active. Four navigation arrows to the left of the sheet tabs let you see names of additional sheets or move the list of sheet names to the left or right.

The status bar, below the sheet tabs, alerts you to data entry status (Ready, Edit), prompts you during the use of some commands, and displays error messages. If cells with values are selected, an AutoCalculate feature displays a total or other statistical measure (average, standard deviation, etc.).

TAKE NOTE

▶ **KEEP TOOL TIPS PRESENT**

Even experienced Excel users are fond of those pop-up tool tips that appear when you point to a toolbar button. If they're not there, click View ⇨ Toolbars ⇨ Customize. In the Toolbars dialog box, click the Options tab and check the box next to Show screen tips on toolbars.

CROSS-REFERENCE
See Chapter 9 for details on multiple-sheet workbooks.

FIND IT ONLINE
Interested in learning more about powers of 2 (like 256 and 65,536)? Check out www.geocities.com/SoHo/Studios/1831/power.html.

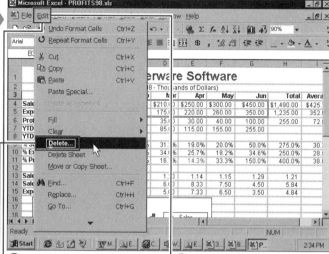

① After starting Excel, you see the empty workbook named Book1 in the title bar.

② The menu bar contains various commands, such as File, Edit, and so on.

③ The Standard and Formatting toolbars contain buttons to get to commands fast.

④ Hover the cursor over a button to find out what it does.

⑤ Click a command to get a list of choices.

⑥ Click the command that you want to use.

⑦ You can press the Esc key (or click the command again) if you decide not to use the command.

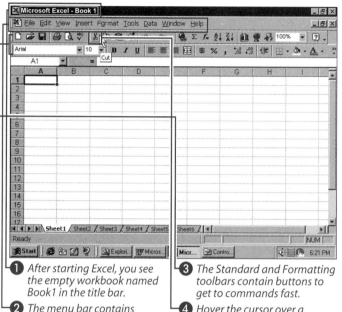

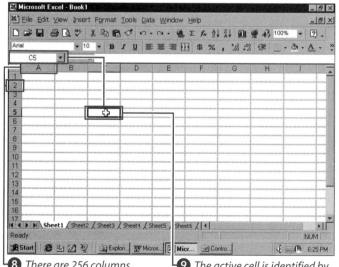

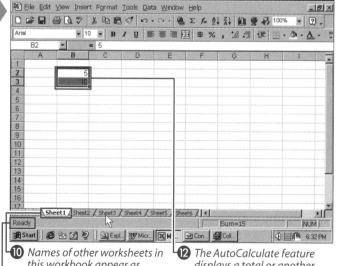

⑧ There are 256 columns, identified by letters and 65,536 rows, identified by numbers.

⑨ The active cell is identified by a thick border. Its address is in the formula bar.

⑩ Names of other worksheets in this workbook appear as sheet tabs.

⑪ Words appear in the status bar to describe the status of your worksheet.

⑫ The AutoCalculate feature displays a total or another statistical measure of the selected cells.

Using the Shortcut Menu

There are so many commands available from the main menu that it can take time to locate one that you need. The shortcut menu gives you a quick look at an abbreviated list of commands and is also context-sensitive — you get a different set of commands in the menu depending on where the mouse is pointing. You can use shortcut menus throughout the Windows environment, particularly in all of the Office 2000 software packages — Word, PowerPoint, Access, and so on. A visual characteristic of most shortcut menus is that they are divided into sections separated by horizontal lines. These sections group commands by their location on the main menu.

You can activate the shortcut menu almost anywhere on the Excel screen by clicking the right mouse button. You can then select the command you need using either mouse button. When you activate the shortcut menu on the menu bar or on a toolbar, you get a list of all toolbars. Those toolbars that are currently visible are identified by a button with a sunken appearance and a check mark; those not currently in use appear flat and unchecked.

You get different menu selections when you activate the shortcut menu from a worksheet cell compared with activating it from a column letter or row number. You can insert, delete, and hide columns and rows faster with the shortcut menu than you can if you use the main menu or the toolbar buttons.

Activate the shortcut menu on the navigation arrows that are located to the left of the worksheet tabs at the bottom of your screen and you will see a vertical list of worksheet names.

Activate the shortcut menu in the status bar just below the worksheet tabs to see a list of functions. If you select one of these, the next time you select (highlight) one or more cells you will see a sum, average, and so on of the numbers in those cells.

When you explore Excel's charting capability in Part III, you will see a variety of shortcut menus as you click on different chart locations.

TAKE NOTE

YOU CAN'T FIND EVERYTHING ON A SHORTCUT MENU

Remember that the shortcut menu is not comprehensive. There will be times when the command that you want does not appear on the shortcut menu. You'll need to explore the menu bar further to find the command you need. Although you can customize the toolbars and the menu bar, there is no way for you to control the contents of a shortcut menu.

USE THE SHORTCUT MENU TO EXPLORE

Besides using the shortcut menu to reach context-sensitive commands, you can use it as a tool for exploring. When working with charts, or printing, activate the shortcut menu and you may see some commands that you haven't seen before.

CROSS-REFERENCE

See Chapter 6 for details on using the shortcut menu to insert, delete, and hide rows and columns.

FIND IT ONLINE

If you come across an acronym that you don't understand, check out **http//www.mtnds.com/af/**.

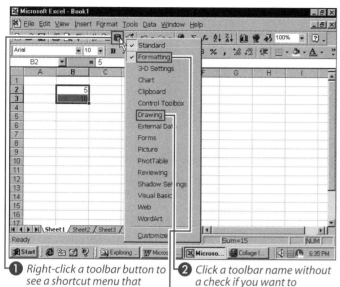

1 Right-click a toolbar button to see a shortcut menu that shows names of other toolbars.

2 Click a toolbar name without a check if you want to activate that toolbar.

3 Click a toolbar name with a check if you want to deactivate that toolbar.

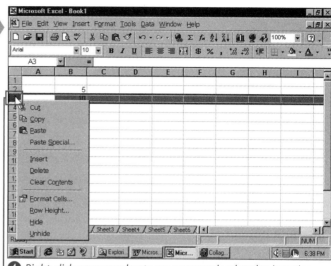

4 Right-click a row number to see commands related to inserting, deleting, and hiding a row.

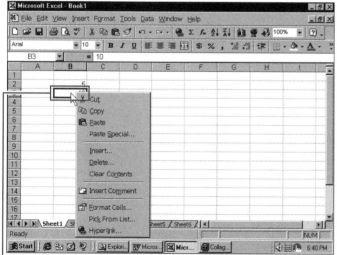

5 Right-click a cell to see commands related to editing and manipulating cells. If you right-click a cell while pointing to the fill handle or an edge, the shortcut menu won't appear. Make sure you point inside the cell and right-click.

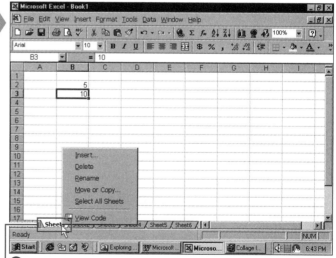

6 Right-click a sheet tab to see commands related to sheet manipulation and macro coding.

Navigating Worksheets and Workbooks

When you enter Excel, you will see the phrase Microsoft Excel — Book1 in the title bar at the top of the screen. The word book, shortened from workbook, emphasizes the idea that an Excel file is a workbook — a book that contains worksheets. Think of a worksheet as a single sheet of paper and a workbook as a number of worksheets. You can store information in one or many worksheets. To gain a better understanding of worksheets and workbooks, you need to become familiar with a few techniques that let you move freely and easily between different workbooks and throughout a given worksheet.

By default, when you enter Excel, or create a new workbook, the workbook will have three sheets in it. Think of worksheets as being stacked on top of each other — Sheet1 on top, followed by Sheet2, Sheet3, and so on. The number of worksheets in your workbook is limited only by the amount of Random Access Memory (RAM) on your computer.

To jump to another worksheet in your workbook, click a different sheet tab at the bottom of the screen. When you have many worksheets, use the navigation arrows to the left of the sheet tabs.

At any given time, there is always one cell that is called the active cell. It's identified by a thicker border and you can see its address on the left side of the formula bar, just above the row numbers. Always keep an eye on the active cell as you switch screen views and jump between worksheets. Whenever you type, the information goes into the active cell.

TAKE NOTE

▶ SCROLL BARS

The vertical scroll bar on the right side of the worksheet and the horizontal scroll bar at the bottom of the worksheet, enable you to move quickly to parts of the screen that are not currently visible. The arrows at either end of the scroll bars and the box, located between the arrows, let you reposition your view of the screen. The scroll box becomes smaller as you utilize more rows in your worksheet.

▶ SETTING A DEFAULT WORKBOOK SIZE

After using Excel for a time, you may want most of your new workbooks to have a specific number of worksheets. You can change the default setting from three to another number (see the lower-right corner of the opposite page). This setting only pertains to new workbooks created thereafter, not current ones.

▶ SCROLL BARS AND THE ACTIVE CELL ARE NOT IN SYNC

When you use scroll bars to see a different part of your worksheet, the location of the active cell remains unchanged. If you make an entry before clicking in the area you scrolled to, whatever you type appears in the active cell.

CROSS-REFERENCE

See Chapter 9 for more information on working with multiple sheet workbooks.

FIND IT ONLINE

Check out **http://www.browserwatch.internet.com/** to learn more about navigating the Web.

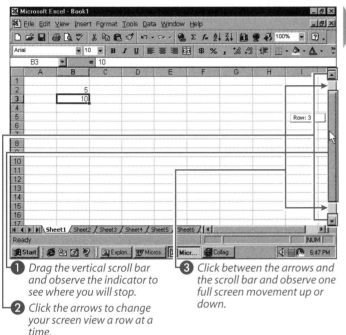

① *Drag the vertical scroll bar and observe the indicator to see where you will stop.*

② *Click the arrows to change your screen view a row at a time.*

③ *Click between the arrows and the scroll bar and observe one full screen movement up or down.*

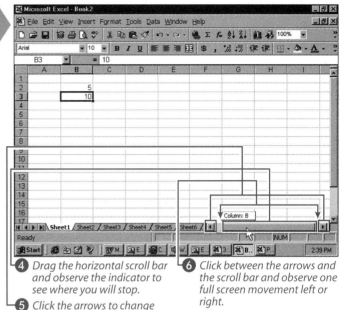

④ *Drag the horizontal scroll bar and observe the indicator to see where you will stop.*

⑤ *Click the arrows to change your screen view a column at a time.*

⑥ *Click between the arrows and the scroll bar and observe one full screen movement left or right.*

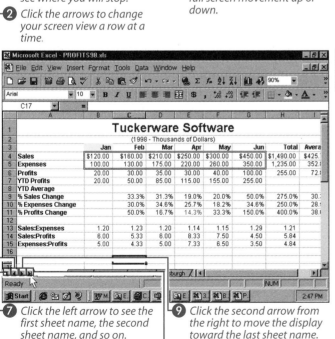

⑦ *Click the left arrow to see the first sheet name, the second sheet name, and so on.*

⑧ *Click the second arrow from the left to move the display toward the first sheet name.*

⑨ *Click the second arrow from the right to move the display toward the last sheet name.*

⑩ *Click the right arrow to see the last sheet name, the second last sheet name, and so on.*

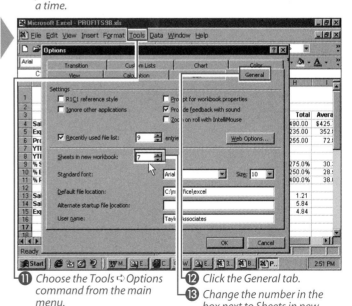

⑪ *Choose the Tools ⇨ Options command from the main menu.*

⑫ *Click the General tab.*

⑬ *Change the number in the box next to Sheets in new workbook.*

Navigating Worksheets and Workbooks *Continued*

Navigation from the Keyboard

Since your hands are often on the keyboard typing entries and changes, it's handy to use the keyboard to navigate to other locations. Some of the more frequently used keys are explained below:

Keys	Action
Arrow keys	Use the up, down, left, or right arrow (located together in their own keypad cluster on many keyboards) to quickly move the active cell in any direction. Movement occurs rapidly if you hold down any of these keys.
Ctrl+Home	Return the active cell to the A1 cell location.
Ctrl+End or End, Home	Move the active cell and screen display to the lower-right corner of the worksheet. You can be sure that there is no data in any column to the right or in any row below this location.
Page Dn	Move the active cell down one full screen.
Page Up	Move the active cell up one full screen.
Home	Move the active cell to Column A in the same row.
Ctrl+Backspace	Redisplay the screen so that the active cell is visible.
Ctrl+Page Dn	Move the active cell down to the next worksheet in this workbook.
Ctrl+Page Up	Move the active cell up to the previous worksheet in this workbook.
Ctrl+Tab or Ctrl+F6	Switch to the next workbook among those currently open.
F5 or Ctrl+G	Activate the Go To dialog box. Type an address and press enter to move the active cell to another location. Most useful when you want to move the active cell a great distance — dragging the mouse or using arrow keys can be time-consuming or unwieldy.

TAKE NOTE

> #### USE THE SCROLL LOCK KEY TO SCROLL WITH THE KEYBOARD
>
> Every time you press the Scroll Lock key, you toggle back and forth between the ability to scroll (or not to scroll) from the keyboard. With Scroll Lock on, you can use the arrow keys to move your screen display in different directions, without changing the location of the active cell, just as if you were using one of the scroll bars with the mouse. With this feature turned on, you can still scroll with the mouse.

CROSS-REFERENCE

See Chapter 9 for details on entering data and formulas on multiple worksheets.

FIND IT ONLINE

Need navigation tips on your palmtop PC? Check out http://www.palmsizepc.com/june8-1.html.

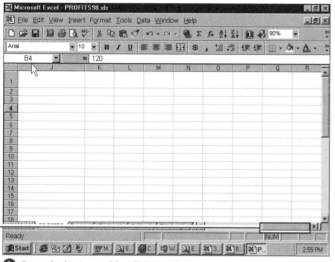

① Drag the horizontal Scroll Bar so that the active cell is not visible on the screen. Press Ctrl+Backspace to redisplay the screen so that it includes the active cell.

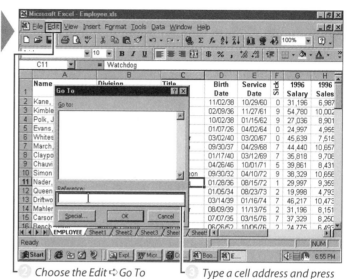

② Choose the Edit ⇨ Go To command from the main menu to display the Go To dialog box.

③ Type a cell address and press Enter.

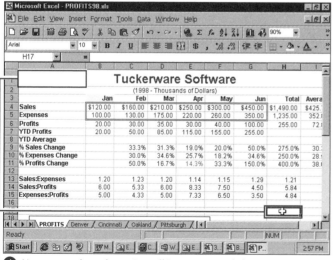

④ No matter where the active cell is on your worksheet, press Ctrl+Home to return to the upper-left corner — cell A1.

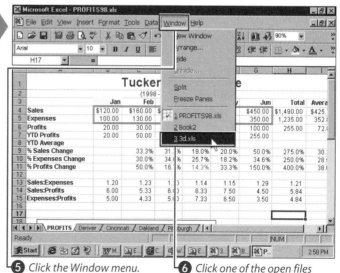

⑤ Click the Window menu.

⑥ Click one of the open files listed at the bottom of the selection to make that file the current workbook

Using the Help Menu

When you need help using Excel, you often want it immediately. The revised Excel Help system gives you an extensive body of Help screens, accessible at almost any time, even in the midst of a procedure or action.

Generally, using Help is an intuitive process. Whenever you need help, you can get to it from the Help menu by selecting Microsoft Excel Help. You can use Help's Contents tab to see a list of major topics, not unlike the table of contents that you see at the beginning of a textbook. You can also type a question using a feature known as the Answer Wizard. Or, use the Index tab that lets you look up topics as you do in the index of a textbook — alphabetically. As you explore the Help system, you will encounter screens that may contain information that you'd like to print. You can copy information from the Help system and paste it into a document in Word and you can print the current Help screen.

If you need information on a menu command, a toolbar button, or any area of your screen, there's a What's This? button in the Help menu.

Most dialog boxes in Excel have a question mark in the upper right corner. When you're in doubt about a particular choice in a dialog box, you can use this symbol to get an immediate pop-up box containing a brief explanation.

You can also get help by connecting to a Microsoft Office Update Web site and other Microsoft Web sites if you select the Office on the Web command on the Help menu.

The Assistant balloon, gives you suggestions on how to phrase a question to the Office Assistant or narrow your search by using keywords. If you still can't find the information you want, you can send feedback to improve future versions of Help, and be automatically connected to the Microsoft Office Update Web site.

Another useful Help feature is the Tip Wizard, which "watches" as you use Excel and frequently displays a tip that is related to an action you just completed. Sometimes this tip is a keystroke shortcut and at other times it's a toolbar or command technique.

TAKE NOTE

▶ COPY A USEFUL FORMULA FROM HELP

If a Help screen contains a useful formula or function, you may want to copy it directly into your current worksheet. You can use menu commands in Help or keystroke combinations to copy and paste information into your worksheet.

▶ USE HELP TO VERIFY WHICH VERSION OF EXCEL YOU'RE USING

Click the Help menu and select About Microsoft Excel. Regardless of which version you're using, the version level will appear.

CROSS-REFERENCE
See Chapter 7 for details on using Help when you're creating a formula.

FIND IT ONLINE
Use your Internet search engine to locate "Excel Help" and discover over 500 locations to explore.

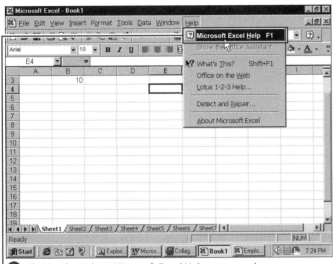

1 Choose the Help ➪ Microsoft Excel Help command.

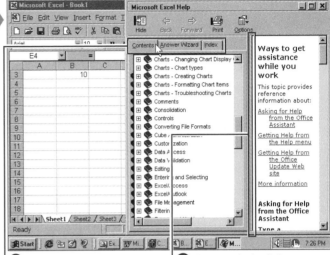

2 Click the Contents, Answer Wizard, or Index tab to use Help in different ways. Contents tab is currently shown.

3 Drag vertical split bars to expand or shrink a panel or edge.

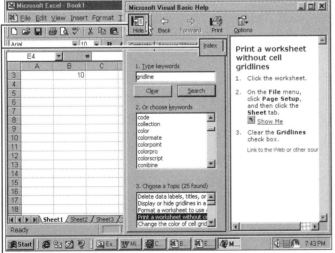

4 Click Hide to shrink the Help Screen, and then click the Show button to expand it. The Index tab is currently shown.

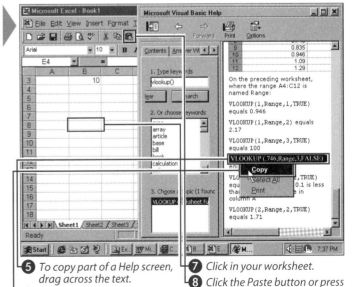

5 To copy part of a Help screen, drag across the text.

6 Right-click and choose Copy from the shortcut menu or press Ctrl+C.

7 Click in your worksheet.

8 Click the Paste button or press Ctrl+V.

Exiting Excel

When you're finished using Excel and wish to exit from the software, the process is simple, but can be fraught with problems if you're not careful of the status of your workbooks.

There are many ways to exit from Excel—by using a command, a keystroke shortcut, or using a couple of different icons. But no matter how you exit, if you have files open, and you've made changes without saving the files, you have unfinished business.

For each open file where there's been any activity since you last saved it, Excel displays a dialog box asking you if you want to save the changes you have made to that particular workbook. You can save the changes you've made to the workbook or close the file without saving changes. A dialog box appears, one by one, for every open workbook that you made changes to but did not save. If at any time you cancel the command, you effectively terminate the exit process at that time and Excel stays active. Some files might still be open.

You may want to save a workbook under a different name, thereby creating an additional copy, although you're more likely to simply allow saving to occur without changing the filename. In effect, exiting from Excel is an ideal opportunity to update the disk version of each open file.

If you are finished using Excel and think you won't need to use it for a while, you should exit from Excel.

When Excel is open it occupies memory space and makes your PC usage less efficient. The measure of all this depends heavily on the specifications of your PC, but most importantly on the amount of RAM installed. As a general rule, the more applications you have open, the less efficient your system becomes. However, if you don't have many other applications open, you will hardly see any difference when you compare performance with Excel closed and with Excel minimized (see Take Note section). It is slightly faster to bring back Excel from the taskbar than it is to do a complete restart.

TAKE NOTE

▶ DO I NEED TO EXIT FROM EXCEL?

If you plan to return to Excel later in the day and are not using many other applications, you can minimize Excel — effectively reducing its presence to a button on the taskbar at the bottom of your screen. To minimize Excel, click the minimize button (it looks like an underscore symbol) located on the right side of the Microsoft Excel title bar.

▶ CLOSE OR EXIT?

If you want to close the file you're working on and keep Excel active, select the File menu and choose Close. You will be prompted to save the file if you have made changes since you created it. Excel remains active after the file is closed.

CROSS-REFERENCE

See Chapter 4 for details on managing files.

FIND IT ONLINE

Check out the One Stop ... Many Exits site at **http//ps.superb.net/WebLinks/**.

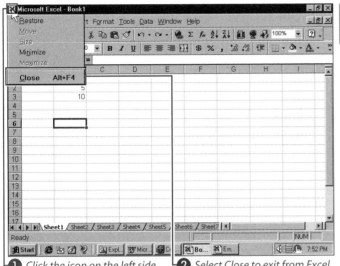

1 Click the icon on the left side of the title bar.

2 Select Close to exit from Excel.

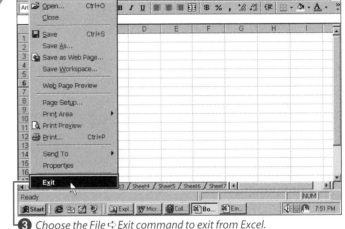

3 Choose the File ⇨ Exit command to exit from Excel.

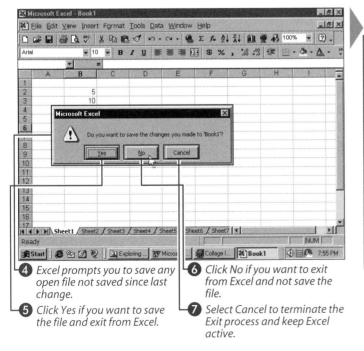

4 Excel prompts you to save any open file not saved since last change.

5 Click Yes if you want to save the file and exit from Excel.

6 Click No if you want to exit from Excel and not save the file.

7 Select Cancel to terminate the Exit process and keep Excel active.

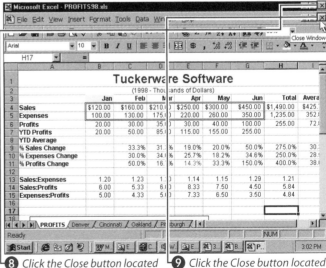

8 Click the Close button located on the right side of the title bar to close Excel.

9 Click the Close button located on the right side of the menu bar to close the current workbook.

Personal Workbook

Q&A

1 If you can't start Excel from the Start button, how can you start the software?

_____

_____

2 True or false: If you don't need all 65,586 rows in a worksheet, you can delete some of them.

_____

_____

_____

3 Will all of your open workbooks be automatically saved when you exit from Excel?

_____

_____

_____

4 If you've finished using Excel, does it make any difference whether you minimize Excel or exit from it?

_____

_____

_____

5 True or false: Like the menu bar and toolbars, you can customize the appearance of shortcut menus.

_____

_____

_____

_____

6 True or False: Keystroke shortcuts are next to every command in the menu system.

_____

_____

_____

_____

7 Why (and when) do some toolbar buttons appear sunken?

_____

_____

_____

_____

ANSWERS: 320

EXTRA PRACTICE

1 Using the shortcut menu, hide the Formatting toolbar; use the same technique to display it.

2 Use the F5 key to jump to cell T2000.

3 Use another keystroke combination to return immediately to cell position A1.

4 Someone has told you that there is a function called STDEV that enables you calculate a Standard Deviation. Using the Help system, find information on this function and print it.

5 If you have more than one workbook open, press Ctrl+F6 to toggle to each of them.

REAL-WORLD APPLICATIONS

✔ You are going to use Excel on a large monitor to make a presentation. You prefer to hide cell gridlines but aren't sure how to do it. Choose the Help ⇨ Microsoft Excel Help command and then click the Answer Wizard tab. Type: **How can I hide cell gridlines?**, and then click the Search button.

✔ You're doing a lot of data entry and alterations on different sheets in your workbook. Since your hands are on the keyboard a lot, you switch from sheet to sheet with the Ctrl+PgUp and Ctrl+PgDn keystroke shortcuts.

✔ You're not sure how many files are currently open so you click the Window menu to see a list of open workbooks.

Visual Quiz

In the screen image shown on the right, the Formatting toolbar is missing. Using the shortcut menu, how do you quickly return the Formatting toolbar to its usual location below the Standard toolbar?

_____

_____

_____

_____

_____

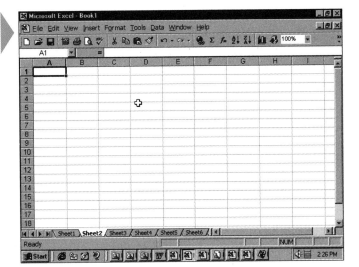

CHAPTER 2

MASTER THESE SKILLS

▶ Entering Text, Numbers, and Dates

▶ Selecting Ranges

▶ Using AutoFill, AutoComplete, and Preselection

▶ Using AutoSum

▶ Creating Simple Formulas

▶ Editing Cells

▶ Naming Cells and Ranges

Basic Worksheet Creation

As you build a worksheet, entering data into it is a task you'll need to perform frequently. To do so, you need to learn the basic methods of getting information into a cell and the general rules about default placement of cell contents — text to the left, numbers, formulas, and dates to the right. Before you learn how to move data and redesign your worksheets, the process of data entry may seem rigid and occasionally even tedious, but there are many shortcuts and techniques to simplify the process.

When you need to designate a group of cells that you're going to use in a formula, or you plan to make formatting changes to cells, you need to select them beforehand. Most of the time, you will use a mouse to perform this all-important task, but there are other methods that work too.

You can use the AutoComplete technique to simplify data entry down a column when the entries include a lot of repeats. With AutoFill, you can quickly enter a series of months or days into a row or column by simply typing an initial entry and dragging across the target cells. If you

select a range of cells prior to data entry, you can restrict active cell movement to the range during data entry. There are other preselection techniques that simplify data entry also.

When you want to add up a column or row of numbers, you can use the AutoSum tool. Summation is likely to be the most common kind of calculation you'll do in a worksheet — when you use this feature you'll be introduced to the concept of a worksheet function.

Invariably, you will need to write formulas, also. As you learn the essentials about formulas, you'll realize why most formulas contain cell addresses rather than just values. You'll also recognize that Excel is capable of handling lengthy, complex formulas if needed.

To edit a cell's content, you need to learn a few concepts and pointers that make this task easier than you might think. In this chapter, you get some exposure to the concept of naming a cell or a range of cells to improve your worksheet's readability and simplify the preparation of formulas and functions.

Entering Text, Numbers, and Dates

As you enter data in worksheet cells, you need to be mindful of the fact that Excel determines the type of entry you're making by the kind of characters you type. Based on these characters, Excel sets some limitations on what you can do with the cell's content.

During data entry, you can make immediate corrections before completing the entry or return later and edit the cell's content. You can also control where the active cell moves to as you finish your entry. Most of the time, you'll want to enter data down a column, but you can adjust the default movement to be across rows instead.

All data that you enter into cells falls into two broad categories: text and values. Text entries include any combination of characters containing at least one alphabetic character and not beginning with an equal (=) sign. In practical terms, we're talking about words and phrases typically used for identifying a column or row of information. Text automatically appears aligned on the left side of the cell, but you can easily make alignment adjustments from the Formatting toolbar.

Values include numbers, dates, formulas, and functions that appear aligned on the right side of cells. When entering a number in a cell, you may precede it with a minus sign if it's negative.

If you enter dates and times using standard styles (see the Take Note section), you open the door to an extremely powerful feature of Excel — the ability to handle date/time arithmetic. Using Excel, you are able to calculate the time elapsed between two dates or times, track hours worked, determine the day of the week, create date or time series, and perform a variety of other analytical tasks revolving around chronological considerations.

TAKE NOTE

STANDARD DATE ENTRY

When entering dates, use commonly accepted formats such as: 5/13/99 or 12-13-99. Dates appear right-aligned in a cell because Excel records them as values. If you enter an impossible date, such as 2/29/99 or 4/31/99, Excel accepts the entry as text and displays it left-aligned. For days in the twenty-first century, you can use 00, 01, etc., to designate the year. Any year from 00 through 29 will be entered as twenty-first century data; years from 30 through 99 will be treated as twentieth century data.

STANDARD TIME ENTRY

To enter a time in a cell, use one of these styles: 11:20, 14:45, 4 pm, or 3:35 am. Omit an am/pm designator for hours 0 through 12 and Excel assumes the entry is am (before noon).

AVOIDING DATA ENTRY ERRORS

Perhaps the most error-prone part of creating a worksheet is the typing that occurs during data entry. Always be on the lookout for methods of copying information from other sources to circumvent this problem.

CROSS-REFERENCE
See Chapter 8 for a fuller discussion of dates and times.

FIND IT ONLINE
Is all that data entry getting you down? Check out http://www.typequick.com.au/ to learn more about touch-typing.

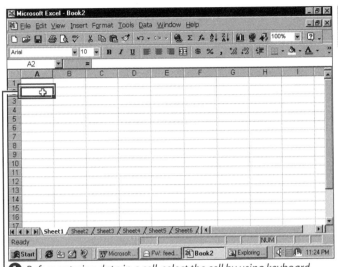

1 *Before entering data in a cell, select the cell by using keyboard arrows or point and click the cell with the mouse.*

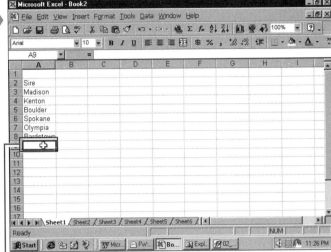

2 *As you enter data in cells down a column, press Enter to complete an entry and move down to the next cell. Press Tab to complete entries and move to the next cell to the right.*

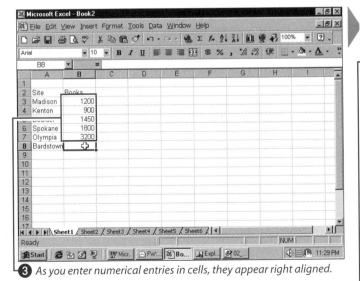

3 *As you enter numerical entries in cells, they appear right aligned.*

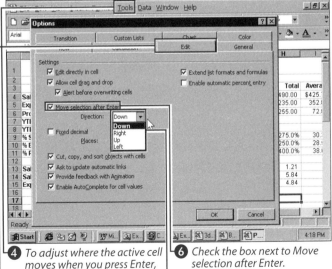

4 *To adjust where the active cell moves when you press Enter, choose the Tools ➪ Options command.*

5 *Click the Edit tab.*

6 *Check the box next to Move selection after Enter.*

7 *Click the drop-down list box next to Direction and make a selection.*

25

Selecting Ranges

In Excel, you really can't get much accomplished beyond basic data entry unless you learn how to select cells. By default, there's always one cell, the active cell, that's selected. This cell is identified by the slightly thicker border on its edges. If you use a command or toolbar button (unless it's a global feature), you are only making changes to that cell. So it is important that you learn how to select a range.

Selecting a range before actually taking some kind of action that affects that range, is a basic concept in Excel. This is generally true in all of the Office 2000 packages. The refrain "Select . . . then do" sums up the way you change a cell or a group of cells.

You can select a range of cells — perhaps you want to delete them, make them bold, copy them, or take any number of actions from the vast possibilities in Excel commands and toolbars — by using the mouse or keyboard.

By definition, a range is a cell or a contiguous rectangular group of cells. If you ever need to select a nonrectangular group, such as the left column and top row of a list, because you intend on giving them a common format, Excel gives you ways to select multiple ranges that are not necessarily contiguous. See the lower left figure on the opposite page.

TAKE NOTE

▶ MOUSE OR KEYBOARD?

The easiest way to select a range of cells is to click and drag across the face of the cells in question. To avoid dragging cell content or mistakenly moving cells, always point inside a cell as you begin to click and drag. As you drag the mouse, the pointer should look like a 3-D plus sign. An alternative method is to position the active cell on one of the imaginary corners of the range, hold down the Shift key and press the arrow keys until the intended range is completely highlighted.

▶ WHY DOES ONE OF MY CELLS IN A SELECTED RANGE LOOK UNSELECTED?

Whenever you select a range of cells, all of the cells except the one that you started with is displayed with a colored background. This cell is the active cell and it's part of your selected range even though it looks different from the others. When entering formulas for all of these cells at once, you need to key the formula to the active cell.

▶ MAKING SOME SELECTIONS CAN BE A REAL DRAG

When selecting a range much larger than your screen display area, it may be impractical to drag the mouse. Before attempting to drag across a large range, click the Zoom control box on the right side of the Standard toolbar. From the list of choices, try 50%, or even 25%. Often your screen display will now include the entire range that you want to select.

CROSS-REFERENCE

See "Naming Cells and Ranges" later in this chapter.

FIND IT ONLINE

Interested in zooming and panning? Look into
http://awmap.vevo.com/.

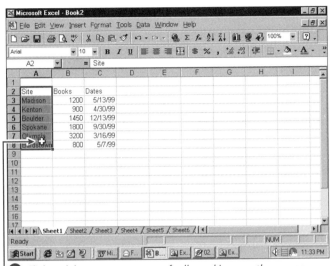

❶ Click and drag across a range of cells, making sure the mouse pointer looks like a 3-D plus sign.

❷ To select large ranges, first click one of the four cells in one corner of the range.

❸ Using the scroll bars if necessary, point to the cell in the diagonally opposite corner of the range.

❹ Press the Shift key and click the cell.

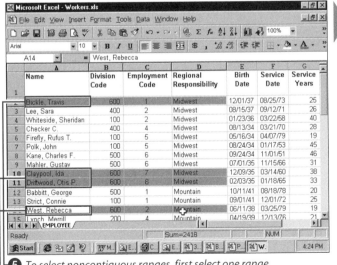

❺ To select noncontiguous ranges, first select one range.

❻ Next, press the Ctrl key as you select each additional range.

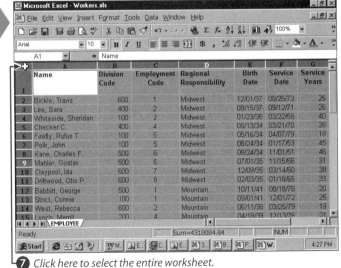

❼ Click here to select the entire worksheet.

Using AutoFill, AutoComplete, and Preselection

There are a number of data entry shortcuts that accelerate data input and reduce errors. If you need to enter a commonly used series, such as names of months, days of the week, or quarters of a year, you can use Excel's AutoFill feature. If many text entries in a column are likely to be repeat entries, you can take advantage of the AutoComplete capability. When you need to enter the same text, value, date, or formula in a number of different cells, there's a handy preselection technique and a keystroke shortcut to simplify the process.

If you want to enter the names of the months, or their abbreviations down a column or across a row, all you need to do is enter the first month or day that starts the series. The AutoFill feature recognizes any month or day of the week or its standard three-letter abbreviation, i.e., Feb, Apr, Tue, Sat, and so on.

If you're about to make column entries in situations where many of the entries will be repeats of previous column entries, you can rely upon Excel's AutoComplete feature. It remembers what you've already typed in a column and attempts to complete any entry that begins with the same letter as a previous column entry. The AutoComplete feature works fine as long as the first letter you type was previously used as an initial letter but used only once. If you entered Jones, then later, Johnson, you won't be able to use AutoComplete for any name beginning with the letter J.

Another way to use AutoComplete is to select from a list of previous entries as you come to the next cell in a series of column entries. You can use either the shortcut menu or a keyboard shortcut combination.

TAKE NOTE

▶ PRESELECTION

Select the range of cells in which you want to make a series of entries, to simplify the process. As you complete each cell entry, press Enter to cause the active cell to move downward until the end of the column and then into the next column. If you press Tab to complete each entry, the active cell will move to the right until the end of the row, and then into the next row. In either case the active cell will never move out of the selected range.

▶ AUTOCOMPLETE IS INCOMPLETE

The AutoComplete feature works only in columns, not rows.

▶ DRAG UP, DOWN, LEFT, OR RIGHT

When you create a series by dragging the mouse from the lower-right corner of a cell, usually you drag the mouse downward or to the right, to create a series that moves ahead in time. Drag up or to the left and you create a series moving backward in time.

CROSS-REFERENCE

See Chapter 8 for information on creating a date series.

FIND IT ONLINE

Download the article on AutoFill at **http://www. computerimages.com/imgs_old.html**

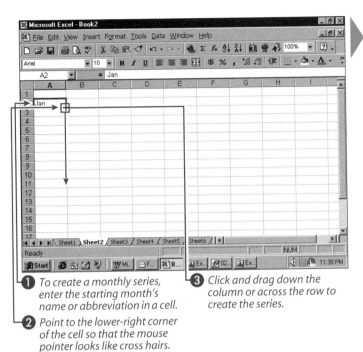

1 To create a monthly series, enter the starting month's name or abbreviation in a cell.

2 Point to the lower-right corner of the cell so that the mouse pointer looks like cross hairs.

3 Click and drag down the column or across the row to create the series.

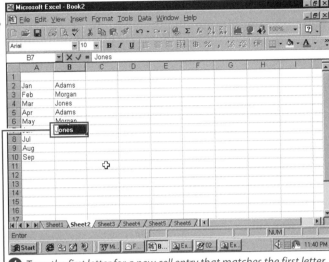

4 Type the first letter for a new cell entry that matches the first letter of a previous entry in the column. Press Enter if you want to use that name again.

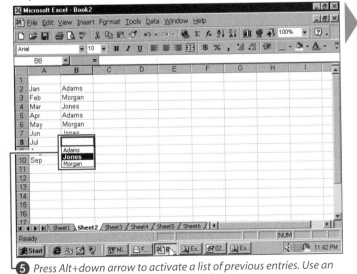

5 Press Alt+down arrow to activate a list of previous entries. Use an arrow key to select an entry and press Enter.

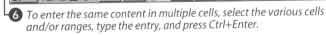

6 To enter the same content in multiple cells, select the various cells and/or ranges, type the entry, and press Ctrl+Enter.

Using AutoSum

The most common kind of calculation that you're likely to need in Excel is addition. Anytime you've got a column or row of values, you will probably want a total below them or in a cell to the right. One way for you to calculate these kinds of totals is to use the most frequently used of all the Excel functions — SUM — but let the AutoSum feature perform the task for you. This way, when you want to add the contents of a column or row, you don't need to type a formula or function and you'll make fewer errors. AutoSum automatically selects those cells that you would choose to total. Using AutoSum automatically invokes the SUM function.

You can create a total for a column or a row of cells if you position the active cell just below the column or to the right of the row of numerical entries. When you use the AutoSum feature, Excel looks above the active cell for a contiguous range of values. If it finds values, it determines the extent of them and displays the range of cells it's about to add. If there's no numerical data in the cells immediately above the active cell, Excel analyzes the data in cells to the left of the active cell.

The AutoSum feature actually works by using the SUM function to add up cells immediately above or to the left of the selected cell. You can even select all of the cells that will be added and the one that will contain the result before activating AutoSum and the feature works even faster.

Similarly, you can use the AutoSum tool to give you a series of answers when you have a series of adjacent columns or adjacent rows with values to be added.

TAKE NOTE

▶ WHAT IF AUTOSUM WANTS TO ADD DIFFERENT CELLS?

If you attempt to use the AutoSum feature where conceivably you could get a total of the cells above the active cell or to the left of the active cell, Excel will create a total for the cells above. You can control the process, however, by clicking once on the AutoSum tool to see which cells are going to be referenced in the total. If the cells referred to are not the ones you want to be added, use the mouse to click and drag across the appropriate cells, and then click again on the AutoSum tool or press Enter.

▶ TRY DOUBLE CLICKING A CELL TO ADD FASTER

If you select just a single cell in which to insert an AutoSum for the adjacent cells, double-click the AutoSum tool to create the result.

CROSS-REFERENCE
For information on this and Excel's other built-in functions, see Chapter 7.

FIND IT ONLINE
If you like adding numbers in your head, look at some of the math tricks at **www.ummed.edu/pub/k/kfletche/tricks.html**.

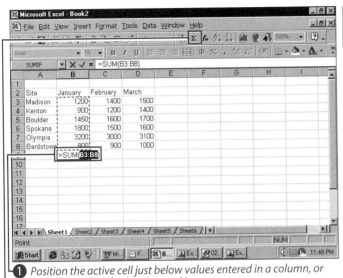

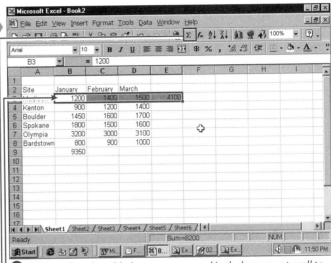

❶ Position the active cell just below values entered in a column, or just to the right of values entered in a row.

❷ Click the AutoSum button and press Enter to complete the function.

❸ Select cells to be added across a row and include an empty cell to contain the total.

❹ Click the AutoSum button once, to produce the result.

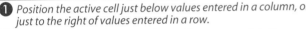

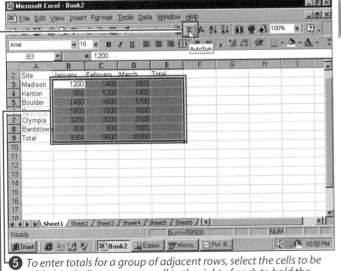

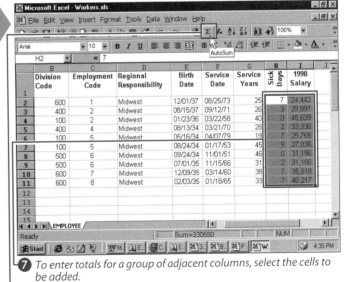

❺ To enter totals for a group of adjacent rows, select the cells to be added, including an empty cell to the right of each to hold the totals.

❻ Click the AutoSum button once.

❼ To enter totals for a group of adjacent columns, select the cells to be added.

❽ Click the AutoSum button once.

Creating Simple Formulas

Excel's capability as a calculator means that your data entry requirements and the opportunity for errors are both reduced. There's no reason for you to manually calculate the sum, difference, product, or quotient of cells when you can easily enter a formula to do the job for you. Usually, formulas make references to other cells, not the values they contain. That means that your formulas react when the contents of any of their references get changed. As you become more familiar with Excel's built-in functions, you'll have the potential to create complex formulas to handle almost any kind of mathematical calculation.

Each of the following formulas calculates a simple result.

=A3+100	the sum of 100 and the contents of cell A3
=5%*B16	5% of the value in B16
=C3*1.03	the product of 1.03 and the content of cell C3
=C4+100-B6	the sum of 100 and content of cell C4 minus the content of cell B6
=B2^3	the value of cell B2 raised to the third power
=(B3+B5+B7)/3	the value of one-third of the sum of B3+B5+B7

The result of the formula is stored in the cell where the formula is written. These operators apply to Excel formulas:

▶ = (**equal sign**) begins each formula
▶ + (**plus sign**) is used for addition
▶ - (**minus sign**) is used for subtraction
▶ * (**asterisk**) signifies multiplication
▶ / (**slash**) signifies division; don't use backslash (\)
▶ ^ (**caret**) signifies exponentiation

When you write a formula involving multiple operators, Excel adheres to a strict order of calculation that might not seem logical to you. Instead of performing operations in a left to right order, Excel operates by first considering the kind of operations it sees in a formula and then performs the calculation according to what are called *rules of precedence*. The major components of these rules are:

▶ Calculations inside of parentheses are performed first, in a left to right order
▶ Exponentiation occurs next
▶ Multiplication and division are performed as they occur from left to right
▶ Addition and subtraction are performed as they occur from left to right

TAKE NOTE

USE SAMPLE DATA WHEN TESTING FORMULAS

To test your formulas, try using small values that you can easily verify by doing the math in your head. Never assume that your formula is correct if you've only tested it once.

CROSS-REFERENCE
Learn more about formulas and functions in Chapter 7.

FIND IT ONLINE
If you need help with basic multiplication and division concepts, check out **www.cne.gmu.edu/modules/ dau/algebra/fractions/frac4_bdy.html**.

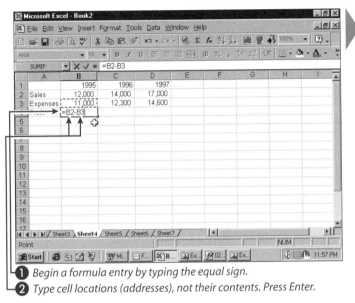

❶ Begin a formula entry by typing the equal sign.

❷ Type cell locations (addresses), not their contents. Press Enter.

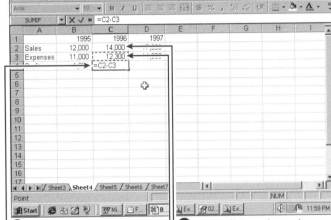

❸ Instead of typing =C2-C3, type the equal sign.

❹ Click cell C2 and type the minus sign (notice the formula emerging in the formula bar as you go through these steps).

❺ Click cell C3 and press Enter.

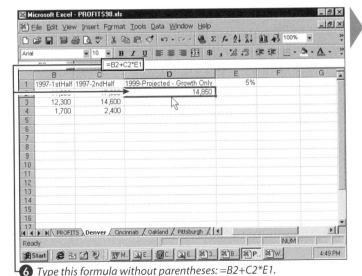

❻ Type this formula without parentheses: =B2+C2*E1.

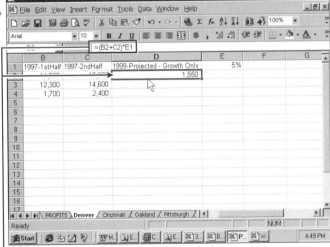

❼ Type this formula with parentheses: =(B2+C2)*E1. Contrast the result here with the previous screen.

Editing Cells

You're probably not error-prone, but you will often need to change the contents of cells, whether they contain text, numbers, formulas, or functions. Usually, the process isn't very complicated. If a cell entry isn't very long, but you want to change part of it, there's no need to do any editing. Simply select the cell, type the correct entry, and press Enter. The process of editing, whereby you alter just part of a cell, is straightforward and something you can achieve in a number of different ways in Excel. Normally, you edit one cell at a time, but you can select a number of different cells, edit the active cell, and, upon completion, effectively change all those selected cells at once.

You can start editing in at least three different ways, but the results are all the same. While editing a cell, a red X and a green check appear on the left side of the formula bar; these not only remind you that you're in "edit mode" but give you mouse methods for escaping from, or completing, editing. Also, while you're editing, the word Edit appears in the status bar at the bottom of the screen.

Don't forget those keystroke shortcuts that seem to work nearly everywhere in the Windows environment — use Ctrl+C to copy, Ctrl+X to cut, and Ctrl+V to paste. They're particularly handy during editing because you can copy or cut information from the cell that you're editing and later paste it into another cell.

If you'd like to edit a group of cells at once so that they will all have the same content, select the cells and then either press the F2 key or click in the formula bar. After making all of the changes you want to make, press Ctrl+Enter.

TAKE NOTE

▶ MOVING THE EDITING CURSOR

Press the Home or End key to move the editing cursor to the beginning or the end of the cell. Use the Ctrl key along with the left or right arrow key to move the editing cursor a word at a time in text cells.

▶ SELECTION WHILE EDITING

Press Shift+Ctrl+Home to select all text from the editing cursor to the beginning of the cell. Press Shift+Ctrl+End to select all text from the editing cursor to the end of the cell. Double-click a word to select it.

▶ DELETING WHILE EDITING

Press the Backspace key to delete a character to the left of the editing cursor, or the Delete key to delete a character to the right of the editing cursor. Press Ctrl+Delete to delete all text from the editing cursor to the end of the cell.

CROSS-REFERENCE

See Chapter 3 for more details on how you can use formatting tools on portions of selected text.

FIND IT ONLINE

If you're interested in editing, look into The Electric Editors homepage at www.ikingston.demon.co.uk/ee/home.htm.

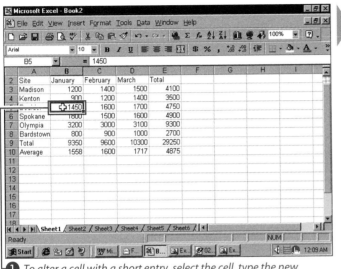

① To alter a cell with a short entry, select the cell, type the new content, and then press Enter. There is no need to erase the cell.

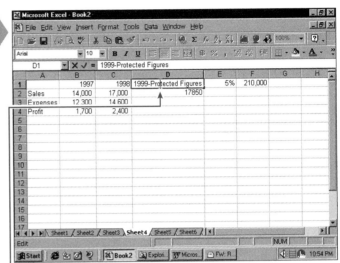

② To start editing a cell at a specific point, double-click the cell at that point in the cell.

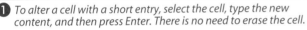

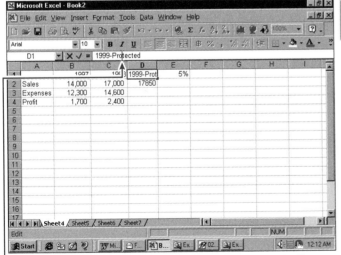

③ Click in the formula bar to activate editing for a selected cell.

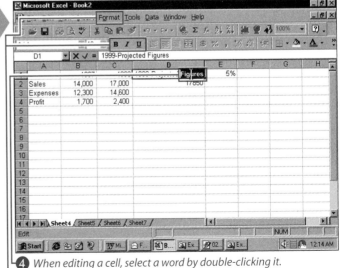

④ When editing a cell, select a word by double-clicking it.

⑤ Apply formats using the formatting buttons or the Format ⇨ Cells command.

Naming Cells and Ranges

Assigning a name to a cell or a range of cells may not seem like an obvious benefit to your worksheet, but properly named ranges produce a number of advantages. They increase the readability of your formulas, simplify your ability to create new formulas, and provide a good "paper trail" as you strive for better worksheet documentation. You can give a name to a single cell or to a group of cells. When you want to use range names in formulas or functions, you use them as if they were addresses. For example, if you assigned the name PCTincrease to cell B5, then, instead of typing the formula =B5*B7, you could type PCTincrease*B7. If you assigned the name Salaries to the range C2:C57, you could type =SUM(Salaries) instead of =Sum(C2:C57).

Range names can be up to 29 characters in length but may not contain spaces or hyphens. Use the underscore character to simulate the look of words. Avoid using special characters in range names, since most of them will not be accepted.

After you have created a range name, not only can you can use it in formulas; you can also move to it quickly, either from the name drop-down box on the formula bar or from the Edit ⇨ Go To command. You can access range names throughout a workbook, even when they refer to locations on different sheets. The ability to move quickly to another part of your workbook is a useful feature.

You can also use cell content as range names if the cells appear along the top or bottom row or the left or right column of a list of data. Although you have a great deal of latitude in creating range names, good judgment dictates the use of short, meaningful names for ease of use and rapid recognition.

TAKE NOTE

HOW CAN I REMEMBER THOSE RANGE NAMES?

If you've forgotten the range name that you need in a formula, or don't want to type it, do the following when it's time to type the name: press the F3 function key to display all range names, and then double-click the appropriate name.

THE F3 KEY AND RANGE NAMES

In addition to the example in the previous note, you can rely on the F3 key for three different uses in relation to range names. Use Ctrl+Shift+F3 after you've highlighted some cells that contain a border row or column that you'd like to use as range names. Use Ctrl+F3 to activate the Edit ⇨ Define Name command. When you're not in the midst of editing, press the F3 key to activate the Edit ⇨ Paste Name dialog box. Here you have the ability to paste a list of range names into your workbook.

CROSS-REFERENCE
Learn about producing range name lists in Chapter 6.

FIND IT ONLINE
If you're running out of creative range names, look into Onomastikon, a dictionary of names from around the world at **http://www.fairacre.demon.co.uk/**.

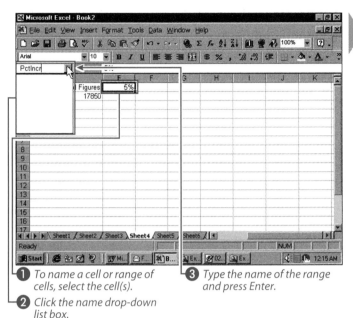

① To name a cell or range of cells, select the cell(s).

② Click the name drop-down list box.

③ Type the name of the range and press Enter.

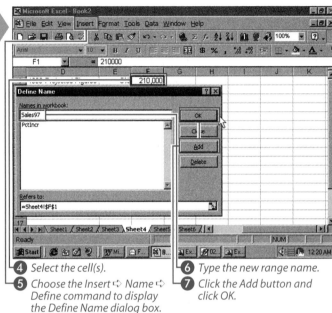

④ Select the cell(s).

⑤ Choose the Insert ➪ Name ➪ Define command to display the Define Name dialog box.

⑥ Type the new range name.

⑦ Click the Add button and click OK.

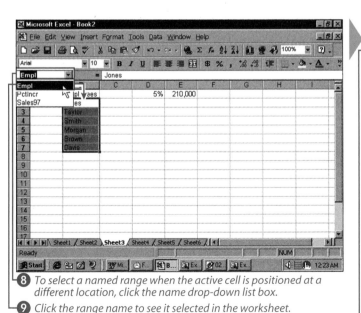

⑧ To select a named range when the active cell is positioned at a different location, click the name drop-down list box.

⑨ Click the range name to see it selected in the worksheet.

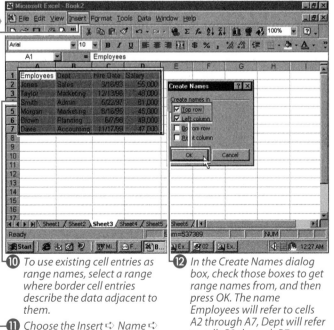

⑩ To use existing cell entries as range names, select a range where border cell entries describe the data adjacent to them.

⑪ Choose the Insert ➪ Name ➪ Create command.

⑫ In the Create Names dialog box, check those boxes to get range names from, and then press OK. The name Employees will refer to cells A2 through A7, Dept will refer to cells B2 through B7, etc.

37

Personal Workbook

Q&A

1 Will a date entry typed as 11/31/99 appear left- or right-aligned in a cell?

_____

_____

_____

2 Describe three ways in which to select a range of cells.

_____

_____

_____

3 How would you create a series of text entries for each month in the second half of the year?

_____

_____

_____

4 What keystroke combination can you use to make a cell entry when you want to select from a list of previous entries?

_____

_____

5 True or False: When you use the AutoSum tool, you can't edit the function it creates.

_____

_____

_____

6 True or False: When you write a formula without parentheses, Excel performs all calculations from left to right.

_____

_____

_____

7 What keystroke combination can you use to display the range names you need when writing a formula?

_____

_____

8 True or False: You can edit a cell that contains text, a number, a formula, a date, or a function.

_____

_____

ANSWERS: 321

EXTRA PRACTICE

1. A cell contains the text Fiscal Year 98 Expenses. Edit it to change 98 to 99.

2. There are sales figures in six consecutive cells in a row. Using AutoSum, put a total in the cell just to the right of these entries.

3. Put the word TOTAL in three separate locations on your worksheet but type it only once.

4. After entering three different department names down a column, you realize the next few entries will simply be using these names again. Use the Alt+Enter keystroke combination to make these entries without typing.

5. Write a formula that calculates a 10% increase over a 1998 salary amount located in cell B7.

REAL-WORLD APPLICATIONS

✔ A formula you've used many times on a calculator requires you to calculate a cube root. You can't find anything in Excel's help commands so you try this formula to get the cube root of cell B3: $=B3^\wedge(1/3)$.

✔ In one of your large worksheets, you frequently need to jump to the summary totals in cell A95. You make cell A95 the active cell, press Ctrl+F3, type the name SUMMARY and press Enter. Thereafter, to go to cell A95, you press the F5 function key and double-click the word SUMMARY.

✔ Column B in you personnel worksheet contains division names. There are only five possible divisions. After at least one occurrence of each exists in Column B, future entries are easy. You press Alt+down arrow to activate the list of previous entries, use the arrow keys to select the appropriate entry and press Enter.

Visual Quiz

In the screen image to the right, you're trying to get a total in cell F5 that sums the cells B5 through E5, but after you clicked the AutoSum tool the function displayed added the cells F2 through F4. What can you do with the mouse to make AutoSum do what you want?

_____

_____

_____

_____

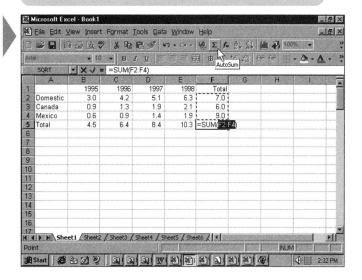

CHAPTER 3

MASTER THESE SKILLS

▶ Applying Font Attributes

▶ Aligning Cell Entries

▶ Formatting Numbers

▶ Applying Border Effects to Cells

▶ Applying Cell Background Colors and Patterns

▶ Adjusting Column Width and Row Height

Formatting Your Worksheet

Once you have most of your worksheet's content in place, you're likely to shift your focus to its appearance. Although content is more important than appearance, a poor design detracts from a worksheet's effectiveness and usability. If your worksheet will be used in a sales presentation or as part of a handout at an important meeting, really focus on clarity. An unattractive worksheet might lack readability, cause confusion, fail to emphasize the points you wish to stress, and, if it looks dull, a worksheet can reflect unfavorably on its creator.

Because formatting is so important in the creation of a worksheet, Excel puts most of the frequently used formatting features on the Formatting toolbar, which most Excel users display onscreen at all times. One thing to remember is that formatting alters a worksheet's appearance, not its content.

Excel gives you many ways to add pizzazz and interest to a worksheet. With color printers becoming more popular, you might want to give some thought to adding color to fonts, borders , and cell backgrounds. The ease with which you can export an Excel chart or worksheet into a PowerPoint presentation also gives credence to incorporating color. You might also want to apply color for a more pleasant onscreen worksheet view.

You can also emphasize parts of a worksheet through the use of patterns and underlining. Different fonts, font styles, and angular text alignment add interest, too.

Not all formatting is strictly for making a worksheet look better. You may need to make columns wider or narrower to improve readability or even visibility. You can use various alignment features to wrap text in a cell, rotate cell content to different angles, and merge cells to create titles that extend across many columns or down many rows. Also consider the implications of numeric displays. Excel allows you to create almost any kind of format imaginable to handle numeric information.

When you create charts with Excel, you'll find that many of the formatting techniques you've learned to apply to worksheets can also be used with charts.

Applying Font Attributes

An easy way to emphasize portions of a worksheet is to change the font, or typeface of the text. Excel gives you many fonts to choose from. You could use unusual or more prominent fonts for title areas in your worksheet and more typical fonts for everything else.

In Excel, the standard font is Arial, a plain, unadorned typeface that is ideal for clearly presenting text and numbers. Arial is similar to fonts that contain Swiss, Helvetica, or Sans in their names. As with most formatting tasks, before you make a font change with the toolbar or menu commands, remember to highlight the affected range of cells.

You can change fonts at any time, using the toolbar or menu bar to choose from a wide selection. Because fonts vary in design, some are more conspicuous and take up more vertical space in a cell. Excel will automatically adjust the height, unless you have specifically altered row height.

The Excel standard font size is 10 points. The Font Size drop-down list box, located just to the right of the Font drop-down list box, allows you to change the font size.

When experimenting with the look of your worksheet, you may also use font sizes that are not listed; just select the cell(s), click the Font drop-down list box, type in a number not shown, and press Enter. As a rule of thumb, 72-point text, when printed without shrinking the page, is one inch tall; 18-point text is ¼ inches tall; and 12-point text is ⅙ inches tall. Most people care about how text looks, not its exact measurement.

It's so quick and easy to change fonts and font sizes - experiment freely with these options until you get the appearance that suits you.

It's also a simple matter to change font color. The text-color selection tool is located to the right of the Formatting toolbar. You can easily spot the icon, a large letter **A**, and it retains the color you selected when you last activated it. Don't use this tool to make negative numbers red until you explore some of the numerical formatting selections that can perform this task for you.

Continued

TAKE NOTE

DON'T GO OVERBOARD

It's fun to be able to change the font, font sizes, and font colors so quickly, but it's easy to get carried away. Using too many font variations in a worksheet creates distractions and makes it difficult to focus on a worksheet's content.

CROSS-REFERENCE

See Chapter 2 for information on selecting ranges.

FIND IT ONLINE

If you're looking for unusual fonts, check out Fonts & Things at **http://www.fontsnthings.com**.

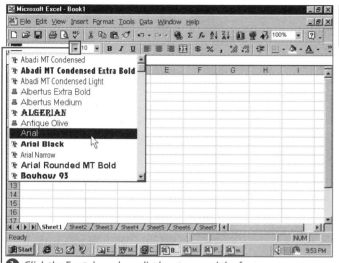

① Click the Font drop-down list box to reveal the fonts you can choose from

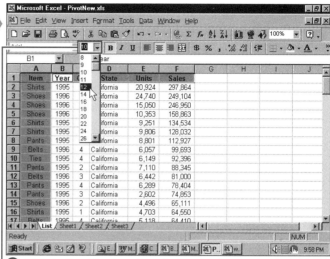

② Click the Font Size drop-down list box to select a point size, or type in a specific size and press Enter

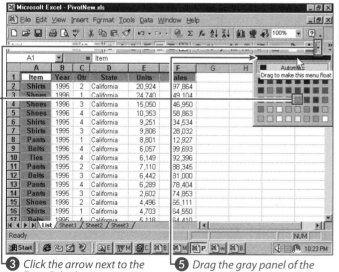

③ Click the arrow next to the Font Color button to activate the Font Color palette.

④ Click a color to change the font color of the selected cell(s).

⑤ Drag the gray panel of the Font Color palette onto the worksheet area if you want to keep it handy.

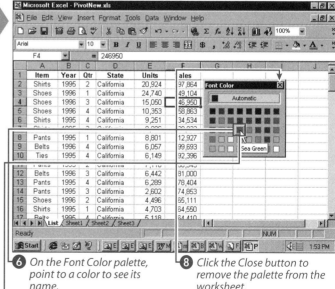

⑥ On the Font Color palette, point to a color to see its name.

⑦ Click a color to apply it to the font of the selected cell(s).

⑧ Click the Close button to remove the palette from the worksheet.

Applying Font Attributes *Continued*

Making Text Bold, Italic, or Underlined

You can make quick changes to the look of cells if you make text bold, italic, or underlined. When you select any of these features, any time the cell is active the toolbar button (whether it's bold, italic, or underlined) appears selected (with a sunken look). It's a good reminder that the cell is formatted. Each of the Bold, Italic, and Underline buttons acts as a toggle switch. Click the button to turn the feature on or off.

Many people prefer to use italics only for text. Italicized numbers may be more difficult to read.

Remember that underlining is different than using a solid line on the bottom of the cell border. Underlining is distinct from cell gridlines also, but when an active cell is underlined, you may have difficulty seeing this effect.

There are two notable byproducts of bolding and italicizing. If you bold a non-numeric cell, the text will require more horizontal space, thus you may have to widen the column. If you use the Italic button, the text will be slightly narrower for some fonts but wider for others. With most fonts, the width of numbers is unaffected by these changes, because, for proper alignment in a column of cells, numbers need to be the same width.

As you may have noticed, you can easily access these formatting features from the toolbar. Because Excel's formatting capabilities are so extensive and varied,

don't overlook the possibilities that the Format ⇨ Cells command presents. You'll also get a preview of your selections in the Format Cells dialog box.

The Font tab of the Format Cells dialog box gives you not only all of the font-related choices found on the Formatting toolbar, but it also presents some other options. Another advantage of the Format ⇨ Cells command is that it displays a preview of a feature before you apply it. This is useful when you are unfamiliar with certain fonts and how they appear in combination with underlining styles and effects.

There's a special section on the Font tab of the Format Cells dialog box that shows an expanded set of underlining variations. Some of the choices are just slightly different than others. The two accounting choices, for example, put the lines farther below the text than the other choices. Superscript and subscript choices are here, but you can't use them with numbers.

TAKE NOTE

▶ FORMATTING WHILE EDITING

You can also use the font formatting toolbar buttons and the Format Cells command when you edit a cell. This means that you can select some of a cell's content and apply a formatting attribute (font, size, bold, italic, underline, color, etc.).

CROSS-REFERENCE

Learn how to apply border effects later in "Applying Border Effects to Cells."

FIND IT ONLINE

Learn more about why some Internet text is underlined at **http://www.ns.sympatico.ca/Sympatico_Help/ Learn/help8.html**.

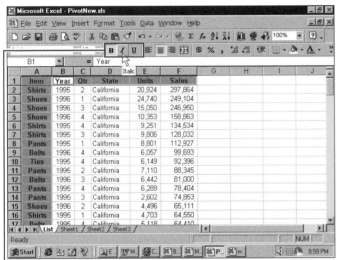

1 Click any of these buttons as needed for Bold, Italic, or Underline style. Try them in combinations.

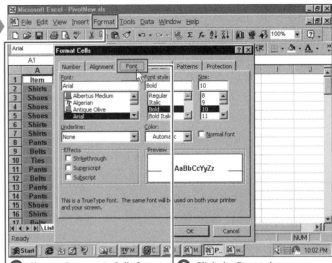

2 Choose Format ⇨ Cells from the menu bar.

3 Click the Font tab to see many formatting choices in one location.

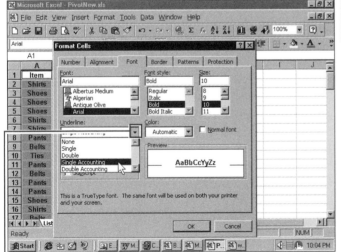

4 Click the arrow in the Underline drop-down list box to see choices not available on the toolbar.

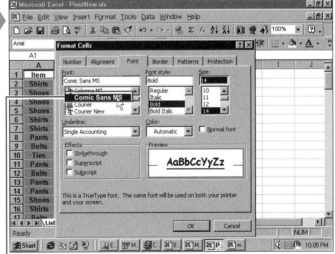

5 Select a font, then switch to the up and down keyboard arrows to get a quicker look at each of the fonts in the Preview window.

Aligning Cell Entries

By default, when you type information into a cell, it will be either right-aligned (numbers, formulas, functions, dates) or left-aligned (text). Often, these default settings are exactly what you want. With numeric information, don't change this alignment. In fact, Excel has made it more difficult to do so. You cannot left-align or center the contents of numeric cells if you applied numeric formatting.

As with other formatting features, you can achieve most of your needs by relying on the Align Left, Center, Align Right, and Center and Merge buttons located near the middle of the Formatting toolbar.

These buttons act as toggle switches and, at a glance, tell you if you chose alignment for the active cell (they appear sunken when activated).

You may want to indent the contents of cells containing text, dates, or numbers. However, if you use any numeric formatting in cells, you will not be able to use either of the indenting tools in those cells. The most logical use of indenting is for row identifiers, typically in Column A. Decrease Indent and Increase Indent buttons complement each other and give you flexibility in moving text around inside cells.

To center a title across multiple columns, click the Merge and Center button in the Formatting toolbar and two actions occur: the title text is centered across the selected columns, and the selected columns in that row merge into a single cell. The merged cells in this row share an address. Unlike other alignment tools, this one is not a toggle switch. If you later decide to make alterations, you'll need to use the Format ⇨ Cells command to deselect the Merge cells option. You can also merge cells in a column, but first you need to learn how to rotate text in a cell.

Continued

TAKE NOTE

ROTATING CELL CONTENTS

If you want to rotate text to shorten the amount of horizontal space that a column requires (at the expense of making the row taller), you can rotate text to be vertical or at any angle between horizontal and vertical. As with the font formatting features, you'll find a wealth of alignment options when you choose Format ⇨ Font from the menu bar, including the capability to rotate cell content. When you rotate text at an angle, the resulting display can have a dramatic effect on your worksheet; you'll probably want to experiment with it, including printing it to assess output quality.

CROSS-REFERENCE

See the next task for information on vertically aligning cell content.

FIND IT ONLINE

Concerned about alignment? Check out the Wheel Alignment Directory at **http://www.wheelalignment.com/**.

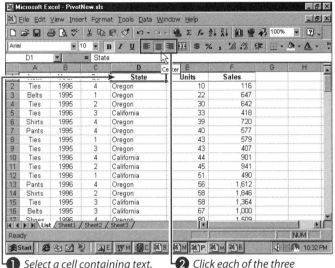

❶ Select a cell containing text.

❷ Click each of the three alignment tools to alter placement of the text in the cell.

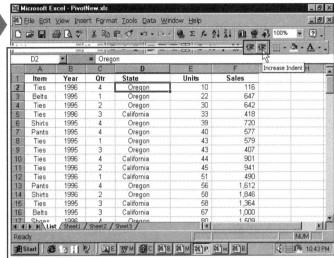

❸ Click the Increase Indent and Decrease Indent buttons to alter the appearance of text cells.

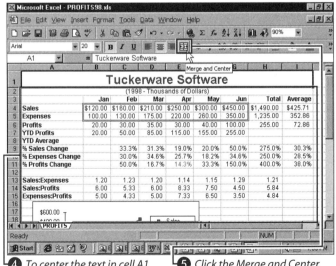

❹ To center the text in cell A1 across columns A through I, select cells A1 through AI.

❺ Click the Merge and Center button.

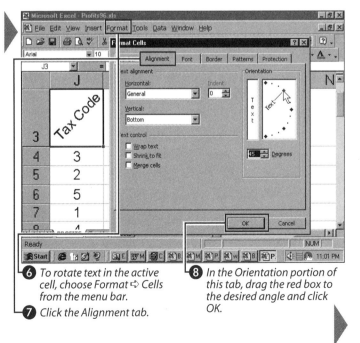

❻ To rotate text in the active cell, choose Format ➪ Cells from the menu bar.

❼ Click the Alignment tab.

❽ In the Orientation portion of this tab, drag the red box to the desired angle and click OK.

Aligning Cell Entries *Continued*

Wrapping Text in a Cell

Larger monitors help you see more information on your screen, but there will be occasions when you'd like to see more columns at one time. You can use techniques such as hiding columns or zooming back, but there are always those situations where a column's width is dictated by a long title. Whenever you have a cell entry that's significantly wider than other entries in the same column, consider wrapping the text in the cell to create a multiline appearance. The row height automatically becomes taller but you can reduce the width of the column.

You can do a line wrap as you type a cell entry or choose the Format ⇨ Cells command to apply a wrap before or after cell entry. The advantage of the former is that you have precise control over where the line split occurs. The advantage of the latter is that you can have the wrap occur in many cells at one time. If the wrapping is not satisfactory, you can edit a cell and press Alt+Enter at the appropriate location to control line breaks.

The Shrink to fit feature lets you shrink the size of the font in a cell when you want to keep the content intact without widening the column. Excel uses whatever font size is necessary to fit the text, but the font size indicator in the Formatting toolbar does not change. You can't see the new font size. If you make the column narrower, the cell content will continue to shrink. If you make the column wider, the cell content will continue to grow, but it won't turn into a font size that's larger than the original setting.

The alignment tools in the Formatting toolbar apply only to horizontal alignment (left-right) in cells. You can control vertical alignment (top-bottom) in cells if you want to make text in a tall cell appear in the top, middle, or bottom of the cell. An example of this is shown on the following page.

TAKE NOTE

LINE WRAPPING

During data entry, press Alt+Enter when you want to split a line. You can do this as often as you want line breaks. Complete cell entry in the normal way with the Enter, Tab, or arrow keys.

WHY IS MY ROTATED TEXT RAGGED-LOOKING?

Depending on the your monitor's resolution, you may be surprised by the look of cells that you've rotated. Often the text looks ragged and sloppy. If you're more concerned with the look of your worksheet on paper, printed material usually has smooth edges and looks cleaner.

WRAP AND ROTATE TOGETHER?

If you're in an experimental frame of mind and you want to both wrap text and rotate it, the features are compatible.

CROSS-REFERENCE
See Chapter 13 for details on using angled text in charts.

FIND IT ONLINE
For a more technical look at shrinking, read Atom Lithography May Shrink Chips at **http://www.nist.gov/ public_affairs/gallery/lithcp.htm.**

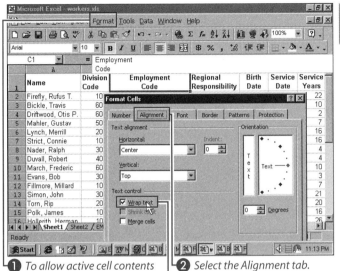

❶ To allow active cell contents to be on multiple lines, choose the Format ➪ Cells command from the menu bar.

❷ Select the Alignment tab.

❸ Click the Wrap text check box and click OK.

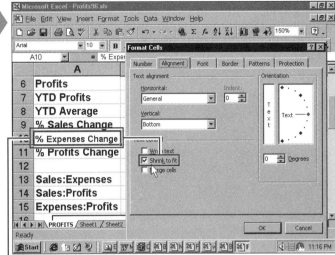

❹ Click the Shrink to fit check box to fit the contents within the column width.

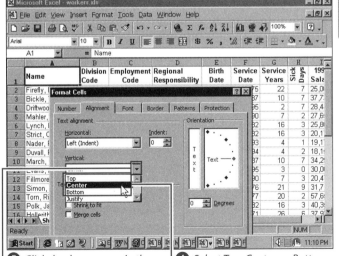

❺ Click the down arrow in the Vertical drop-down list box, contained in the Alignment tab.

❻ Select Top, Center, or Bottom to place text in that part of the cell.

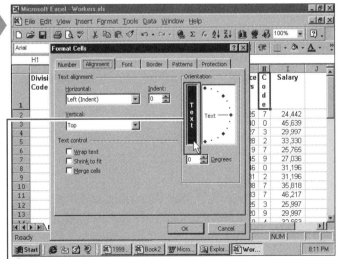

❼ Click the text box on the left side of the Orientation portion of the tab to rotate and stack text.

Formatting Numbers

Displaying numbers is a critical consideration in any worksheet. For example, you may need to decide if currency symbols and decimal places are appropriate for certain cells in a financial worksheet or whether it makes sense to show more decimal places in a scientific worksheet. You can easily make most of these kinds of changes from the numerical formatting buttons on the Formatting toolbar.

Excel's default formatting for numbers displays as many decimal places as you type, but it does not use commas or currency symbols. When you type in currency symbols and/or commas, Excel formats the cell and displays the information as entered. Rather than attempting to apply formatting during data entry, it's more efficient to format cells either before or after data entry.

For many people, the Comma Style button, located just to the right of the Currency Style button on the Formatting toolbar, is an ideal selection. Two decimal places appear, and commas, if necessary, appear after every three display positions to the left of the decimal point. Novice users are sometimes unnerved when they see the result of using this button, because a series of pound signs (#) fills cells where the column is not wide enough. Don't worry—no data is destroyed. Remedies include using fewer decimal places or widening the column, both of which are addressed in this chapter.

The Currency Style button is similar to the Comma Style button, but it displays a leading dollar sign. Here, too, you may see cells filled with pound signs, making you want to take corrective action.

Use the Percent Style button to convert the display of formulas that calculate a percent. You may want a formula such as =G3/G9 to result in a display of 12.4% instead of124. The Percent Style button does not initially display decimal places.

The Increase Decimal and Decrease Decimal buttons in the Formatting toolbar let you display more or fewer decimal places in cells. For some financial worksheets, you may want to display large numbers with no decimal places, so you'll decrease the number of decimal places displayed. In scientific worksheets, you may want more decimal places.

The Number tab in the Format Cells dialog box gives you an unlimited set of numerical formatting possibilities. There is a list of categories along with a set of variations for each. The Custom category shows existing formats that you can use to build your own customized formats.

TAKE NOTE

▶ SPECIAL FORMATS

Check out the built-in formats in the Special category on the Number tab in the Format Cells dialog box. If you're entering a series of phone numbers, ZIP codes, or social security numbers, these formats provide all the special characters. All you do is type the numbers. Leading zeros are also handled properly.

CROSS-REFERENCE

See Chapter 8 for details on special formatting variations of date cells.

FIND IT ONLINE

To learn more about how we have come to use numbers, look at the History of Numbers at http://members.xoom.com/Wei_21/.

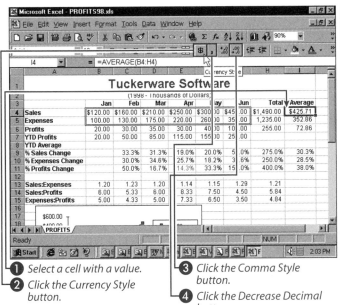

1. *Select a cell with a value.*
2. *Click the Currency Style button.*
3. *Click the Comma Style button.*
4. *Click the Decrease Decimal button.*

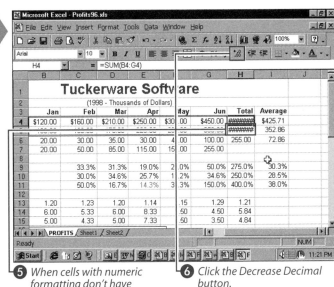

5. *When cells with numeric formatting don't have enough display space, they display #####.*
6. *Click the Decrease Decimal button.*

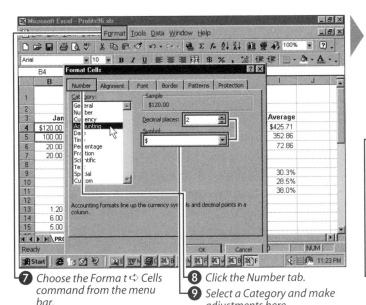

7. *Choose the Format ⇨ Cells command from the menu bar.*
8. *Click the Number tab.*
9. *Select a Category and make adjustments here.*

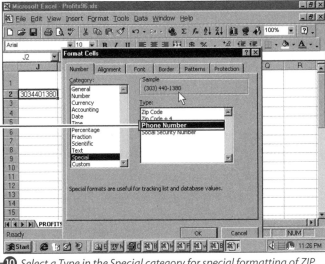

10. *Select a Type in the Special category for special formatting of ZIP codes, phone numbers, and social security numbers.*

Applying Border Effects to Cells

You can add emphasis to certain areas of your worksheet if you apply border effects to the perimeter of individual cells in a selected range. These effects include thicker lines, selectively placed lines, colored lines, or different line types (dashed, dotted, combination).

There is only one toolbar button to consider when you want to make border changes. It's the Borders button located on the right side of the Formatting toolbar, just to the left of the Fill Color button. Normally it's the third button from the right and, like the Font Color and Fill Color buttons, the appearance of this button changes as you use the feature.

The choices on the Borders palette are almost self-explanatory, but it's best to experiment with them. The button in the lower-right corner (Thick Box Border) creates a perimeter border on the outer edges of your selected range. Choose the second button from the left in the bottom row (All Borders) if you want a border on every side of every cell in your range. Another useful button is the one in the upper-left corner (No Border), used to remove all border styles currently in your selected cells. The last style you use will be the one that the Borders button displays.

If you want to use color borders, have more line-type and thickness options, apply more than a single border style at a time, and be able to use angled border lines, use the Format Cells dialog box and select the Border tab. There are so many choices and combinations available that you'll want to experiment in the preview area of the dialog box.

CROSS-REFERENCE

See Chapter 5 for details on displaying and hiding gridlines on printed output.

FIND IT ONLINE

Get leads on a ton of borders and backgrounds at http://webclipart.tqn.com/msub3.htm.

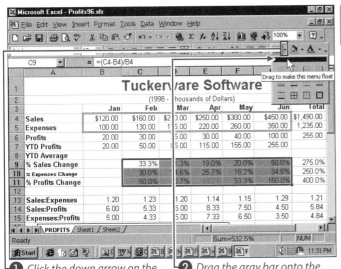

1 Click the down arrow on the right side of the Borders button, which is located on the Formatting toolbar.

2 Drag the gray bar onto the worksheet for handier use.

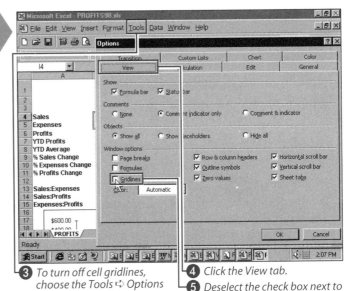

3 To turn off cell gridlines, choose the Tools ⇨ Options from the menu bar.

4 Click the View tab.

5 Deselect the check box next to Gridlines.

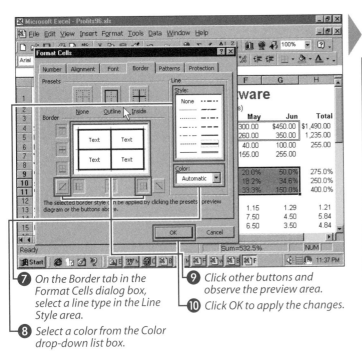

7 On the Border tab in the Format Cells dialog box, select a line type in the Line Style area.

8 Select a color from the Color drop-down list box.

9 Click other buttons and observe the preview area.

10 Click OK to apply the changes.

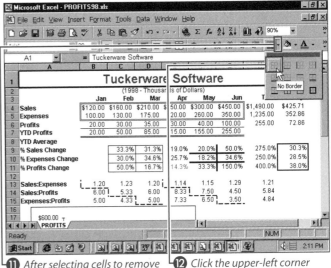

11 After selecting cells to remove border effects, click the down arrow next to the Borders button.

12 Click the upper-left corner button to remove all border effects from the selected cells.

Applying Cell Background Colors and Patterns

As with many other formatting features, color cell backgrounds and patterns, sometimes used separately, sometimes together, add variety and interest to a worksheet. It can be a significant factor in color printouts and presentations where you use a monitor or projection system to display a worksheet. There are other times when it's just more pleasant and interesting to work with a colorful screen.

To apply a color background to your selected range, click the Fill Color button (it's got a bucket on it) located on the right side of the Formatting toolbar. Like the buttons on either side of it, it has these characteristics: the color displayed is the one you last used, and, if you click on the down arrow to expose the palette, you can make it float by dragging it onto the worksheet.

Although you can choose to have either patterned or color backgrounds in cells, you may want to experiment with a combination of the two. You can achieve a variety of effects by using patterns in cells, although many are not subtle. When used in occupied cells they may hamper your view of the data. It is not uncommon, therefore, to see patterns applied to empty cells that separate, delineate, or isolate different sections of a worksheet. There is no way to apply patterns to worksheet cells from the Formatting toolbar, but a Patterns tab appears when you choose the Format ⇨ Cells command from the menu bar select. There are 18 different patterns and

you can try them in combination with the different color choices.

Just as the presence of gridlines poses visual problems for viewing border styles, a similar effect sometimes occurs when using color backgrounds and borders. Review the previous section on turning off gridlines if you have difficulty viewing your color and pattern changes.

TAKE NOTE

GRAPHIC BACKGROUND

You can add a graphic background to your entire worksheet, somewhat like a watermark, if you choose Format from the main menu, then choose Sheet and drag to the right to choose Background. Unlike a background color that resembles like a painted a wall, a sheet background can include shading and give a transparent look. You can select from a variety of file types and locations on your system. The clouds background familiar to Windows users is one of the available choices. If your selection is unsatisfactory, use the same command and choose Delete Background.

COLORS HIDE GRIDLINES

You might be surprised when adding a color background to a cell to realize that the cell gridlines seem to be missing. Actually they're not — they're hidden behind the colors. To simulate the look of cell gridlines, use the border features referred to in the last set of tasks.

CROSS-REFERENCE

See Chapter 5 to learn about problems that occur with some color backgrounds when printing.

FIND IT ONLINE

There's a wealth of patterns at http://www.connectedlines.com/.

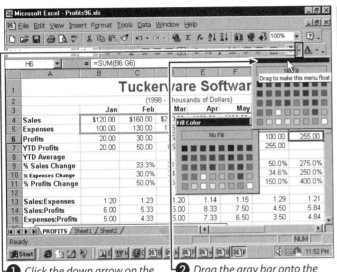

1 Click the down arrow on the right side of the Fill Color button on the Formatting toolbar.

2 Drag the gray bar onto the worksheet for handier use.

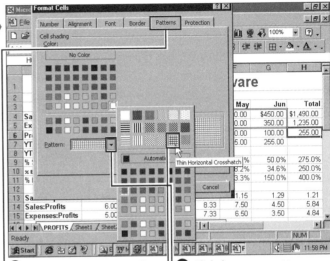

3 Choose the Format ⇨ Cells command and select the Patterns tab.

4 Click the arrow next to Pattern.

5 Select a pattern.

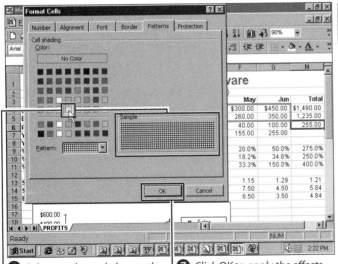

6 Select a color and observe the sample that shows the mix of pattern and color.

7 Click OK to apply the effects.

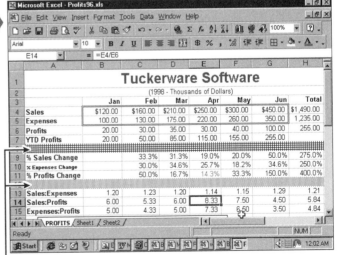

8 A pattern can be used to separate sections of a worksheet.

Adjusting Column Width and Row Height

You can easily adjust the width of a column or the height of a row. Most of the time your rationale is obvious—a cell isn't wide enough to display its contents without truncating it or, worse in the case of values, displaying it as a bunch of pound signs. Therefore, make the column wider. On other occasions, you might remove a wide cell entry, leaving the column unnecessarily wide; so you'll want to make the column narrower. In Excel, you never really adjust the width or height of cells—all cells in any specific column are always the same width and all cells in the same row are always the same height. Because Excel automatically makes many row-height adjustments, the focus is on adjusting column width.

Excel's method for adjusting column width is so intuitive that many people are not even aware that there is a command method available. By using the mouse, you can either drag a column to make it wider or narrower or use a double-clicking technique to let Excel apply a best-fit—the column will accommodate the widest entry. When you drag a column to a specific width, you see an indicator just above the column that tells you how many characters and how many pixels wide the column will be if you release the mouse at that point.

You can adjust the width of a number of columns at once, whether they're adjacent to each other or dispersed throughout your worksheet. When you adjust the width of multiple columns, you also have the option to set them all to be the exact same width or make each one of then be a so-called "best-fit". You may need to choose the Format ⇨ Column command when you want one column to be exactly the same width as another.

Adjusting the height of a row is very similar to adjusting the width of a column. The same concepts used when adjusting column widths apply here also. You can drag rows to a specific height or get a best-fit. You can adjust multiple rows at the same time and in the same way as you can with columns. Unlike columns, however, row heights automatically adjust to a taller setting if you use a larger font and the row height automatically shrinks if you use a smaller font.

TAKE NOTE

ADJUSTING ALL COLUMNS OR ALL ROWS AT THE SAME TIME

If you'd like to adjust the width of all columns at one time, first select the entire worksheet with the keystroke combination Ctrl+A. Then double-click any column boundary (between the column letters at the top of the column) to get a "best-fit," or drag any column boundary to a width that's suitable for all columns.

CROSS-REFERENCE

See Chapter 6 for details on hiding columns and rows.

FIND IT ONLINE

Learn about Greek columns at **http://eghs.dist214. k12.il.us/html/academics/english/humanities/ grkcol.html**.

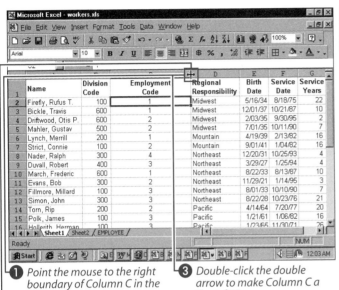

1 Point the mouse to the right boundary of Column C in the column headings.

2 Click and drag to the left or right to shrink or expand the width of Column C.

3 Double-click the double arrow to make Column C a "best-fit."

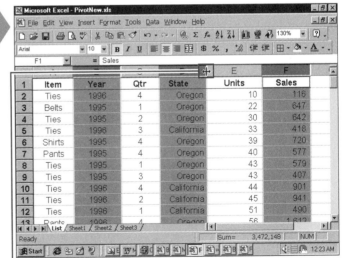

4 Click and drag up or down on the bottom boundary of Row 2 to shrink or expand its height.

5 Double-click the double arrow to make Row 2 a "best-fit."

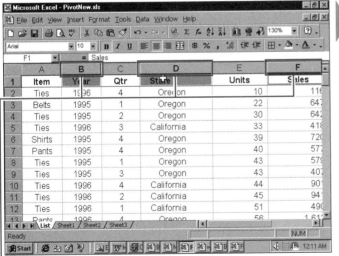

6 Click different column letters with the Ctrl key held down prior to adjusting the width of all columns you select.

7 Drag one of the right boundaries to adjust all of the selected columns to the same width as the column whose boundary you're adjusting.

Personal Workbook

Q&A

1 Can you select fonts from a toolbar or do you need to use the Font tab in the Format Cells dialog box?

_____

_____

_____

2 True or False: Bold print doesn't take up more space, it just looks bigger.

_____

_____

3 Why does Excel make it difficult to center numbers in a cell?

_____

_____

_____

4 Can you rotate the contents of a cell containing formulas to a 45 degree angle?

_____

_____

_____

5 True or False: Numeric formatting, unlike other kinds of formatting, can actually alter content.

_____

_____

_____

6 What's the difference between putting a bottom border on a cell and underlining a cell?

_____

_____

7 What do you need to do when you see a cell filled with ##### ?

_____

_____

_____

8 Once you use the best-fit technique on a column, will it automatically expand when you type a long entry in one of its cells?

_____

_____

_____

ANSWERS: 321

EXTRA PRACTICE

❶ In one of your worksheets, change a cell's font to 14-point Times New Roman.

❷ Apply bold formatting to a cell with text. Does the cell need more space? Try this on a cell with values. Is the situation the same?

❸ Type the phrase "Tax Code" in a cell so it appears on two lines within the same cell.

❹ Change the width of columns containing some cells with text and others with values. Notice the different effects when you make the columns narrower.

❺ Press Ctrl+A to select the entire worksheet. Then double-click the vertical line between two column letters to adjust all column widths.

REAL-WORLD APPLICATIONS

✔ You want your worksheet to have a series of alternating columns showing "Projected" and "Actual" for a 12-month period. In columns C through Z, make every other column the same color, but different than the interspersed columns. Use the Ctrl key to select every other column and apply a light yellow background.

✔ A Column in your worksheet contains single-digit employment codes, but the column is wide because the top cell contains the text "Empl. Code." Use the Wrap text feature to make the entry appear on two lines, thus making the column narrower.

✔ You want to calculate batting averages, so you'd like to see a display such as .318 instead of the 0.31831 that appears now. Use the Number tab in the Format Cells dialog box to get to the Custom category and enter .000 in the Type area.

Visual Quiz

In the screen shown to the right, can you create this border effect from the Borders palette in the Formatting toolbar? If not, which command can you use?

_____

_____

_____

_____

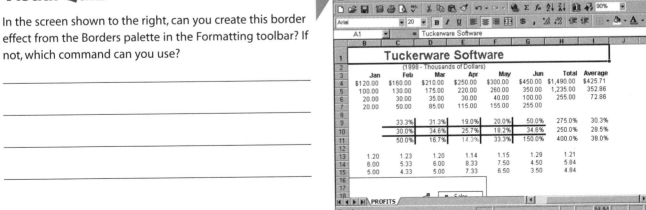

CHAPTER 4

MASTER THESE SKILLS

▶ Saving a Workbook

▶ Creating a New Workbook

▶ Finding and Opening a Workbook

▶ Closing a Workbook

▶ Renaming a Workbook

Managing Your Files

Keeping track of your files is not the most exciting aspect of working with Excel, or with any software for that matter. Fortunately, all you need to do in Excel is familiarize yourself with just a few basic commands in order to create, save, open, and close files seamlessly.

Outside of Excel, you can use commands available in Windows Explorer to clarify the names and locations of files. The Find feature, accessible from the Windows Start button, is also useful in locating files that you may have misplaced. Excel's Find feature is similar, although not as comprehensive. Windows file management capabilities won't be covered extensively in this material, so you may want to explore classes or books on that topic to give yourself some help on these features. However, as a casual user of Excel, you can learn how to use file management commands and toolbar buttons and get along just fine.

The Excel file-related features, such as those used for opening and saving files, are visually oriented and filled with command tips that simplify their usage. Many of the visual features

in these commands reflect the style used in Windows and in Internet applications. File activity is centered around the File menu or toolbar equivalents, but you will also be using the Window menu to monitor open files.

For compatibility reasons, you may need to open files created in software other then Excel. Excel is able to handle a variety of file formats when opening files. You can also save your Excel workbook as an HTML file suitable for the Internet or in a format that needs to be readable by another party that does not have Excel.

For ease in creating new workbook files, you should explore some of Excel's built-in template files that you can open, adjust for your needs, and save for future use. The template files Invoice and Expenses are two which have wide applicability.

A key factor in sensible file management is having control over the names of your Excel files. Whenever you save an existing workbook file, you can adjust its name if it seems inappropriate. Also, when you're opening files you can pause during that operation and change the names of files.

Saving a Workbook

If you've opened Excel and started to enter data into the default workbook (Book1), you have created something that really only exists in one place — random access memory (RAM) in your computer. Until you make a copy of this information somewhere else, such as a diskette, a zip drive disk, a CD, or a hard drive location, your work is vulnerable to power failures, unintended exits from the software, battery failure (on portable computers), and accidentally pulled plugs. Sure, most of these disasters are avoidable and this won't happen often, but you must be aware of the potential for losing not only a lot of data but also a lot of time if you need to recreate the information lost.

It's recommended that you save your work shortly after you've created it and frequently thereafter. The word save may sound a little strange when you use it in the context of making additions to an existing workbook and then saving it. The word update may be what you're thinking — that's actually what you do when you save a file that already exists. You update the file on disk (or other medium) to include the latest changes, additions, and deletions since the last time you saved the workbook. An AutoSave feature in Excel automatically saves your workbook on a periodic basis (every five or ten minutes, for example).

For new files, use either the File ➪ Save or the File ➪ Save As command and Excel automatically activates the same dialog box. When you save a file for the first time, you will no doubt want to override the default name of Book 1 and create a meaningful name to suit your needs. Excel filenames can be up to 218 characters long, but sensible usage suggests any readable name up to about 20 characters.

TAKE NOTE

▶ SAVE OFTEN

If you're working with a file that's already been saved, you should save the file frequently to ensure that your recent changes become part of the file. Click the Save button (third from the left on the Standard toolbar) or use its command equivalent — File ➪ Save.

▶ FILE➪SAVE AS

Use the File ➪ Save As command when you want to save your file with a different name, location, or file format. Save your file with a different name and you create a new file while keeping a copy of your file with its original name. Save your file at a different location and you have two files with the same name in two locations. Save your file in a different format and you have two files with the same filename but with different 3-letter file extensions and different formats.

CROSS-REFERENCE

See "Closing Files" later in this chapter, for information on how File ➪ Save As appears when you close a file for the first time.

SHORTCUT

Use Ctrl+S as a shortcut for the File ➪ Save command and the F12 key to activate the File ➪ Save As dialog box.

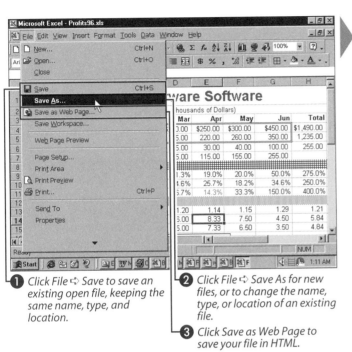

❶ Click File ➪ Save to save an existing open file, keeping the same name, type, and location.

❷ Click File ➪ Save As for new files, or to change the name, type, or location of an existing file.

❸ Click Save as Web Page to save your file in HTML.

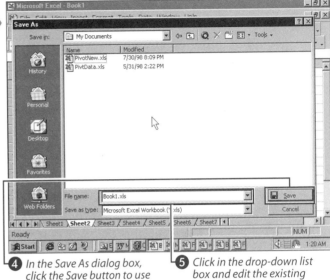

❹ In the Save As dialog box, click the Save button to use the name displayed.

❺ Click in the drop-down list box and edit the existing name or type a new name (there's no requirement to type .xls).

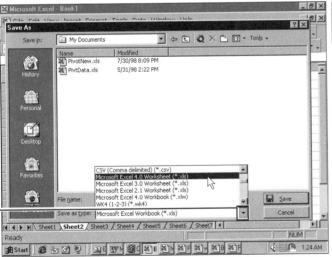

❻ In the Save As dialog box, click the arrow in the Save as type drop-down list box and select a format to save your file in.

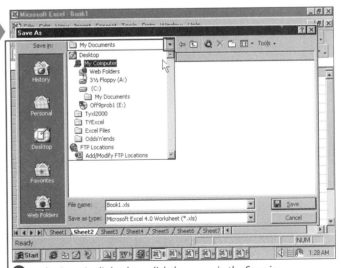

❼ In the Save As dialog box, click the arrow in the Save in drop-down list box to select any folder on any drive as a location to save your file.

Creating a New Workbook

When you enter Excel, a new workbook is already waiting to be used. There will be many times, however, when you're already using Excel that you need to create a new workbook. Maybe you realize that one of the workbooks that you have open is too large or has a worksheet that really doesn't belong there. You may want to move data or a whole worksheet into a new workbook.

A toolbar button exists that creates a new blank workbook with no questions asked. A command — File ⇨ New — that seemingly does the same thing, but actually is much more expansive. Instead of simply creating a new empty workbook, you get the opportunity to create a new workbook based on a template.

A number of template files ship with Excel 2000. With these templates, you can get a jump-start in creating a workbook. Some of these files are very professional-looking and have formulas set up so that you can enter data in many cells with little need to customize the formulas or to redesign the layout. These templates are also useful as a source of information on using functions and formats. You'll get lots of ideas just by navigating around these workbooks. Before opening any of these templates, you can see a preview to get some idea of the appearance of the workbook. When you select one of these files and open it, Excel does not really open the template file, but opens a copy of it with a temporary name. This prevents you from accidentally deleting the template. If you don't see any templates here and want to make them available, you need to rerun the Office 2000 setup utility and add the spreadsheet template.

TAKE NOTE

▶ TEMPLATE WORKBOOKS

If you have a particular workbook that you want to use as a skeleton, or template, for other workbooks, you can save such a workbook by using the File ⇨ Save As command and selecting template as the file type. In the future, these files will then appear in the New dialog box on the General tab when you use the File ⇨ New command. When you open a template file from the General tab, Excel opens a copy of the template file and gives it a temporary name that looks like the template name with a numerical suffix. For example, open the template file INVOICE and the workbook on your screen is named INVOICE1.

▶ ADD A TAB TO THE NEW DIALOG BOX

If you want to store template files in a tab in the New dialog box, create a subfolder of the Templates folder, located in the Microsoft Office folder. When you save Excel files as templates, you can store them there.

CROSS-REFERENCE

See Chapter 10 to learn how to move a worksheet from one workbook to another.

SHORTCUT

Press Ctrl+N to create a new, empty workbook.

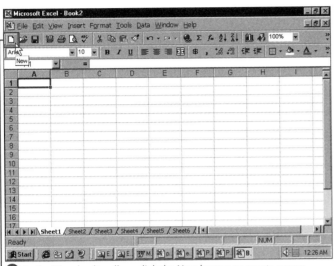

1 In the Standard toolbar, click the New button to create a new, empty workbook.

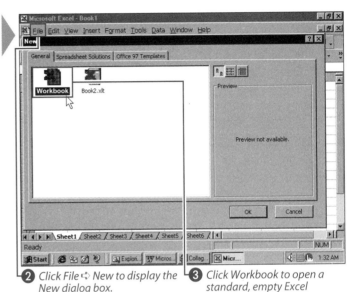

2 Click File ➪ New to display the New dialog box.

3 Click Workbook to open a standard, empty Excel workbook.

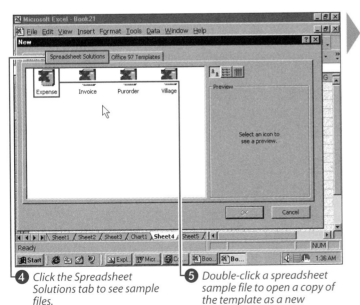

4 Click the Spreadsheet Solutions tab to see sample files.

5 Double-click a spreadsheet sample file to open a copy of the template as a new workbook.

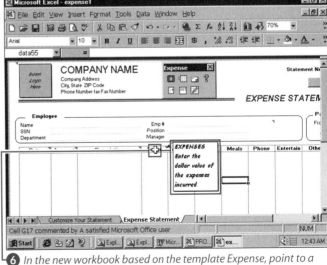

6 In the new workbook based on the template Expense, point to a cell with a red triangle on it to see a comment.

Finding and Opening a Workbook

When working in Excel, you will handle files that have already been created and that you're in the process of refining and changing. You probably gave some thought as to the most convenient location to keep these files. Depending on your work habits and your own particular or business needs, you're most likely to save your files on a hard drive location on your own computer, or on a network on one of the servers found in most companies today. In any case, you need to get to your files at a later time and you need to feel comfortable that you can find any file, no matter where it's located. The most obvious advice to anyone about saving files is to save them in the same folder. You can make that folder the default location in the File ⇨ Open dialog box.

The process of opening a file should be simple and straightforward. However, there will be times when you need to open a workbook but you only have a vague idea where it's located. Analysis of almost anyone's use of Excel will turn up this fact: When you want to open a file, it's often a file that you used recently. By default, Excel's File ⇨ Open command recognizes this fact, and can show you up to as many as nine of the files that you opened most recently.

When you use either the command or toolbar method to open a file, Excel only shows you the names of Excel files, but you can open files not created in Excel also.

If you're not sure where to find a file, but know something about its name, creation date, or size, you can use Excel's Find capability to locate the file.

TAKE NOTE

OPENING MULTIPLE FILES SIMULTANEOUSLY

When using the Open dialog box, you can select several consecutive files by holding down the Shift key and clicking the first and then the last file in group you want to select. To select nonconsecutive files, hold down the Ctrl key as you click the different filenames. When you click the Open button you will open all of the selected files.

DEFAULT FILE LOCATION

To set a default file location, select Tools ⇨ Options, then on the General tab, and in the panel next to Default file location, type the file path. You may need some additional help on what to type here, but if you want to store your files in a folder named Excel that's inside a folder named Office on your hard drive, then you would type c:\Office\Excel.

CROSS-REFERENCE

See Chapter 18 for information on how you can use a hyperlink in one workbook to open another workbook.

SHORTCUT

Press Ctrl+O to activate the File ⇨ Open command.

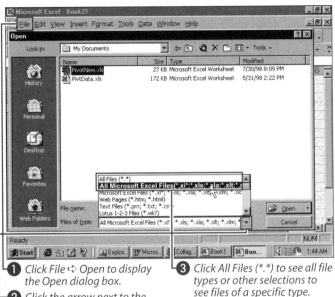

➊ Click File ➪ Open to display the Open dialog box.

➋ Click the arrow next to the Files of type drop-down list box.

➌ Click All Files (*.*) to see all file types or other selections to see files of a specific type.

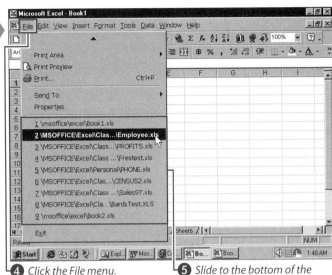

➍ Click the File menu.

➎ Slide to the bottom of the menu to see a list of up to 9 of the files opened most recently.

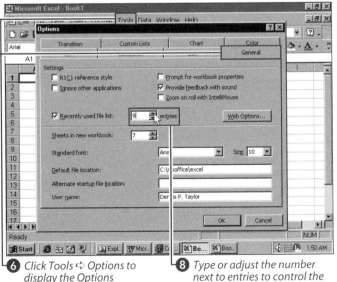

➏ Click Tools ➪ Options to display the Options dialog box.

➐ Click the General tab.

➑ Type or adjust the number next to entries to control the number of recent filenames that appear on the File menu.

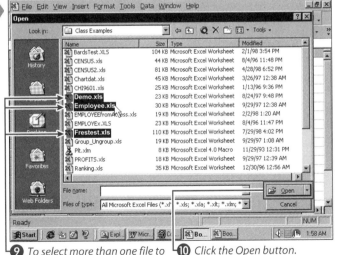

➒ To select more than one file to open at once, hold down the Ctrl key as you click files you want to open.

➓ Click the Open button.

Closing a Workbook

When you've finished working with a workbook file, you can leave it open indefinitely and continue to open and create other files, or you can close it. Closing a file means that the file no longer uses any space in memory and is no longer visible on your screen.

Be sure not to use the terms Exit and Close interchangeably. Use the File ⇨ Exit command to shut down Excel, and in the process, close all workbooks that may be open. Confusion may arise if you click the application icon located on the left side of Excel's title bar. The menu also includes the selection Close. In this case, Close means to close the Excel application.

You can close a workbook with a command or icon, or using one of two keystroke shortcuts, all of which are referred to in the images on the opposite page or in the notes below. You can also close all currently open workbooks at once, a handy feature when you realize that you have too many open workbooks that could be affecting the efficiency of your Excel usage.

When you close a file that you have made changes to and not yet saved, a warning appears. If you indicate that you want to save the file, no additional dialog box will appear and your file will be updated. However, if the workbook has never been saved before and you attempt to close it, you'll be confronted with the same kind of warning, if you indicate you want to save the workbook, the Save As dialog box will appear. This is so that you can assign a filename, file location, and file type, as necessary.

TAKE NOTE

CLOSING A FILE FROM THE KEYBOARD

In addition to closing a workbook by using the File ⇨ Close command or the Close button on the right side of the workbook's title bar, you can also use a keystroke shortcut that works throughout the Windows environment — Ctrl+F4. Use this keystroke shortcut to close a file in Excel, Word, Access, and so on. Remember its companion, Alt+F4, which you can use to exit the current application.

FINDING THE CLOSE DOCUMENT BUTTON

If the current workbook is maximized, there is only one title bar in Excel, but there are two sets of icons in the upper-right corner of your Excel screen. Click the lower of the two X icons to close the current workbook. If the current workbook is not maximized, it will have its own title bar, which will be located beneath the formula bar. To close this workbook, click the X icon on the right side of the workbook's title bar. With multiple workbooks open and displayed together, each workbook will have its own title bar, including a close document button.

CROSS-REFERENCE

Review Chapter 1 for information on the File ⇨ Exit command.

SHORTCUT

To close the current workbook, press Ctrl+W.

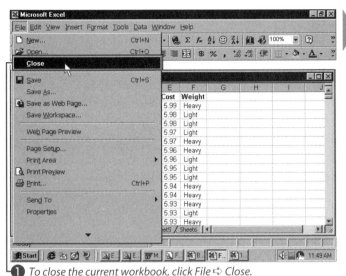

1 To close the current workbook, click File ➪ Close.

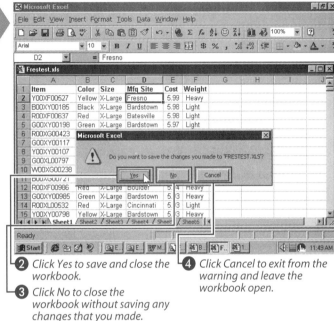

2 Click Yes to save and close the workbook.

3 Click No to close the workbook without saving any changes that you made.

4 Click Cancel to exit from the warning and leave the workbook open.

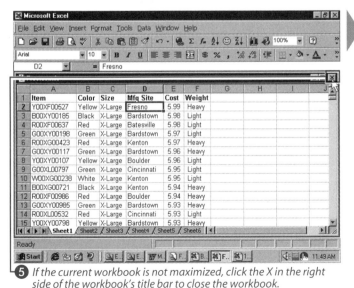

5 If the current workbook is not maximized, click the X in the right side of the workbook's title bar to close the workbook.

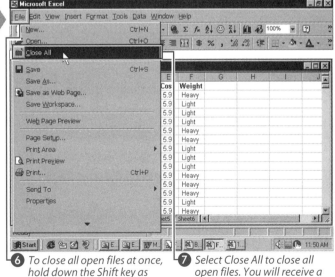

6 To close all open files at once, hold down the Shift key as you click to File menu.

7 Select Close All to close all open files. You will receive a warning (like the one shown in Step 2) for all open files where changes occurred.

Renaming a Workbook

One of the keys to managing your files intelligently is to use sensible filenames. There can be good reasons for using long filenames. Long names are more likely to be descriptive, they can contain the name of the creator, or they might contain the date of original creation. All of these kinds of naming techniques help you find a file at a later time. Short names have their advantages too — you don't need to readjust screen displays to see their complete names, they're easier to refer to when used in Excel formulas, and, if they're eight characters or fewer in length, they won't get truncated as they get copied or transmitted through different file systems.

There are many reasons for wanting to change the name of a file. Sometimes a name you created just isn't as descriptive as it should be. Occasionally, you will name a file identically to a file stored in a different directory. Although this is acceptable, common sense suggests changing the name of one of them. Some users are frequent recipients of files from others. Files named by other users often don't fit your needs, so you'll want to change those names also.

It's important to note the difference between renaming a file and saving a file under a different name. When you rename a file, you are not creating a new file, you're simply changing the name of an existing file. If you save an existing file with a new name you will actually have two files that are identical in content but with different names.

In Excel, you can rename a file whenever you're in the process of opening files, even though renaming and opening are two completely different actions. Renaming techniques are consistent with the file renaming methods available in Windows explorer.

TAKE NOTE

▶ DON'T FORGET FILE EXTENSIONS

When renaming a file, don't forget to include the period (.) and file extension (usually xls). If the name you use does not include the three-letter extension that was part of the original filename, you will get a warning message.

▶ A DOWNSIDE TO RENAMING

If you've become a proficient Excel user and have started to link files, when you rename a file that's referenced by other workbooks, you will encounter problems when you open those workbooks. Excel has commands and techniques to minimize this potential problem, but as a general rule, it's not a great idea to rename workbooks referenced by other workbooks.

▶ DON'T FORGET COPY/CUT/PASTE TECHNIQUES

If you're about to rename a group of files to have similar names, you can use Ctrl+C to copy one of the names while you're editing. As you start to rename each of the others, press Ctrl+V to paste in the name and adjust as necessary.

CROSS-REFERENCE

For information on renaming files that are linked, see "Linking Workbooks" in Chapter 17.

FIND IT ONLINE

See how some well-known musical figures have been renaming themselves at **http://www.partypros.com/musicmagic/Realnam.htm.**

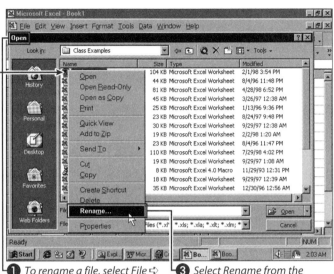

① To rename a file, select File ⇨ Open to display the Open dialog box.

② Right-click a filename you want to rename.

③ Select Rename from the shortcut menu.

④ You can also rename a file if you click it twice without double-clicking. When the file appears with a frame around it, retype it or click in the name to start editing.

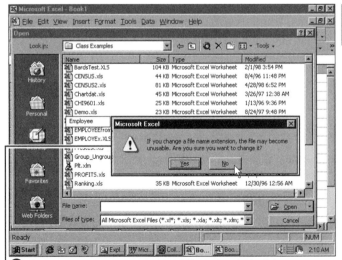

⑤ If you attempt to rename an Excel file and omit the 3-letter extension, this warning occurs. Click the No button and rename with the .xls extension.

⑥ If you attempt to rename a file and it duplicates the name of another file in the same folder, you get this warning.

⑦ Click the OK button and rename the file without duplicating it.

Personal Workbook

Q&A

① What toolbar button can you use to update the changes you've been making to your worksheet?

_____

_____

_____

_____

_____

② True or False: Use the File ⇨ New command to open a file you previously created and saved.

_____

_____

_____

③ How do you make Excel display recently opened filenames on the File menu?

_____

_____

_____

_____

④ How many previously used files can you see on the File menu?

_____

_____

_____

_____

⑤ True or False: The three-letter .xls file extension, automatically appears.

_____

_____

_____

⑥ Does it make any difference if you rename an Excel file and omit the three-letter extension?

_____

_____

_____

_____

ANSWERS: PAGE 322

EXTRA PRACTICE

❶ Create a small Excel file and save it on the desktop.

❷ Open an Excel file that you stored on the desktop.

❸ When using the File ⇨ Open command, you see that one of your files needs to be renamed. You want to rename it with the three-letter extension .act because it's an accounting application. Rename the file and observe the prompt and reconsider your action.

❹ Use the File ⇨ Save As command to save the current Excel file you're working with. Save the file under a different name. Use the File ⇨ Open command to see that you still have a file with the original name available.

REAL-WORLD APPLICATIONS

✔ You need to develop an invoice for your billing system. Using the File ⇨ New command, you find an Invoice template on the Spreadsheet Solutions tab and use it as the basis for your own invoice.

✔ You often open four of your files at the same time. You rename them so each begins with the same three letters. When you use the File ⇨ Open command, they appear together. You click the first one, then use the Shift key as you click the last one. Next, you click the Open button to open all four at once.

✔ You frequently find that you have many files open. When this happens, you hold down the Shift key as you select the File menu. Then you choose Close All.

Visual Quiz

In the screen shown below, what's the most efficient action you can take to find and open the Lotus 1-2-3 files that you want to convert into Excel files?

_____

_____

_____

_____

_____

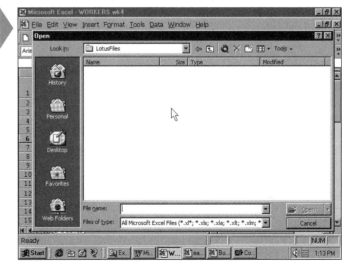

CHAPTER 5

MASTER THESE SKILLS

- Selecting What to Print
- Using Print Preview and Page Setup
- Selecting Orientation and Shrinking Print Ranges
- Setting Print Margins and Centering Output
- Controlling Headers and Footers
- Controlling Gridlines and Column/Row Headings
- Adjusting Page Breaks with Page Break Preview

Printing

Many of the display features that you use in Excel revolve around the way they appear on your screen. Although you may be thinking about the appearance of your worksheet on paper, it's not until you print your worksheet that you can truly judge its suitability for publication or as a handout in that all-important meeting. In particular, color and shading selections may create some surprising results. But before you print, you should always go through the Print Preview capability to get an onscreen preview of your worksheet.

By using Print Preview and Page Setup together, you can deal with the more obvious issues of orientation and size. Orientation refers to the direction that the printed image appears on paper, either parallel with the short edge of paper, like most letters, or rotated 90 degrees to be parallel with the long side of the paper. In Excel, the former is referred to as portrait, the latter as landscape. You also need to consider the placement of the material on the printed page. Centering is often preferred, but adjusting margins to allow more white space along the four edges of the paper is also a factor if you want to allow room for notations. Headers and footers are particularly useful with multipage output and gridlines. Row and column headings and page breaks are other printing features you need to give some thought to.

Except for the occasional surprise with color or shading, printing isn't really all guesswork. The various print commands and buttons give you firm control. In addition to Print Preview, you should also explore Excel's Page Break Preview feature, which offers some significant onscreen advantages and may be a better choice for some users than Print Preview.

When you're about to print, you may need to rethink your worksheet layout. What seems reasonable on the screen doesn't always pan out that way on paper. With onscreen usage, you tend to favor wide worksheets over tall ones — your monitor is wider than taller. On paper, you might prefer tall (portrait) over wide (landscape).

With Excel's print commands, you can print some or all of a worksheet, selected worksheets, or the entire workbook. In addition, if you are printing just one worksheet, you have control over which ranges on the worksheet to print.

Selecting What to Print

You can print workbooks and worksheets in many ways, but before printing, the first question to consider is: What do I want to print? If you immediately start printing without considering this, you might print more than you expect. It's not uncommon to have part of your worksheet set aside for comments or notes and not want that part included on your printed output. Situations also arise where you want to print only the summary part of your worksheet and not the detailed section. At other times, your needs may be the opposite.

Most often, you probably want to print a single worksheet, but there are some other variations that you should consider. You may want to print all of the worksheets in the current workbook or just a few of them. You can select just part of the current worksheet to print or you may decide to select a number of different ranges on the same worksheet. And to expand the possibilities even further, you might want to print a number of different ranges from a number of different worksheets in the current workbook.

If you make no selection before printing, the print commands assume you want to print the entire active area of the current worksheet.

TAKE NOTE

THE PRINT TOOLBAR BUTTON

If you use the Print toolbar button (fourth from the left in the Standard toolbar), printing starts immediately. If you didn't take the time to define the range of worksheets or cells to print, you will get an unexpectedly large and often unattractive printout. Define what you want to print before you use this button. Once you have spent some time preparing printed output and have printed your output at least once, you'll have a pretty good feel for how the current worksheet will appear on the printed page. You can make numerous nonformatting changes to your worksheet and click this button for no-questions-asked printing.

AN AUTOMATICALLY NAMED PRINT RANGE AREA

Select an area to print and then select File ➪ Print Area ➪ Set Print Area and you automatically create a range named Print Area. You can use this name like any other named range.

WHAT PRINTS IF I SELECT ALL OR A FEW WORKSHEETS?

If you want to print all of the worksheets in the current workbook or just a few, Excel checks each worksheet to see if you've selected a part of that worksheet to be printed. On those sheets where you do not indicate a range to print, Excel assumes that you want to print the entire active area of the worksheet.

CROSS-REFERENCE

Get more information on selecting and manipulating worksheets in Chapter 9.

FIND IT ONLINE

To learn about the development of print technology, take a look at **http://communication.ucsd.edu/ bjones/Books/printech.html.**

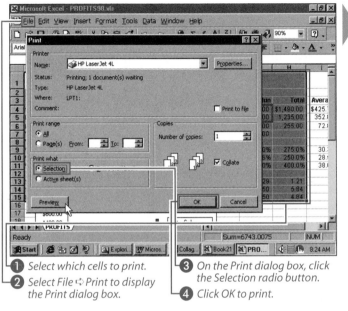

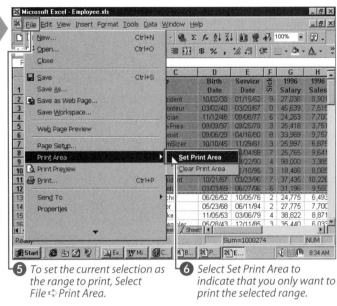

1 Select which cells to print.

2 Select File ➪ Print to display the Print dialog box.

3 On the Print dialog box, click the Selection radio button.

4 Click OK to print.

5 To set the current selection as the range to print, Select File ➪ Print Area.

6 Select Set Print Area to indicate that you only want to print the selected range.

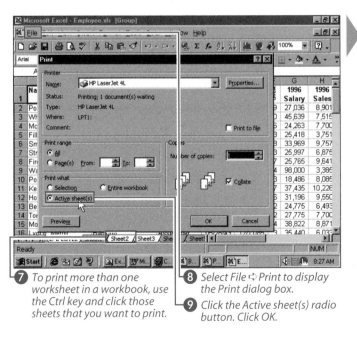

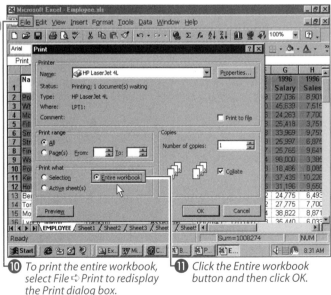

7 To print more than one worksheet in a workbook, use the Ctrl key and click those sheets that you want to print.

8 Select File ➪ Print to display the Print dialog box.

9 Click the Active sheet(s) radio button. Click OK.

10 To print the entire workbook, select File ➪ Print to redisplay the Print dialog box.

11 Click the Entire workbook button and then click OK.

Using Print Preview and Page Setup

In order to see what you're about to print and also have a quick way to adjust the prospective printout, you need to have a readily available set of features that work well together. One way is to rely on the Print Preview and Page Setup commands, both available on the File menu. Print Preview (which is also accessible from the Standard toolbar), enables you to see what you're about to print, while Page Setup gives you most of the tools to adjust how the printing will appear. You can work in a cyclical manner with these two features — making adjustments and viewing the results repeatedly until you're ready to print. In the Print Preview dialog box, you can find a quick way to activate Page Setup; when you've finished with Page Setup adjustments, your display returns you to Print Preview.

Whenever you use Print Preview, look to see how many pages printing will require. You may very well want to print fewer pages. Be sure to look at the images of each page of the printout. If some pages have just a slight amount of information on them, you may want to explore the Page Setup options that reduce the size of your printout. Or, you may want to return to the worksheet and make some adjustments there.

Back in your worksheet, it may be feasible to hide some columns or rows, or make some of the columns narrower. You might also decide to select a smaller range to print or reduce font sizes. All this considered, you shouldn't always be trying to squeeze your printed output onto fewer pages. The printed version may look too crowded and some worksheets look better on multiple pages anyhow. Return to Print Preview occasionally to assess the changes that you've made.

TAKE NOTE

COLLATING COPIES

If you want to print more than one copy of your output, indicate the number of copies on the right side of the Print dialog box. Also, when there's more than one page to be printed, consider whether to check or uncheck the collate box. For a five-page printout, for example, collate means print pages one through five, five times. With collate unchecked, you will get five copies of page one, five copies of page two, and so on.

VIEWING MULTIPLE PAGES IN PRINT PREVIEW

Unlike a number of the other packages in Office 2000, Excel doesn't have the capability in Print Preview to let you view more than one page at a time. Similarly, Excel has no way to control the percent of zooming that occurs when you zoom in and zoom out.

CROSS-REFERENCE

See the "Page Break Preview" task later in this chapter for a contrasting approach to previewing printed output.

FIND IT ONLINE

To get a preview of what will be printed in the next edition of the New York Times, go to **http://www. nytimes.com/**.

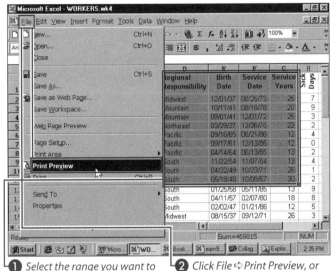

1 Select the range you want to print.

2 Click File ➪ Print Preview, or click the Print Preview button (fifth button from the left on the Standard toolbar).

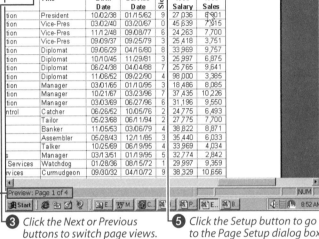

3 Click the Next or Previous buttons to switch page views.

4 Look in the lower-left corner for page count.

5 Click the Setup button to go to the Page Setup dialog box.

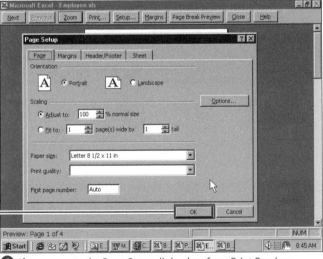

6 If you came to the Page Setup dialog box from Print Preview, make adjustments, and click OK to return to Print Preview.

7 Click the Zoom button or click the paper image to zoom in and out.

Selecting Orientation and Shrinking Print Ranges

When you're using Print Preview, you need to consider the implications of how the printed output might appear if it were rotated 90 degrees and printed horizontally along the long side of the paper. Experience may be your best judge here as to what will look best, but never overlook the opportunity to view your presentation from a different perspective. Choosing between the Portrait and Landscape modes of orientation is such an easy decision to make that you might as well try it just to see how the two displays compare. Another group of choices that you should explore stem from the need to fit your printed output to fewer pages or perhaps even one page. At times, your objective could be the reverse — you'd like to expand your printed output to fill up the page more than it currently does.

The Page Setup dialog box, accessible directly from the File menu or from the Print Preview screen is where you make all the choices related to rotating your output or adjusting its shrinkage factor. You are able to choose either of the mutually exclusive Portrait or Landscape buttons there. Helpful preview images describe the look of the output — landscape allows more columns and fewer rows than portrait. In times when you're not sure which way is best, try both.

Page Setup gives you the opportunity to simply shrink your print range to fit on a single page or to shrink a tall print range to a one page tall by two pages wide output or a wide print range to two pages tall by one page wide. As always, when you look at the preview after making your choice, it will be easier for you to decide which scaling to consider. After you see the preview and return, notice that Excel has applied a certain percentage of shrinkage to meet your objective. Initially, the number may seem trivial, but over time, you become familiar with such numbers as a predictor of how the printed output will actually appear. Be sure to check this number when you're exploring portrait/landscape options and trying to use shrinkage.

TAKE NOTE

▶ EXPAND TO FIT?

Excel has no expand-to-fit option. If you want your printout to fill the page, you'll just have to experiment with the scaling numbers in the Page Setup dialog box, noting each time in the preview if more than one page is required.

▶ SCALING NUMBERS

Scaling settings in Page Setup, just like in the worksheet environment, can range from 10 to 400. Through experience, you'll come to recognize what range of numbers produces acceptable output.

CROSS-REFERENCE

Check out the Page Break Preview task at the end of this chapter for a way to see a portrait or landscape preview as you continue to work with your data.

FIND IT ONLINE

If you'd like to look into the technical side of page orientation, check out **http://archive.nlm.nih.gov/ pubs/doc_class/prword.html** on the Web.

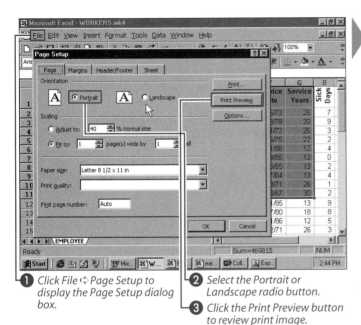

❶ Click File ➪ Page Setup to display the Page Setup dialog box.

❷ Select the Portrait or Landscape radio button.

❸ Click the Print Preview button to review print image.

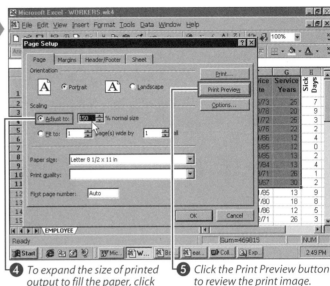

❹ To expand the size of printed output to fill the paper, click the Adjust to radio button and try a number larger than 100.

❺ Click the Print Preview button to review the print image.

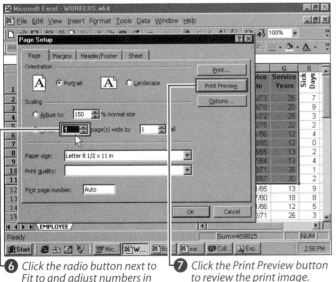

❻ Click the radio button next to Fit to and adjust numbers in both of the drop-down list boxes.

❼ Click the Print Preview button to review the print image. Return to Page Setup to see the percentage that Excel used for shrinking.

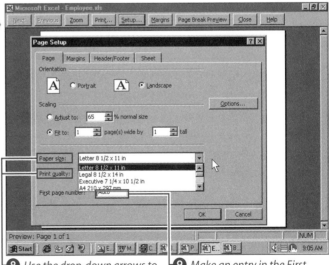

❽ Use the drop-down arrows to select paper size and print quality choices.

❾ Make an entry in the First page number box if you need a value other than 1.

Setting Print Margins and Centering Output

If your printed output is destined for publication or for use as handouts in a class, seminar, or meeting, you probably don't want information crowding the edges of the paper. You should leave plenty of room for notations, punched holes, or binding—basically, you want larger margins. Wider margins, if not overdone, give a lighter, less cluttered look that works well in certain situations.

If you're printing a large database and need to see a lot information on one or all pages, maybe your objective is different—use as much of the paper for printing as possible. Using smaller fonts and hiding columns will help to a certain extent, but shrinking the size of margins will make a more significant difference.

Margin adjustment, whereby you adjust the amount of space outside of the printed area on the paper, is a key component of printing. With margin adjustments, you can set the top, bottom, left, and right margins as well as the space allocated for a header and footer.

Margin settings are measured in inches. Most printers can handle margins as small as a ¼ inch, but the print may look like it's crowding the edge of the page. Remember also, that if you plan to use headers and footers, your settings for top and bottom margins need to be larger than your settings for headers and footers.

You can approach margin setting in two ways. If you're more likely to remember the numerical measure of the margin, you can use the Margins tab in the Page Setup dialog box. Here you can set a specific decimal value for the amount of margin space that you want. If you tend to make choices on a visual basis, and would prefer to drag margin boundaries and observe the changes to the page, then you can adjust margins from Print Preview. This method is similar to adjusting them on your worksheet—it even includes a number to represent the width in characters, the same kind of measure you see when you drag column widths in your worksheet.

TAKE NOTE

CENTERING YOUR PRINTOUT

If your printed output doesn't fill the page, you can adjust the margin settings to be larger so as to control placement of your output on the page. But, there's an easier way—rely upon the two check boxes available on the Page Setup dialog box. If you choose Horizontally, your output will be centered midway between the left and right margins (not the edges of the page). If you choose Vertically, your output will be centered midway between the top and bottom margins.

CROSS-REFERENCE
See the next task to learn how to use headers and footers.

FIND IT ONLINE
Learn about two great basketball centers at http://www.letsfindout.com/subjects/sports/tallmen.html.

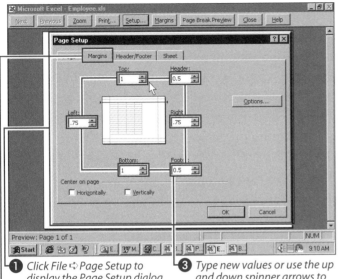

① Click File ➪ Page Setup to display the Page Setup dialog box.

② Click the Margins tab.

③ Type new values or use the up and down spinner arrows to adjust the sizes of margins, headers, and footers.

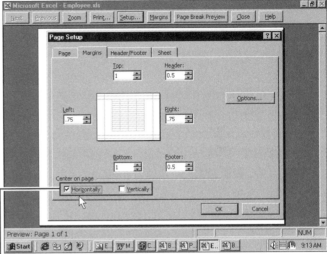

④ Click in the Horizontally or Vertically check boxes to center output left-right and top-down. Observe effects in the sample area.

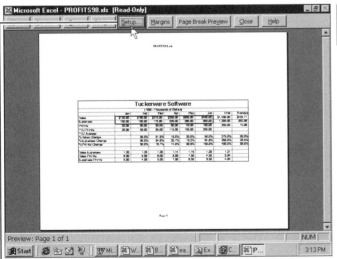

⑤ Click the Setup button to return to Page Setup and adjust the scaling number if necessary.

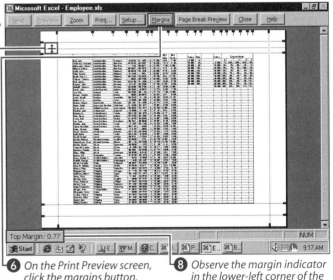

⑥ On the Print Preview screen, click the margins button.

⑦ Drag the margin line to increase or decrease the size of the margin.

⑧ Observe the margin indicator in the lower-left corner of the status bar.

Controlling Headers and Footers

When you first see a print preview of your output, you may be surprised to see a header line above the top of the worksheet image and a footer below the bottom. By default, Excel includes these in your printed output, even if you never asked for them. You can select from a list of different headers and footers or you can create your own.

The location of headers and footers is initially set to a half inch, but you can alter this spacing by going to the Margins tab in the Page Setup dialog box. (See the previous task.) If you want to allow more room for a header or footer (you can expand to occupy more than one line) be sure to enlarge the corresponding top and bottom margin settings as well as the header and footer settings. You can adjust all of these settings in a more visual way with the Margins button on the Print Preview screen.

The Header/Footer tab in Page Setup has a wealth of built-in headers and footers that include page numbers, sheet names, workbook names, your name, your company name, and dates in a variety of combinations. You can select from a list of one-line entries for both header and footer. You can create your own custom header or footer, either from scratch or by using one of the built-in headers or footers as a starting point and then editing it.

When you create a new header or footer, you can decide to include information in three separate areas: a left section with information aligned on the left margin; a middle section with information centered horizontally between the left and right margins; and a right section for entries that will appear aligned on the right margin. You can type anything in these three panels and you can activate codes from toolbar-like buttons to display the number of the current page, the total number of pages, the current date, the current time, the current workbook name, and the current worksheet name. Using a button, you can also adjust the font and font size.

TAKE NOTE

▶ DYNAMIC OR FROZEN DATE/TIME

When you use a button to insert a date or time into a customized header or footer, it's as if you're inserting a running clock into the printout. When you print, the current date and time are printed according to the actual time. If you'd prefer to set a specific date or time in your header or footer that will not react to your system clock, type it using the exact content that you want to see on the printout.

CROSS-REFERENCE

See Chapter 6 for a way to show all formulas in your worksheet.

SHORTCUT

When reviewing the list of built-in headers and footers, press the Home key to go to the top of the list, the End key to get to the bottom.

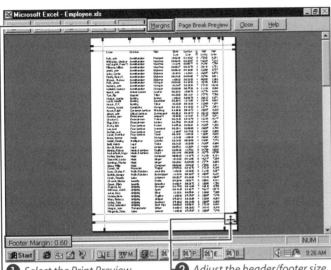

1 Select the Print Preview button from the Standard toolbar and click the Margins button.

2 Adjust the header/footer size by dragging the header or footer margin line up or down.

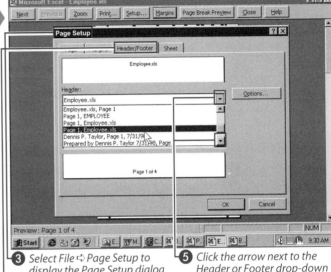

3 Select File ➪ Page Setup to display the Page Setup dialog box.

4 Click the Header/Footer tab.

5 Click the arrow next to the Header or Footer drop-down list box to see other built-in choices.

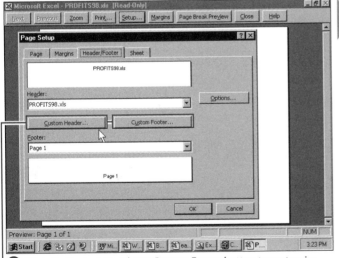

6 Click the Custom Header or Custom Footer button to customize your header or footer.

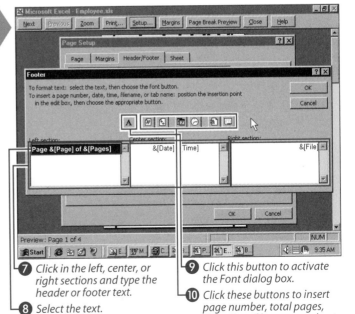

7 Click in the left, center, or right sections and type the header or footer text.

8 Select the text.

9 Click this button to activate the Font dialog box.

10 Click these buttons to insert page number, total pages, date, time, filename, or sheet name.

Controlling Gridlines and Column/Row Headings

Most Excel users favor the display of cell gridlines, column letters, and row numbers as they use their worksheets. Gridlines help you read a worksheet more easily and there's a natural tendency to want them on your printed output also. You may be surprised, therefore, when you view your print preview, to see that the cell gridlines are not there. After you add gridlines to your printed output and view the results on paper, you may have a change of heart. Gridlines on your screen represent a visible, but nonetheless subtle and understated presence. On paper, they may turn out to be more prominent than you wish. You be the judge, but there's ample reason to try printing your worksheet both ways so that you can make the comparison on paper.

Using gridlines on the screen and using them on your printed output are two separate choices, independent of each other. The same is true of your column and row headings, but for these settings, the rationale is quite different. Rare is the worksheet that doesn't have the column letters and row numbers displayed on the screen. It's the default setting and most users don't know or care how to remove them. For most users, however, it's a different story when it comes to printing. Usually, you don't want to see column letters and row numbers on your printout. If your worksheet is the centerpiece of an important budget meeting, such indicators may be unnecessary and could distract from the focus of your

presentation. If you're in the development stages of your worksheet, however, it makes good sense to display the row and column headings. If you display all of the worksheet formulas instead of the results of those formulas, it's useful to display the row and column headings also, which makes your printout a useful debugging tool.

TAKE NOTE

▶ WHAT HAPPENS TO HIDDEN COLUMNS AND ROWS ON YOUR PRINTOUT?

If you hide a column or row on your worksheet, it will not appear in your print preview or on your printout (if it's included in the range you're going to print). There won't be a gaping hole or anything else to indicate that anything is missing. However, if you choose to display row and column headings, any hidden columns and rows will be conspicuous because you will notice missing row numbers and column letters on your preview and printout.

▶ GRIDLINES TAKE TIME

It may not be intuitive, but large worksheets take longer to print if you choose to have the gridlines present.

▶ PARTIAL GRIDLINES

If you want a gridline effect on part of your printed output, you can apply border features to a selected range and then turn off the display of gridlines in the Page Setup dialog box. The border features will appear somewhat like gridlines.

CROSS-REFERENCE

See Chapter 3 to review the use of border effects in your worksheet.

FIND IT ONLINE

Learn about grid design at **http://www.griddesign.com/Pages/indexP.htm**.

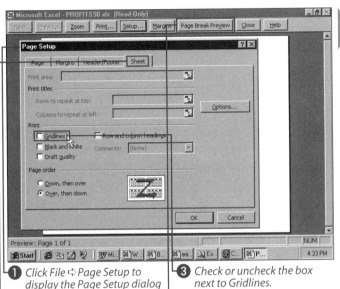

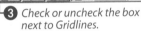

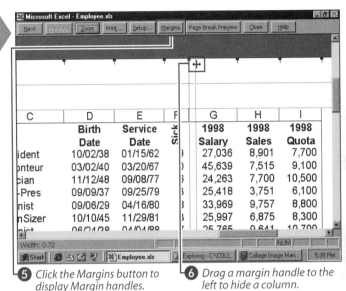

① *Click File ➪ Page Setup to display the Page Setup dialog box.*

② *Click the Sheet tab.*

③ *Check or uncheck the box next to Gridlines.*

④ *Click Print Preview.*

⑤ *Click the Margins button to display Margin handles.*

⑥ *Drag a margin handle to the left to hide a column.*

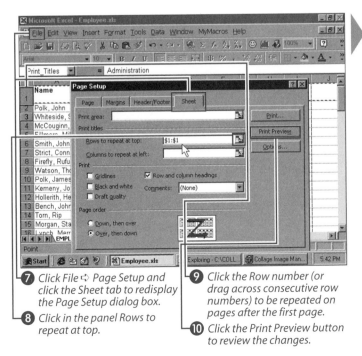

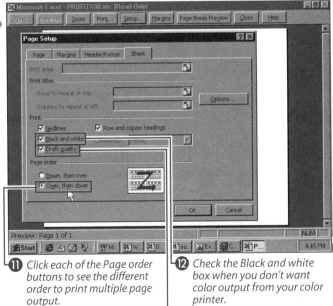

⑦ *Click File ➪ Page Setup and click the Sheet tab to redisplay the Page Setup dialog box.*

⑧ *Click in the panel Rows to repeat at top.*

⑨ *Click the Row number (or drag across consecutive row numbers) to be repeated on pages after the first page.*

⑩ *Click the Print Preview button to review the changes.*

⑪ *Click each of the Page order buttons to see the different order to print multiple page output.*

⑫ *Check the Black and white box when you don't want color output from your color printer.*

⑬ *Check the Draft quality box for faster printing; uncheck it for higher quality printing.*

87

Adjusting Page Breaks with Page Break Preview

On multiple page output, page breaks sometimes occur exactly where you don't want them to. You can adjust page breaks in Excel in a number of ways. One such way is through an explicit command, whereby you indicate that a page break will occur above a certain row, even if you later insert new rows above it. You can also control some page breaks indirectly, by shrinking your display to squeeze it onto fewer pages, adjusting margins, or switching portrait/landscape settings.

With Excel's Page Break Preview feature, however, you can get an easy-to-read, coherent image of your entire worksheet with the print range clearly delineated with page break lines. Best of all, you can drag these lines easily to adjust the page breaks. You can also continue to make changes to your worksheet (changing cell content, column widths, inserting rows, and so on) while using the preview feature.

Page Break Preview is actually just an alternate way to view your worksheet. Either you view your worksheet in Normal view or you view it in Page Break Preview. You can toggle back and forth between the two from the View menu.

When you activate Page Break Preview, your worksheet image shrinks and you clearly see page names in gray print and page breaks indicated by dashed blue lines. You can easily change these default page break lines to include more or less of your worksheet. If you move page break lines to a different location, you're setting an explicit page break (see Take Note). You can also drag the print range boundaries on the perimeter to include more or fewer columns and rows in the print range.

TAKE NOTE

▶ EXPLICIT PAGE BREAKS

If you want a certain row to be the first row at the top of a page, you can insert a page break there. Click the row number and then select Insert ⇨ Page Break. If you've activated Page Break Preview, you'll see a solid blue horizontal line indicating the page break. If you're viewing the screen in Normal view, you'll see a dotted line across the top of the row. To remove the break, click the row number and select Insert ⇨ Remove Break.

▶ SOLID OR DASHED LINES

In Page Break Preview, the solid blue lines represent breaks you have set, and the dashed blue lines are the default page break lines controlled by Page Break Preview. Drag a page break line up or down and you may see a new default page break line (dashed) emerge on the preview above or below the line you drag.

CROSS-REFERENCE

Compare Page Break Preview with Print Preview, covered earlier in this chapter.

FIND IT ONLINE

Check out the Page Break Paradise at **http://www. clipartcastle.com/bars.htm.**

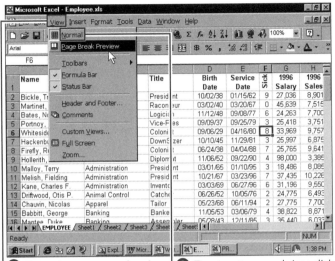

❶ To preview your page breaks, click View ➪ Page Break Preview.

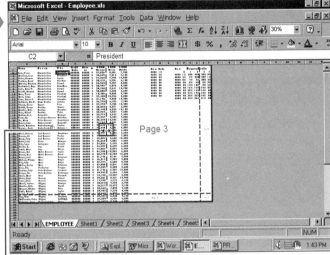

❷ To return to normal view, click View ➪ Normal.

❸ Click and drag page boundaries (dashed lines) to squeeze more on the page or push data onto other pages.

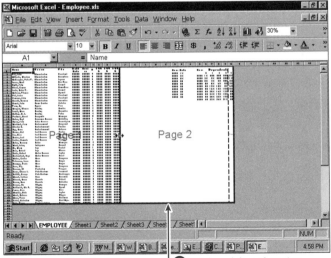

■ After you drag dashed lines to adjust page boundaries, they become solid lines.

❹ Click and drag the print selection edge to include more or less of your worksheet.

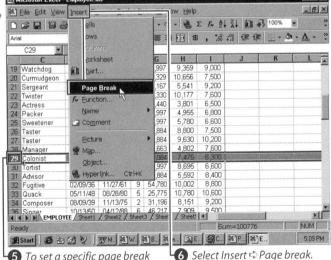

❺ To set a specific page break location in normal view, click the row number of the row that will follow the page break.

❻ Select Insert ➪ Page break.

Personal Workbook

Q&A

1 Is there an expand-to-fit button in Excel's Page Setup command?

_____

_____

_____

_____

2 Do hidden columns and rows appear on printed output if they are within the range selected for printing?

_____

_____

_____

_____

3 How can you start page numbering at a number other than 1?

_____

_____

_____

_____

4 What button must you use to get total pages in a header or footer, so that you can use a phrase like Page 2 of 5?

_____

_____

_____

_____

5 If you include cell gridlines on your printed output, does it take up more space? What about row and column headings?

_____

_____

_____

_____

6 If you want to be able to make worksheet changes as you observe page breaks, do you use Print Preview or Page Break Preview?

_____

_____

_____

ANSWERS: PAGE 322

PRINTING

Personal Workbook

EXTRA PRACTICE

① Hide some columns and rows, then click the Print Preview button to see your printed output.

② Prepare output that is in landscape orientation, shows gridlines and row/column headings, and is centered vertically and horizontally.

③ Shrink a column so that it's too narrow to display the contents properly. Activate Print Preview and click the Margins button. Adjust the width of the column by dragging the handles.

④ Prepare a header with your name on the left side, a date in the middle, and automatic page numbering on the right.

⑤ Using the File ⇨ Page Setup command, expand a one-page printout to take up two pages.

REAL-WORLD APPLICATIONS

✔ You often want a printout just for yourself so that everything squeezes onto one page. Routinely, you use the Scaling option on the Page tab of the Page Setup dialog box, setting the Fit to option to 1 by 1.

✔ Rather than using Print Preview to find out how many pages your printout will require, you switch to Page Break Preview mode where you have a clear image of pages required. Every month you print a 20-page report. The title page is prepared in Word. You want the Excel part of the report to have page numbers starting with page 2. Through the Page Setup command, you change the First page number setting on the Page tab to the number 2.

Visual Quiz

How do you center the output between the left and right side of the paper and between the top and bottom of the paper? Can you expand it to fill out the page better? How would you remove the column letters and row numbers and show gridlines instead?

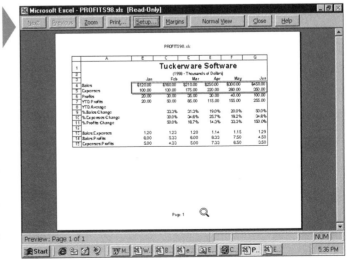

PART

II

Contents of 'Desktop'

Name

My Computer

Network Neigh

Internet Explore

Microsoft Outloo

Recycle Bin

My Briefcase

3252-9

3259-6

3261-8

3262-6

3281-2

3286-3

DE Phone List

Device Manager

In

Iomega Tools

Enhancing Excel Worksheets

Many of Excel's enhancement features spring from the fact that worksheets are dynamic creatures. Rare is the worksheet that remains unchanged after you create it. You will always want to do more with your worksheets, whether it's adding new rows and columns because you want to include new data, or using functions and formulas to derive additional information out of the data already in your worksheet. At certain times, you may also want to display your worksheet in certain ways so you can see widely dispersed cells or view data in different worksheets.

Creative opportunities both with your data and how it's displayed become more apparent with Excel's date handling and display features. You'll become interested in the benefits of using graphical features as you encounter the myriad of graphics creation and manipulation commands.

As your data handling needs expand, Excel's multiple-sheet workbook concept opens new vistas for dealing with related data in more sophisticated and productive ways.

CHAPTER 6

MASTER THESE SKILLS

▶ Undo and Redo

▶ Finding and Replacing Data

▶ Inserting and Deleting Columns and Rows

▶ Moving Data Within or Across Worksheets

▶ Copying Data Within or Across Worksheets

▶ Copying Formulas to Adjacent Cells

▶ Hiding and Revealing Columns and Rows

▶ Auditing and Documenting a Worksheet

▶ Finding Dependent and Precedent Cells

Modifying Your Worksheet

Even when you set out with a clear vision of how you want your worksheet to look, you invariably need to make changes to it. In Chapter 3 you learned how to make changes to your worksheet by adjusting column widths, realigning cell entries, applying color to text and cell backgrounds, using borders and patterns, and a variety of other formatting techniques. In this chapter the focus shifts to modifying the structure and content of your worksheet and using powerful commands to make major changes quickly. The Copy, Cut, and Paste commands, for example, let you copy or reposition large ranges of data without deleting and reentering data. And copying a formula into adjacent cells is one of the most powerful and frequently used commands in Excel.

As you take more adventurous steps with Excel, occasionally you will make some unintended changes that result in undesirable effects. With Excel's Undo capability, you are able to step back and undo the damage. If you have second thoughts about what you "undid", you can activate Excel's Redo capability.

To ease the chore of data entry and making massive content changes, you can use Excel's Replace capability, a feature normally associated with word processing. With Excel's AutoCorrect command, you can create codes that, when typed, automatically cause words or phrases to be entered into cells.

If you have confidential data in your worksheet and want to prevent this information from appearing on the screen and in printed output, you can hide columns and rows and readily redisplay them whenever necessary.

As your worksheets grow and mature, you'll want to be able to monitor changes. Sometimes you need to review formulas throughout a worksheet. You may want to find all of the cells that can contribute to the content of a specific cell. You can also find all of the cells that could be affected if you change the content of the active cell. You can use Excel's Auditing toolbar or use a quick keystroke method to locate these cells.

For better onscreen documentation, you need to learn about attaching comments to specific cells to remind you or others about a cell's content or usage.

Undo and Redo

Whenever you make mistakes when using Excel commands or toolbar buttons, you can recover from them by using the Undo capability. This feature is also useful when you're experimenting with a command or formula, trying to assess its accuracy by seeing the effect and deciding whether to go on or undo it and try it again with modifications. It's also handy when you want to view a worksheet where many cells are dependent on the value of an index that could change; change the index and watch the worksheet change. Undo the action and the worksheet returns to its former look. You can repeat such a cycle using Undo's companion feature — Redo.

Every time you use the Undo feature, those actions that you undo are placed in the Redo category. This is a useful feature because you may accidentally undo more actions than necessary. The Redo feature is structured just like Undo, occupying an adjacent position on the toolbar and in the Edit menu. Potentially, you have the ability to Redo up to 16 of the most recent actions that you "undid."

Similar to the Redo feature, Excel's Undo feature also lets you undo up to 16 of the last consecutive actions that you took while using the menu commands or the toolbar buttons. Some kinds of commands are irreversible. Commands that involve worksheet manipulation, such as inserting and deleting worksheets, cannot be undone. Some of the settings available through the Tools ⇨ Options command, such as turning gridlines on or off, are also actions that cannot be undone. You can't un-save a file or un-print a worksheet. Also, when you take certain actions, such as saving a file, the commands you used before them are not reversible.

The Undo feature can be used in two ways: to quickly reverse your last action, and to select from a list of up to 16 of your last reversible actions. When taking the latter approach, you get the chance to review these last 16 actions before deciding how many of them to undo.

The Undo feature is available from the Edit menu and from the Standard toolbar, but no matter which method you use, this capability is an essential tool in any Excel user's day-to-day usage.

TAKE NOTE

REDO OR REPEAT?

If you need to repeat your last action (as long as it wasn't an Undo), select the Edit command from the main menu. The second choice will be the word Repeat followed by the action you just took. This takes a few seconds, so you might want to use the keystroke shortcut — Ctrl+y — whenever you want to repeat an action. Remember, most of the time, your last action was not an Undo.

CROSS-REFERENCE

See Chapter 9 for more information on worksheet display features that you can't undo.

FIND IT ONLINE

For a more philosophical approach to Undo, read about "The Power of the Undo" at **http://michaeII. nscad.ns.ca/undo.html**.

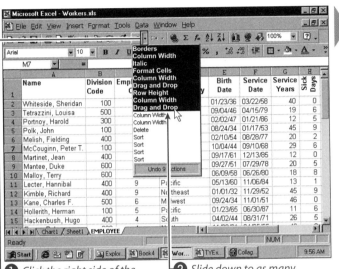

① Click the right side of the Undo button to see a list of up to 16 consecutive actions you can undo.

② Slide down to as many actions as you want to undo.

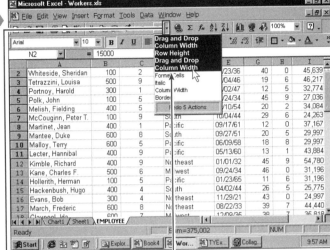

③ Click the right side of the Redo button to see a list of up to 16 consecutive actions you "undid" with the Undo command or button.

④ Slide down to as many actions as you'd like to redo.

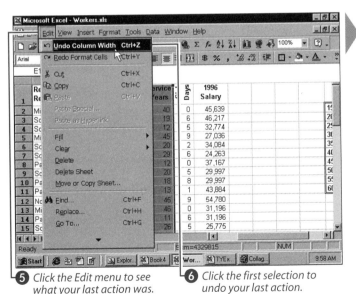

⑤ Click the Edit menu to see what your last action was.

⑥ Click the first selection to undo your last action.

⑦ If your last action did not use the Redo command or button, the second command on the Edit menu will tell you what action you can repeat. Click it to repeat your last action.

Finding and Replacing Data

Use Excel's Find capability to locate any word, phrase, cell reference, formula, or character string anywhere in the current worksheet. You may be adept at locating some of these things visually but normally you don't see formulas on the screen so it would be a time-consuming task to attempt to locate text or an address within formulas. In addition to finding information, you may need to replace it. If you need to have a cell reference or word replaced many times in a worksheet, Excel's Replace command is invaluable, fast, and accurate.

You may want to search through the entire worksheet or confine your search to a particular range. In a large worksheet, it's definitely advisable to keep the search restricted to a small area, thereby reducing the search time.

You can control your searching so that it's limited to an exact match (case sensitive). So if you search for US, you won't find us. If what you're looking for occupies an entire cell, you can make sure that searching only finds those cells where your search string fills the cell. With this restriction in place, you could find cells where US fills the cell but your search ignores AUSTRIA, AUSTRALIA, and RUSSIA.

Excel's Edit ⇨ Replace command is very similar to the Edit ⇨ Find command but with the added ability to substitute one string of characters for another. After indicating what you want to find and what you want to replace it with, consider these possibilities:

▶ You can replace the first occurrence of what you're looking for and then proceed to the next occurrence before deciding what to do there.

▶ If you don't want to replace the first occurrence of the string, you can skip over it to find the next occurrence of the string.

▶ You can replace all occurrences of the search string with the replacement string in one go.

▶ You can confine your use of Find and Replace to the current worksheet or you can expand it to a group of selected sheets.

TAKE NOTE

INSTANT REPLACEMENT

With Excel's AutoCorrect feature, you can develop a list of abbreviations or codes to represent long strings. Select Tools ⇨ AutoCorrect. Click the Replace box and type a code (making sure that it isn't a word or cell address that could lead to complications). In the With box, type the complete replacement word or phrase, then click the OK button. Thereafter, whenever you type the code, followed by a comma, period, or space, the replacement will occur instantly.

You can do your own form of ad hoc replacement by using this technique. Whenever you need to type a word or phrase you know you'll use frequently, make up a code on the spot and use it consistently. Occasionally, use the Edit ⇨ Replace command to find your code and replace it with the word(s) you really want.

CROSS-REFERENCE

See "Auditing and Documenting a Worksheet" later in this chapter to learn how to view a worksheet's formulas.

SHORTCUT

To repeat the last use of Edit ⇨ Find or Edit ⇨ Replace, press the F4 key.

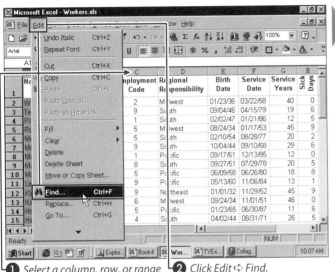

❶ Select a column, row, or range to minimize the worksheet area to search.

❷ Click Edit ➪ Find.

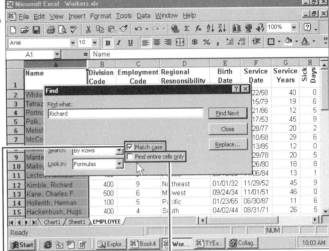

❸ Make a text search case sensitive by checking the Match case box.

❹ Check the Find entire cells only box if you're only looking for cells where the search string occupies the entire cell.

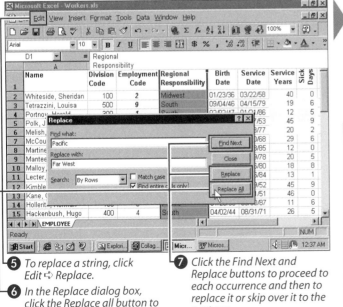

❺ To replace a string, click Edit ➪ Replace.

❻ In the Replace dialog box, click the Replace all button to replace all occurrences of one entry with another.

❼ Click the Find Next and Replace buttons to proceed to each occurrence and then to replace it or skip over it to the next one.

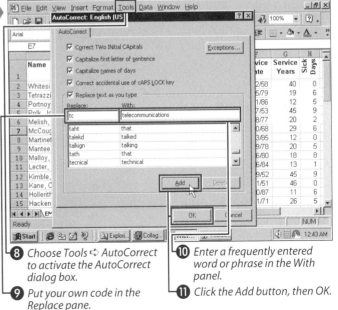

❽ Choose Tools ➪ AutoCorrect to activate the AutoCorrect dialog box.

❾ Put your own code in the Replace pane.

❿ Enter a frequently entered word or phrase in the With panel.

⓫ Click the Add button, then OK.

Inserting and Deleting Columns and Rows

One of the basic techniques you need when redesigning a worksheet's layout is a way to insert columns and rows, either because you want to add additional data or you need a more spacious look for your worksheet. It's equally important to be able to delete an entire column or row.

Imagine that you've built a worksheet to present monthly sales data in 12 columns, followed by a column for a yearly total. You later decide that you want to have quarterly totals after the end of each quarter. You now need a new column to the right of your March, June, September, and December columns.

When you insert a new column, it's an entirely new column extending all the way down the worksheet. All formulas anywhere in the worksheet that refer to data in columns to the right of the new column adjust automatically. In a similar way, any new row you insert extends entirely across the worksheet and affects all formulas that reference cells below the new row.

You can insert a single column or row at a time, or if necessary, insert multiple columns or rows at once. Excel allows you to insert a consecutive cluster or a scattered group of columns or rows. Although you might be worried about what might be happening to your formulas, Excel makes all formula adjustments automatically. In effect, cell references travel with the layout changes you make when inserting columns and rows.

When you delete a column or row, you are not simply erasing its contents, you are actually eliminating the column or row. Before deleting a row or column, make sure you are aware of any data that may exist in the row or column that's not displayed on your screen. You can delete a single column or row at a time, as well as a group of consecutive or nonconsecutive columns or rows.

> ## TAKE NOTE
>
> ### ▶ WHY CAN'T I INSERT A ROW OR COLUMN?
>
> If you ever try to insert a row, a column, or cells and are confronted with a message that says, "…Microsoft Excel cannot shift nonblank cells off the worksheet," you may have mistakenly entered data into the last row (row 65,556) or the last column (IV). There's an easy remedy — delete the unnecessary last row or column. You're then free to insert rows, columns, and cells.

CROSS-REFERENCE

See Chapter 7 for information on how formulas adjust to worksheet changes.

SHORTCUT

Select a row using Shift+spacebar and a column with Ctrl+spacebar and then insert with Ctrl+plus sign (from the numeric keypad) or delete with Ctrl+minus sign.

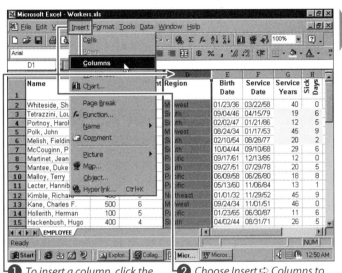

① To insert a column, click the column letter to the right of where you want the new column.

② Choose Insert ⇨ Columns to insert a new column to the left of the selected column.

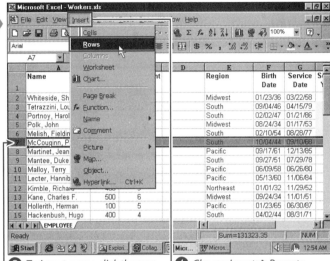

③ To insert a row, click the row number just below where you want the new row.

④ Choose Insert ⇨ Rows to insert a new row above the selected row.

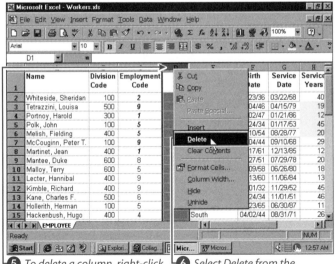

⑤ To delete a column, right-click the column letter or row number.

⑥ Select Delete from the shortcut menu.

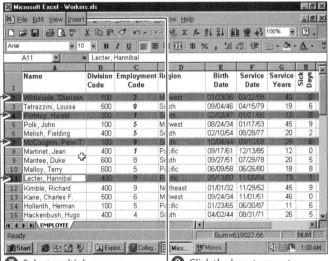

⑦ Select multiple rows or multiple columns together (using the Ctrl key with the mouse).

⑧ Click the Insert menu to proceed with inserting or right-click any selected row/column and select Delete.

101

Moving Data Within or Across Worksheets

A frequent task you need to perform as you redesign your worksheet is moving a range of data from one worksheet location to another. In some situations, you may find it more useful to move a large range of data instead of inserting a column or row. In Excel, if you want to move the contents (and formats) of a range, you can use Cut and Paste menu commands, toolbar buttons, or a sequence of keystroke combinations.

Cutting and pasting are two separate actions. When you cut data you remove it from your worksheet and place it on the Clipboard, a holding area in your computer's memory. You then paste the data from the Clipboard to another location on the current worksheet, to another worksheet in the same workbook, or to a worksheet in another workbook.

Formulas in the moved cells do not change. Formulas that refer to any cells in the cut area get adjusted to refer to cells in the paste area, and formulas that refer to cells in the paste area become illegal references when the paste is completed.

The cut-and–paste sequence is neither the fastest nor the most intuitive way to move data. When you drag a range of cells with the mouse, you may see what you are dragging and where you're dragging it to, but you can't select multiple ranges and drag them in one action.

If you drag cells to a destination where any of the cells are occupied, you will see the warning, "Do you want to replace the contents of the destination cells?"

You can also move a range of cells and insert them between other cells in one action.

TAKE NOTE

▶ DON'T LET DRAGGING BECOME A DRAG

It's tricky to drag a range of cells to a distant worksheet location. Make the process easier by first selecting the cells you want to move, and then clicking the Zoom control arrow in the Standard toolbar and selecting 50% or even 25%. Point to an edge of your selection so that you see an arrow and begin to click and drag. You won't need to drag too far if you've zoomed way back. Zoom back after the move.

▶ MOVE AND INSERT TOGETHER

If you'd like to move a range of data and at the same time insert it between cells, hold down the Shift key as you point to the edge of your selected range. As you drag the data to the destination, the onscreen indicator appears as a line so that you can position it between the cells where you want inserting to occur. Be sure to release the mouse button before the Shift key to complete the action.

CROSS-REFERENCE
See Chapter 10 for more information on opening multiple workbooks.

SHORTCUT
To learn more about moving data over the airwaves, check out **http://www.businessweek.com/1995/26/ b343019.htm.**

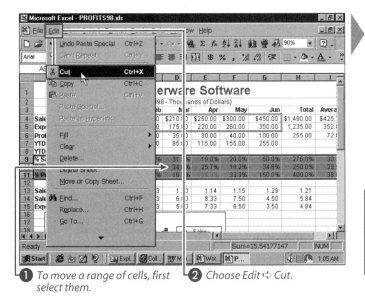

1 To move a range of cells, first select them.

2 Choose Edit ⇨ Cut.

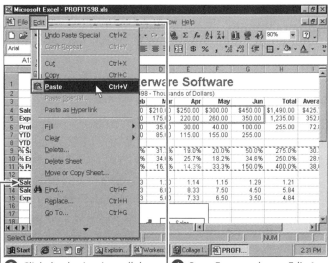

3 Click the destination cell that represents the upper-left corner of the range.

4 Press Enter or choose Edit ⇨ Paste.

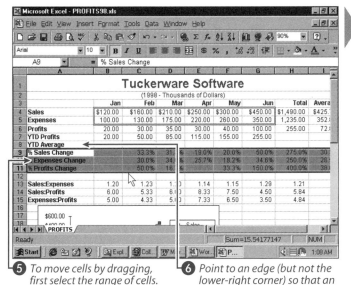

5 To move cells by dragging, first select the range of cells.

6 Point to an edge (but not the lower-right corner) so that an arrow appears and drag to the destination.

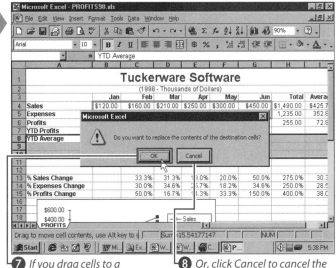

7 If you drag cells to a destination where any cells are occupied, you see a warning message. Click OK to complete the move.

8 Or, click Cancel to cancel the move and leave cells in place.

Copying Data Within or Across Worksheets

Although copy and move are often mentioned in the same breath, your need to use these capabilities varies widely and, in many respects, they are quite different. In general, the idea of copying means that you want to keep data in one location and create a duplicate elsewhere. If the cells to be copied contain raw data, the meaning is clear. However, if the cells that you want to copy contain formulas, you're more likely to want to copy the formulas. This kind of action is referred to as a relative copy. Imagine a cell containing a formula that adds three cells to its left. Do you want to copy the result that you see in the cell or do you want to copy the formula that's the real content of the cell? So, whenever you're about to copy some cells where any formulas are included, you should ask yourself this question — Do I want to make a copy of the data as it appears in the cells, or do I want to copy the formulas?

Excel gives you the ability to handle both kinds of situations through its Copy ⇨ Paste Special command. However, when you use mouse methods, you get copies of formulas adjusted to the destination area, with no questions asked. As with moving, you can copy information from one part of your worksheet to another, on the current worksheet, to a different worksheet in the same workbook, or to a worksheet in another open workbook. Unlike moving, however, you can copy information and then repeatedly paste it in different locations — in effect, one copy, many pastes.

Formulas that arrive in the paste location are adjusted relatively. Formulas that refer to cells in the copy area remain unchanged, and formulas that refer to cells in the paste area continue to refer to cells in the paste area and react to the new contents.

TAKE NOTE

COPYING WITH THE MOUSE

Despite the ease of using the Cut and Copy commands or their toolbar equivalents, copying with the mouse is usually faster and almost as easy as moving cells with the mouse. Hold down the Ctrl key, point to the edge of the range (that you've selected to copy) and drag it to the destination, releasing the mouse first. If you drag cells to a destination where any of the cells are occupied, you will see the warning, "Do you want to replace the contents of the destination cells?"

CROSS-REFERENCE

Refer to the next task in this chapter to learn about relative and absolute references and their roles in copying formulas.

FIND IT ONLINE

If you're concerned about the legal issues of copying, go to http://www.ariadne.ac.uk/issue2/copyright/.

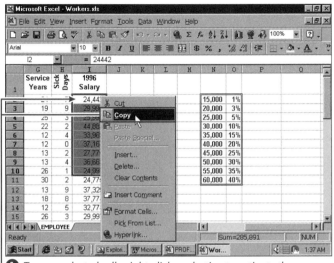

1 To copy selected cells, right-click a selection to activate the Shortcut menu and select Copy.

2 Right-click the destination to activate the Shortcut menu and select Paste.

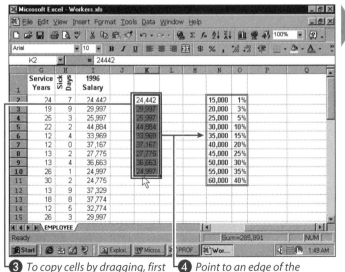

3 To copy cells by dragging, first select the cells.

4 Point to an edge of the selection and drag to the destination with the Ctrl key held down. Release the mouse before the Ctrl key.

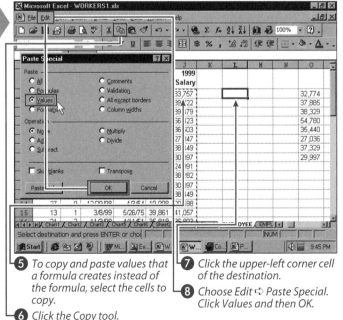

5 To copy and paste values that a formula creates instead of the formula, select the cells to copy.

6 Click the Copy tool.

7 Click the upper-left corner cell of the destination.

8 Choose Edit ⇨ Paste Special. Click Values and then OK.

Copying Formulas to Adjacent Cells

If you analyze situations where you have created formulas, you will see a common scenario: Create a formula in one cell and then copy it into contiguous cells either down a column or across a row. You can use all of the standard copy and paste methods available to handle the situation, but the need to copy formulas to adjacent cells is something you'll use so frequently that Excel has two commands, Edit ⇨ Fill Right and Edit ⇨ Fill Down, that are designed just for this purpose.

To copy formulas into adjacent cells, you should have some understanding of how Excel handles formulas during this kind of action. When you make a copy of a cell that contains a formula, you get a formula that is adjusted relatively. If you're copying a formula that subtracts the two cells above it, you expect to get a formula that takes the same relative action of subtracting the two cells above it. Whenever you use any of the standard copy techniques, you get this kind of result. It is referred to as a relative copy.

If you need to copy a formula and want to make sure that a cell reference does not get adjusted relatively, you need to make that reference absolute. Imagine a worksheet where you're about to create a series of formulas that refer to an index value in cell B6. If you create a formula that refers to cell B6 and then copy that formula to the right, you will get subsequent formulas that refer to C6, D6, E6, and so on. You must change your original formula so that B6 becomes an absolute reference. You can change the

formula and make B6 look like B6, or use the shortcut described in the note that follows. If you copy the cell, all of the destination cells refer to B6 also.

TAKE NOTE

▶ CELL REFERENCES, ABSOLUTELY

To make a reference absolute, edit the cell, select the cell address, and press the F4 key. This causes dollar signs to appear; a cell address such as C3 will appear as C3. Press Enter to complete editing. When you copy the cell to any other location, the absolute reference stays intact.

▶ COPYING DOWN A COLUMN

If you need to copy a formula down a long column into adjacent cells quickly, a handy trick is to point to the fill handle and double-click. This action causes your selected cell to be copied down the column into as many cells as are occupied in the column to the left. If the cell to the left of the active cell is empty, Excel will copy the active cell's content downward into as many cells as are occupied in the column to the right.

CROSS-REFERENCE

Refer to the previous task in this chapter for information on copying formulas and copying values.

SHORTCUT

When selecting a cell to copy, select it and the adjacent destination together. Next, press Ctrl+R to copy it to the right or Ctrl+D to copy it down.

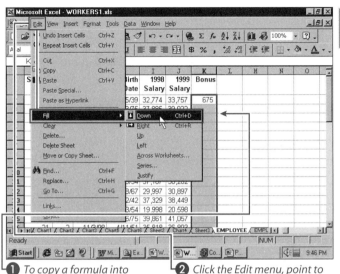

1 To copy a formula into adjacent cells using commands, first select the cell to copy and the adjacent destination cells.

2 Click the Edit menu, point to Fill and slide to Down (if you selected cells in a column) or Right (if you selected cells in a row).

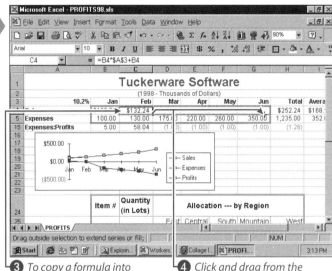

3 To copy a formula into adjacent cells using the mouse, first select the cell to copy.

4 Click and drag from the lower-right corner (the fill handle) of the active cell into the adjacent cells.

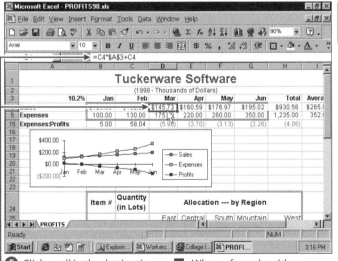

5 Click a cell in the destination range to see a relative copy of the formula that was copied.

■ When a formula with an absolute reference is copied, the absolute reference — A3 — stays the same in the destination cells.

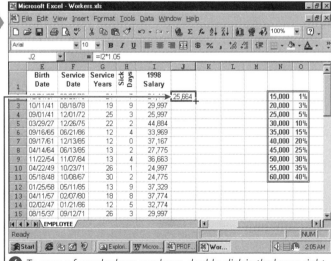

6 To copy a formula down a column, double-click in the lower-right corner (on the fill handle) of the cell that contains the formula.

Hiding and Revealing Columns and Rows

Hiding a column or row might not be something that's critical to worksheet development, but it's extremely useful in a variety of situations. Here are a few examples:

- ▶ Your monitor is visible to others and you often have sensitive or confidential data in your worksheets that you'd like to keep out of sight.
- ▶ You only occasionally refer to data in a particular column, so you might as well hide that column.
- ▶ You want to see more columns currently off the right side of the screen while retaining those on the left side of the screen and split-screen techniques are too unwieldy to use.
- ▶ You want to print your worksheet and leave out certain columns or rows inside your print range.

When you hide a column or row it is no longer visible and other columns and rows appear to have moved over or up to fill in the space. At first, you will see a thick vertical line where the hidden column or row had been, but after you move the active cell elsewhere, the line disappears. A subtle display difference is that the boundary between column letters and row numbers appear slightly thicker if there's a hidden column or row there. A more obvious difference, but one that you sometimes may overlook, is that there are missing letters in the column headings and missing numbers in the row headings. You can also hide a series of consecutive or nonconsecutive columns or rows.

When you print a worksheet that has hidden columns and rows within the printed range, the hidden information does not appear on your printout and there's no gaping hole to suggest that anything is missing. However, if you choose the Print ⇨ Setup option that displays column and row headings, the column letters and row numbers referring to the hidden elements will be notable by their absence.

You can easily reveal a hidden column or hidden row, but not both at once. You can also reveal a number of selected columns or rows at a time.

TAKE NOTE

▶ HIDING IS NOT DELETING

Contents of cells that are part of hidden columns and rows are part of the worksheet and you can refer to them in formulas whenever necessary. Active cell movement, however, is restricted. You can't move to hidden cells with the arrow keys or select one with the mouse.

▶ HIDING CELLS

There is no command to hide a range of cells, but a number of techniques exist to achieve this goal. Perhaps the easiest way is to select the cells you want to hide and then, from the Font Color toolbar button, choose white as the font color.

CROSS-REFERENCE

See Chapter 9 to learn how to set up split screens and panes.

SHORTCUT

Press Ctrl+0 to hide the column of the active cell; press Ctrl+9 to hide the row of the active cell.

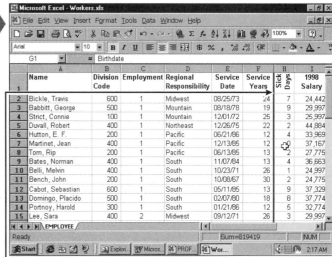

1 To hide selected columns or rows, choose Format ⇨ Column or Row.

2 Select Hide.

■ A thick vertical line appears on the worksheet just after you hide the column or row.

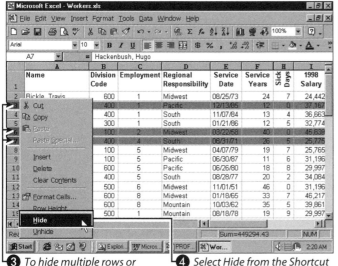

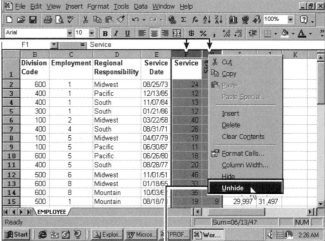

3 To hide multiple rows or columns, hold the Ctrl key down and click them. Right-click any selected row number or column letter.

4 Select Hide from the Shortcut menu.

5 To reveal a hidden column, drag across surrounding column letters.

6 Right-click to activate the Shortcut menu and select Unhide.

Auditing and Documenting a Worksheet

When you're looking at a worksheet that someone else created or one of your own that you haven't used in a while, you need some help in understanding where formulas are and what cells they relate to. For more efficient use of your worksheet, you may need to provide some information on how it's structured, how you've organized data, or how an unusual formula works. Excel has a number of auditing and documentation tools that will help.

You can find formulas as you move the active cell around a worksheet and observe the formula bar, but this becomes an unthinkable task in a large worksheet and who's guaranteeing that you'll find every cell with a formula? Furthermore, you'd like to see the entire worksheet with formulas clearly visible on the screen so that you can analyze it and perhaps print it that way also. Excel gives you a way to see the formulas in a worksheet displayed in their cells where you usually see results. All column widths are twice as wide as usual. With some formulas, you may still need to make the columns wider to see the entire formula. For documentation or debugging reasons, you can print your worksheet with the formulas exposed.

If you use a lot of range names in a worksheet, it's easy to lose track of them and the drop-down box on the left side of the formula bar only shows you seven of them until you start scrolling, but it doesn't give you their locations. You can create a copy of all your range names and their locations, placing them right on the worksheet. If you anticipate using this feature, first put the active cell in a location where you have enough open cells to accommodate a two-column list.

TAKE NOTE

▶ TOGGLING BETWEEN FORMULAS AND RESULTS

One of Excel's best keystroke shortcuts lets you toggle back and forth between displaying formulas and displaying results. Ctrl+` uses the key just above Tab and below Esc on most keyboards. Usually it's on the same key with tilde (~). Try it a few times and you'll forget there's a command.

▶ HOW BIG IS THIS WORKSHEET?

Press Ctrl+End as you encounter an unfamiliar worksheet. The active cell will appear in the lower-right corner of the active part of the worksheet. You can be sure that all columns to the right of this cell and all rows below this cell are empty and that there is at least one entry in the row and column of this cell.

CROSS-REFERENCE

Refer to Chapter 2 for information on creating range names.

FIND IT ONLINE

To get the real scoop on auditing and other accounting terminology, go to the Auditing Glossary of Terms at **http://www.ais-cpa.com/glosa.html**.

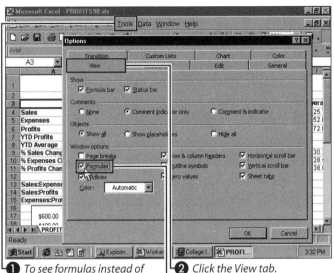

1 To see formulas instead of results in worksheet cells, choose Tools ➪ Options to display the Options dialog box.

2 Click the View tab.

3 Check the box next to Formulas in the Windows options section.

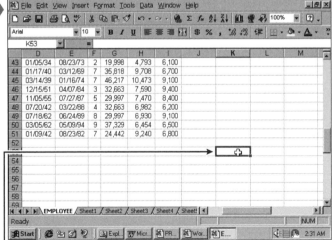

4 To preview the printed version of the worksheet showing formulas, click the Print Preview toolbar button.

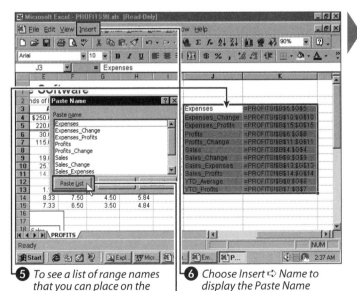

5 To see a list of range names that you can place on the worksheet, position the active cell in an open area.

6 Choose Insert ➪ Name to display the Paste Name dialog box.

7 Click the Paste List button.

8 Press Ctrl+End to move the active cell to the lower-right corner of the active worksheet.

■ All cells in columns to the right and rows below this cell are empty.

Finding Dependent and Precedent Cells

It's not always easy to anticipate what impact changing one cell is going to have on cells throughout the worksheet and perhaps to other worksheets in the current workbook or to cells in other workbooks. Excel's auditing capability, primarily in the form of the Auditing toolbar, gives you an easy way to trace all dependent cells. On other occasions, you may need to assess the accuracy of a cell by tracking the source of its formula. This can become a voluminous task when you realize that many cells contribute to the cell in question. The 3 also lets you trace these precedent cells.

With the Auditing toolbar, you can find all of the cells that depend on the value in the active cell. If there are dependent cells, one or more arrows, pointing to these cells, will appear. You can see these dependencies emerge on your screen, step by step.

The Auditing toolbar also lets you track down precedents — all cells that contribute to the result that you see in a particular cell. Here too, you will see arrows on your worksheet that point to the different cells in the current worksheet that impact the selected cell. You can see these arrows emerge, in stages, to represent different levels of dependence. Sometimes this question is just as important as finding dependents.

If you want to explain what a cell contains, or provide a warning about a cell's content, you can attach a comment to a cell. You can type a comment for a selected cell so that in the future, anytime you slide the mouse over the cell, the comment will pop up in a yellow box. Slide away from the box and the comment disappears. You can easily edit comments whenever necessary. A cell with a comment is instantly identified by the red triangle in the upper-right corner. Techniques also make it possible to display the comments on top of the worksheet and enable you to print a worksheet with all of the comments visible. Standard printing of a worksheet will not reveal the triangle in the upper corner of cells with comments.

TAKE NOTE

▶ AUDITING ON OTHER WORKSHEETS IN THE SAME WORKBOOK

When you use the Auditing toolbar to locate dependent or precedent cells, you will sometimes see an arrow pointing to a grid image. This is actually a reference to a cell on another worksheet in the current workbook. You can double-click the arrow line to display the Go To dialog box, which shows the location on the other worksheet. You will not, however, get a series of references across different worksheets, even if they exist.

CROSS-REFERENCE

See Chapter 15 to learn how to use the Auditing toolbar to check for valid data.

FIND IT ONLINE

To learn about dependent cells from an anatomical perspective, go to **http://www.synthecon.com/ bioreactor.htm**.

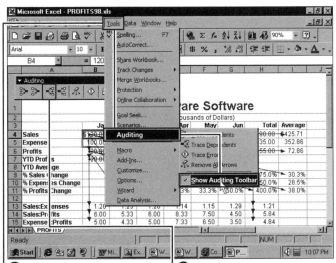

❶ Choose Tools ⇨ Auditing ⇨ Show Auditing Toolbar.

❷ Click repeatedly on the Trace dependents button to reveal layers of cells dependent on the active cell.

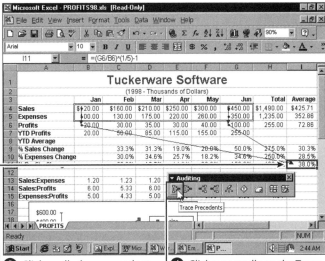

❸ Click a cell whose precedents you want to find.

❹ Click repeatedly on the Trace precedents button on the Auditing toolbar to reveal layers of cells that contribute to the content of the active cell.

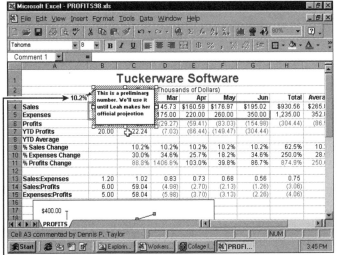

❺ To create a comment in a cell, press Shift+F2, then type a comment.

■ Click elsewhere to end the comment.

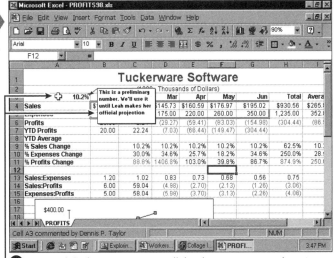

❻ As you slide the mouse over a cell that has a comment, the comment pops up.

Personal Workbook

Q&A

1 Can you use the Undo feature to Undo the File ⇨ Save command?

_____

_____

_____

2 Is deleting a row equivalent to erasing all data in that row?

_____

_____

_____

3 Do you need to adjust any worksheet formulas if you insert a row or column?

_____

_____

_____

4 True or False: If you don't see the destination on your screen, you can't move a range of cells by dragging them.

_____

_____

5 Can you copy formulas up or to the left of adjacent cells just as you can copy them down or across to adjacent cells?

_____

_____

_____

_____

6 Can you write formulas that refer to data in hidden columns or rows?

_____

_____

_____

_____

7 What's a quick way to display all formulas in your worksheet?

_____

_____

_____

_____

ANSWERS: PAGE 323

EXTRA PRACTICE

1. Using the Tools ⇨ Options command, click the General tab and uncheck the Gridlines box. Use the Undo button to verify that you can't undo all actions.

2. Using the AutoCorrect feature, create a 2-letter code for the word Overhead. Use the code as you type a cell entry and observe the result.

3. Insert a new row above Row 1 and use it for a worksheet title.

4. Using the Cut and Paste toolbar buttons, move data from one worksheet to another.

REAL-WORLD APPLICATIONS

✔ Your worksheet has 12 columns of data for a year. You want quarterly totals, so you insert new columns to the left of April, July, etc. After writing total formulas for the first quarter you copy these formulas into the new cells for the remaining quarters.

✔ You're about to make a correction to a sales figure in a worksheet that you've just assumed responsibility for. You're concerned about the impact of this change on other cells. You activate the Auditing toolbar and check for all cells that are dependent on the one you're about to change.

✔ You frequently use a worksheet that contains the birth dates and salaries of employees in your organization. Other people can see your monitor, so you hide the columns that contain this data.

Visual Quiz

You want to replace all occurrences of US with USA in Column D. Do you need to select Column D first? How do you activate the dialog box shown? Do you need to check the Match case box? Should you also check the box next to Find entire cells only? What will happen if you leave both boxes unchecked and click the Replace all button?

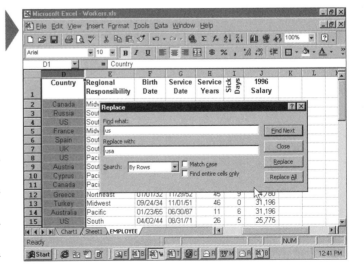

CHAPTER 7

Using Formulas and Functions

For many Excel users, mastering the use of formulas and functions is the centerpiece of this software. This is where you turn mere numbers into more meaningful information. Whether your math skills are good or just so-so, you'll be writing formulas, using some of Excel's 325 functions, or using a combination of both. You can't really think of functions as separate from formulas.

For the most part, Excel functions are formulas that have been written for you to handle commonly needed calculations. While it's true that many functions are mathematically oriented, a lot of them have little to do with your math skills, so don't be intimidated by the idea of using functions.

The beauty of many Excel functions is that they perform complex calculations that you don't really see or need to understand in detail. A case in point is the PMT function, whereby you can determine the monthly payment on a car or house loan simply by providing the interest rate, the number of payments, and the amount borrowed. You don't necessarily know that the math performed by this function involves raising a number to a negative power.

Certainly, there will be times when you need to write a formula to arrive at a result and without functions that can assist you. Many of the formulas that you need are ones that you can create using the most basic math skills, but at other times, you may need to call upon a friend or just keep trying until a formula works. Fortunately, the Excel environment is ideal for testing and retesting, using sample data, and setting up formulas with simple values for rapid evaluation. It's not a bad idea to use an empty worksheet in your workbook as an area for experimenting with formulas and functions.

In this chapter you see a few examples of commonly used formulas and learn how to use the extremely helpful Paste Function tool to get a jump-start on using functions. In addition to getting some exposure to the major types of functions in Excel, you also learn how some selected functions give you powerful analytical tools to become a more productive user of Excel.

Using Formulas to Calculate YTD and Percentage Changes

Two kinds of formulas exist that may come in handy in a variety a situations. The first one calculates a year-to-date (YTD) total. The second calculates a percentage change. Learning how to set up formulas like these (neither is very lengthy) teaches lessons about formula building that include the concept of relative formulas, the idea of testing and evaluating, and the importance of parentheses to control order of operation.

The key idea behind a year-to-date calculation is the idea of cumulative totals. Use it if you'd like to maintain a running total of sales, profits, or some other amount. Whether your data is in a column or row makes no real difference — the concept is the same.

Imagine a column of sales figures for the first few months of the year. You plan to record the sales for each additional month as you review your receipts. You have set a yearly goal and want to keep an eye on what's happening from month to month and you need to see your yearly total so far. A YTD column will show you two useful pieces of information: The total for the year so far — just look at the total next to the last month recorded — and the YTD total up to any given point in the year. This could be useful when comparing this year's totals with last year's.

For the first month, the YTD total is simply equal to the first month's amount. For the other 11 months, you need a formula to add the most recent month's YTD total to the previous YTD total.

You can calculate percentage of change in a variety of situations where you're trying to perceive the rate of change, perhaps on a month-to-month basis. Rather than just seeing the amount of change occurring month-to-month, you'd like a better measure of change — one that shows the percent of change each month.

The first obvious aspect about percentage change is the fact that you need to be comparing the figures of two periods in order to make a calculation. Therefore, you can't really calculate a value for the first month because there's no previous value to compare it to.

The standard method of calculating percentage change is: (Second period - First period)/(First Period Value).

TAKE NOTE

USING PARENTHESES

Don't forget the critical role that parentheses play in this and many formulas. Without parentheses in this example, division occurs first, creating an obvious calculation error. Be sure to use parentheses to control the order of operation; you need to have the subtraction occur before the division.

AN ALTERNATE METHOD

Another way to handle percentage change is: First Period Value/Second Period Value – 1.

CROSS-REFERENCE

Read more about the rules of precedence in formulas in Chapter 2.

FIND IT ONLINE

If you're troubled by basic math concepts and fundamentals, take a look at **http://edie.cprost.sfu.ca/~rhlogan/basicmth.html**.

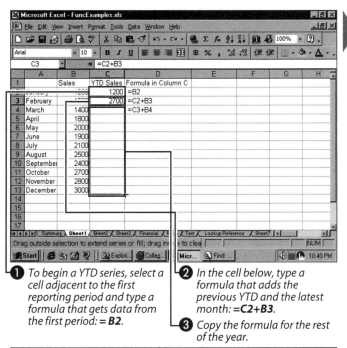

① To begin a YTD series, select a cell adjacent to the first reporting period and type a formula that gets data from the first period: **= B2**.

② In the cell below, type a formula that adds the previous YTD and the latest month: **=C2+B3**.

③ Copy the formula for the rest of the year.

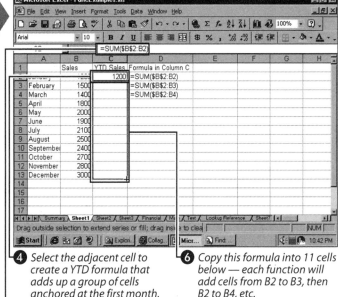

④ Select the adjacent cell to create a YTD formula that adds up a group of cells anchored at the first month.

⑤ Type = **sum(B2:B2)** to add up all the cells from B2 to B3.

⑥ Copy this formula into 11 cells below — each function will add cells from B2 to B3, then B2 to B4, etc.

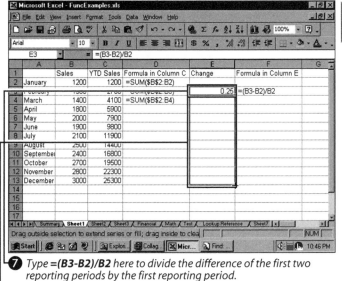

⑦ Type =**(B3-B2)/B2** here to divide the difference of the first two reporting periods by the first reporting period.

⑧ Copy the formula for the remaining 10 months.

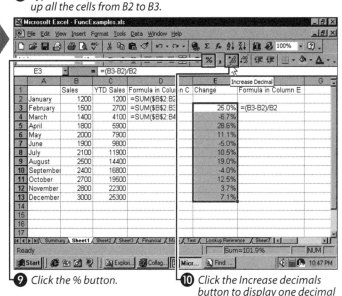

⑨ Click the % button.

⑩ Click the Increase decimals button to display one decimal place; repeat for additional places.

Using the Paste Function Tool

ecause there are so many functions in Excel, it can be a daunting task to know which functions exist, what their names are, and how to use them. A useful Excel feature, the Paste Function button in the Standard toolbar, can help with this problem and serves as an on-the-spot aid during formula writing.

Whether you're an Excel novice or an experienced user, you can find the Paste Function tool to be of enormous help. Often, you'll be in situations where either you think, or you have been told, that a function exists that's just what you need to derive a particular result. When you activate the Paste Function, you open the door to all functions. If you happen to know the specific name of a function, or at least the kind of category it's included in (Financial, Mathematical, Text, Logical, etc.), your search is quick indeed. Otherwise, you may need to explore a bit, but even then, the structure of this feature is logically organized.

The Paste Function dialog box provides you with an alphabetical list of all functions, for those situations when you know the function you want, and a grouping of functions by category, which is ideal when you know the kind of function you need but don't know its name.

When you select the function you're interested in, you get a brief description of it and a way to activate a help screen that ultimately gives you a full description and some examples. You can even copy some of these examples into your worksheet. Even more useful is the second screen in the Paste Function sequence, where you get prompting for each argument that the function requires. Instead of typing in cell addresses, you can use the mouse to highlight pertinent cells.

Functions vary widely in their complexity and number of arguments, so there's a wide range of argument types and options. A key aspect of using the Paste Function feature, however, is the idea that you get onscreen help on each step of the way in using an unfamiliar function. After using a certain function a few times, you may find it faster to bypass the Paste Function feature and simply type the function in your worksheet. The feature is always there when you need it, though.

TAKE NOTE

PASTE FUNCTION'S MEMORY

Once you've used the Paste Function a few times, you'll want access it a little faster, and you can if you click the equal sign that's in the formula bar. It won't be obvious at first, but you can then click a drop-down list box that shows you the functions you've used most recently. Click one to use it again.

CROSS-REFERENCE

Review information in Chapter 1 on using the Help system — a source of information on all functions.

SHORTCUT

After typing a function name, press Ctrl+A to activate the Paste Function dialog box.

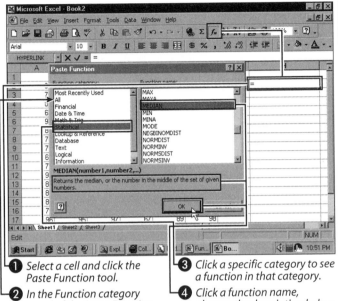

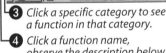

1 Select a cell and click the Paste Function tool.

2 In the Function category panel of the Paste Function dialog box, click All to see a list of all functions.

3 Click a specific category to see a function in that category.

4 Click a function name, observe the description below and click OK.

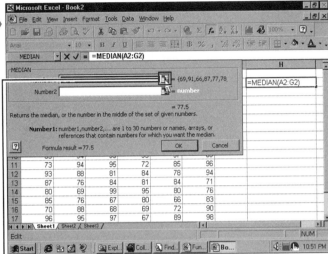

5 Click the range box on the right side of the dialog box; for some functions, type an address or value here.

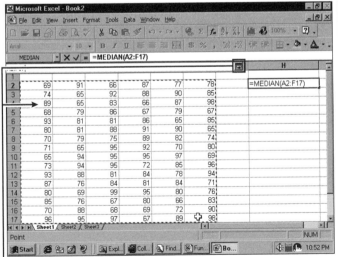

6 With the dialog box shrunk, select a cell range and click the range box to restore the dialog box.

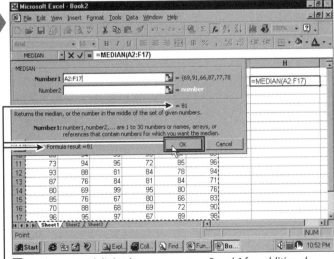

■ In the restored dialog box, repeat steps 5 and 6 for additional arguments if necessary.

7 Observe the result in the dialog box; click OK to complete the function entry.

Using Statistical Functions

Even if you're not a statistician, you'll want to use some of Excel's 80 statistical functions, many of which are applicable in multiple workbooks.

The AVERAGE function, which calculates the arithmetic mean, is probably the most widely used function after SUM. Most users approach this function with little concern for its meaning and operation — doesn't everybody know what an average is? You must, however, consider how this function calculates averages when blank cells are included in the range being averaged. For example, if you use the AVERAGE function to evaluate three cells, two of which contain the value 15 and the third of which is a blank cell, you get 15 as an answer. But if the cells contain 15, 0, and 15, you get 10. Sometimes, you'll overlook this fact and your incorrect answer will appear credible.

Use the COUNT function to find out how many cells in a range contain values. You can use this function as a validity check to uncover non-numeric entries, such as a lowercase L (l) in place of the number one (1) or a capital O in place of zero (0). Use the COUNTA function to find out how many cells in a range are not empty.

Sometimes, you want to sort data so that highest or lowest values are on top, but it's often not practical to do this. The MIN function returns the lowest value in a range without indicating where the value occurred. Similarly, the MAX function returns the highest value in a range.

The SMALL and LARGE functions are variations on MIN and MAX. They return the *nth* smallest and the *nth* largest values in a range, respectively. Usually, you'll be looking for the second or third highest (or lowest) value in a range, but you can use any number that's no larger than the range size. Like MIN and MAX, these functions don't return the location of the result.

The RANK function returns a number representing the rank of a cell's value compared to all of the other values in the range that the cell is part of. If the rank of a cell is tied with another, they both have the same ranking and the next ranking value is omitted.

Calculating the standard deviation of a range of values is one of the most commonly used statistical measures and certainly one of the most error-prone if done manually. STDEV and STDEVP provide you with two widely used methods of calculating standard deviation. Explore the VAR and VARP functions if you need to calculate the variance of a range of values.

TAKE NOTE

RANGES IN FUNCTIONS

In statistical functions, the range you select to analyze can be a series of ranges and may also include values. The function =AVERAGE (A2:A9,100,B4,C2:D4) is valid and averages eight values in the range A2:A9, the value 100, the value in B4, and the six cells in the range C2:D4. The result is an average of 16 values. Similarly, the function MAX(A4:B7,E4:G7) returns the highest value in the 20 cells referred to between the parentheses.

CROSS-REFERENCE

Read more about selecting ranges in Chapter 2.

FIND IT ONLINE

Learn about the law of averages at **http:// www. nils.com/rupps/3540.htm**.

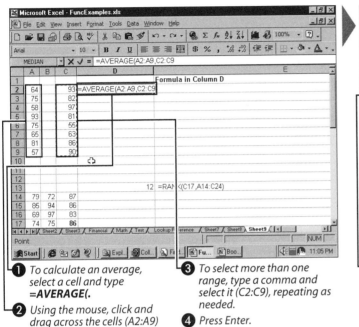

1 To calculate an average, select a cell and type **=AVERAGE(.**

2 Using the mouse, click and drag across the cells (A2:A9) that you want to average.

3 To select more than one range, type a comma and select it (C2:C9), repeating as needed.

4 Press Enter.

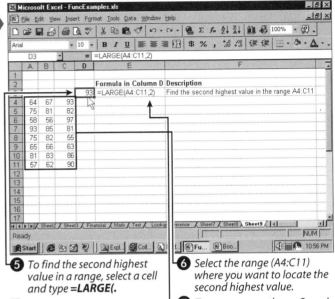

5 To find the second highest value in a range, select a cell and type **=LARGE(.**

■ Function names are not case sensitive but Excel displays them as uppercase.

6 Select the range (A4:C11) where you want to locate the second highest value.

7 Type a comma, then a **2**, and then press Enter.

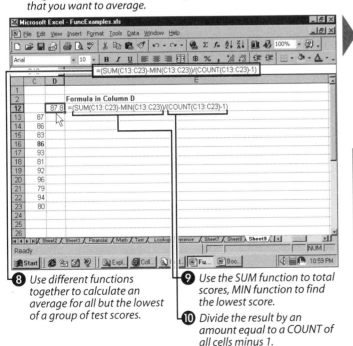

8 Use different functions together to calculate an average for all but the lowest of a group of test scores.

9 Use the SUM function to total scores, MIN function to find the lowest score.

10 Divide the result by an amount equal to a COUNT of all cells minus 1.

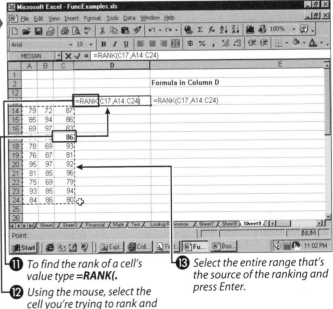

11 To find the rank of a cell's value type **=RANK(.**

12 Using the mouse, select the cell you're trying to rank and type a comma.

13 Select the entire range that's the source of the ranking and press Enter.

Using Financial Functions

Excel has many useful financial functions. Some of them involve annuities (cash flows over time), others solve depreciation calculations, and others are for calculating the rate of return.

Many of the financial functions require you to enter interest rates in terms of their payment. If you're paying 7.5 percent interest, it's usually stated as a yearly rate, but applied on a monthly basis, as are most home and car loans. In financial functions, the rate is expressed as 7.5%/12 or .075/12. In addition, the time period is usually expressed in months, so that when you refer to a 5-year loan, the number of periods covered is 60 months.

One of the most widely used of these functions is PMT, which can calculate the monthly payment (principal and interest) on a loan, perhaps for your house or car. This function needs three pieces of information: the interest rate, the number of periods, and the amount you're borrowing. After using the function a few times, experiment with it freely so you can find out how much that extra quarter percent really means to your monthly payment. Equally useful, is the way you can experiment with the meaning of a shorter loan or a larger loan.

The FV (Future Value) function, which computes the future value of a series of equal cash flows made on a regular basis, gives you a quick way to find out how much that $200 a month you're setting aside into an interest-bearing account will amount to after a selected number of months. Like many of the financial functions, it allows you to include a lump sum that's there at the start of the term.

The FV (Future Value) function, in layman's terms, gives you an easy method of calculating how much you can borrow if you've set a monthly payment that you think you can handle, taking into account a specific interest rate and term.

The RATE function will tell you what rate you need if you're going to make a specific monthly payment for a set term to pay off a loan. This function, like many other financial functions, has additional arguments that allow you to make guesses and assumptions.

Another group of financial functions is related to depreciation calculations. Use the SLN function for straight-line depreciation, the SYD function for a sum-of-the-years depreciation method, and the DDB function for the double-declining balance method.

TAKE NOTE

FINANCIAL TERMINOLOGY

If you're not conversant with financial terminology, you may initially be put off when you see some of the descriptions of financial functions in Excel's Help system. But usually, you will find an example or two written in layman's terms, which you can copy into your worksheet.

CROSS-REFERENCE
Read more about the Help system in Chapter 1.

FIND IT ONLINE
Check out CNBC's Market and Financial Terminology site at **http://www.cnbc.com/tickerguide/termin.html.**

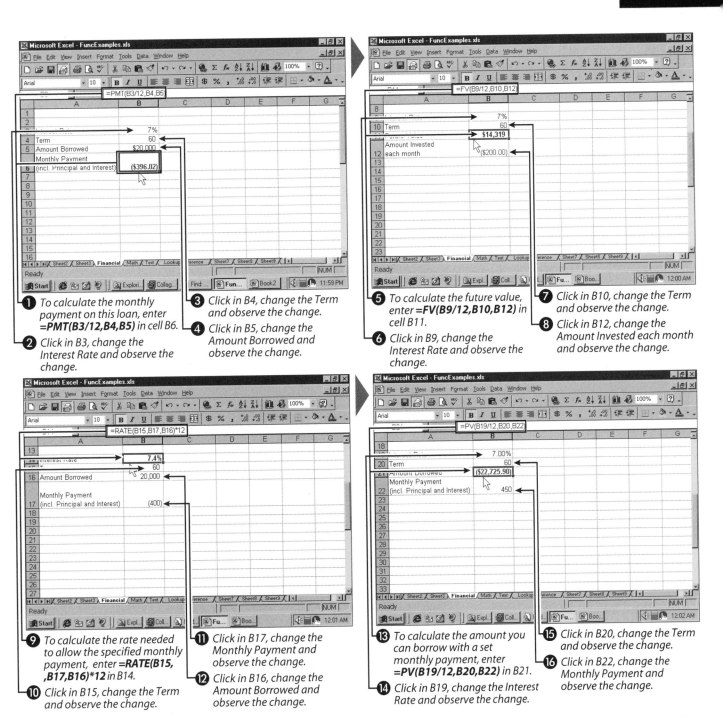

① To calculate the monthly payment on this loan, enter =**PMT(B3/12,B4,B5)** in cell B6.

② Click in B3, change the Interest Rate and observe the change.

③ Click in B4, change the Term and observe the change.

④ Click in B5, change the Amount Borrowed and observe the change.

⑤ To calculate the future value, enter =**FV(B9/12,B10,B12)** in cell B11.

⑥ Click in B9, change the Interest Rate and observe the change.

⑦ Click in B10, change the Term and observe the change.

⑧ Click in B12, change the Amount Invested each month and observe the change.

⑨ To calculate the rate needed to allow the specified monthly payment, enter =**RATE(B15, ,B17,B16)*12** in B14.

⑩ Click in B15, change the Term and observe the change.

⑪ Click in B17, change the Monthly Payment and observe the change.

⑫ Click in B16, change the Amount Borrowed and observe the change.

⑬ To calculate the amount you can borrow with a set monthly payment, enter =**PV(B19/12,B20,B22)** in B21.

⑭ Click in B19, change the Interest Rate and observe the change.

⑮ Click in B20, change the Term and observe the change.

⑯ Click in B22, change the Monthly Payment and observe the change.

Using Mathematical Functions

Mathematical functions include a variety of sophisticated functions suitable for scientific usage. There are functions for logarithms (natural and base 10), radian and degree conversion, and all of the standard trigonometric and geometric functions. But there are also a number of functions useful and necessary in many nonscientific workbooks. Rounding functions, for example, have wide applicability, particularly in accounting worksheets.

The ROUND function is exactly what you need when you're trying to change the actual value of a calculated cell by mathematical rounding, and not just its appearance through formatting. With the ROUND function, you can round a calculation to a specified number of digits — to the nearest tenth, hundredth, thousandth, and so on — to the right of the decimal point or to the left of the decimal point.

Similar functions, such as ROUNDUP and ROUNDDOWN are designed for those occasions when you'd prefer to round up or down to the nearest decimal place or integer place. Related functions such as FLOOR and CEILING, give you rounding possibilities keyed to specific values instead of to decimal or integer values. You may want to raise the price of all items to the nearest nickel, for example. The functions ODD and EVEN, provide more rounding possibilities to the nearest odd or even number.

When you want to round down to the nearest integer (ignore the decimal portion of a positive value), use the INT (short for integer) function. When applied to a cell or calculation, the INT function returns the nearest whole number after rounding down. The TRUNC function, nearly identical, simply discards the decimal portion, and is different from INT in the way it treats negative numbers.

The RAND function generates a random number between zero and 1, a fact not instantly appreciated by everyone. The function could be useful in situations where you want to rearrange data in no apparent order. Imagine a workbook which keeps a record of all of your invoices. For reasons of quality control, you would periodically like to pick 20 of them at random so that you can review them in detail. You can fill an adjacent column with random numbers and sort the records based on the random values in this column so that the records appear in random order. You can then use the first 20 records to review.

TAKE NOTE

ADD MORE FUNCTIONS

The Excel add-in package, Analysis ToolPak, adds financial, statistical, and engineering analysis functions that you may find useful. After installing this feature, you will have more functions to choose from when you use the Paste Function button. To add the ToolPak, click Tools ➪ Add-Ins. Check the Analysis ToolPak box and click OK. If you don't see Analysis ToolPak in the list of Add-Ins, click Browse and locate the filename for the Analysis ToolPak add-in or run the Setup program.

CROSS-REFERENCE
Read more about sorting in Chapter 15.

FIND IT ONLINE
For an in-depth discussion, and a different perspective on rounding rules, go to: **http://dbhs.wvusd. k12.ca.us/Rounding.html.**

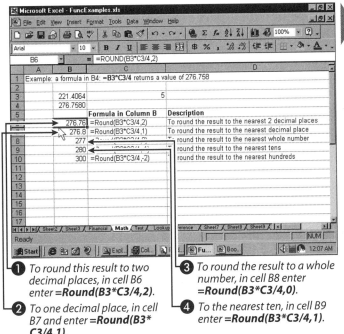

❶ To round this result to two decimal places, in cell B6 enter =**Round(B3*C3/4,2)**.

❷ To one decimal place, in cell B7 and enter =**Round(B3*C3/4,1)**.

❸ To round the result to a whole number, in cell B8 enter =**Round(B3*C3/4,0)**.

❹ To the nearest ten, in cell B9 enter =**Round(B3*C3/4,1)**.

❺ To round the result down to two decimal places, click in cell B13 and enter =**Rounddown(B3*C3/4,2)**.

❻ To round the result down to one decimal place, click in cell B14 and enter =**Rounddown(B3*C3/4,1)**.

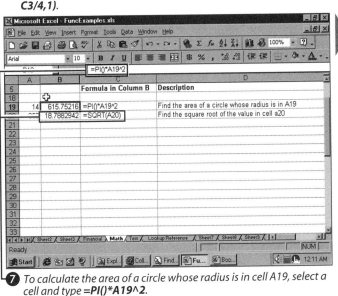

❼ To calculate the area of a circle whose radius is in cell A19, select a cell and type =**PI()*A19^2**.

❽ To calculate the square root of a value in A20, select a cell and type =**SQRT(A20)**.

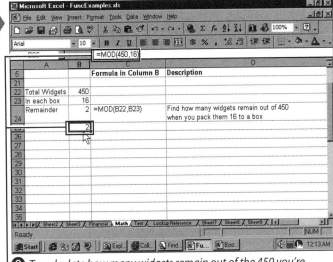

❾ To calculate how many widgets remain out of the 450 you're putting in boxes that hold 16 each, type =**MOD(450,16)**.

127

Using Text Functions

Text functions give you the ability to operate on the characters within a cell, primarily for extraction and analysis. Sometimes, you'll find it necessary to extract last names from cells that contain full names in address style; you can then sort a list on this information. You can also use these functions to deal with product codes which are often designed so that certain character positions in the code pertain to color, size, manufacturing site, or date of manufacture. Text functions deal with upper- and lower-case issues, and the elimination of spaces. In many situations, you will need to use a series of text functions, not necessarily in the same formula, to find and extract the text you need.

The FIND function will return the specific position of a character that you're looking for in a string of characters. If you're looking at cell that contains a first and last name separated by a space, you need to find the space as a prelude to using other functions that need this location to extract text.

The MID function, derived from the word middle, gives you the ability to extract a copy of characters starting at a particular location in the cell, perhaps the location of the space.

With the LEFT function you can extract a specific number of characters from the left side of a cell. In a similar fashion, use the RIGHT function to extract a specific number of characters from the right side of a cell. If you had used the FIND function to locate a space in the sixth character position of a cell containing names, you could use the LEFT function to extract a copy of five characters from the left side of a cell, and thereby extract a first name.

Sometimes, you get data from another source and the text in some cells is all uppercase or all lowercase. For a variety of reasons you may need to see the information in another form but you don't want to retype entries. The function UPPER returns the contents of a cell with all characters in uppercase; the LOWER function returns the contents of a cell with all characters in lowercase. The PROPER function returns the contents of a cell with all characters in lowercase other than the first character of each word, which is uppercase.

Use the TRIM function to return a cell's content with all leading and trailing spaces removed and all other multiple spaces between words reduced to a single space.

TAKE NOTE

CONCATENATE TEXT

Concatenation, a useful technique for combining text information from different cells, isn't really a function, but is frequently used with text functions and often with pure text strings. The entry =A3&" "&A4 extracts the content of cell A3, adds a space, and then appends the content of cell A4.

CROSS-REFERENCE

Read more about sorting, useful when analyzing text strings, in Chapter 15.

FIND IT ONLINE

To learn more about concatenation and other computer terminology, go to http://webopedia.internet.com/TERM/c/concatenate.html.

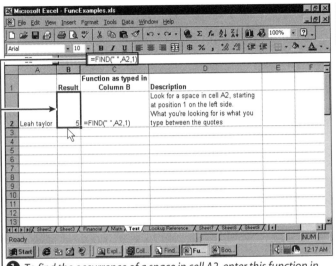

1 To find the occurrence of a space in cell A2, enter this function in cell B2: **=FIND(" ",A2,1)**. Note the space between the quotes.

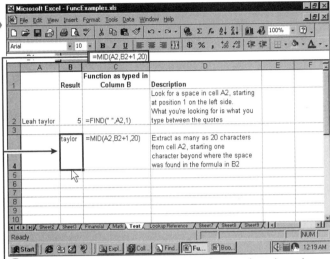

2 To extract a copy of up to 20 characters from A2, based on where you found the space, enter the function **=MID(A2,B2+1,20)**.

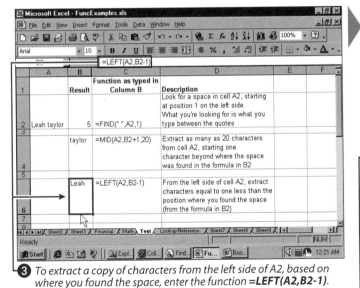

3 To extract a copy of characters from the left side of A2, based on where you found the space, enter the function **=LEFT(A2,B2-1)**.

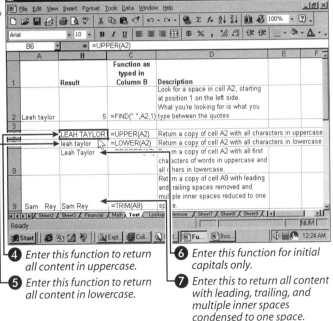

4 Enter this function to return all content in uppercase.

5 Enter this function to return all content in lowercase.

6 Enter this function for initial capitals only.

7 Enter this to return all content with leading, trailing, and multiple inner spaces condensed to one space.

Using Logical Functions

Logical functions introduce a new dimension to workbook development. You can use these functions to create alternate results based on the value of cells, formulas, or calculations in your workbook. If you have had any experience with programming languages or other spreadsheet or database software, you have probably encountered some variation on the IF function.

The most prominent of the logical functions is the IF function. Its typical use is to test for a condition and provide an answer when the condition is true and provide a different answer when the condition is false. Conditions often involve comparisons between two cells, between a cell and a value, between a formula (or function) and a value, or between a cell and a formula. Most conditional testing revolves around numerical comparisons, but text strings (embedded in quotes) can also be involved in conditions.

The results of the possible conditions can be any of the following: a value, the content of another cell, a formula or function that calculates a value, a text string in quotes. Sometimes the result is an empty string, which displays as a blank.

The IF function relies on logical operators to express conditions. These include: greater than (>), less than (<), equal to (=), not equal to (< >), greater than or equal to (> =), and less than or equal to (< =).

IF functions can become quite complex when you need to test for a set of hierarchical conditions. Imagine a situation where all salespeople with sales greater than $50,000 get a ten percent raise, those who reach the $25,000 level get a five percent raise, and all others get a two percent raise. To solve this problem, you need to use a technique called nesting, whereby you embed IF functions within IF functions. Although Excel allows you to nest as many as seven IF functions in one statement, functions with as many as three nested IFs become difficult for most people to comprehend.

The AND, OR, and NOT functions increase the capability and complexity of IF functions by allowing you to set up compound and negative testing. If, for example, you want to give a bonus based on longevity, performance, and current salary level, you may need to set up an AND condition that requires three conditions to be true (service years >15, performance evaluation >3, salary >40000). If any one of these conditions can trigger a bonus, you would use the OR function instead.

TAKE NOTE

STAND-ALONE FUNCTIONS
Although AND and OR frequently are used with the IF function, they can be used by themselves. The entry =AND(B7>10,D7="Sales") results in the answer TRUE if both conditions are true, or FALSE if either condition is false. The entry =OR(B7>10,D7="Sales") results in the answer TRUE if either condition is true or FALSE if both conditions are false.

CROSS-REFERENCE
Learn how the VLOOKUP function is better than the IF function (when you're trying to provide multiple answers) in the next task.

FIND IT ONLINE
If you're a logical thinker and like logical puzzles, look at http://www.geocities.com/Athens/Acropolis/3565/puzzle.htm.

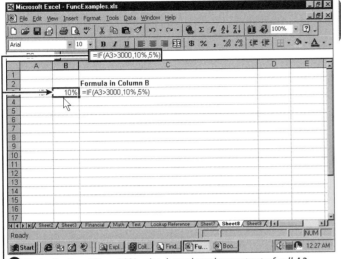

① To indicate a 5% or 10% raise, based on the content of cell A3, enter **=IF(A3>3000,10%,5%)**.

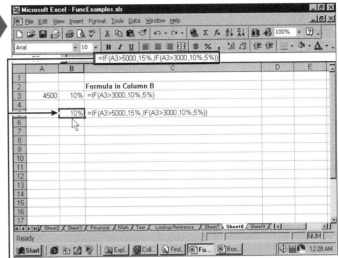

② To indicate a 5%, 10%, or 15% raise, based on the content of cell A3, enter **=IF(A3>=5000,15%,IF(A3>=3000,10%,5%))**.

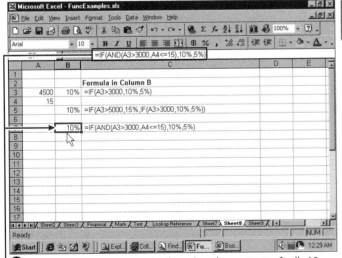

③ To indicate a 5% or 10% raise, based on the contents of cells A3 and A4, enter **=IF(AND(A3>3000,A4<=15),10%,5%)**.

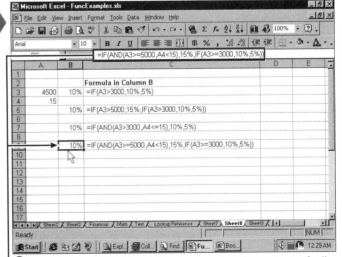

④ To indicate a 5%, 10%, or 15% raise, based on the contents of cells A3 and A4, enter **=IF(AND(A3>=5000,A4<15),15%,IF(A3>=3000,10%,5%))**.

Using Lookup Functions

Excel has a number of lookup and reference functions that return information by looking into tables or at worksheet information. The most widely used of these is VLOOKUP, which performs a vertical table lookup based on a table located in your workbook.

You will realize that the IF function has limitations, particularly with comprehension issues when you test for more than three possibilities, and this is when VLOOKUP is particularly helpful. Lookup tables typically contain values or text and can have many entries in them, allowing you to far exceed the number of possible answers you could get from a heavily nested IF statement.

Imagine if you had a column of items listed with their respective weights. You need to know what the mailing charge is for each item. You use the VLOOKUP function to compare the weight of each item with a table on your worksheet that shows a list of increasing weights in one column and the postal rate for each in the adjacent column.

Your table might also have a number of additional columns, one for each postal zone in the country. The VLOOKUP functions can be used to return the answer from the appropriate column in the table keyed to the row that represents the item's weight.

VLOOKUP can handle these two kinds of situation: If the values you're looking up don't need to match exactly what's in the left column of the table — Excel will use the lower value. Or, if the values you're looking up need to match one of the values in the left column of the table exactly.

Normally, VLOOKUP is used with values, but you can use it to provide text strings as answers. For example, to look up number grades in a table that shows their letter (A+, A, A-, B+, B, B-, C+, etc.) equivalent. You can even use text as the lookup item, such as looking up rates for zones that are identified by letters.

If your table would be more sensibly organized in rows, rather than in columns, you could use the HLOOKUP function instead.

The CHOOSE function is a variation on the concept of lookup tables. It is much more limited in its capabilities but has one major advantage — there is no need to create a table anywhere on the worksheet. The function is self-contained and can hold up to 29 items (values or text strings).

TAKE NOTE

TIPS FOR TABLES

Values in the far-left column of the table must be in ascending order as you read downward (unless you're using the optional fourth argument of VLOOKUP, which finds an exact match). If the value to be looked up is lower than the first value in the far-left column of the table, #VALUE! is returned as the result. If the value to be looked up is higher than the highest value in the far-left column of the table, the answer comes from the last row in the table.

CROSS-REFERENCE

Review how to apply a range name in Chapter 2.

FIND IT ONLINE

Need a table lookup for area codes by state? Check out http://www.nwrdc.fsu.edu/nwr/gdqf/areacode.htm.

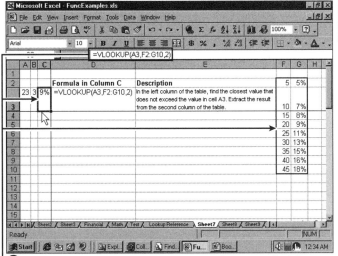

1 Based on a table in cells F2:G10, enter this function to find the rate for the item in cell **A3: =VLOOKUP(A3,F2:G10,2).**

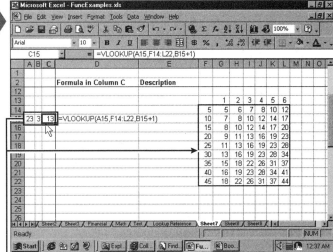

2 Based on a table in cells F14:L22, enter this function to find the rate for the item in cell A15 whose zone is in B15: **=VLOOKUP(A15, F14:L22,B15+1).**

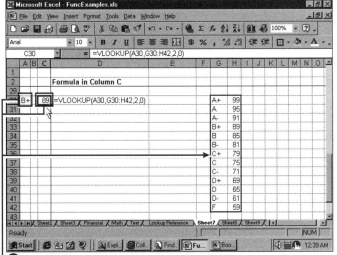

3 Based on a table in cells G30:H42, enter this function to find the score for the grade in cell A30: **=VLOOKUP(A30,G30:H42,2,0).**

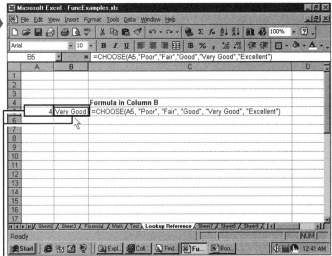

4 Based on the rating in cell A5, enter this function to display the description: **=CHOOSE(A5, "Poor", "Fair", "Good", "Very Good", "Excellent").**

Personal Workbook

Q&A

1 Cells B3 through B6 contain these entries: 20, 0, Blank, and 70. If you write this function =AVERAGE(B3:B6) what value is displayed?

_____

_____

2 How should you adjust this function to make the result appear more reasonable?

_____

_____

_____

3 The range C3:C10 contains these values: 20, 30, 85, 26, 82, 45, 61, and 47. If you type the function =LARGE (C3:C10,2) what value is displayed?

_____

_____

_____

4 If you type =RIGHT(A5,3) and cell A5 contains the text string A423B6765, what will you see?

_____

_____

5 If cell B3 contains 100, what does this function display =IF(_B3>100,10%,5%)?

_____

_____

_____

6 If you click the equal sign (=) in the formula bar, what happens?

_____

_____

_____

7 True or False: The CHOOSE function, unlike VLOOKUP, doesn't require you to have a table in your worksheet.

_____

_____

8 If cell A5 contains the value 27.571, what does the function =ROUND(A5,2) return?

_____

_____

ANSWERS: PAGE 324

EXTRA PRACTICE

① Write a formula to calculate the percent of change between January Sales of $15,000 and February Sales of $19,000.

② Average a range of cells, one of which is blank. Note the result and then enter a zero in blank cell and compare with the previous result. Type a word instead of zero and compare the results.

③ Cell A4 contains the text MALLOY and cell B4 contains the text TERRY. Using concatenation, write a formula to display the result TERRY MALLOY.

④ Using the function PMT, calculate the monthly payment to pay off a 4-year $18,000 loan with an interest rate of 71/2 percent.

REAL-WORLD APPLICATIONS

✔ You need to arrange your product list by the manufacturing site. The 10-character product codes in Column A use the characters in position 6, 7, and 8 to identify the manufacturing site. In a new column you enter this function: =MID(A3,6,3) in row 3 opposite the first record. You apply this function to other cells in Column A and sort your list on the new column.

✔ Your database has a column containing evaluation scores. You'd rather see words like Excellent, Good, Fair, and so on instead. Using the CHOOSE function in a new column, you display descriptive words.

✔ In your list of employees, salaries occur in Column G. You would like to see the ranking of each salary among the 200 salaries. In a new column you use the RANK function to calculate the salary rankings.

Visual Quiz

What formula is in cell E11? Why is the result negative? If March or April profits were zero, would this affect the formula in E11 in any unusual way?

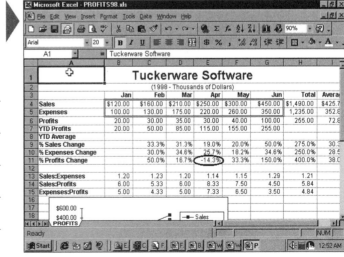

135

CHAPTER 8

Using Dates and Times

A valuable but sometimes overlooked feature of spreadsheet software is its ability to handle dates and times in a mathematical way, as well as displaying them in a way suitable for spreadsheet, report, and database use.

Whenever you make date or time entries in a variety of acceptable methods, Excel stores the information numerically but displays it chronologically. That means that you can sort data in true chronological order because sorting considers the numerical value, not the appearance. You have a lot of choices, too, about how you want dates and times displayed. The Number tab of the Format Cells command not only has a list of date/time variations, but gives you the ability to create the kinds of date and time displays most suitable for your needs.

As you grow accustomed to using dates and times in numerical way, you are more likely to use them in formulas and functions. You can calculate the amount of time elapsed between two dates, calculate a date that's so many days into the future or past, and use dates and times along with the powerful IF function as you test for target or completion dates.

A time-saving aspect of Excel's date and time usage is the ease with which you can build a series of dates. Need a list of Mondays for the next year? How about a series consisting of the last day of every month for the next two years? Do you need a list of the first days of the next 12 quarters? Or, a list of times at 15-minute intervals? You can create all these kinds of series and more, usually with Excel's AutoFill feature. You can also use the Edit ⇨ Fill Series command to create date and time series.

There are special Date and Time functions that will help you analyze information on the basis of monthly numbers, hours of the day, or days of the week. Some of these functions are also useful for converting date/time information (created in text form) into numerical units.

As you might expect, all of the date and time features of Excel are designed to handle the oddities of our chronological system, including February 29 and the crossover into the next century.

Entering Dates and Times

If you have already entered dates into an Excel worksheet, you've seen how simple and logical it is. Type 5-13-99 or 5/13/99 and 5/13/99 appears in the cell. But that's not always the way you want dates to appear. If you're showing a regional sales report, it's clearer to show just the month and the year, not specific days in that month. If the entire worksheet is devoted to the current year, you might want to show just the month and the day of the month. Take advantage of the fact that you can reduce errors and save typing time because Excel makes certain assumptions about dates and times during data entry.

If you're entering dates and they're all assumed to be within the calendar year, you can omit the year and you won't see it displayed in the worksheet. Like all date formats, you can change this to show the year, but whether you see the year or not, information about it is stored as part of the cell's content. Similarly, you can keep track of entries by month, by omitting the day of the month in your entry the first day of the month is automatically used.

Excel handles dates from 1900 until the year 10000. When you type a date, Excel translates your entry into a value equivalent to the number of days since the beginning of 1900.

To enter times of the day, type entries like 10:35, 6:40 AM, 4:30 PM, or 17:30. If you omit the AM/PM indicator for hours 1 through 12, Excel assumes you mean morning hours. Excel stores time information as a fractional portion of a day. Noon is recorded as .5, 3 PM as .625, and 6 PM as .75. As with dates, your more immediate concern is the way this information appears on your worksheet.

TAKE NOTE

▶ DELETING DATE ENTRIES

If you use the Delete key to erase a cell with a date, the formatting remains. If you later enter data into the cell, formatting may cause the result to seem illogical. If you want to delete a cell containing a date, use the Edit ➪ Clear All command.

▶ DATES THAT LOOK LIKE 35000

If you mistakenly use numeric formatting on cells that contain dates, they may look like numbers in the 35-37,000 range if you're dealing with dates around the turn of the century. The date May 13, 2000 could appear as 36659 — it's the number of days since the date system's start in 1900. Reformat it as a date to display it coherently.

▶ HOURS, MINUTES, AND SECONDS

For some worksheet applications, particularly scientific, you may need to record times in seconds. Use a second set of colons to separate minutes from seconds. The entry 10:30:15 AM represents 15 seconds after 10:30 a.m. and 3:35:45 PM is 45 seconds after 3:35 p.m.

CROSS-REFERENCE

Learn about entering a series of monthly names (not treated as dates) in Chapter 2.

FIND IT ONLINE

Isn't it time you learned more about how we keep track of time? Read all about the Gregorian calendar at http://es.rice.edu/ES/humsoc/Galileo/Things/gregorian_calendar.html.

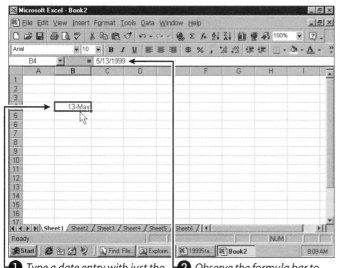

① *Type a date entry with just the day and month, i.e. 5/13. Observe the worksheet to see the display there.*

② *Observe the formula bar to see that the current year is automatically included.*

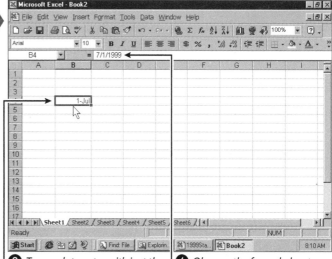

③ *Type a date entry with just the month and year, i.e. 7/99. Observe the worksheet to see the display there.*

④ *Observe the formula bar to see that the first day of the month is automatically included.*

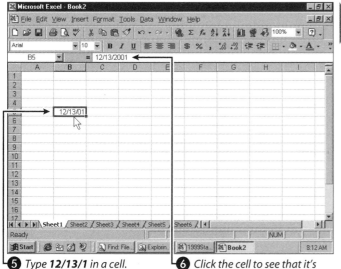

⑤ *Type **12/13/1** in a cell.*

⑥ *Click the cell to see that it's recorded as 12/13/2001 in the formula bar and 12/13/01 in the worksheet (years 0 through 29 are treated as the twenty-first century.*

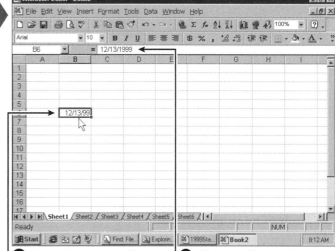

⑦ *Type **12/13/99** in a cell.*

⑧ *Click the cell to see that it's recorded as 12/13/1999 in the formula bar and 12/13/99 in the worksheet.*

Formatting Dates and Times

Unlike much of the formatting that you can do in Excel from the toolbar buttons, there are no formatting buttons to handle dates or times. Fortunately, when you type date or time entries, automatic formatting occurs. As you've seen, type an entry like 8/13/99 or 8-13-99 and it looks like 8/13/99 on your screen. Type 10/99 or Oct-99 and the display looks like Oct-99. Automatic formatting is fine, but you can also use a variety of built-in formats and, based on them, create your own special formats for dates and times.

Before trying to build your own date formats, you can check out some of the built-in formats available in the Format Cells command and decide which ones work best for you. As always, you never really change the content of cells when you format them.

When you need to display date or time information in a style other than the standard ones, use the Custom category of the Format ⇨ Cells command, which gives you an unlimited set of possibilities.

Here, you can use the letters m, d, and y in ways that are not immediately obvious. Used singly, the letter m refers to the month number (1 to 12) and will display 7 for July and 10 for October. The letters mm will display July as 07 and October as 10. Use mmm to get the standard three-letter abbreviation for the month, such as Jul or Oct. Use mmmm to get the full spelling, such as July or October.

The letter d refers to the day of the month; dd displays 09 for the 9th. Use ddd and you get the standard abbreviation for the day of the week (Sun, Mon, etc.). Use dddd to get the full spelling of the day. Use yyyy to display the full year, such as 1999.

You can use these forms in combinations. For example, use dddd, mmmm d, yyyy for 3/4/99 and Thursday, March 4, 1999 is displayed.

When applying formatting to times, consider the implications of seconds and tenths (or hundredths, thousandths, etc.). A format of mm:ss.00 allows you to type an entry of 3:48.14 to refer to a time of 3 minutes, 48 seconds and 14 one-hundredths of a second.

TAKE NOTE

▶ DELETING DATE ENTRIES

It's easy to use the Delete key to erase a cell's content, but if the cell contains a date or time, the formatting remains. If you later enter data into the cell, the date formatting may seem illogical. To delete a cell containing a date or time, use the Edit Clear All command.

▶ FOUR-DIGIT YEARS

If you're concerned about confusion over how years get recorded, enter 4-digit years, such as: 12/13/1925 or 5/13/2035. The dates will display as 12/13/25 and 5/13/35 respectively but will retain the four-digit year information. If you wish, create a format with yyyy to show a 4-digit year.

CROSS-REFERENCE
Learn about deleting the content of a cell in Chapter 2.

FIND IT ONLINE
Read about date formatting and related Y2K problems at **http://www.isaca.org/yr2k_cor.htm** .

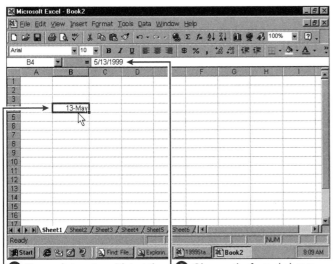

① Type a date entry with just the day and month, i.e. 5/13. Observe the worksheet to see the display there.

② Observe the formula bar to see that the current year is automatically included.

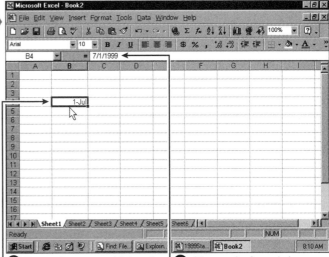

③ Type a date entry with just the month and year, i.e. 7/99. Observe the worksheet to see the display there.

④ Observe the formula bar to see that the first day of the month is automatically included.

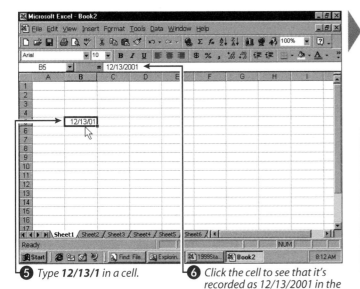

⑤ Type **12/13/1** in a cell.

⑥ Click the cell to see that it's recorded as 12/13/2001 in the formula bar and 12/13/01 in the worksheet (years 0 through 29 are treated as the twenty-first century.

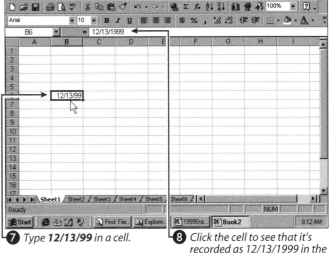

⑦ Type **12/13/99** in a cell.

⑧ Click the cell to see that it's recorded as 12/13/1999 in the formula bar and 12/13/99 in the worksheet.

Using Date and Time Entries in Formulas

I f you need to use dates and times in formulas, it's best to remember that they really are values, specifically, the number of days from the beginning of the year 1900. A later date is represented by a larger number than an earlier date. You can compare the contents of different cells containing dates or you might need to compare a date cell with a target date whose value exists only in a formula.

If you need to find a date that is a specific number of days after a date in a cell, simply write a formula in another cell that adds the cell address and the number. To find a day that's a specific number of days before the date in a cell, write a formula in another cell that subtracts that number from the date. Just as easily, you can find the amount of elapsed time between two dates by writing a formula that subtracts the contents of two different cells with dates. The answer is in days, but if the cell where you write the formula had previously contained a date, the date format remains and the result, which might look like a day in the early 1900s, is irrelevant and misleading. A quick way to adjust this is by clicking the comma button in the Formatting toolbar, the cell should then display a value instead of a date.

The same kinds of display problems occur with times. Calculating elapsed time sometimes gives the result as a time of day. Reformat such a result so that the am/pm indicator is not present and the answer makes sense.

TAKE NOTE

► ELAPSED TIME ACROSS DAYS

If you're trying to measure elapsed time (hours and minutes) across more than a day, you need a special format — [h]:mm — to produce the correct result. If you subtract two cells containing the date/time entries 8/7/99 2:43 PM and 8/5/99 4:49, the result is 9:54 with standard time formatting. Use the [h]:mm format and you get the correct answer: 57:54 – 57 hours and 54 minutes.

► SUBTRACTING DATES AND TIMES

Warning: When you subtract two different dates and the result is negative, simply ignore the minus sign and the result is clear. But if you write a formula subtracting a later time from an earlier time, the result is useless. Rewrite the formula, reversing the reference, and the result is workable.

► SPECIFIC DATES IN FORMULAS

To use a specific date in a formula, such as when you're comparing a cell's content with a specific date, embed the date in double quotes and use the Datevalue function as follows: =if(B17>Datevalue ("8/15/99"),"Overdue","Not Due").

CROSS-REFERENCE

Learn about using the IF function (useful when comparing dates) in Chapter 7.

SHORTCUT

When writing a formula, if you need to enter a date that's near the current date, press Ctrl+; and then edit it as needed.

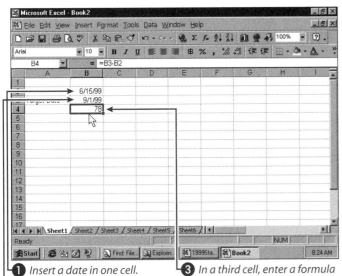

1 Insert a date in one cell.

2 Type a target (later) date in another cell.

3 In a third cell, enter a formula that subtracts the first date from the second date. The answer reflects the number of days between the two dates.

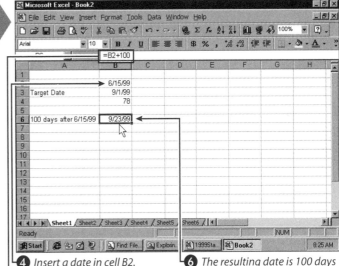

4 Insert a date in cell B2.

5 In a nearby cell, type a formula that calculates a date that's 100 days later: **=B2+100**.

6 The resulting date is 100 days after the initial date.

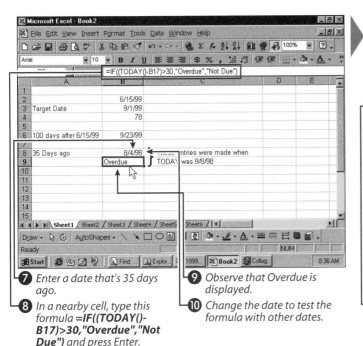

7 Enter a date that's 35 days ago.

8 In a nearby cell, type this formula **=IF((TODAY()- B17)>30,"Overdue","Not Due")** and press Enter.

9 Observe that Overdue is displayed.

10 Change the date to test the formula with other dates.

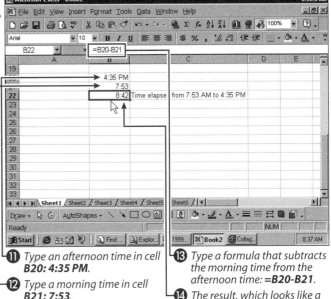

11 Type an afternoon time in cell **B20: 4:35 PM**.

12 Type a morning time in cell **B21: 7:53**.

13 Type a formula that subtracts the morning time from the afternoon time: **=B20-B21**.

14 The result, which looks like a time, represents elapsed time between the two entries.

Creating Date Series

Creating a series of dates sounds like a painstaking chore, but Excel's AutoFill feature seems to be custom-designed for just this. The Edit ⇨ Fill ⇨ Series command has its benefits too, but AutoFill will meet most of your needs. But remember, AutoFill is not a command sequence; It is a technique that creates answers by analyzing your selected entries and extending that series into additional cells that you select when you drag the mouse.

You might need to create a date series in any number of situations. A series that simply consists of consecutive days is the most obvious one. But you might also need a series of equally spaced dates (every 5 days, every 7 days, etc.), a series of dates consisting of the same day every month, or a series consisting of the last day of each month or the last day of each quarter.

The key to creating most date series is to enter dates in two consecutive cells, either in a column or in a row. The interval between the two will be recognized and expanded upon when you extend the series by dragging with the mouse.

You can create a series of times at one-hour intervals by starting with a single entry or you can create a series of equally incremented times by starting with two adjacent cells that have times entered at the desired interval.

The AutoFill feature can be a little untidy in the sense that you don't really assign a stop value, you just guess at how far you think you want to drag the mouse. Also, there is no easy way to create a series with AutoFill that just includes Mondays through Fridays.

The Edit ⇨ Fill ⇨ Series command sequence meets these needs. With it, you can create a date series by designating a larger than necessary range but with a definite stopping date. You can also create a series designed to fill a selected range of cells when you don't know or care what the stopping date is. When creating a series of either type, you can consider limiting your results so that only standard weekdays (Monday through Friday) appear in the series.

TAKE NOTE

ENTERING THE SAME DATE IN A SERIES

To create a series of entries that are the same date or time, select the range, type the date or time, and press Ctrl+Enter.

VALUES, NOT FORMULAS

Although you can create a date or time series by setting up formulas, when you create a date or time series using either AutoFill or the Edit ⇨ Fill ⇨ Series command, you fill cells with actual values, not formulas.

CROSS-REFERENCE

Refer to Chapter 2 to learn how to create a series of monthly or daily text entries.

SHORTCUT

To start or extend a series down a column as far as there are entries in the column to the left, double-click the fill handle.

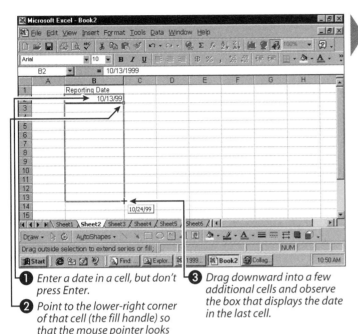

1 *Enter a date in a cell, but don't press Enter.*

2 *Point to the lower-right corner of that cell (the fill handle) so that the mouse pointer looks like a small plus sign.*

3 *Drag downward into a few additional cells and observe the box that displays the date in the last cell.*

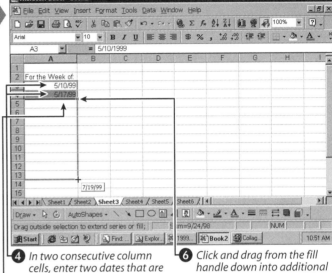

4 *In two consecutive column cells, enter two dates that are seven days apart.*

5 *Select both cells.*

6 *Click and drag from the fill handle down into additional cells to create a series of dates that are the same day of the week.*

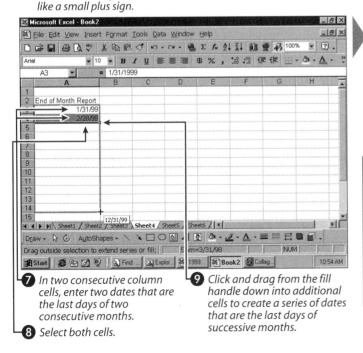

7 *In two consecutive column cells, enter two dates that are the last days of two consecutive months.*

8 *Select both cells.*

9 *Click and drag from the fill handle down into additional cells to create a series of dates that are the last days of successive months.*

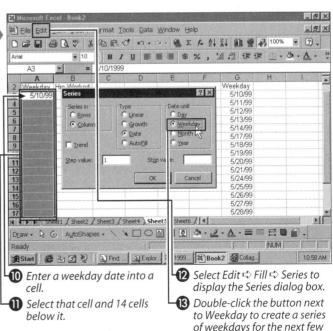

10 *Enter a weekday date into a cell.*

11 *Select that cell and 14 cells below it.*

12 *Select Edit ➪ Fill ➪ Series to display the Series dialog box.*

13 *Double-click the button next to Weekday to create a series of weekdays for the next few weeks.*

Date and Time Functions

Date functions are extremely useful in all kinds of worksheets. If you're analyzing workflow, for example, you may need to find out which day of the week is heaviest for phone orders. Perhaps you want to calculate a future date and make sure it's not on a Saturday or Sunday. For a variety of reasons, you may need to extract the month number or the day number from a date. You can use functions for dynamic date and time entry, and for converting imported data into readable dates and times.

When used in a formula with another date, the WEEKDAY function returns a value from 1 to 7 representing Sunday, Monday, and so on. If you have a column of date entries that you need to sort by day of the week, create a new column filled with the WEEKDAY function referring to each of those dates and then sort on this new column.

The MONTH and DAY functions extract the number of the month and the day of the month respectively. If you have a database containing hire dates, and want to work out which correspond to review dates, you may want to sort them in order by month of hire so that you can create a list each month of people who are due for a review. Create a new column, as in the previous example, and use the MONTH function to create an entry in each cell that returns the number of the month for each date.

You can use the TODAY and NOW functions as date and time stamps. Type the TODAY function in a cell and you will see the current date. The TODAY function looks at your system calendar to see the date and holds that information. Whenever you make a worksheet change, the function again checks the calendar and records the date. Save the file and open it tomorrow and it will have tomorrow's date there. In a similar fashion, the TIME function looks at your system's internal clock and displays the current time. Make a worksheet change and the time will change. If you print your worksheet with these cells in the print range, they represent an accurate date and time stamp as to when the worksheet was printed.

When you get data from sources other than Excel, you sometimes need to be able to convert what look like valid dates and times into forms readable by Excel. Some dates for example, may contain a leading space or quote. Use Datevalue and Timevalue to derive usable dates and times.

TAKE NOTE

DON'T FORGET PARENTHESES WHEN USING TODAY() AND NOW()

Both of these functions require parentheses even though you don't put anything between them. When they're in cells where no other parentheses are used, however, you can omit the closing parenthesis and the function works anyway.

CROSS-REFERENCE

Learn about sorting in Chapter 15.

FIND IT ONLINE

Learn about the origin of weekday names at http://www.stepstones.com/week.htm .

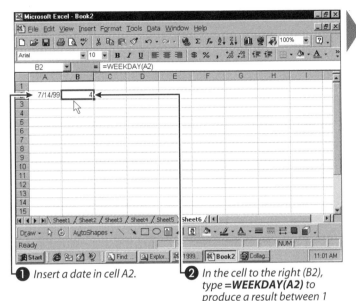

1 Insert a date in cell A2.

2 In the cell to the right (B2), type **=WEEKDAY(A2)** to produce a result between 1 and 7; 1=Sunday, 2=Monday, etc.

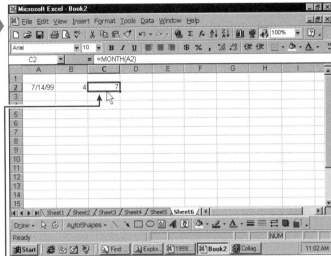

3 In cell C2, type **=MONTH(A2)** to produce a result between 1 and 12; 1=January, 2=February, etc.

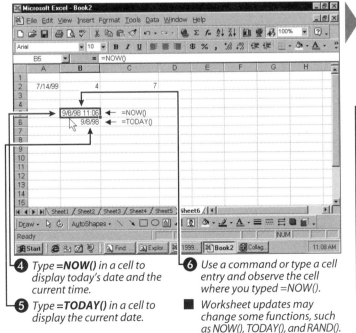

4 Type **=NOW()** in a cell to display today's date and the current time.

5 Type **=TODAY()** in a cell to display the current date.

6 Use a command or type a cell entry and observe the cell where you typed =NOW().

■ Worksheet updates may change some functions, such as NOW(), TODAY(), and RAND().

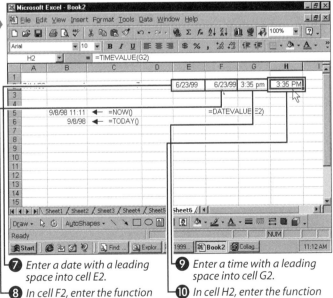

7 Enter a date with a leading space into cell E2.

8 In cell F2, enter the function **=DATEVALUE(E2)** to display the correct date.

9 Enter a time with a leading space into cell G2.

10 In cell H2, enter the function **=TIMEVALUE(G2)** to display the correct time.

147

Personal Workbook

Q&A

1 True or False: To enter the time 2:30 (afternoon) into a cell, you should type 14:30.

_____

_____

_____

_____

2 What keystroke combination can you use to enter today's date into a cell?

_____

_____

_____

_____

3 What's the difference between using ddd and dddd in a custom date format?

_____

_____

_____

_____

4 On what date will you be (or were you) 10,000 days old?

_____

_____

_____

_____

5 True or False: If you're not sure about whether a date is going to be recorded as twentieth or twenty-first century, use a 4-digit year during data entry.

_____

_____

6 What day of the week is March 17, 2001? (Use the WEEKDAY function.)

_____

_____

_____

7 How many days are there between 5/28/99 and 9/13/99?

_____

_____

_____

ANSWERS: PAGE 325

148

EXTRA PRACTICE

1. Try these entries in six separate cells to see which ones are interpreted as dates: 9Jun, 9 Jun, 9-Jun, Jun9, Jun 9, and Jun-9.

2. Create a series consisting of the first day of each quarter for the next five years.

3. Enter the time 8 p.m. into a cell.

4. Use a built-in format that displays today's date like 5-Dec-99.

5. Create a format that would display July 4 in 1999 as Sun July 4, 1999.

REAL-WORLD APPLICATIONS

✔ Your yearly summary has a column for each week. You want every Monday for the whole year in the column. You enter the first two Mondays, select them both and drag the fill handle downward to include 52 cells.

✔ A column in your database is headed: Last Review Date. You insert a new column and write a formula that calculates the days elapsed since the last review. You use the TODAY function in your calculation so that whenever you view the file, the number of days elapsed is accurate.

✔ Whenever you print a certain worksheet, you want to see the current date and time displayed in cell A1. So, you type the function =NOW() in cell A1.

Visual Quiz

In the screen shown to the right, cell B3 formerly contained a date. You selected the cell and pressed the Delete key to erase it. Later you typed the value 20000 here. Why does the cell contain the date 10/3/54? Is that the date you had typed there before erasing the cell? What's a quick way to adjust the format so that the value 20000 appears there?

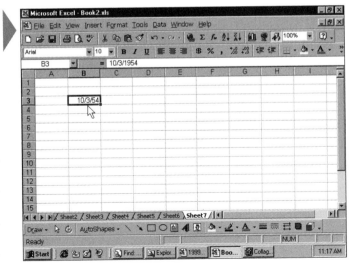

CHAPTER 9

MASTER THESE SKILLS

▶ Displaying Multiple Worksheets

▶ Displaying Multiple Workbooks

▶ Setting Up Horizontal and Vertical Split Screens

▶ Setting Up Horizontal and Vertical Title Panes

▶ Using Zoom Control

▶ Customizing and Moving Toolbars

Adjusting Window and Worksheet Display

Despite all of the important content and formatting changes that you make as you create, refine, and consolidate worksheets, there are times when the way your worksheets appear onscreen is critical.

You've no doubt already learned some tricks about seeing more information on your screen by using smaller fonts or hiding columns and rows. But most of the tasks in this chapter have more to do with the manipulation of workbooks, worksheets, and windows so you can see the information you want in a more convenient way. As you expand your Excel usage, you are more likely to want to be able to see more than one worksheet in a current workbook and to have more than one workbook open at a given time.

Excel's zoom capability is instantly available when you want to see more of your worksheet at a glance or when you prefer to enlarge a smaller area for easier viewing. You can also optimize your view of a selected range to have it expand within the screen or shrink to fit within the screen. A related feature essentially strips the Excel screen of menus, toolbars, and other features to allow a so-called Full Screen view.

Being able to see different sheets of the same workbook is immeasurably helpful, not only when creating worksheets, but also when copying or moving data from one worksheet to another. For similar reasons, you may sometimes need to see and manipulate different workbooks together onscreen. A side benefit of this kind of capability is that you gain a greater sense of control when handling multiple workbooks at one time. This may lead to consolidation and linking efficiencies that would be less likely if you weren't aware of these viewing features.

A number of display features enable you to keep part of a worksheet visible when scrolling through other parts of the worksheet. In different ways, you can freeze panes, set up split screens, or open additional windows for the same workbook in order to do this.

Another screen adjustment, moving and customizing toolbars, has implications in two areas: providing more worksheet space for data, and improving your use of commands by enabling you to remove toolbar buttons from existing toolbars and add buttons for frequently used commands.

Displaying Multiple Worksheets

No matter how many worksheets there are in your current workbook, there may be times when you'll want to see parts of more than one of them at a time. For example, when you're writing a formula in one worksheet that depends on data in another. Or, if you plan to either copy or move a range of cells from one worksheet to another. When you can see both the sending and receiving areas onscreen, you can drag data from one sheet to another, without relying on commands or toolbar buttons.

A less obvious reason to display multiple worksheets is for when you want to view different parts of the same worksheet in two separate windows. Split-screen techniques, covered later in this chapter, may prove to be a more appealing approach, but opening a new window is a method that works for two situations: to show two different sheets in separate windows or to show two different parts of the same sheet in separate windows.

When you view more than one worksheet at a time, you have the option of viewing the sheets in a vertical (side-by-side) or horizontal (top-bottom) arrangement. With just two worksheets onscreen, these are sensible options, but displaying three or more sheets horizontally or vertically is a visual disaster. With three or more sheets displayed, create your own windows arrangement or choose a Tile option. There's also a cascade option that displays worksheets in an overlapping diagonal layout as if they were sheets stacked on top of each other.

You can improve the readability of onscreen multiple sheets by clicking in each sheet and reducing the zoom factor. You can also hide toolbars. Both of these tasks are covered later in this chapter.

After you create windows to enable multiple-sheet viewing, check the Window drop-down list box for a list of currently open windows. You may be accustomed to using this to obtain a list of currently open files, but it also shows you open windows.

TAKE NOTE

CLOSING A WINDOW

When you have more than one window displayed from the same workbook and you're viewing multiple sheets, it may seem that if you click the X in the upper-right corner of a window, you'll close the file. As long as more than one workbook window is open, closing one will not close the workbook.

CROSS-REFERENCE

Learn about copying and moving worksheets in Chapter 10.

FIND IT ONLINE

As you open new windows to display more worksheets, pause and take a brief look at the history of Windows at **http:// www.zdnet.com/pcmag/features/windows98/history6.html**.

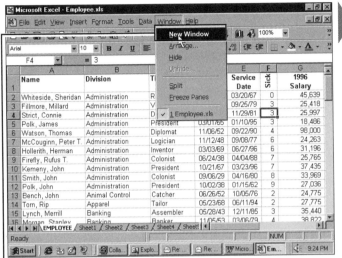

1 To create a new worksheet window, choose the Window ➪ New Window command.

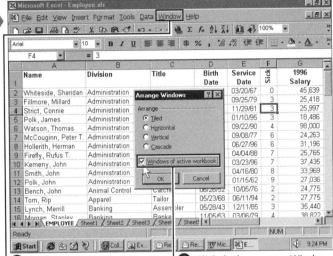

2 To display more than one window, choose Window ➪ Arrange to display the Arrange Windows dialog box.

3 Click the box next to Windows of active workbook, select Tiled, Horizontal, Vertical, or Cascade, and click OK.

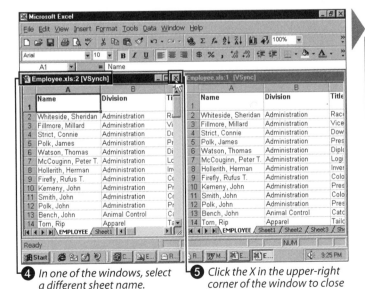

4 In one of the windows, select a different sheet name.

5 Click the X in the upper-right corner of the window to close it, not the file.

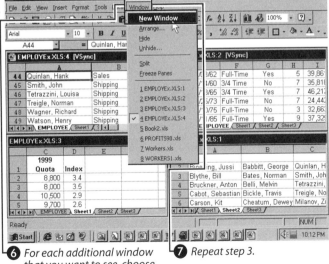

6 For each additional window that you want to see, choose the Window ➪ New Window command.

7 Repeat step 3.

Displaying Multiple Workbooks

You can have many workbooks open at once. The only real limitations come from the amount of memory on your computer and the current availability of system resources. Reasons abound for having more than one workbook open. Perhaps you want to consolidate a number of workbooks, or perhaps there are pieces of information in one workbook that logically belong in another. Just as it makes good sense to be able to view more than one worksheet onscreen at a given time, it's also useful to see parts of different workbooks. Being able to drag a sheet or range (for copying or moving) from one workbook to another is a more attractive alternative than using cut and paste commands or buttons. Achieving multiple-workbook displays requires essentially the same techniques used to display more than one worksheet at a time.

A side benefit of displaying multiple workbooks together is that you're then more likely to see consolidation possibilities. It's not always true that fewer workbooks is better, but often you can be more efficient after you move sheets from one workbook to another and discard unneeded workbooks.

With more than one workbook open, it's easy to switch between them even when you don't see them together at the same time. The Window drop-down list box always maintains a list of all open files — it's not a bad idea to occasionally click the Window drop-down list box to help you remember which files are open.

The display possibilities for multiple workbooks are the same as those for multiple worksheets: you can arrange workbooks in a horizontal, vertical, tiled, or cascade display. If you want to temporarily remove one of your open workbooks from a multiple workbook display, you can minimize that workbook (unlike worksheets, which you can hide, there is no way to hide a workbook) and redisplay the other open files in the most suitable layout.

TAKE NOTE

KEYSTROKE SWITCHING

You can jump to the next open workbook by pressing Ctrl+F6. Repeatedly press this combination to "make the rounds" of all open workbooks, but you don't control the order. Press Ctrl+Shift+F6 to move to each open workbook in the opposite order. Both combinations work when you have one workbook or many workbooks displayed onscreen.

SAVE YOUR SPACE

If you frequently need to see the same two workbooks open together, open them and arrange them onscreen the way you'd like. Next, choose File ⇨ Save Workspace, which prompts you to save each file if you made changes. Then you can open this workspace file (it's actually a shortcut that opens your two workbooks) to view both workbooks onscreen in their saved arrangements.

CROSS-REFERENCE

Read more about copying and moving sheets to different workbooks in Chapter 10.

FIND IT ONLINE

If you're interested in the history of tiles, take a look at **http://francha.com/essenza/histo2.htm**.

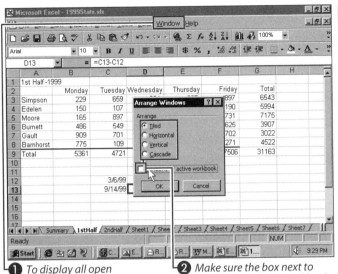

1 To display all open workbooks, choose Window ➪ Arrange to display the Arrange Windows dialog box.

2 Make sure the box next to Windows of active workbook is not checked; select Tiled, Horizontal, Vertical, or Cascade and click OK.

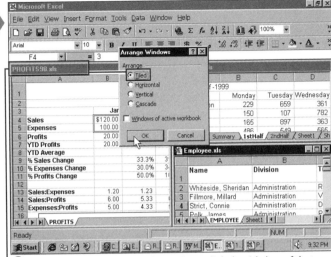

3 To make a window larger than others, click the title bar of that window, repeat step 1, and select Tiled.

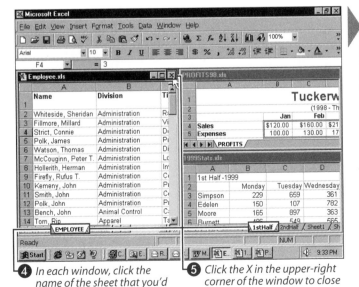

4 In each window, click the name of the sheet that you'd like to see.

5 Click the X in the upper-right corner of the window to close it and the workbook.

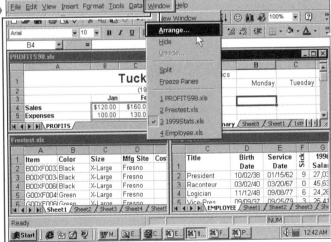

6 Choose Window ➪ Arrange and repeat step 2. (Image shows Tiled option.)

Setting Up Horizontal and Vertical Split Screens

If you'd like to keep an eye on one part of your worksheet while working on another, you can use a number of different split screen techniques. There are many analogies that liken creating and using worksheets in Excel to creating and using spreadsheets on paper. But some split screen techniques really don't have a paper comparison. On paper, can you imagine seeing column T, which has your yearly totals, and column V, which has your five-year totals, both appearing to the left of column A, which contains your row identifiers?

When you establish a horizontal split screen, you have two separate vertical scroll bars, one for each pane. When you establish a vertical split screen, you have two separate horizontal scroll bars, one for each pane. With both types of split screens in effect, you have four scroll bars so you can manipulate any part of the worksheet that you wish to view.

You can manipulate column display by using vertical split features, and row display using horizontal split features. If you want to adjust row 17, which contains data on profits in China, and row 45, which contains profit data on Russia, so that they appear in adjacent rows onscreen, create a horizontal pane and adjust the display. Although it may be confusing at first, you can even use both horizontal and vertical split screens and ultimately be able to see any two parts of a worksheet, no matter how far apart, onscreen at the same time.

At all times, when using the various combinations of split screens, you retain your ability to enter data, make formatting changes, copy and move ranges, and perform all other standard methods of operations. Setting up a split screen does not create new cells, columns, rows, or sheets.

TAKE NOTE

CREATING PANES WITH THE MOUSE

You can quickly create vertical and horizontal splits with the mouse. Position the active cell just below where you want a horizontal split. Double-click the horizontal split screen indicator that's just above the vertical scroll bar. Double-click the vertical split screen indicator that's just to the right of the horizontal scroll bar to create a vertical split.

MOVING (AND REMOVING) PANES WITH THE MOUSE

Click and drag either a vertical or horizontal split bar to move it to a different screen location. With both kinds of panes in effect, you can drag the intersection of the two to adjust both horizontal and vertical panes. Double-click either a vertical or horizontal split bar to remove it. If you want to remove both bars at once, double-click their intersection.

CROSS-REFERENCE

See Chapter 6 for details on hiding columns and rows as a way of assisting with split screen techniques.

SHORTCUT

Press F6 to jump to a different pane in a clockwise direction; use Shift+F6 to jump in a counterclockwise direction.

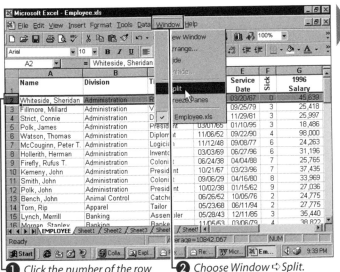

1 Click the number of the row just below where you want to horizontally split the screen.

2 Choose Window ⇨ Split.

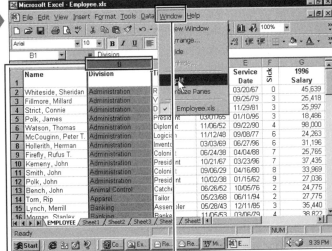

3 Click the letter of the column just to the right of where you want to vertically split the screen.

4 Choose Window ⇨ Split.

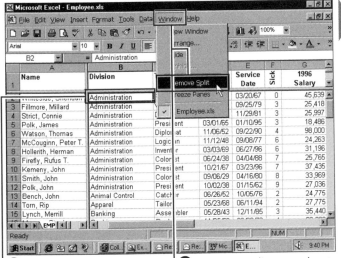

5 On a screen with a split in effect, click and drag scroll bars as needed to scroll in any of the panes.

6 To remove split panes, choose Window ⇨ Remove Split.

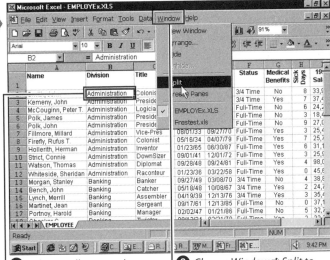

7 Select a cell or range just below a desired horizontal split and just to the right of a desired vertical split.

8 Choose Window ⇨ Split to apply both a horizontal and vertical split.

Setting Up Horizontal and Vertical Title Panes

There are many worksheets where all the columns don't fit onscreen. You can hide columns, make some of them narrower, use the zoom capability to shrink the display size and employ other techniques to help achieve your objective. But often, a better way is to freeze a portion of your worksheet so that you can freely navigate elsewhere. The freeze capability, unlike using split screen features, is keyed to the left side of your worksheet, the top of your worksheet, or both, and is primarily used for keeping column and row headings visible while you scroll elsewhere.

Frequently, you need this capability when you're looking in column T and you want to see column A, which contains information that identifies each row. If you rotate the image 90 degrees, you sometimes have a similar need to keep row 1 "frozen" at the top of the screen while you scroll elsewhere.

There are times when it's desirable to keep multiple rows or multiple columns "frozen" at the top or left side of your screen. There is no requirement that the rows or columns be at the edge of your worksheet. If you need to keep rows 5 and 6 visible as you scroll elsewhere, use the scroll bars until these rows appear at the top of your screen and then activate the freeze feature to keep them there.

You can use Excel's freeze capability along with the split screen techniques covered in the previous task, but you can also use them alone. You can apply freezing either horizontally, or vertically, or both at once.

When you freeze panes instead of using split-screen techniques, you create a cleaner looking display without the double set of scroll bars. If you save a workbook that has frozen panes, the panes will still be there the next time you open it.

TAKE NOTE

YOU CAN UNFREEZE BUT YOU CAN'T UNDO A FREEZE

Excel gives you an Unfreeze command to get rid of any kind of frozen panes. But if you attempt to reverse recent actions by performing a series of Undos from the toolbar button, Excel will skip over any freeze-related commands, but you can undo any actions taken before them.

GROUPING AND FREEZING

Although you can group one or more worksheets and freeze panes and not get any system message, the command only goes into effect on the active sheet, not the other grouped sheets.

CROSS REFERENCE

Learn more about Excel's zoom capability later in this chapter.

FIND IT ONLINE

Learn about multi-pane windows at **http:// www.thewindowplace.inter.net/DOE.HTML/EREC.ENERGY. EFFICIENT.WIND.html.**

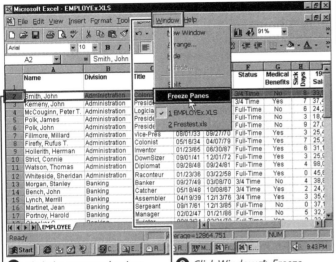

1 Click the row number just below where you want to freeze the screen horizontally.

2 Click Window ➪ Freeze Panes.

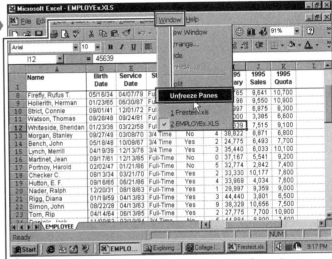

3 If Freeze Panes is activated, select Window ➪ Unfreeze Panes.

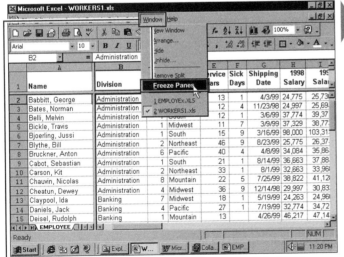

4 In a worksheet that has a dual split screen, select Window ➪ Freeze Panes.

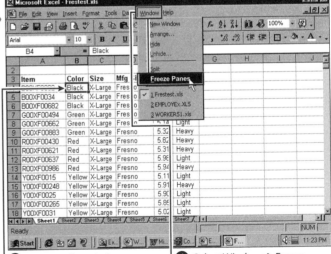

5 Click a cell just below a desired horizontal freeze and just to the right of a desired vertical freeze.

6 Select Window ➪ Freeze Panes to apply both a horizontal and vertical freeze.

Using Zoom Control

Your ability to zoom in and out of a worksheet is an extremely handy feature. You can view your worksheet up close so that it appears larger (but you see fewer rows and columns) or step back and see more of it (but with more difficulty in reading it because it's smaller). Excel's zoom capability is numerically limited to the extremes of 400% and 10%, but you can choose any zoom factor between these two values.

Excel's Zoom drop-down list box gives you choices of 200%, 100%, 75%, 50%, 25%, and Selection (see Take Note). For the most part these choices are adequate and most users are comfortable with a setting of 100% or 75%. Because you have some control over your screen's resolution through Windows settings, using 75% on one computer may look more or less satisfactory than the same setting on another computer. You can also type in any value from 10 to 400.

It's unlikely that you will use a 400% zoom setting very often, but if you display part of a worksheet on a monitor in a conference room or through a projection system during a meeting, a momentary screen enlargement enables you to emphasize part of a worksheet's contents or formulas.

It's equally unlikely that you'll frequently use a 10% setting, but zooming out that far helps you get a finer sense of a worksheet's layout and design. Because 25% is listed in the Zoom drop-down list box, try it first.

Regardless of what zoom selection is in effect, your worksheet is operative. You can continue to enter data and make formatting changes.

When you group worksheets and apply a zoom setting, it applies to all selected worksheets.

TAKE NOTE

▶ SELECTIVE ZOOMING

If you want to see a selected range appear as large as possible yet have it fit onscreen, click the Zoom drop-down list box and go to Selection. Excel either expands or shrinks the screen display so that the selected area fills the screen. The display retains the same aspect ratio (height to width), as if enlarging or shrinking a photograph.

▶ MAXIMIZE YOUR VIEWING AREA WITH FULL SCREEN DISPLAY

You can maximize your worksheet area (at the expense of hiding the toolbars, formula bar, sheet tabs, and Status Bar) if you choose View ⇨ Full Screen. A special menu bar appears so that you can return to the standard display.

▶ WHERE ARE THE GRIDLINES?

If you set the zoom percentage to 39 or lower, you will not see gridlines on your screen.

CROSS-REFERENCE

Read more about grouping workbooks in Chapter 10.

FIND IT ONLINE

For information on serious zooming, learn about the history of telescopes at **http://www.yesmag.bc.ca/telescope.html** .

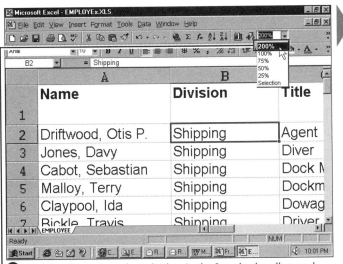

1 Click the Zoom drop-down list box in the Standard toolbar and select 200% to greatly enlarge the view of the worksheet.

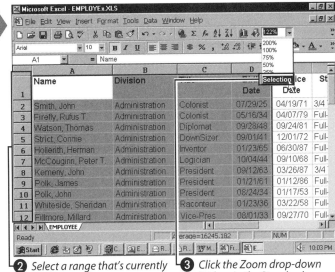

2 Select a range that's currently too large to fit onscreen.

3 Click the Zoom drop-down list box in the Standard toolbar and go to Selection.

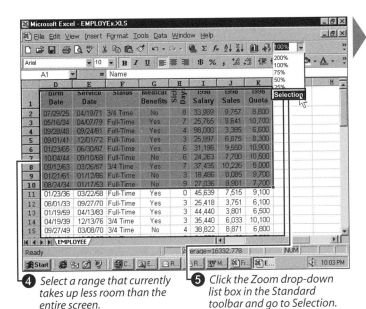

4 Select a range that currently takes up less room than the entire screen.

5 Click the Zoom drop-down list box in the Standard toolbar and go to Selection.

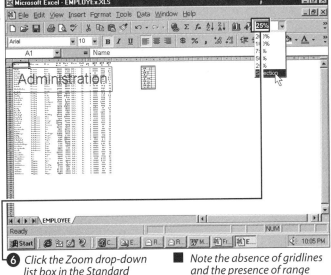

6 Click the Zoom drop-down list box in the Standard toolbar and choose 25% to greatly reduce the view of the worksheet.

■ Note the absence of gridlines and the presence of range names.

Customizing and Moving Toolbars

Toolbars give you fast and easy access to commands, often saving you time and making you a more efficient Excel user. Even after a short time as an Excel user, you are probably familiar with many of the buttons on the Standard and Formatting toolbars. For a variety of reasons, you may want to move a toolbar to a different part of the screen, hide it from view to maximize screen usage (and bring it back later), or reshape it for optimum screen usage. Also, you may want the toolbar buttons to be larger or smaller.

The default location for toolbars is at the top of your screen just below the menu bar and just above the formula bar. When you activate certain toolbars you may be surprised to see them appear at the bottom of a worksheet, but you can easily move them. You can position toolbars at any of a worksheet's four sides or make them "float" on the worksheet. This can be handy when you intensively use a particular toolbar for a short time and need to quickly get to the buttons. You can reshape a floating toolbar by dragging its edges, making it less oblong or tall and more compact as it approaches a square shape.

Excel has many toolbar buttons that you can add to existing toolbars or use with familiar buttons to build a customized toolbar. The more you use Excel,

the more curious you may become about the images that appear to the left of some commands. Many are buttons that appear on the Standard and Formatting toolbars. Others are not, but could be. For example, in the Edit drop-down list box you see binoculars next to Find. In the Insert drop-down list box there's a yellow sheet next to Comment. If you frequently use these commands, why not have them easily available as toolbar buttons? Check other drop-down list boxes to see what's at the left of command choices.

When you customize a toolbar, you can explore a huge list of buttons and menu commands — any one could go on one of your existing toolbars. When customizing, you can also remove buttons from toolbars if you don't use them, thus freeing up space for new buttons.

TAKE NOTE

▶ RETURNING A TOOLBAR TO ITS RIGHTFUL PLACE

If you dragged a toolbar onto a worksheet for handier use, you can rapidly return it to the edge of the screen where it was last located; just double-click the toolbar's title banner.

CROSS-REFERENCE
See Chapter 2 for information on hiding and displaying toolbars via the shortcut menu.

FIND IT ONLINE
For information on customizing automobiles, look at http://www.jandcmotorsport.com/.

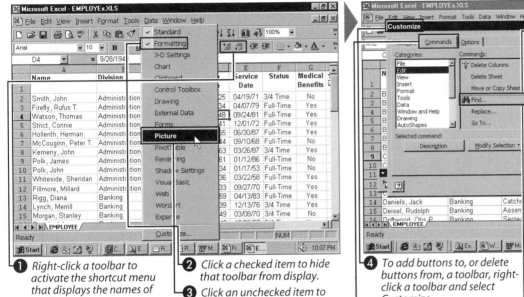

① *Right-click a toolbar to activate the shortcut menu that displays the names of toolbars.*

② *Click a checked item to hide that toolbar from display.*

③ *Click an unchecked item to display that toolbar.*

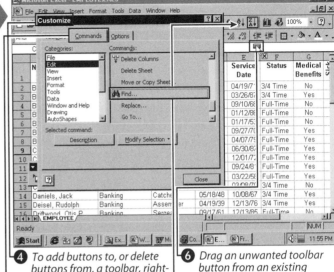

④ *To add buttons to, or delete buttons from, a toolbar, right-click a toolbar and select Customize.*

⑤ *Select the Commands tab.*

⑥ *Drag an unwanted toolbar button from an existing toolbar onto the worksheet.*

⑦ *Click a command and drag it onto an existing toolbar.*

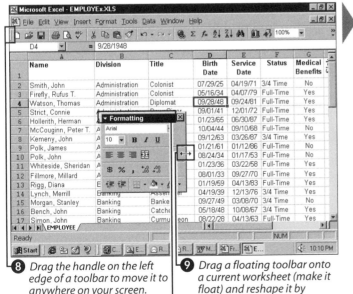

⑧ *Drag the handle on the left edge of a toolbar to move it to anywhere on your screen.*

⑨ *Drag a floating toolbar onto a current worksheet (make it float) and reshape it by dragging any of its edges.*

⑩ *Drag a floating toolbar by its banner to a different location.*

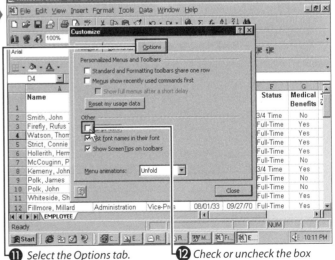

⑪ *Select the Options tab.*

⑫ *Check or uncheck the box next to Large icons.*

Personal Workbook

Q&A

1 True or False: If you're viewing more than one workbook, you can't display multiple worksheets for any of the open workbooks.

_____

_____

2 What's the fastest way to eliminate a dual split screen?

_____

_____

_____

3 The Window drop-down list box shows you the names of open workbooks, but does it show you how many windows are open for the current workbook?

_____

_____

_____

4 What keystroke combination enables you to jump from one open workbook to another or from one window to another?

_____

_____

_____

5 If you'd like to see row 13 and row 75 onscreen at the same time, what kind of split would you activate?

_____

_____

_____

_____

6 If you mistakenly set up a split screen at the wrong location, can you use Undo to reverse your action?

_____

_____

_____

_____

7 What keystroke combination moves an active cell from pane to pane on a split screen?

_____

_____

_____

ANSWERS: PAGE 326

EXTRA PRACTICE

1 Drag the Formatting toolbar onto you worksheet and resize it. Double-click its title banner to return it to its usual spot at the top of your screen.

2 Create a vertical split and display column M to the left of the split bar and column A to the right of the split bar.

3 Imagining column headings in rows 4 and 5, freeze these two rows at the top of your screen.

4 Select a four-row-by-six-column range and, using the Zoom drop-down list box, use Selection to optimally display your range.

REAL-WORLD APPLICATIONS

✓ You need to see rows 1 and 2 and column A indefinitely onscreen. You press Ctrl+Home, select Cell B3, and click the Window drop-down list box. You select Freeze Panes so you can scroll anywhere while retaining the desired rows and column.

✓ You're about to copy Sheet3 from one workbook to another, so you open both workbooks and click the Window drop-down list box, select Arrange, and click OK in order to see both workbooks.

✓ You need a dual split screen just above and to the left of Cell C3. You click Cell C3, click the Window drop-down list box and select Split.

✓ Frequently, you like to see more rows on your worksheet, so you choose Edit ➪ Full Screen.

Visual Quiz

In the screen shown to the right, how many workbooks are open?

_____

_____

_____

_____

_____

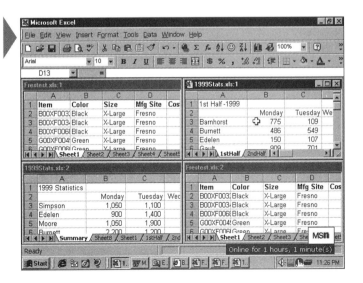

CHAPTER 10

MASTER THESE SKILLS

▶ Inserting and Deleting Worksheets

▶ Renaming Worksheets

▶ Copying Worksheets

▶ Moving Worksheets

▶ Creating Multiple-Sheet Formulas

▶ Grouping Worksheets

Working with Multiple-Sheet Workbooks

You may be a bit intimidated by the idea of a multiple-sheet workbook. After all, there are so many things to learn with just a single sheet. Nevertheless, many of the concepts and ideas behind using more than one sheet in a workbook are simply extensions of what you have already learned about using Excel in a two-dimensional environment.

Those extra sheets, which maybe you think you won't need, can be used as working space — a place for you to experiment with formulas and to try features or functions that you're unfamiliar with and would like to explore. You may come to think of those sheets as a place to hold certain kinds of lookup tables or reference information, or as a repository of documentation about the rest of the workbook.

By far the most common concept for multiple-sheet workbooks, however, is that it is a sensible and convenient place to keep information for different periods of time, different locations, or different organizational units. For example, you could use each sheet to keep track of similar data, but for a different fiscal year; or use each sheet to hold similar information about different departments in a company; or use each sheet to keep track of sales figures for a different region in your organization.

As you start to use these kinds of workbooks, you need to know how to add and remove sheets and rename and reposition them. You also need to learn how to take advantage of shortcuts, formulas, functions, and how to link workbooks.

Inserting and Deleting Worksheets

Excel limits you to 255 worksheets as a default size for new workbooks, but new workbooks automatically have three sheets. If your workbook is such that everything you need from it can be sensibly stored and organized on one sheet, you may decide to eliminate the unnecessary sheets. But if you'd like to keep data for each 12 months on separate sheets, you need to add sheets, possibly using 13 sheets — one set aside for a summary.

When you enter Excel, the first workbook you see has three sheets in it. You might decide that this is either too large or too small — it all depends upon your needs. For a time, accept this number of sheets until you begin to understand why these sheets might be useful to you. Eventually, you may decide that a five-sheet workbook will suit your needs; many of your workbooks may deal with data on a quarterly basis and you want to have a sheet for each quarter and a summary sheet that shows yearly totals.

When you insert a single worksheet, it appears to the left of (or above) whichever sheet you choose. The sheet tabs at the bottom of your worksheet read left to right but can also, if you think about it, be read from top to bottom. You can also insert more than one sheet at a time; in fact, if you're anticipating a workbook with 13 worksheets, it's likely that you will insert many at once rather than one at a time.

As always, when erasing or deleting, proceed with caution. Deleting a sheet with data in it may cause problems later. You can delete one or many worksheets at a time, but you get a firm warning that "...the sheets will be permanently deleted." A phrase that means that you cannot use the Undo button or Edit ⇨ Undo command to reverse this action. However, the warning does not state this in explicit terms.

TAKE NOTE

DELETING UNNECESSARY SHEETS

A few empty worksheets incur a small cost in terms of file size and memory usage. Add a sheet and it uses about 300 bytes, a veritable drop in the bucket. A seven-sheet workbook that's empty takes up about 14,000 bytes, but a 255-sheet workbook with nothing in it requires about 85,000 bytes of space.

MORE THAN 255 SHEETS?

Even though Excel will not allow you to set the default number of sheets for new workbooks to exceed 255, you actually can keep adding sheets to a workbook well beyond that number. Eventually, your computer's memory will limit the number of sheets you can add.

CROSS-REFERENCE

Learn about displaying multiple worksheets in Chapter 9.

FIND IT ONLINE

Check out **http://www.idgb.com/** for other Excel books.

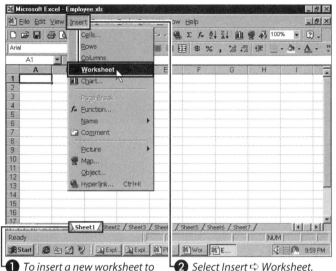

1 To insert a new worksheet to the left (above) of a worksheet, click the worksheet tab that will follow the new worksheet.

2 Select Insert ⇨ Worksheet.

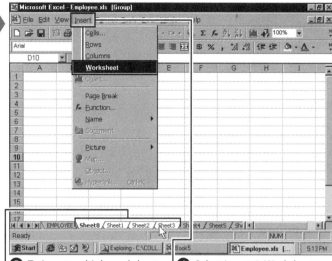

3 To insert multiple worksheets to the left (above) of a worksheet, use the Ctrl key and click consecutive sheet tabs.

4 Select Insert ⇨ Worksheet to add as many sheets as you selected in the previous step.

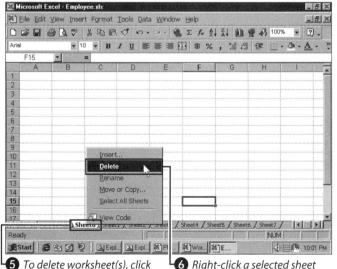

5 To delete worksheet(s), click the single sheet you want to delete, or press Ctrl as you click additional sheets.

6 Right-click a selected sheet tab to expose the shortcut menu and click Delete.

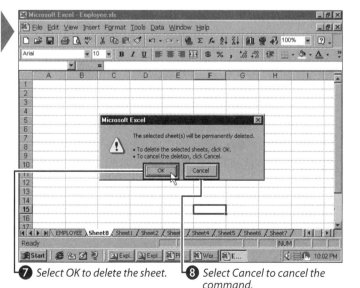

7 Select OK to delete the sheet.

8 Select Cancel to cancel the command.

Renaming Worksheets

By now, you have probably noticed that the default sheet names on the tabs at the bottom of a worksheet are generic and not at all descriptive. It makes good sense to change these sheet names so that they reflect their contents. Renaming is fast and easy.

You can create sheet names as long as 31 characters and, unlike range names, they may contain spaces. Use upper and lowercase letters as you choose, SHEET7 and Sheet7 would be considered identical and couldn't exist in the same workbook. You may feel inclined to use long worksheet names for greater clarity, but remember, you won't be able to see very many of them across the bottom of your worksheet. The Paste List feature allows you to create a list of range names on your worksheet. However, if you use short names for the worksheets in your workbook, you will be able to see more, if not all, names across the bottom of your worksheet.

You can use sheet names in formulas and functions, but if you use long names, it makes formulas more difficult to read and manipulate. It may be sensible to use names such as Alabama, Alaska, Arizona, for sheets pertaining to those states instead of Sheet1, Sheet2, and so on, but names such as AL01, AK02, and AZ03 combine the idea of alphabetizing and numeric order together. Excel offers no way to sort worksheet tabs except through obscure macros. With this in mind, you may want to maintain some sense of the order by naming conventions based either on the aforementioned alphabetic or numeric ordering or some other scheme, such as age, geography, or size. You can avoid unnecessary confusion if you make sure that when you name a sheet, you are not duplicating a range name or using a name that's the same as a cell address.

No matter how long your sheet names are, if they are referenced in formulas, the references will be readjusted automatically when you rename the sheets.

TAKE NOTE

THE EDIT⇨UNDO COMMAND AND WORKSHEET MANIPULATION

Most worksheet manipulation is outside of the realm of actions that you can reverse with the Undo command or toolbar button. You have already learned that you can't undo a worksheet deletion. You also cannot use the Undo feature to undo any of these worksheet actions: insert, rename, copy, or move.

PASTING A SHEET NAME

Standard cut/copy/paste techniques work when you're renaming sheets. You can use a name you've copied from a cell as a name to paste as a sheet name.

CROSS-REFERENCE

Read more about using sheet names in the task "Creating Multiple-Sheet Formulas" later in this chapter.

FIND IT ONLINE

If you want to rename yourself, start by looking at:
http://www.usafe.af.mil/bases/ramstein/legal/ethics/name.htm.

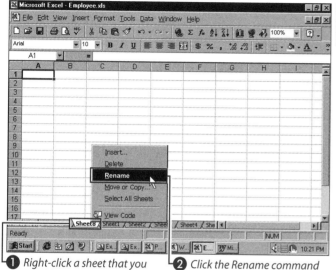

1 Right-click a sheet that you want to rename.

2 Click the Rename command and type the new name or click in the old name and edit it.

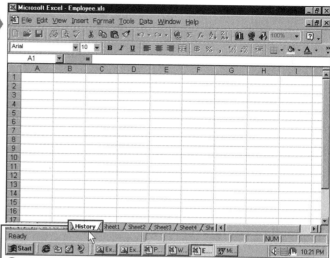

3 A faster method — double-click the name of the worksheet you want to rename and then type the new name.

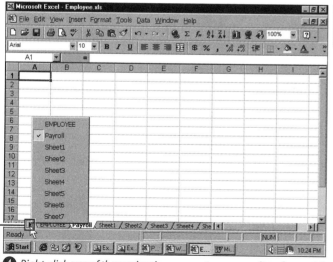

4 Right-click one of the navigation arrows to expose a list of up to 16 worksheet names in the current workbook.

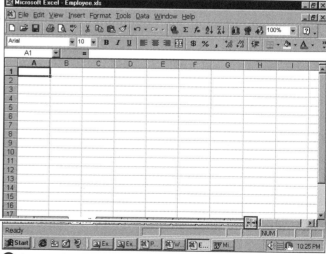

5 Point to the vertical line that separates worksheet names and the horizontal scrollbar. Drag the pointer to show more or fewer worksheet names while shrinking or expanding the horizontal scrollbar.

Copying Worksheets

Just as the ability to copy cells from one location to another is handy and efficient, so is the ability to copy an entire sheet. In effect, what you achieve is a new worksheet that initially looks exactly like the one you copied. You may want to do this so that you can experiment with a copy of your data while preserving the original. At other times, you need to duplicate a sheet of information and use it as a starting point for a new region, a new quarter, a new state, and so on. You can quickly rename the sheet and then edit its contents.

You can make a copy of a worksheet in the current workbook or in another open workbook. If you copy a worksheet by dragging, it has a decided advantage over the more deliberate action of selecting worksheet cells and copying them with cut and paste tools or commands. Not only is copying the entire worksheet easier than a copy-and-paste scenario, it also includes formatting features such as column widths and row heights as part of the copied information. In addition, when you copy an entire sheet, you are more likely to be copying all of the cells referenced by formulas in the copied sheet. If you copy a range of cells that refer to other cells that you're not copying, the references get adjusted to the destination sheet, often pointing to empty cells.

You can copy a worksheet to any location (before or after any specific worksheet) in the current workbook or in another workbook. If you copy a sheet to the current workbook, the new sheet name will be the same as the original with the exception that the number 2 (in parentheses) will follow the new name. For each additional copy you make of the same sheet, the numbers 3, 4, and so on will be used. If you copy a sheet to another workbook, the new sheet name will be identical to the original unless there's already a sheet there with that name.

Using the drag and drop method, copying a worksheet is simple and straightforward. But if you need to copy a sheet to a location that's many sheets away (differences in screen settings and the length of sheet names makes this a vague measure) you may prefer to use a more lengthy command method.

TAKE NOTE

COPYING MULTIPLE WORKSHEETS

You can make a copy of more than one sheet at a time, even sheets that aren't adjacent to each other. The newly created copies will appear in consecutive order and each will have the repeated sheet name followed by the number in parentheses.

CROSS-REFERENCE

See Chapter 6 for details on various copy and paste methods.

FIND IT ONLINE

If you want to know more about copying, get an overview and some history, at **http://www.sciam.com/1096issue/1096working.html.**

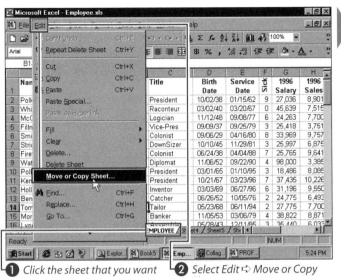

① Click the sheet that you want to copy.

② Select Edit ➪ Move or Copy Sheet.

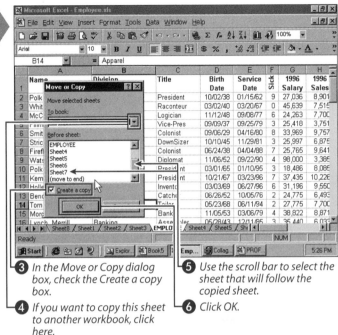

③ In the Move or Copy dialog box, check the Create a copy box.

④ If you want to copy this sheet to another workbook, click here.

⑤ Use the scroll bar to select the sheet that will follow the copied sheet.

⑥ Click OK.

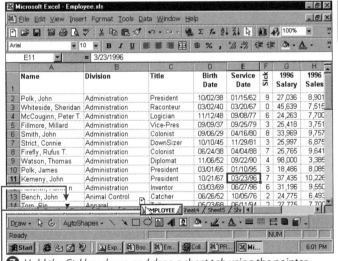

⑦ Hold the Ctrl key down and drag a sheet tab using the pointer to designate the destination; release the mouse button before the Ctrl key.

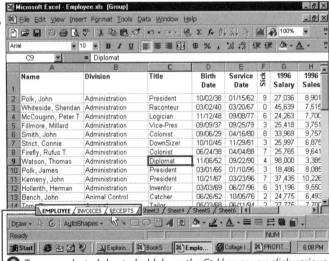

⑧ To copy selected sheets, hold down the Ctrl key as you click various sheet tabs; repeat steps 2 through 7.

173

Moving Worksheets

If your worksheets aren't in a logical or useful order, you will want to move them around. The way you move a sheet is very similar to the way you copy one. You can either use the drag and drop method to move a sheet quickly and easily (the name of the sheet you move will remain the same), or the command method, which is lengthier but often necessary. To move a sheet to a location that's many sheets away, you need to be able to specifically pick the location by seeing a list of sheet names.

Whenever you need data in one workbook that's already available in another workbook, it may be advantageous to copy a worksheet from one workbook to another. If you move a worksheet from one workbook to another and close the source workbook (without saving it), you have, in effect, copied the worksheet. At other times, when reassessing the structure of a workbook, you may decide to move a worksheet from one workbook to another. In either case, drag-and-drop techniques work quickly and easily. If there are no sheet names at the destination workbook like the one you're moving, the sheet name stays the same. But, if the name already exists, you will get a sheet name just like the old one, with the addition of the number 2 (in parentheses).

Whenever you want to move a worksheet to a different workbook, it's better to have the destination workbook open so that you can clearly see the sending and destination locations on your screen. In the destination workbook, it's useful to see the sheet tab names near the intended receiving area. When you move a worksheet to another workbook, any reference to cells in that worksheet will now refer to locations in the new workbook.

TAKE NOTE

▶ **MOVING MULTIPLE WORKSHEETS**

If you move nonadjacent sheets, they appear in consecutive order at the new location. Formulas that refer to a consecutive group of worksheets may become inoperative if you move some, but not all, of the sheets that are referenced in those formulas.

▶ **HIDDEN WORKSHEETS**

You can hide a worksheet with the command Format ➪ Worksheet ➪ Hide. If you move a group of consecutive worksheets that includes a hidden worksheet, that worksheet will not be moved.

CROSS-REFERENCE

See Chapter 9 to learn how to arrange or display more than one workbook on your screen at the same time.

SHORTCUT

If you drag worksheet tabs from the current workbook onto the Excel background, you instantly create a new workbook with as many sheets as you dragged.

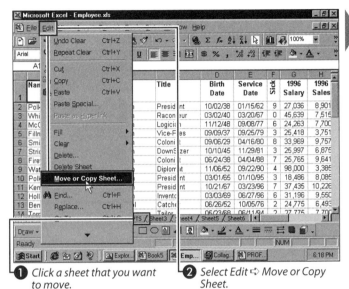

① Click a sheet that you want to move.

② Select Edit ➪ Move or Copy Sheet.

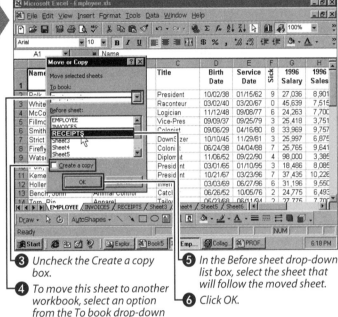

③ Uncheck the Create a copy box.

④ To move this sheet to another workbook, select an option from the To book drop-down list box.

⑤ In the Before sheet drop-down list box, select the sheet that will follow the moved sheet.

⑥ Click OK.

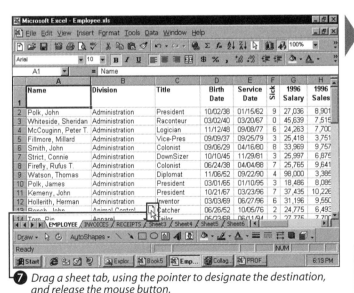

⑦ Drag a sheet tab, using the pointer to designate the destination, and release the mouse button.

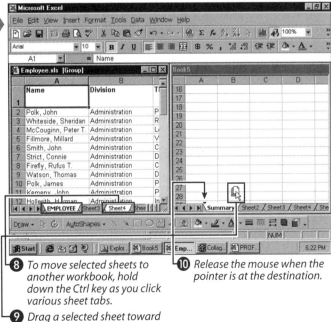

⑧ To move selected sheets to another workbook, hold down the Ctrl key as you click various sheet tabs.

⑨ Drag a selected sheet toward the destination workbook.

⑩ Release the mouse when the pointer is at the destination.

Creating Multiple-Sheet Formulas

As you gain familiarity and proficiency with using multiple-sheet workbooks, the idea of writing a formula or function in one worksheet that gets information from another worksheet seems less unusual and increasingly useful. In some workbooks, you can't imagine *not* using them.

A key point to setting up multiple-sheet workbook formulas is so that you don't have to type sheet names and addresses in your formulas, even though they're always required. The point-and-click method of writing formulas may seem strained when all cell references reside in the same worksheet. But when formulas refer to locations beyond the current worksheet, this method comes into its own, and is the recommended way to prepare such formulas.

There are many situations where you might want to gather data from other worksheets. For example, you may have a summary sheet where you plan to total all of the various entries from each of the four quarters for the year. The data for each quarter resides on a different sheet. You write a single formula on the summary sheet that adds data from each of the four sheets. You might do this for a single cell on the summary sheet or you might do this for an entire range of cells. In either case, you essentially write the formula once.

Other examples of worksheets like this include when the summary sheet serves as the total for data from 12 sheets for each month, or five sheets for the past five years, or eight sheets for each of the divisions in your company, and so on.

Not all formulas that refer to other sheets are as structured as discussed here. If you use a worksheet as a working area for experiments and sample work, you might need a formula there that refers to data on two of your five other sheets. Undoubtedly, you will encounter other useful times for these kinds of formulas.

TAKE NOTE

MOVING AND DELETING SHEETS REFERRED TO BY FORMULAS

If you move a sheet that is referred to by a formula in another sheet, the reference follows the sheet. If you delete a sheet that is referred to by a formula in another sheet, the formula displays #REF!, which indicates that the cell reference isn't valid.

GROUPING FORMULAS

Just as you can create a function such as =SUM(B2:B7) that refers only to the outer cells in a range yet includes all the cells between them, so too, can you write a function that refers only to the outer sheets in a workbook yet includes all the worksheets between them.

3-D FORMULAS

A formula such as =SUM(Quarter1:Quarter4!C3), which adds the content of cell C3 from four separate sheets, is often referred to as a 3-D formula. Moving or deleting any of the four quarterly sheets does not generate an error or warning message.

CROSS-REFERENCE
Read more about writing formulas that refer to other workbooks in Chapter 17.

FIND IT ONLINE
Learn more about three-dimensionality at
http://www.liglobal.com/ent_fun/3d/about3d/.

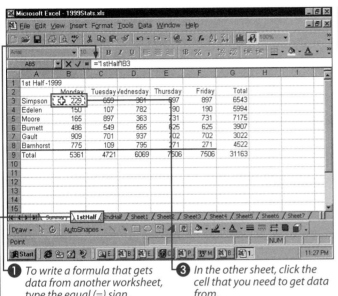

1 To write a formula that gets data from another worksheet, type the equal (=) sign.

2 Click the sheet tab where the other cell is located.

3 In the other sheet, click the cell that you need to get data from.

4 Type the operator needed (+ - * / or ^). Repeat steps 2 and 3 as necessary and press Enter.

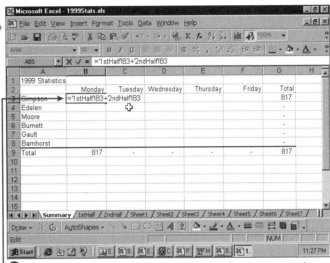

5 Double-click the cell in the previous image where you wrote the formula and observe the references to cells in other worksheets.

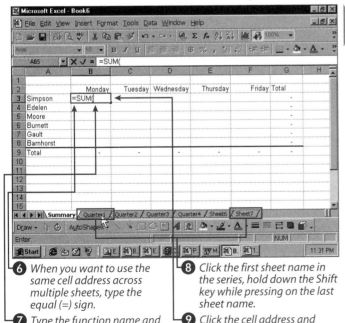

6 When you want to use the same cell address across multiple sheets, type the equal (=) sign.

7 Type the function name and the left parentheses.

8 Click the first sheet name in the series, hold down the Shift key while pressing on the last sheet name.

9 Click the cell address and press Enter.

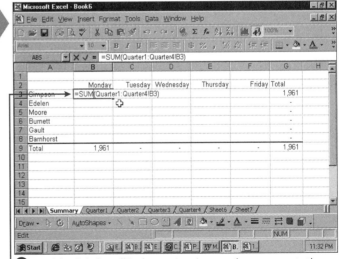

10 Double-click the cell in the previous image where you wrote the formula and observe the references to a cell range across multiple worksheets.

177

Grouping Worksheets

Another advantage of multiple-sheet workbooks is that you can temporarily treat some, or all, as a unit. Do you need to make column B in a number of these sheets be the same width? Should row 2 in these sheets be bold? Do you want to enter the same date in cell C3 of each of these sheets? How about the same title in cells A1 through J1 in each of the same sheets centered across those cells? The possibilities seem endless. In those workbooks where you want a group of sheets to have the same formatting characteristics, the same kind of data, and the same relative formulas, the concept of grouping is just what the doctor ordered.

The best situation for grouping worksheets is when you're about to design layout and data characteristics for a number of sheets before you've entered any text or formulas in them. Imagine a workbook that's like a yearly report based on quarterly data in four consecutive sheets named Q1, Q2, Q3, and Q4 and a fifth sheet named Summary. Column and row identifiers in all five sheets will be identical with the possible exception of a title to distinguish each sheet, particularly when printed. You also want all of your totals in a specific column and in a specific row — the same respective columns and rows in each worksheet.

When you group these sheets, the word Group will appear in the title bar at the top of your screen and the sheet tabs for all worksheets selected will have a white background instead of the usual gray. It won't be obvious as you start data entry and continue with entering formulas and making formatting selections, but your actions will occur in all of the selected sheets. When you're ready to make changes to a single sheet only, you can ungroup the sheets quickly.

When the need for grouping arises you're more likely to want to group a consecutive set of sheets, but you can also select a nonconsecutive group of sheets easily.

TAKE NOTE

▶ REMOVING/ADDING A SHEET FROM/TO THE SELECTED GROUP

If you included a sheet in a grouping of sheets and want to deselect it, hold down the Ctrl key as you click that sheet. Similarly, if you want to include a sheet along with others currently grouped, press Ctrl as you click that sheet.

▶ KEEP YOUR EYE ON THE TITLE BAR

Get in the habit of checking for the word Group in the title bar to remind yourself that grouping is (or isn't) in effect. Using the navigation arrows and sheet tabs is not reliable as they do not always show you which sheets, if any, are selected.

CROSS-REFERENCE

See Chapter 5 for information on printing multiple sheets in one printing action.

FIND IT ONLINE

A group of lions is a pride but what about a group of ravens or kangaroos? Find out at **http://www.interline. com.au/~nudge/GroupTerms.html**.

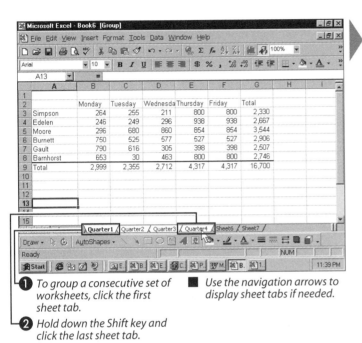

① To group a consecutive set of worksheets, click the first sheet tab.

■ Use the navigation arrows to display sheet tabs if needed.

② Hold down the Shift key and click the last sheet tab.

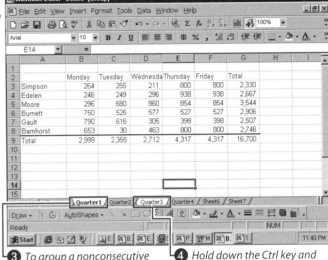

③ To group a nonconsecutive set of worksheets, click the first sheet tab.

④ Hold down the Ctrl key and click the other sheet tabs.

■ To group all sheets, right-click a sheet tab and choose Select all Sheets.

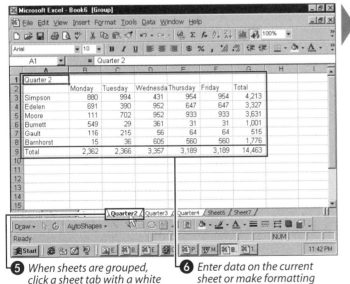

⑤ When sheets are grouped, click a sheet tab with a white background to see a sheet in the group.

⑥ Enter data on the current sheet or make formatting changes and all selected sheets will be affected.

⑦ To ungroup all sheets that are grouped, right-click a sheet that's part of the selected group.

⑧ From the shortcut menu, select Ungroup Sheets. Alternatively, click a sheet that is not part of the grouped sheets.

Personal Workbook

Q&A

1 Can you undo the action you just took to delete a worksheet?

_____

_____

_____

2 How many sheets can you insert at a time?

_____

_____

_____

3 What's a good reason for using short, rather than long names for worksheets?

_____

_____

_____

_____

4 True or False: There's not really any difference between copying a worksheet and using the copy-and-paste technique to copy all the cells of a worksheet to another worksheet.

_____

_____

5 Can you copy more than one worksheet at a time? Can you move more than one worksheet at a time?

_____

_____

_____

_____

6 True or False: If you're writing a formula that refers to a cell in another worksheet, you must type the name of that worksheet in your formula.

_____

_____

_____

7 In your workbook that has 12 worksheets named after each month and one called Summary, what happens to the formula =SUM(JANUARY:DECEMBER!B17) if you delete the sheet named OCTOBER?

_____

_____

_____

ANSWERS: PAGE 326

EXTRA PRACTICE

1 In a multiple-sheet workbook, type a formula to add cells A3 on Sheet2, B6 on Sheet3, and D4 on Sheet4. Do not type sheet names or the exclamation point (!) when writing your formula. Observe the formula after you've completed it.

2 Select two worksheets in a new workbook and double the width of column A. Verify that the action took place on both worksheets.

3 With a workbook open, create a new workbook. Use the Window ⇨ Arrange command to display a portion of each workbook on your screen. Copy a worksheet from one workbook to another.

4 Make a copy of Sheet1. Rename the copied sheet as Sheet1Backup.

REAL-WORLD APPLICATIONS

✔ You're about to rename four sheets to be Quarter1, Quarter2, and so on. After renaming the first one, you select the text and press Ctrl+C to copy the text. As you rename the next three sheets, you use Ctrl+V to paste the test Quarter1, which you then edit to adjust the quarter number.

✔ You frequently need to change the index value in cell C1 of Sheet1. Formulas in other worksheets refer to this cell. Whenever you're looking at another sheet, you'd like to see this index value. You select all other sheets, click C1 and type =Sheet1!C1.

✔ You often open the Invoice and Sales workbooks together. You move each of the two worksheets from the Sales workbook to the Invoice workbook. Next, you save the Invoice workbook and later delete the Sales workbook.

Visual Quiz

In the screen shown below, can you change the name of the sheets Quarter1, Quarter2, and so on to Q1, Q2, and so on without worrying about formulas working properly?

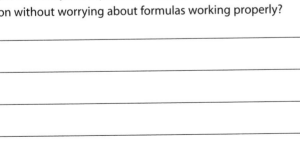

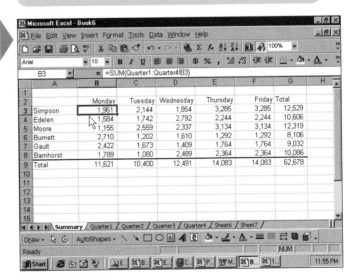

CHAPTER **11**

MASTER THESE SKILLS

▶ **Creating Graphic Objects**

▶ **Manipulating Objects**

▶ **Formatting Objects**

▶ **Using WordArt**

▶ **Annotating Data with Arrows and Boxes**

▶ **Inserting Pictures into a Workbook**

Creating Graphics and Pictures

Excel's graphical capabilities are more than just cosmetic. If your worksheet is going to be part of a publication or part of a slide presentation, you need to have the ability to emphasize portions of it using visual techniques that are not just bells and whistles. A good explanatory newspaper article, for example, is accompanied by diagrams, statistics, arrows, boxes, and special text to highlight one feature or another. When you need to present worksheet information either to readers or listeners, you also need some of these techniques.

Creating graphic objects is just the beginning of the process. You need to learn how to control colors (including shading, textures, and patterns) and line edges (including color, thickness, and dashes). There's a special toolbar for each of these options that provides additional settings. You have many other design considerations, including the ability to apply one of 20 different shadow options or one of 20 different 3-D settings. Also, you should learn how to copy objects and move them around the screen. Resizing and reshaping objects, either from their centers or from opposite corners, are also useful capabilities.

It's also worth learning the role that graphics can play in the production of your workbooks. Creating text boxes with arrows can go a long way toward adding coherence, as well as attractiveness to a worksheet that you're going to use for presentation or publication purposes.

You can also use clip art images, photographs from digital cameras, and pictures from other parts of the current worksheet (or from other worksheets) to enhance your worksheet presentation. Many of the techniques in this chapter are related to some of the ways that you manipulate information on Excel charts. If you're a current or potential user of PowerPoint, you will notice that many of the concepts presented here are identical or similar.

If you need to build a logo or simply to present a title in a more eye-catching and appealing way, using WordArt will give you most of the features you need. This add-in package, also a component of Word and PowerPoint, is well integrated with the Drawing toolbar that is the starting point for using most graphical objects.

Creating Graphic Objects

Before actually working with graphic objects, you should think of them as images that sit on top of a worksheet, not embedded in it as part of the cell structure. The boxes, buttons, circles, lines, and other objects that you will be creating have impact not only on the appearance of your worksheets, but the content of some menu commands — you will see new commands on the menu when you're dealing with objects. If you have worked with PowerPoint or other graphics packages, you will be familiar with many of the methods of creating and modifying objects.

The starting point for creating a graphic object is the Drawing toolbar. You can access it, just like any other toolbar, by right-clicking a toolbar button and selecting Drawing, but it also has its own button in the Standard toolbar which acts as a toggle switch to show or hide the toolbar quickly.

The five basic objects that you can create from the Drawing toolbar are: line, arrow, rectangle (including a square), oval (including a circle), and text box. There are many more shapes, however, accessible from an AutoShapes button, available in tear-off palettes so that you can park them on your worksheet for an indefinite time.

You have access to 32 basic shapes, 28 block arrows, 28 flowchart shapes, 8 stars, 8 banners, and 20 callouts (various boxes, ovals, and clouds with connectors as used in cartoons). Also, you will find connectors (9 to choose from) that you can click and drag between two objects that you've already drawn so that whenever you move the objects, the lines move (and grow or shrink as needed) to remain connected to the objects.

TAKE NOTE

SQUARES, CIRCLES, AND EQUILATERAL SHAPES

When dragging a rectangle, hold down the Shift key to confine the shape to a square; when dragging an oval, hold down the Shift key to confine the shape to a circle. As you complete the drawing, be sure to release the mouse button before the Shift key. Use the Shift key with some of the other geometric shapes, such as the pentagon, hexagon, and octagon to make them equilateral. Use the Shift key when creating a line or an arrow to ensure that the object lines up with an angle that's a multiple of 15 degrees.

CREATE A SHAPE FROM ITS CENTER

To create a shape whose center must be at a certain point, click the shape and hold down the Ctrl key as you click and drag from the desired center point in your worksheet. You can also hold down the Shift key at the same time to create the effects mentioned in the previous note. Release the mouse before the keyboard as you complete the drawing.

CROSS-REFERENCE
Learn about the placement of toolbars on your worksheet in Chapter 9.

FIND IT ONLINE
Review your knowledge of polygons http://www.li.net/ ~george/virtual-polyhedra/polygons.html .

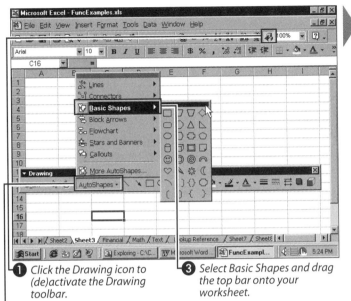

1 Click the Drawing icon to (de)activate the Drawing toolbar.

2 Click the AutoShapes arrow in the Drawing toolbar to activate the list of shapes.

3 Select Basic Shapes and drag the top bar onto your worksheet.

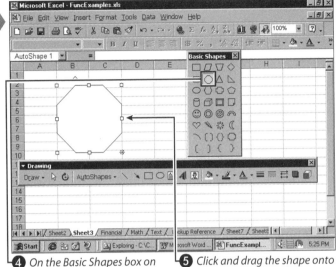

4 On the Basic Shapes box on your worksheet, click a shape.

5 Click and drag the shape onto your worksheet and release the mouse.

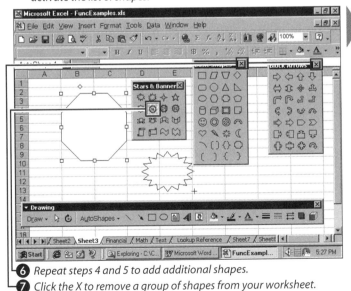

6 Repeat steps 4 and 5 to add additional shapes.

7 Click the X to remove a group of shapes from your worksheet.

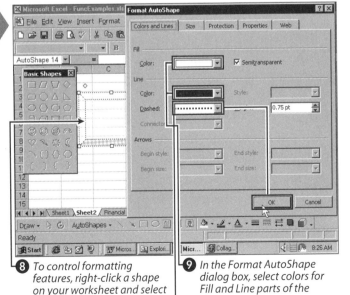

8 To control formatting features, right-click a shape on your worksheet and select Format AutoShape.

9 In the Format AutoShape dialog box, select colors for Fill and Line parts of the shape.

10 Select options for Dashed and Weight and click OK.

Manipulating Objects

Once you've created some graphic objects, you will want to manipulate them. This includes reshaping, moving, copying, rotating, flipping, nudging, and numerous other possibilities.

When you reshape an object, you have the option to retain the same aspect ratio (height to width ratio) or to enlarge or shrink it from its center or from its sides. You can also combine these capabilities. After you've refined the look of an object, you can duplicate it once or many times, or move it to a different part of your worksheet, to a different sheet, or to a different workbook. You can also rotate objects either in 15-degree increments or freely to any angle.

When manipulating objects, whether they're shapes, arrows, pictures, or WordArt (covered later in this chapter), you may need to overlap them. As you move objects around your screen, overlap may occur, but also, you may want a specific object either in front or behind another. Either option is available. When you want to move an object, sometimes you want to move it just a bit. Depending on screen resolution, this can be awkward, but there's a nudge feature on the Drawing toolbar that simplifies this task.

When you've got more than one shape on your screen, you can choose to align two or more of them so that their edges align. When overlapping shapes, you can choose to align them on their respective centers and middles.

TAKE NOTE

▶ HANDLES

The eight tiny rectangles that appear on an object's corners and sides when it's selected are called handles.

▶ GROW OR SHRINK PROPORTIONALLY

To expand or shrink an object proportionally, hold the Shift key down as you drag a corner handle. Release the mouse before the Shift key.

▶ GROW OR SHRINK FROM THE CENTER

To expand or shrink an object while keeping the object centered at the same spot, hold the Ctrl key down as you drag any handle. To keep the object at the same proportion while retaining the same center, hold the Shift key down as you drag a corner. In both cases, release the mouse before the keys. To enable the shape to become taller or shorter around the same center, hold down the Ctrl key and drag a top or bottom handle. Drag the right or left edge to allow the object to become wider or narrower.

▶ ROTATE FROM THE CENTER OR FROM THE OPPOSITE CORNER

To rotate an object around its center, select the object, click the rotate button in the Drawing toolbar and click and drag any of the green circles that appear on the object. To rotate an object from the opposite corner, hold down the Ctrl key as you rotate the object. Hold down the Shift key during rotation to ensure that all rotation occurs in 15-degree increments.

CROSS-REFERENCE

Review copy, move, and paste concepts (usable with graphic objects) in Chapter 6.

FIND IT ONLINE

Learn all about aspect ratio at **http://www.yanman.com/ HomeTheater/HTAspect.htm** .

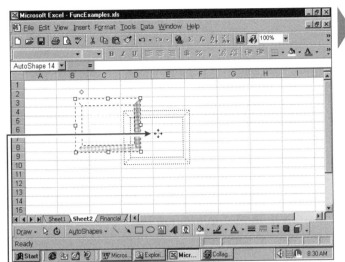

1 To move an object, click and drag it in any direction.

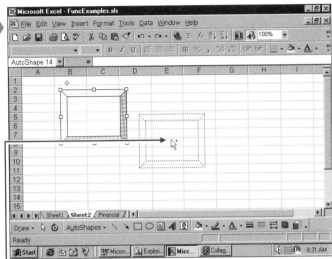

2 To copy an object, hold down the Ctrl key — a plus sign (+) appears — and drag the object in any direction. Release the mouse first.

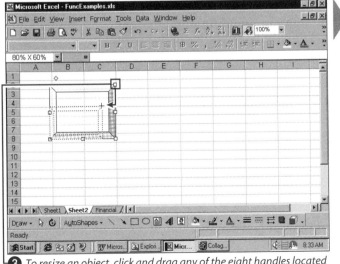

3 To resize an object, click and drag any of the eight handles located on the corners and sides.

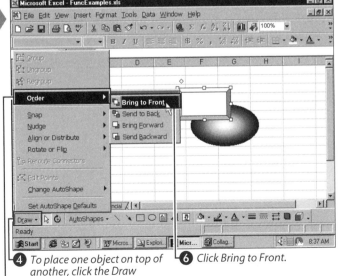

4 To place one object on top of another, click the Draw button in the Drawing toolbar.

5 Click Order.

6 Click Bring to Front.

187

Formatting Objects

When you create a text entry, it doesn't take you long to recognize the need for changing its appearance, either by making it bold, italic, underlined, or any of a number of additional formatting features. With graphic objects, you have these same kinds of needs. You have access to similar color palettes to those you have for text and cell backgrounds, but additionally, you have a palette for line color. You can apply 3-D effects and even control the direction of the imaginary light that determines which sides of 3-D objects are in shadow. Be aware that when you apply these enhancing features to an object, it's easy to duplicate the object or copy its formatting characteristics to another object.

Color choices for objects are unlimited. If, for example, you deal in marble products and want to create a banner design that appears as if it's made from marble, you have a choice of three patterns. The same goes for wood. Gradient choices, whereby you can get light and dark color effects in various receding styles, offers a wealth of interesting possibilities also. You can even make colors transparent. This means that when you want to have overlapping objects on the screen, the colors and shapes will show through the overlap.

To accentuate the edges of shapes, you can choose not only the color of the line comprising the edge, but also the thickness of the line, or, if you want to use dashed lines, the style of the dashed lines. Most of these features are accessible from the Drawing toolbar or from the Format menu; the latter has more choices but is more time-consuming to use.

Another feature, sometimes used with dramatic effect, is shadows. You can apply any color to a shadow and you can use a semi-transparent effect that allows background elements, such as gridlines or overlapped objects, to remain visible.

The possibilities available with 3-D formatting also seem without end. Not only will you find 20 different ways to convert a shape into a 3-D shape, you can also decide on oblique or perspective projection, the angle and intensity of light direction, and the angle and length of depth.

TAKE NOTE

SELECT ALL OR SOME OF YOUR OBJECTS

If you're about to apply a particular formatting feature to all objects on your screen, first click the Select Objects arrow on the Drawing toolbar. Next, click and drag a rectangle to encompass all objects — you can even drag beyond screen boundaries to include objects not currently visible.

To select more than one object prior to formatting or grouping, hold the Shift key down and click the objects you want to format.

CROSS-REFERENCE

See Chapter 6 to review how to use the color background and color text palettes.

FIND IT ONLINE

To learn all about shadow effects during an eclipse, look at **http://www.earthview.com/tutorial/effects.htm**.

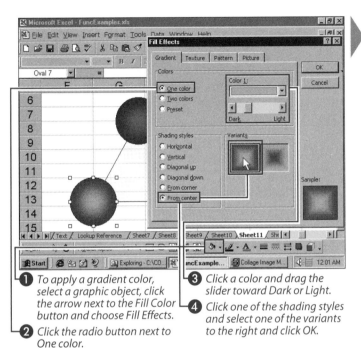

① To apply a gradient color, select a graphic object, click the arrow next to the Fill Color button and choose Fill Effects.

② Click the radio button next to One color.

③ Click a color and drag the slider toward Dark or Light.

④ Click one of the shading styles and select one of the variants to the right and click OK.

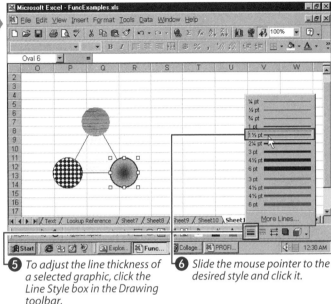

⑤ To adjust the line thickness of a selected graphic, click the Line Style box in the Drawing toolbar.

⑥ Slide the mouse pointer to the desired style and click it.

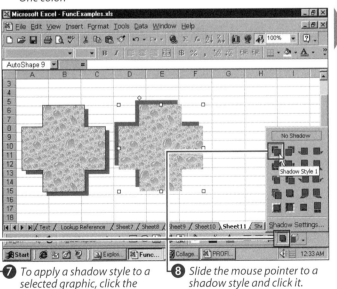

⑦ To apply a shadow style to a selected graphic, click the Shadow box in the Drawing toolbar.

⑧ Slide the mouse pointer to a shadow style and click it.

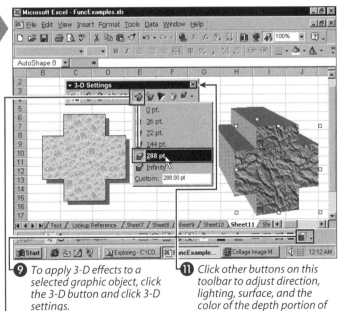

⑨ To apply 3-D effects to a selected graphic object, click the 3-D button and click 3-D settings.

⑩ Click the depth button and click a depth selection.

⑪ Click other buttons on this toolbar to adjust direction, lighting, surface, and the color of the depth portion of the object.

Using WordArt

WordArt, as its name suggests, gives you the ability to manipulate text in creative and artistic ways. For example, you might want to use WordArt to design a logo or create some eye-catching effect for a worksheet title. Maybe you want three-dimensional text? Or, how about text that looks like it's written across the face of a cylinder or ball? Perhaps you'd like the letters to appear as if they're made out of bricks. Whether as an attention-grabber or as something that represents the business you're in, WordArt offers a staggering number of possibilities. WordArt is not unique to Excel—you can find it in Word and PowerPoint also, so you can easily copy a WordArt object from one package to another and still have the menu structure easily accessible.

Most often, you'll use WordArt for one or two word titles, company names, or short phrases. As with drawing objects and pictures, when you use WordArt, you create an object that's on your worksheet rather than in it. WordArt gives you many options, but you can use it effectively with just a few decisions. WordArt gives you 30 separate styles at startup; the emphasis is on color, curved text shapes, and shadows.

After picking a style and providing text, you may be perfectly content with the appearance of what you see. As with objects, you'll often see a yellow diamond when a WordArt object is selected, and you can drag this diamond in different directions to get different shape effects. Some shapes have two diamonds to provide both horizontal and vertical adjustments.

WordArt has its own toolbar that appears every time you click a WordArt object. From this toolbar, you can select one of 40 different shapes so that your text can appear in some of these ways: as if written on a cylindrical strip of paper; in the shape of an octagon; on the perimeter of a circle or semicircle; across a button; as wavy text; in the shape of a trapezoid or triangle.

You can rotate WordArt (just like graphic objects), choose to have all letters be the same height, rotate all of the letters making them vertical, and control character spacing. At any time, you can return to one of the 30 basic startup styles and start over.

TAKE NOTE

▶ DON'T LIMIT WORDART FORMATTING TO THE WORDART TOOLBAR

Despite the tremendous number of choices available from the WordArt toolbar, most of the formatting features available for graphic objects work for WordArt objects also. Don't hesitate to try some of the shadow, color, and 3-D effects readily available from the Drawing toolbar.

CROSS-REFERENCE

See "Inserting Pictures into a Workbook" later in this chapter to learn how to create a picture link.

FIND IT ONLINE

For additional word art inspiration, check out some of the computer-aided calligraphy samples at **http://dspace.dial.p ipex.com/georgethomson/GALLERY1.HTM.**

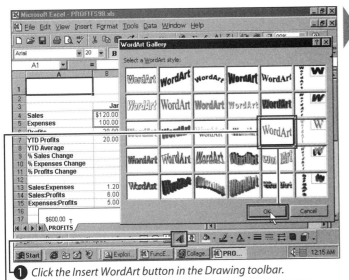

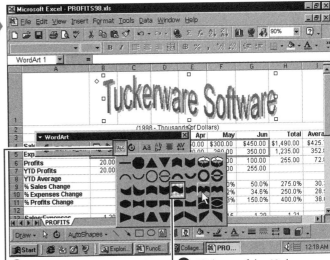

1 Click the Insert WordArt button in the Drawing toolbar.

2 Click one of the 30 styles in the WordArt Gallery and click OK.

3 After typing your text, click the WordArt Shape button in the WordArt toolbar.

4 Click one of the 40 shapes.

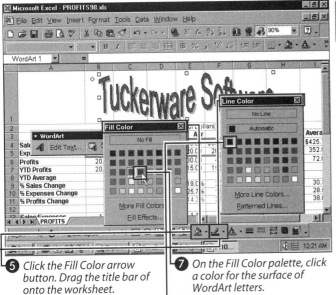

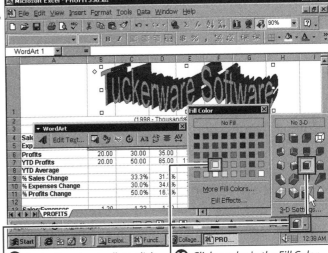

5 Click the Fill Color arrow button. Drag the title bar of onto the worksheet.

6 Click the Line Color arrow button and drag the palette onto the worksheet.

7 On the Fill Color palette, click a color for the surface of WordArt letters.

8 On the Line Color palette, click a color for the edges of WordArt letters.

9 In the Drawing toolbar, click the 3-D button and select an image to apply depth to WordArt letters.

10 Click a color in the Fill Color palette to apply to the surface of WordArt letters.

Annotating Data with Arrows and Boxes

For paper presentations, the use of arrows and boxes (and possibly other shapes) goes a long way toward minimizing the written explanation that you often need to bring out talking points. You can either create boxes and arrows separately or use an AutoShapes group called callouts — reminiscent of cartoon balloons. Either method gives you a way to annotate cells or areas on your worksheet.

As you might expect, both the number and the types of choices that Excel gives you are enormous and infinitely flexible. You can create double-ended arrows if you want to emphasize the relationship between two cells or worksheet sections. When differentiating a series of arrows, you can change the arrow style (maybe using a circle or diamond instead), control the thickness of the line, or adjust the type of line (solid, dashed, or dotted). Sometimes you will create an arrow and decide to retain just the line with no arrow symbols at either end.

You might want a bulletin or box on your worksheet that explains a result, a methodology, a numerical index, a trend, or some other item. You could use one of these boxes tied to an arrow or simply in a stand-alone fashion, almost like a comment box.

One big advantage of using a box or a shape with text is that you have much more flexibility in terms of where you put it and how it's formatted than you do with a standard description in worksheet cells. An explanatory box can have a stylized border, a color background and shadow, and be connected to an arrow that points to the part of the worksheet that contains the pertinent information.

When deciding to put a box on your screen so that you can add text to it, you need to decide between adding a text box and another kind of shape. With a text box, you can only choose between a rectangle or a square. Choose other shapes for variety if you wish, you can still enter text in them.

TAKE NOTE

TEXT IN A BOX

After adding an AutoShape to your screen, you can begin typing and the text will appear inside of the shape, except when the shape is unusual, such as an arc. If you click the edge of the shape you can attempt to center the text, both horizontally and vertically, in the shape by clicking the Format menu and selecting AutoShape. Click the Alignment tab and put a check in the box next to Automatic size and adjust both text alignment settings to Center.

ROTATING TEXT

Although you can't rotate a text box, you can rotate all of the shapes that you can create from the AutoShapes toolbar. However, when you rotate a shape with text in it, the text remains as is. If the shape is rotated 90 degrees, you can separately rotate the text to fit it but you can't rotate text to fit other angles.

CROSS-REFERENCE
Learn about annotating a cell in "Auditing and Documenting" in Chapter 6.

FIND IT ONLINE
Check out online comics at **http://www.zark.com/**.

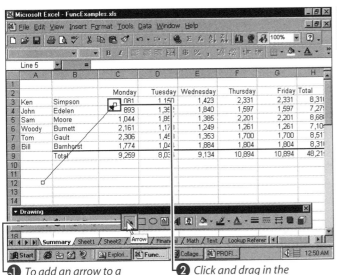

① To add an arrow to a worksheet, click the arrow button in the Drawing toolbar.

② Click and drag in the worksheet, releasing the mouse where you want the arrow point to be.

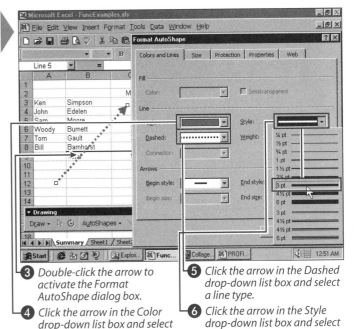

③ Double-click the arrow to activate the Format AutoShape dialog box.

④ Click the arrow in the Color drop-down list box and select a color.

⑤ Click the arrow in the Dashed drop-down list box and select a line type.

⑥ Click the arrow in the Style drop-down list box and select a line style.

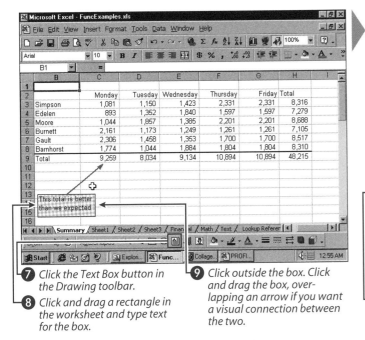

⑦ Click the Text Box button in the Drawing toolbar.

⑧ Click and drag a rectangle in the worksheet and type text for the box.

⑨ Click outside the box. Click and drag the box, overlapping an arrow if you want a visual connection between the two.

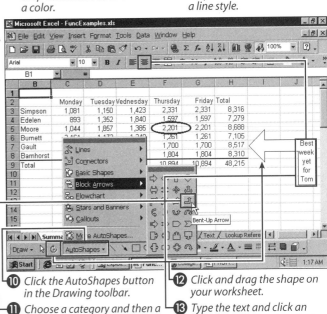

⑩ Click the AutoShapes button in the Drawing toolbar.

⑪ Choose a category and then a specific shape and click it.

⑫ Click and drag the shape on your worksheet.

⑬ Type the text and click an alignment button to adjust the text.

Inserting Pictures into a Workbook

If you believe in the old adage that a picture is worth a thousand words, you don't need to be told how important a picture can be in a worksheet. However, you have more than just the ability to import pictures from other sources, as rich as that feature is. You can also take pictures of part of your worksheet and use them elsewhere in the current worksheet, or another worksheet altogether.

You can get pictures from many sources — other applications such as Paint and PowerPoint, built-in clip art files, Internet screens, scanners, and digital cameras. Once you have inserted a picture into your worksheet, you have many of the same capabilities in manipulating it that you do with other graphic objects. Furthermore, you can crop the image from any of the four edges and you can adjust the brightness and contrast in the picture.

If there's a portion of your worksheet that you'd like to keep in the same location but would like to see an image of that portion displayed elsewhere, you can take a picture of that portion and paste it at another location. Because the picture is an object, you can do more with it in terms of formatting than you can with the original data. For example, imagine a worksheet that's designed to show a number of different sections found on other worksheets in the same workbook. If Sheet1 contains sales data, Sheet2 contains information about sales people, and Sheet3 has information on sales trends, it might make sense to have a summary sheet that shows the important parts of each of these sheets.

You can set up the summary to be either a snapshot arrangement, whereby the information is accurate at the time of placement only, or, you can provide a link between your pasted images on the summary sheet to keep them updated.

TAKE NOTE

▶ PASTE A PICTURE LINK

If a picture is pasted with a link, not only do you get a completely accurate representation of the copied cell content, you also get all of the formatting characteristics too. Any formatting or content changes you make to the area that's copied are immediately reflected in the picture.

▶ USE YOUR CAMERA

The Camera toolbar button is ideal when you want to create a picture link. Select the range to copy and click the Camera button to take the picture. Next, click where you want to paste the upper-left corner of the selection. This links the pasted picture to the original selected range. Review Chapter 9 to learn how to add a button to an existing toolbar. The Camera button is located in the Tools category.

CROSS-REFERENCE
See Chapter 17 for information on other kinds of links.

FIND IT ONLINE
Learn about the benefits of digital cameras at
http://www.dcforum.com/dc/new/benefits.shtml .

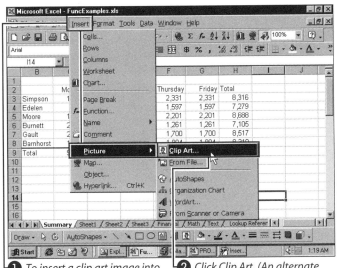

❶ To insert a clip art image into your worksheet, select Insert ➪ Picture.

❷ Click Clip Art. (An alternate method is to click the Clip Art button in the Drawing toolbar.)

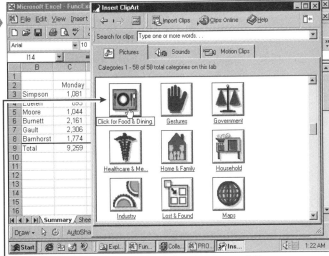

❸ Click a category and double-click an image to add it to your worksheet.

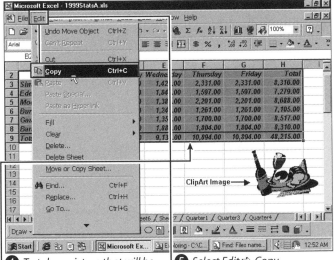

❹ To take a picture that will be pasted at another workbook location, select the range.

❺ Select Edit ➪ Copy.

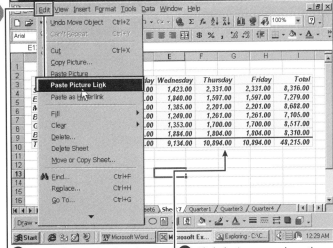

❻ At the destination location, hold down the Shift key and select Edit ➪ Paste Picture Link.

❼ Click the image and use the Fill Color button to apply a color background. The picture is linked to the source; changes in the source will appear in the picture image.

Personal Workbook

Q&A

1 True or False: To edit two objects at the same time, you can select just those objects by holding down the Shift key as you click each one.

_____

_____

_____

2 When you want to make changes to a WordArt image on your screen, how do you activate the WordArt toolbar?

_____

_____

_____

_____

3 When creating an arrow or line, how can you insure that it's at a 45-degree angle?

_____

_____

_____

_____

4 If you use one of the choices in the Connectors palette (found in AutoShapes) to connect two graphical objects, what happens when you move one of the objects?

_____

_____

_____

_____

_____

5 True or False: You can rotate an object from its center or from any of its corners.

_____

_____

_____

6 What happens when you click an object and press Ctrl+D?

_____

_____

_____

_____

ANSWERS: PAGE 327

EXTRA PRACTICE

1 Create a text box in the lower-right corner of your screen. Enter the words: **Better than Expected**. Create an arrow from the box pointing to cell B3.

2 Draw a WordArt image and change its shape to a semicircle (like the letter U).

3 Make a rectangle whose boundary lines up exactly with the cell boundaries of a range that's four cells wide by three cells high.

4 Create an equilateral hexagon centered exactly on the lower-right corner of cell D8.

5 Draw an equilateral triangle and create three circles — each one centered on a corner of the triangle.

REAL-WORLD APPLICATIONS

✔ Two text boxes on your screen are the same size but one's higher than the other. You Shift+click each text box, click the Draw button in the Drawing toolbar, select Align or Distribute, and click Align Top to make them even.

✔ Three cells in your company sales report worksheet appear questionable. You create an oval to surround each of them, and print a few copies of the report for your sales meeting tomorrow.

✔ Your company sells swimming pools. To add a little humor to your worksheet, you select all of your text boxes, click the Fill Color button and select Fill Effects. You click the Texture tab and select the Water droplets choice.

Visual Quiz

In the screen shown at the right, how do you change the selected arrow's text to be bold? Which button in which toolbar do you use to make the arrow's perimeter line thicker? Which button can you use to apply a background color to the arrow?

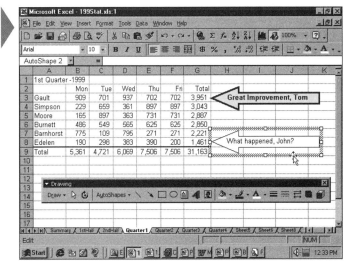

_____

_____

_____

PART

III

Creating Charts with Excel

One of the joys of using Excel is the ease and simplicity with which you can create a chart from your worksheet data. Charting offers enormous possibilities to display worksheet data in colorful and enlightening ways.

As you explore this feature, don't lose track of the fact that charting is considerably more than a way to create colorful images of your data. Charting not only has analytical capabilities, it enables you to see information in illuminating and different ways that often provides insight into the nature of your data. Charting has become a popular tool that's widely used in presentations to both enliven and educate your audience.

Just as you frequently change the content and layout of your worksheet data, you will also want to change the appearances of your charts. When you learn how easy it is to change chart types and how valuable the new perspective can be, experimentation becomes your basic mode of operation.

Another productive side of charting comes from the ability to manipulate charts in ways that alter worksheet data.

CHAPTER 12

MASTER
THESE
SKILLS

▶ Selecting Data for a Chart

▶ Creating a New Chart Instantly
or with the Chart Wizard

▶ Selecting a Chart Type

▶ Moving, Copying, and Resizing
a Chart on the Worksheet

▶ Creating Gridlines, Titles, and Legends

▶ Printing Charts

Creating a Chart

Excel's charting capability is both easy and sophisticated. These terms are not contradictory, but complementary. The ease with which you can convert numerical worksheet data into an impressive chart, with legends, titles, and colors is undeniable. And when your needs are more sophisticated, Excel has an impressive array of commands and features from which to choose.

Key concepts in creating charts include: how and what to select from your worksheet to be displayed in the chart; which chart types work best for the data you've selected from your worksheet; whether to put the chart on your worksheet or on a separate sheet; how best to arrange multiple charts on a worksheet; and how to print your charts.

Many people feel that a worksheet filled with numbers is boring. Add a chart and immediately the visual appeal increases. But charts offer more than just colorful splashes in the midst of a sea of numbers. Some people can look at numbers on a worksheet and never quite grasp the potential trends that might be lurking there. Display those same numbers in the form of a chart and trends and other relationships may seem immediately apparent.

Because Excel has so many chart types and variations on them, charting may seem more experimental than other aspects of this software. Column charts offer bold and colorful displays and are good for illustrating volume. Line charts do a better job than most other types in showing trends over periods of time. Pie charts offer concise depictions of the pieces that comprise a total. Combination charts let you mix chart types, perhaps a line and column chart together for contrasting data. Make a change to the chart type and sometimes what had seemed elusive is now crystal-clear. Charting gives you that extra tool to help clarify and illuminate worksheet data.

To be a proficient user of Excel charts, you need to learn some of the mechanics of manipulation — how to change the appearance of a chart not only by changing its type but also by moving, copying, and reshaping it. Through intelligent use of gridlines, titles, and legends, you have even more tools to polish your charts.

Selecting Data for a Chart

The most critical step of all in creating a chart is to decide what is to appear in your chart. After you create a chart or two, it's quite likely that you'll reconsider the layout of your worksheet to accommodate easier data selection for charts.

To be at all useful in depicting information, an Excel chart must be based on values. You could create a chart totally devoid of numerical data, but it would simply be a shell, an empty grid. On the other hand, if you selected a range of numbers and then created a chart, you would essentially have the opposite of a shell — a group of columns, bars, or lines with no outer information identifying what was being depicted.

Fortunately, when you lay out worksheet data, you nearly always have a row or two of information across the top of your values that explains what's in each column. Also, you nearly always have a column of information along the left side of your data that explains what's in each row. If you adhere to this kind of layout — numerical data with a row of labels across the top and a column of data on the left side — creating the chart will be immeasurably easier.

Not all chart data, however, should be subject to the constraints just described. It's only slightly more time-consuming to select noncontiguous cells and display them in a chart. Imagine a multicolumn report, which contains data for each month in columns and also includes a column showing quarterly totals. It would be sensible to include the row identifiers from the first column, and also identifiers for each of the four quarterly totals.

TAKE NOTE

EXCEL CAN GUESS WHICH CELLS YOU WANT TO APPEAR IN YOUR CHART

If you attempt to create a chart with only the active cell selected, Excel analyzes the location of the active cell and includes all surrounding cells that contain data. Excel will not include any cells beyond empty rows or columns. If what you want charted is neatly encompassed in a range delineated by empty columns and rows and worksheet boundaries, simply click a cell in that range and proceed with chart creation.

CHART DATA FROM DIFFERENT SHEETS

You can't really select ranges from different sheets to appear in a chart, but you can set up formulas on a new sheet that simply get data from a number of different sheets. You can then use this sheet as a source for a chart.

CROSS-REFERENCE
Learn about lists and how they're used in database worksheets in Chapter 15.

SHORTCUT
With just the active cell selected, press Ctrl+* to see which cells Excel will include in a chart.

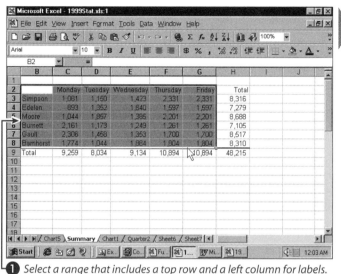

1 Select a range that includes a top row and a left column for labels.

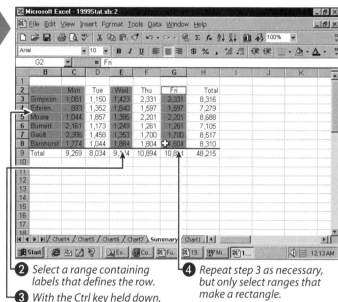

2 Select a range containing labels that defines the row.

3 With the Ctrl key held down, select additional ranges.

4 Repeat step 3 as necessary, but only select ranges that make a rectangle.

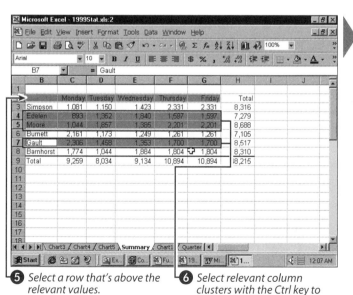

5 Select a row that's above the relevant values.

6 Select relevant column clusters with the Ctrl key to include additional ranges.

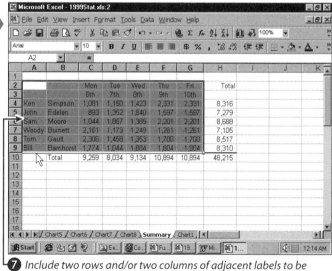

7 Include two rows and/or two columns of adjacent labels to be included in the chart data.

Creating a New Chart Instantly or with the Chart Wizard

You can create charts so rapidly that you may find yourself discarding some of them just as quickly. But, while it's easy to create a chart with little thought or planning, it might make more sense for you to create a chart methodically.

Two major questions need consideration before you create your chart. First, do you want your chart created as quickly as possible with only a minimum of alteration necessary to complete it, or do you want to take a more deliberate approach and make design and layout choices using a step-by-step methodology? Second, if you take the deliberate approach, do you want to create a chart on a totally new and separate sheet or do you want it on your worksheet, side-by-side with your data?

After selecting the data for a chart, it's time to confront the first question above. If you take the quick approach to creating a chart, Excel asks you no questions and automatically creates the chart on a new sheet. The chart will be called Chart1 and any subsequent charts you create in this manner will be named sequentially, Chart2, Chart3, and so on. These charts often only need a title or an occasional descriptor to be understandable. Until you decide otherwise, the default chart type is column — probably the most common type of chart used in business today.

The more deliberate approach to creating a chart is through the Chart Wizard, a four-step process that guides you through various choices related to:

- ▶ What type of chart you'd like (see the task in this chapter on chart types).
- ▶ The data you want included and how it should be oriented.
- ▶ The selection of titles, adjustment of axes, display of gridlines, placement of the legend, and display of source data.
- ▶ Whether to put the chart on a new sheet or in the current worksheet.

Excel's wizard concept is highly interactive. As you make choices, you see the effects on a preview screen of the chart. At any time, you can return to a previous step and make changes as necessary. As you gain proficiency with the Chart Wizard, you'll be able to zip through it quickly to create a chart you won't need to refine.

TAKE NOTE

▶ USE THE WIZARD TO CREATE A QUICK CHART ON YOUR WORKSHEET

Although the Chart Wizard is designed to allow you to proceed intelligently through step-by-step chart creation, you can also use it for instant chart creation. Select your data, click the Chart Wizard tool, and in Step 1 of the wizard sequence, click the Finish button. A chart appears on your worksheet immediately.

CROSS-REFERENCE
Look at Chapter 16 to learn how to create a pivot chart.

FIND IT ONLINE
Learn about another well-known wizard at the Wonderful Wizard of Oz site at http://www.eskimo.com/~tiktok/.

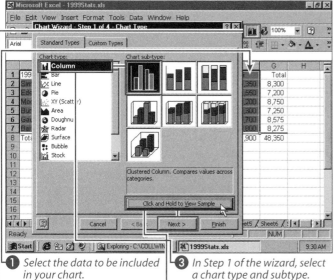

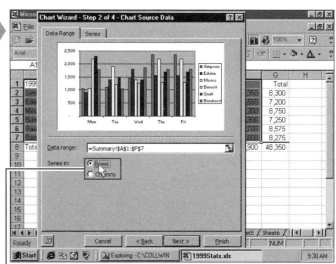

1 Select the data to be included in your chart.

2 Press the F11 key to immediately create a new chart on a separate sheet, or click the Chart Wizard button.

3 In Step 1 of the wizard, select a chart type and subtype.

4 Click and hold the button to get a preview that uses your data. Click the Next button.

5 In Step 2 of the wizard, click rows and columns and observe the different chart orientations.

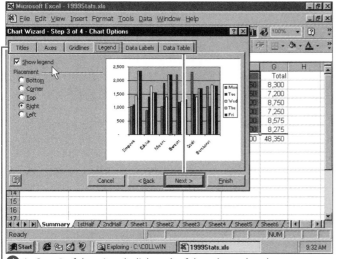

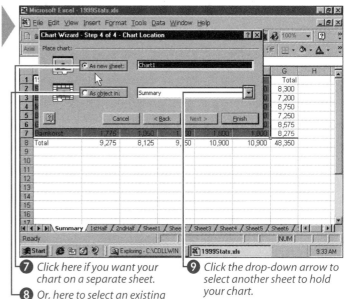

6 In Step 3 of the wizard, click each of the tabs and make adjustments before clicking Next.

7 Click here if you want your chart on a separate sheet.

8 Or, here to select an existing sheet.

9 Click the drop-down arrow to select another sheet to hold your chart.

Selecting a Chart Type

The manner in which you display your data in a chart is equally as important as the data you're presenting. Excel has nearly 100 different built-in standard and custom chart types. You can choose from a quick toolbar button with 15 selections or pursue the more comprehensive list. As you might expect, the design and layout of any of your charts is infinitely changeable.

When you create charts quickly, they appear in vertical columns and often that's not a bad choice. Excel refers to these charts as Column charts — they're ideal for showing volume, whether it's widgets or sales, and they're prominent and bold. Choose a horizontal arrangement instead and it's called a bar chart. With either type, you can choose a stacking variation that can show totals comprised of segments, but this won't work well if negative values are included in the source data.

If you're trying to show a trend, a line chart is likely to be the better choice, because you see the path of a line over a series of dates. When you need to see the parts that comprise a total, a pie chart might be an ideal choice, but be aware that if there's negative data involved (there's no such thing as a negative piece of pie) — the data will be treated as positive.

Excel chart types usually come in flat and 3-D versions. The latter are nearly always more dramatic, but when you're trying to show a lot of data, they can appear crowded and indecipherable. You can rotate, twist, turn, and tilt these charts for optimum viewing angles and you can explode one or more pieces of the pie chart. You should be careful to not let the attractiveness of 3-D charts overwhelm the content and meaning.

When you use the Chart Wizard to create a chart, you are able to see all the built-in and custom types and get a preview as you try different options. In addition to the aforementioned chart types, you may want to consider XY charts (ideal for scientific and engineering data), surface charts (reminiscent of topographic maps), stock charts (which show you high, low, and close readings), and cylinder, cone, and pyramid charts, all three of which are variations on column charts.

Because changing your chart after it's created is so easy, you should approach chart selection experimentally, knowing that you can always choose another.

TAKE NOTE

TWO CHARTS DEPICTING IDENTICAL DATA

If you're not sure which type of chart is going to best portray your data, use the Chart Wizard to create a chart on your worksheet, make a copy of it and change the chart type of the copy. Comparing two charts side by side will help you decide which is better. It's not unthinkable to have two charts of different types that show the same data.

CROSS-REFERENCE
To learn more about showing trends via line charts, learn how to add trendlines in Chapter 14

FIND IT ONLINE
If you're interested in charts that cover all kinds of popular music, go to **http://www.rronline.com/charts/**.

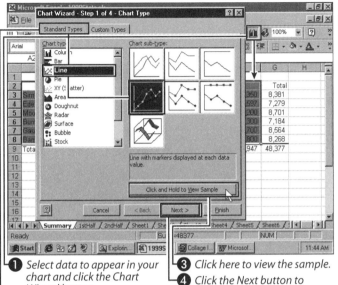

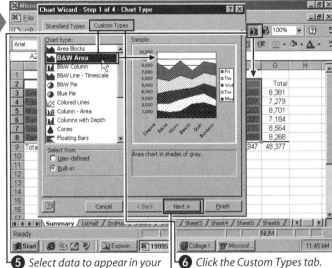

➊ *Select data to appear in your chart and click the Chart Wizard button.*

➋ *Click the Standard Types tab, click a chart type, and then a chart subtype.*

➌ *Click here to view the sample.*

➍ *Click the Next button to proceed.*

➎ *Select data to appear in your chart and click the Chart Wizard button.*

➏ *Click the Custom Types tab. Click a chart type and observe the sample with your data.*

➐ *Click the Next button to proceed.*

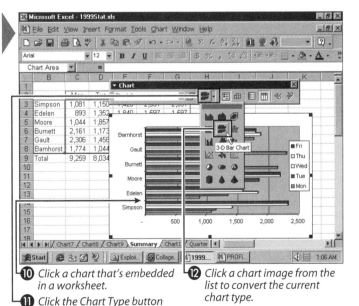

➑ *On a chart sheet, click the Chart Type button in the Chart toolbar.*

➒ *Click one of the 15 major types to convert the current style to that style.*

➓ *Click a chart that's embedded in a worksheet.*

⓫ *Click the Chart Type button (it's appearance reflects the choice you made last time).*

⓬ *Click a chart image from the list to convert the current chart type.*

Moving, Copying, and Resizing a Chart on the Worksheet

When you create a chart on a worksheet, it is likely to overlap your data. That can be acceptable in some cases but you need to be able to move it elsewhere, make a copy of it, or perhaps reshape and resize it. Your ultimate goal may be to have three charts alongside your data, arranged in quadrant fashion with the worksheet data in the upper-left quadrant and the three charts in the other three quadrants.

You can easily change the overall appearance and formatting characteristics of any chart on your worksheet. When you have more than one chart on the worksheet, it's possible that they depict the same data in different ways or that they are based on data in different parts of the worksheet.

Depending on the nature of the data being shown, you may want to resize one chart so that it's larger than another one. Resizing is also necessary sometimes to improve the readability of the chart. It's not uncommon to see a worksheet chart that's entirely too small, causing the legend and horizontal axis labels to appear gigantic, overwhelming the rest of the chart.

If you're resizing a line chart, be aware that you can inadvertently, or purposefully, accentuate the slope of the line(s) shown. When you make your chart taller, lines appear steeper and the amount of change more noticeable. When you make your line chart wider than taller, the lines flatten, thereby suggesting that less change has occurred over time.

TAKE NOTE

▶ MOVING AND COPYING EMBEDDED CHARTS

To move a chart that's on your worksheet, simply point to it and then click and drag it in any direction. If you'd like to copy it, hold down the Ctrl key as you drag the chart to a different location, releasing the mouse before the Ctrl key. To make one or more copies faster, click a chart and press Ctrl+D.

▶ ADJUSTING YOUR CHART EDGES TO MATCH CELL BOUNDARIES

If you'd like the boundaries of your embedded chart to coincide with the cell boundaries of the underlying worksheet, hold down the Alt key as you drag a chart handle (one of the eight squares on the sides or corners on the chart). Instead of doing this four times, drag once each on opposite corners to take care of two sides at once.

▶ RESIZE AND SHAPING CONSIDERATIONS

When resizing a chart, keep an eye on the left side of the formula bar. The numbers you'll see there reflect the percentage of resizing you're doing. To keep height-width proportions the same, hold the Shift key down as you drag one of the corner handles. To keep the same center, hold down the Ctrl key.

CROSS-REFERENCE
See Chapter 11 to review moving and copying objects.

FIND IT ONLINE
See some implications of resizing a chart at
http://noppa5.pc.helsinki.fi/koe/aratio1.html.

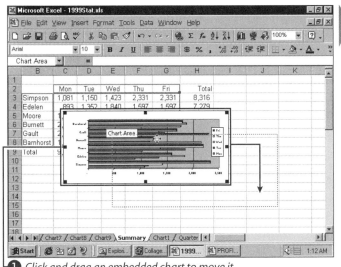
❶ Click and drag an embedded chart to move it.

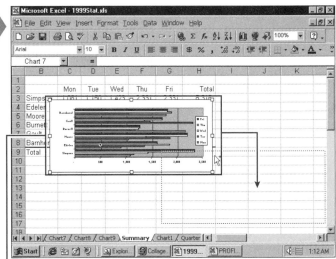
❷ Click and drag an embedded chart with the Ctrl key held down to copy it.

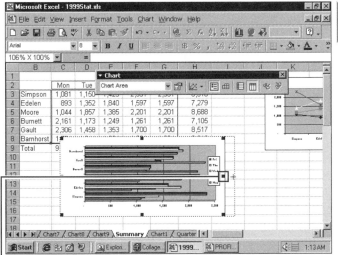
❸ Resize an embedded chart by clicking and dragging any of its eight handles.

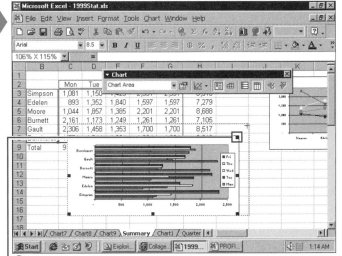
❹ To enlarge or shrink an embedded chart, yet keep the same aspect (height to width) ratio, hold down the Shift key as you drag a corner handle.

Creating Gridlines, Titles, and Legends

Some of the many selections you can make when you create a chart using the Chart Wizard include gridlines (horizontal and vertical), chart titles (for the top and each axis in the chart), and the chart legend. Every chart requires titles of some sort; gridlines enhance column charts but are nonexistent on pie and doughnut charts, and a legend appears on most charts except where pie chart sectors preclude the need for a legend.

When you create a chart with the quick method, you automatically get horizontal gridlines (if you haven't changed the default chart type) and a legend. The most glaring omissions on a quickly created chart are the titles that identify the axes and the main title, frequently used for a company name or to describe the content or reporting period of the chart.

Horizontal gridlines are nearly always present on column, line, and similar charts. Their main purpose is to help you gauge the value associated with a column's height or a point on the chart. For greater accuracy in reading these values, but at the risk of cluttering your chart, try minor gridlines also. You're less likely to use vertical gridlines, but they could be helpful in some column charts to segregate clusters of columns.

A chart tends to look incomplete if you don't have a title. When you create a chart with the quick method, this should be one of the first things you do.

On many charts you'll want to have a title for the Y-axis (vertical) on the left side. Usually, you need to explain the numerical measure depicted on this axis — dollars, thousands of dollars, items sold, items in stock, and so on. Titles for the X-axis (horizontal) tend to be less critical. For example, if X-axis entries are months, it does little good to create the title "Months." On 3-D charts, there is also a Z-axis, and you can provide a title for it also. If you're using the Chart Wizard, Step 3 gives you the opportunity to provide these titles.

A legend is usually necessary. It explains what the colors on a chart stand for. Its default location is on the right side of the chart but you can drag it anywhere, resize it, adjust its fonts, give it a color background and shadow, or hide it. On some charts, it may look presentable sitting right on top of columns or bars.

TAKE NOTE

RETURN THE LEGEND TO ITS LEGENDARY PLACE

To quickly return a legend to the right side of a chart when it's located elsewhere, click the Legend button in the Chart toolbar. Click the button again to make the legend appear — it will always go to the right side of the chart.

CROSS-REFERENCE

Learn about annotating a cell with a comment in Chapter 6.

FIND IT ONLINE

Interested in computer legends? Take a look at The Historical Computer Society site at http://www.getty.net/texts/obsolete.txt.

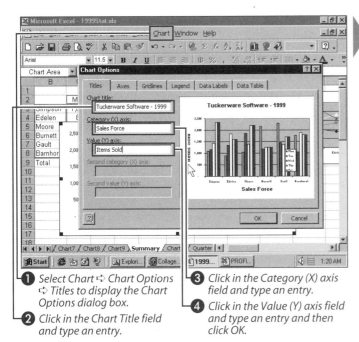

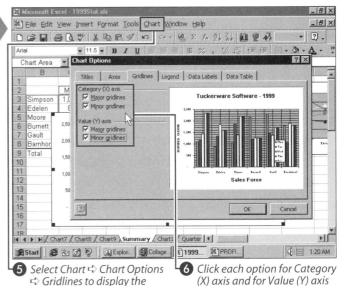

① *Select Chart ⇨ Chart Options ⇨ Titles to display the Chart Options dialog box.*

② *Click in the Chart Title field and type an entry.*

③ *Click in the Category (X) axis field and type an entry.*

④ *Click in the Value (Y) axis field and type an entry and then click OK.*

⑤ *Select Chart ⇨ Chart Options ⇨ Gridlines to display the Chart Options dialog box.*

⑥ *Click each option for Category (X) axis and for Value (Y) axis and observe the resulting image.*

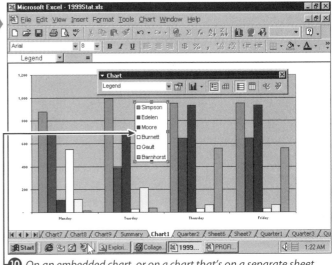

⑦ *Select Chart ⇨ Chart Options ⇨ Legend.*

⑧ *Check the box next to Show legend.*

⑨ *Click each of the Placement buttons while observing the legend relocation in the sample area.*

⑩ *On an embedded chart, or on a chart that's on a separate sheet, click and drag a legend anywhere on the chart.*

Printing Charts

When the time comes to print your chart, the big question is: Do you want your chart to be printed alone or along with your worksheet data? If the chart in question is on a separate sheet, the question is irrelevant. When you print a chart that's on its own sheet, the choices you have revolve around whether you want it to fill the whole page or whether you want it to retain its onscreen proportions. You also have some customizing options, but all of these variations refer to printing the chart only.

When your chart is on a worksheet, the printing choices are more complex. Here too, you can decide to print just a chart, but you can also decide to print your data along with one, two, three, or however many charts are on the worksheet. Because what you get on paper when you print and what you can see on the screen are often different, you need to use some of the same print preview options available when printing a simple worksheet.

Don't hesitate to reshape, resize, and move your charts around the screen. The more charts you attempt to show on a single sheet of paper, the more difficult they will be to read. If you do need to show multiple charts on a single sheet, simplify each one of them as much as possible.

CROSS-REFERENCE
See Chapter 5 for information on printing a worksheet.

FIND IT ONLINE
If you like printing charts and are interested in weather phenomena, visit the Hurricane Tracking Chart Printing site at **http://www.bcinet.net/abennett/hurricane/chart1.htm** .

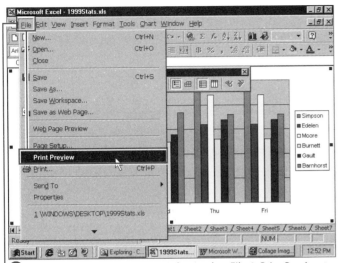

1 On a chart that's on a separate sheet, select File ➪ Print Preview to see how the chart will appear on paper.

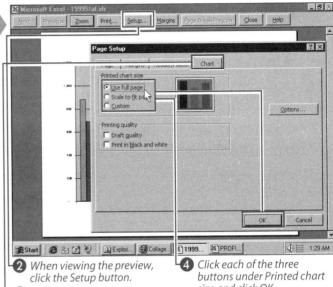

2 When viewing the preview, click the Setup button.

3 Click the Chart tab.

4 Click each of the three buttons under Printed chart size and click OK.

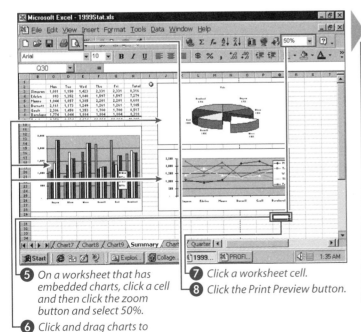

5 On a worksheet that has embedded charts, click a cell and then click the zoom button and select 50%.

6 Click and drag charts to arrange them in the most convenient order.

7 Click a worksheet cell.

8 Click the Print Preview button.

9 Click the image to zoom in or out.

10 Click the Setup button to explore Page Setup options.

11 Click the Close button to return to your worksheet display.

12 Click the Print button to print the preview.

Personal Workbook

Q&A

1 True or False: You can drag a legend anywhere on your chart.

_____

_____

2 What key do you press to create a chart instantly on a new sheet?

_____

_____

_____

3 When resizing a chart on your worksheet, how do you make the chart's edges align with the worksheet's cell boundaries?

_____

_____

_____

4 Can you use a pie chart to show negative data?

_____

_____

_____

5 Is there a way to print a chart that's on a worksheet so that you don't see the worksheet data or gridlines?

_____

_____

_____

_____

6 If you need to create a chart that shows a trend over time, what would be a good chart type to use?

_____

_____

_____

_____

7 How do you resize an embedded chart proportionally?

_____

_____

_____

_____

ANSWERS: PAGE 327

EXTRA PRACTICE

1 Select cells from rows 5, 7, and 9 (but not from rows 6 and 8) to appear in a chart.

2 On a column chart, add minor gridlines for both axes and decide whether one or both kinds are useful in your chart.

3 On a worksheet where you have more than one chart, use the zoom control box and select 50%. Move charts to different locations then zoom back to 75% or 100%.

4 Create a chart using the Chart Wizard. In Step 3, click the Data Table tab and then check the box next to Show data table.

REAL-WORLD APPLICATIONS

✔ You need to create a chart on your worksheet quickly. You select a range, click the Chart Wizard button, and then click the Finish button.

✔ You want to create both a line chart and a column chart on your worksheet that show the same data. You create one chart. Next, you click and drag it with the Ctrl key to create a copy of it. You then click the Chart type button in the Chart toolbar and select a different type.

✔ An embedded chart on your worksheet is small and difficult to manipulate. You right-click the chart and select Chart Window. When the window appears, you enlarge it, make changes, and then close the window.

Visual Quiz

In the screen shown below, which cells in the worksheet were selected to create this pie chart?

_____

_____

_____

_____

_____

_____

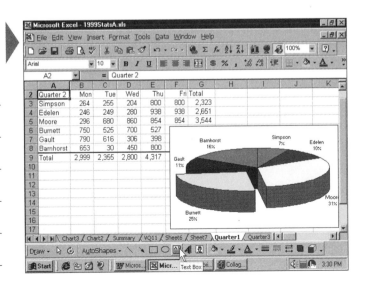

CHAPTER **13**

Changing the Look of Your Chart

As fast and easy as it is to create a chart in Excel, there will still be many occasions when you want to make alterations, additions, and deletions to the appearance of your chart. The integration of the Excel package is increasingly better, and as a result, the way you format your chart is very similar to the way you format your worksheet. Similar menu commands exist and you use the Formatting toolbar buttons to make adjustments. Some appearance features, such as the placement of titles and legends, are unique to charting, yet you'll find that manipulating them is similar to the way you control graphic objects.

As you gain fluency in working with charts, you'll learn the terminology that's long been associated with charts and graphs — gridlines, legend, Y-axis, and soon. This version of Excel has plenty of onscreen memory-jogging to help you learn the charting vocabulary. Tips appear on the screen as you point to different chart elements, and the formula bar is an omnipresent reminder as to which element is currently selected. You can also use the arrow keys on your keyboard to select the various chart elements.

In addition to formatting that involves text and color changes, you also learn more about the mechanics of altering the chart itself. Adjusting axes alters the very structure of the chart and may enhance the presentation of your information. For some scientific charts, using logarithmic scaling on one, or both, axes, offers additional presentation opportunities. As you make these types of changes, you develop a certain creativity, which ultimately makes you feel more confident in controlling your charts.

Nowhere does this increased sense of creativity seem more pronounced than when you work with three-dimensional charts. Whether you're rotating them to get a better view of an exploding piece of a pie chart, adjusting the height of a column or line chart for a bolder image, or changing the perspective angle of any of the 3-D charts, these images can brighten any presentation, either on paper or on a projection system.

Selecting and Manipulating Chart Elements

As a prelude to manipulating various elements of a chart, you need to become observant of what the different pieces (elements) of a chart are called. This should not be an effort at memorization — fortunately, Excel provides you with many visual clues as you use chart menu commands and toolbar buttons. Also, as you point to various screen locations, a chart tip identifies the element. Furthermore, if you click a chart element, observe the left side of the formula bar to see the actual name of that element. If these reminders aren't enough, there's also a button on the Chart toolbar that enables you to select an element.

Some of the chart elements that you'll use include: chart area, plot area, legend, gridline, series, value axis, chart title, category axis, corners, wall, floor, and value (or category) axis minor (or major) gridlines.

It might not seem methodical, but you can begin to change a chart element simply by double-clicking it. A dialog box appears with the appropriate array of choices. There are still some menu commands to pursue, but much of what you need comes from the dialog boxes that appear when you double-click an element.

To alter the color of most chart elements, you can use the color background button from the Formatting toolbar. Many elements have edges or borders that you can also alter — the edges of columns, bars, and pie sectors, for example. If on your chart, each month is represented by a column,

and one person is represented by the color red, you can change all of the red bars at once, or you can select just one of those bars and change its color or pattern. Most of chart elements that you can select have color and line attributes.

TAKE NOTE

USING THE ARROW KEYS TO IDENTIFY CHART ELEMENTS

Whether you're in an inquisitive mood or you just need to find a chart element and don't know what it is, you can use the up and down arrows on your keyboard to survey all element names in a chart. Every time you press one of these keys, a different word or phrase appears on the left side of the formula bar and a different element in the chart (identified by handles) is selected.

CHART TIPS

If Chart tips are not present when you point to various elements, turn the feature on by selecting Tools ⇨ Options. Click the Chart tab and check the box next to Show names. It's also recommended that you check the box next to Show values. It's a handy indicator of a bar, column, line, sector, or point value.

CROSS-REFERENCE

Learn about color formatting in Chapter 3.

SHORTCUT

When a series (of columns, lines, bars, etc.) is selected, use the left and right keyboard arrows to select a specific column, line, bar, and so on.

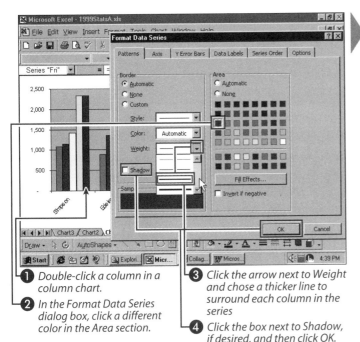

① Double-click a column in a column chart.

② In the Format Data Series dialog box, click a different color in the Area section.

③ Click the arrow next to Weight and chose a thicker line to surround each column in the series

④ Click the box next to Shadow, if desired, and then click OK.

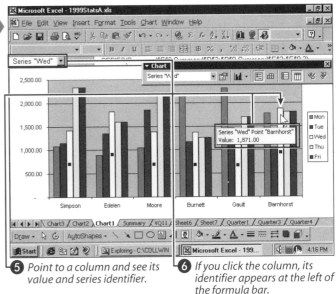

⑤ Point to a column and see its value and series identifier.

⑥ If you click the column, its identifier appears at the left of the formula bar.

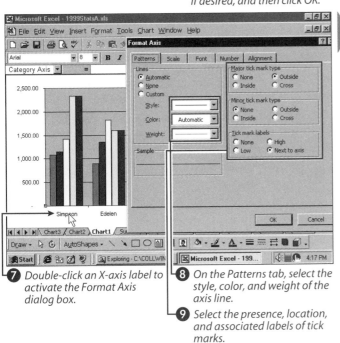

⑦ Double-click an X-axis label to activate the Format Axis dialog box.

⑧ On the Patterns tab, select the style, color, and weight of the axis line.

⑨ Select the presence, location, and associated labels of tick marks.

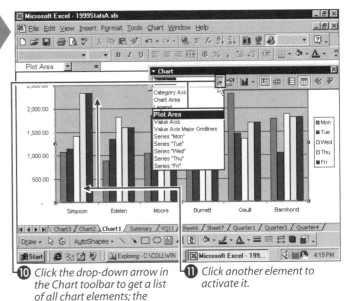

⑩ Click the drop-down arrow in the Chart toolbar to get a list of all chart elements; the current one is highlighted.

⑪ Click another element to activate it.

219

Formatting Text and Numbers

Your chart makes a visual statement and you will spend much time refining those aspects of it. The format of text and numerical information complements the visual side of charting, and invariably, you will need to make adjustments to them, too. This is particularly the case with charts embedded on your worksheet. These charts often display text and numbers out of proportion (they're much too large) to the size of the chart. As you increase the size of your chart, the need for size adjustment lessens, but you should think of adjusting the size of text and numbers as a given in these circumstances.

Formatting text and numbers on the chart is nearly identical to standard worksheet usage — rely on the Formatting toolbar as much as possible and use the Format Cells command for refinements.

Therefore, the basic concepts of worksheet formatting apply — select the element you want to change and click the Formatting toolbar button that's appropriate. Some of these buttons can't be used, though. You can't use the Border toolbar button or the alignment and indent buttons. Other buttons are selectable based on which element is currently selected. Remember that text appears in a variety of screen locations. In addition to the text that appears in titles and legends (covered later in this chapter), text also appears along the X- and Y-axes (and the Z-axis on 3-D charts), and on data labels and values that you may have chosen as you used the Chart Wizard. Most of the numerical data you use will be associated with the X- and Y-axes.

TAKE NOTE

Y-AXIS DATA CAN BE PROBLEMATICAL

The values that define the Y-axis (vertical) on the left side of most charts come from your worksheet and retain the formatting found there. You may, however, change the formatting of these values in your chart without affecting the formatting in the worksheet. But, once you make a single formatting change to the numbers in the chart, any formatting changes you make in the worksheet do not change the appearance of your chart values. A numerical display with currency and two decimal places may look fine in your worksheet, but it may add unnecessary detail and clutter in your chart.

ANGLED TEXT SETTINGS ON THE CHART TOOLBAR

The Chart toolbar has two handy buttons that let you rotate text at 45 degrees upward or downward. You can use these on axis labels and values, the main chart title, and the titles for each of the chart axes. The buttons are mutually exclusive and when neither is checked, the text is not angled. For precise angle-setting, double-click the text and in the resulting dialog box, click the Alignment tab and use the rotate tool.

CROSS-REFERENCE

See Chapter 3 for more information on rotating text.

SHORTCUT

Press Ctrl+1 to activate the Format Cells command.

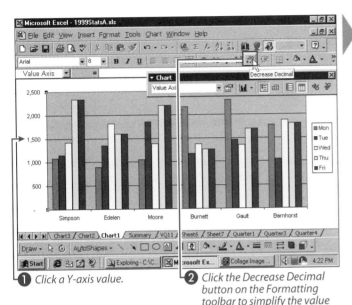

❶ Click a Y-axis value.

❷ Click the Decrease Decimal button on the Formatting toolbar to simplify the value display and increase the size of the plot area.

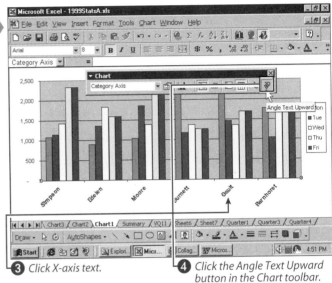

❸ Click X-axis text.

❹ Click the Angle Text Upward button in the Chart toolbar.

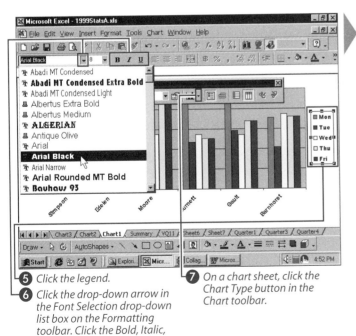

❺ Click the legend.

❻ Click the drop-down arrow in the Font Selection drop-down list box on the Formatting toolbar. Click the Bold, Italic, and Underline buttons also.

❼ On a chart sheet, click the Chart Type button in the Chart toolbar.

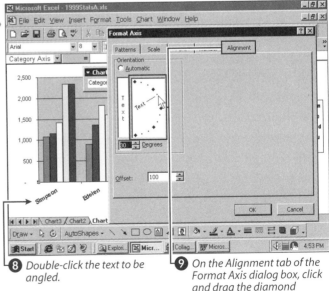

❽ Double-click the text to be angled.

❾ On the Alignment tab of the Format Axis dialog box, click and drag the diamond pointer to adjust the angle of the selected text.

Controlling the Appearance and Scaling of Axes

When you need to emphasize the numerical aspects of a chart, look to the Y-axis and consider not only its color, thickness, and numerical format, but also its scaling. Does it begin at zero? Does its height only barely exceed the tallest column? Do you want more white space above the columns and lines in the body of the chart? These are the kinds of issues that occur when considering a rescaling of the Y-axis. If you're a user of XY charts, you may also have some concerns about scaling the X-axis, but to a much lesser extent. In three-dimensional charts, you may need to make visual adjustments to the Y-axis, X-axis, and to the Z-axis.

Excel's default scaling, analyzes the highest value in the data you're charting and sets a maximum value slightly above it. You can select a higher value to create more space above the bars and charts. Unless negative values are present, the chart begins at zero. You can change the minimum and maximum values and the interval between them. When you change the scaling of an axis, the gridlines travel to the new locations.

Another appearance adjustment you'll want to make is to the location of tick marks (tiny lines at the axis that separate bars and columns) and the text labels that accompany them. You can choose to have major and minor tick marks appear on any axis, either on the inside or outside of the axis, or crossing it. You can also choose to place the text labels on top of the plot area, underneath it, or right near the axis.

TAKE NOTE

▶ DON'T START THE Y-AXIS ABOVE ZERO FOR COLUMN AND BAR CHARTS

Whether by mistake or design, you may send a loaded message if you start column or bar charts above zero. By their nature, these kinds of charts display volume or size. If all values in a chart are in the 6,000 to 10,000 range, it may initially seem reasonable to adjust the Y-axis to begin at 5,000. Try this and you'll see that a value of 7,000 will appear twice as tall as 6,000. Even though you can read the axis values and see what the real values are, the 2:1 visual ratio is hard to overcome.

▶ CONSIDER ADJUSTING THE SCALING FOR LINE CHARTS

In contrast to the previous note, if your line chart contains values between 6,000 and 10,000, it makes good sense to adjust the scaling for the Y-axis. Start the axis at 5,000 and you'll see all of the lines and points more clearly than if you stay with the default setting of zero as the Y-axis starting point.

CROSS-REFERENCE

See the next task in this chapter to learn how to adjust the size of the plot area that encompasses the axes.

FIND IT ONLINE

Learn all about scaling at http://trochim.human. cornell.edu/kb/scalgen.htm.

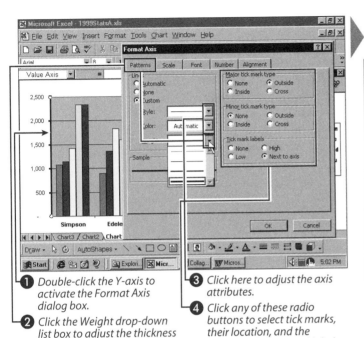

① *Double-click the Y-axis to activate the Format Axis dialog box.*

② *Click the Weight drop-down list box to adjust the thickness of the axis.*

③ *Click here to adjust the axis attributes.*

④ *Click any of these radio buttons to select tick marks, their location, and the location of associated labels.*

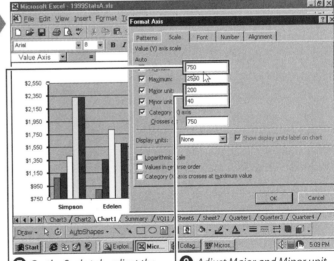

⑤ *To create more space above columns, click the Scale tab and select a maximum value higher than the automatic setting.*

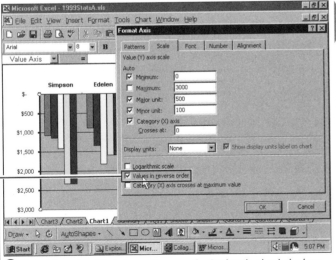

⑥ *To achieve the effect shown here, on the Scale tab, check the box next to Values in reverse order.*

⑦ *On the Scale tab, adjust the minimum value to start the base of the chart higher. Not recommended for column charts but okay for line charts.*

⑧ *Adjust Major and Minor unit settings to control quantity of Y-axis labels and corresponding display of gridlines.*

Controlling Titles and Legends

You can manipulate titles and legends in a variety of ways to provide important information on your chart. The three title areas on most Excel charts include: the chart title, typically placed along the top of the chart, the Y-axis title, placed on the left side of the chart, and the X-axis title, which runs across the bottom of the chart. Pie charts, doughnut charts, and radar charts only have the chart title option.

Two possibilities are available for your chart title that are not immediately obvious. One is the ability to make your chart title a multiple-line entry. When you create a chart with the Chart Wizard, you can only create a single-line chart title. Likewise, when you need to add a title to a chart on a separate sheet, you use the Chart menu, and on the Chart Options dialog box, you can only enter a single-line title. However, after you have your title in place, you can edit it and add more text, possibly including additional lines.

The second chart title option that's not part of standard title creation is linking the chart title to a worksheet cell. This can save some retyping when creating a title, but like multiple-line titles, you need to edit an existing title and type a formula that refers to a worksheet cell.

You can move a chart's legend anywhere on the screen, resize it using the handles, and format it easily through command and toolbar buttons. But don't overlook the fact that each entry in the legend box is selectable and can be formatted.

TAKE NOTE

▶ MOVING CHART TITLES AND LEGENDS

To move a chart title, click the title and drag one of the edges of the rectangular block that surrounds the title. Even though there are handles on this boundary, they serve no purpose. You cannot resize a chart title area with these handles. Change the font size or alter the text and the size of the box will change if necessary.

To move a legend, click it and drag it. To resize it, click it and drag one of the eight handles in any direction.

▶ USING A CELL AS A TITLE SOURCE

To create a title that's based on a cell, first create a title in the regular way (in step 3 of the Chart Wizard or, after a chart's created, using the Chart ⇨ Chart Options command) using just a single character, so that you can see it. Next, select the title, click in the formula bar and type the equal sign(=). Click the worksheet that's the source of the title (the source of the chart is not always the same sheet), click the cell that has the title data and press Enter.

CROSS-REFERENCE
To learn about the placement of the chart legend, refer to Chapter 12.

FIND IT ONLINE
Learn about the place of legends in history, literature, folklore, fiction, and the arts at http://www.legends.dm.net/.

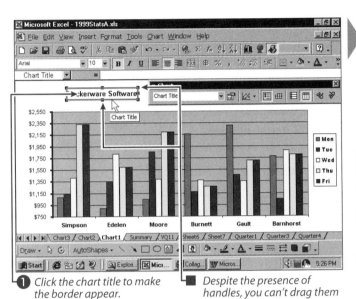

1 Click the chart title to make the border appear.

■ Despite the presence of handles, you can't drag them to resize the box.

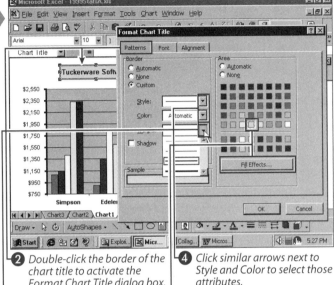

2 Double-click the border of the chart title to activate the Format Chart Title dialog box.

3 Click the arrow next to the Weight drop-down list box to select a title border.

4 Click similar arrows next to Style and Color to select those attributes.

5 Click a color selection or Fill Effects to provide a background color.

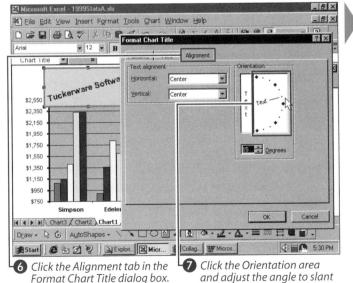

6 Click the Alignment tab in the Format Chart Title dialog box.

7 Click the Orientation area and adjust the angle to slant the title.

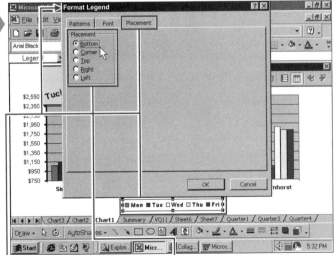

8 Double-click the legend to activate the Format Legend dialog box and select the Placement tab.

9 Click a placement radio button to relocate the legend to a different part of the chart area.

Formatting Plot and Chart Areas

The two biggest areas on your chart, and therefore, the areas with the largest potential for impacting design, are the plot area and the chart area. The plot area (which is always rectangular) is that part of your chart delineated by the height of the Y-axis and the width of the X-axis on most charts; on pie, doughnut, and radar charts, it's determined by the height and width of the shape. The chart area refers to the large rectangle that serves as a platform for your plot area, chart title and legend. You can resize the plot area and provide any number of colors, textures, and fill gradients to it. You can also provide a picture as a backdrop for the various chart elements.

The chart area, the largest element in any chart, and therefore, the one you want to be the most careful with when setting the tone for your chart's presentation, can also be formatted in a number of interesting ways. Because it's so large, it's the ideal element with which to experiment with color, textures, and gradients because you can see the results so clearly.

If you're interested in enhancing or distorting the meaning of a line chart that shows values over time, you need to resize the plot area and possibly the chart area also. If a line chart is much wider than it is tall, the lines don't slope as much and the change from period to period appears to be slight. If you alter the shape of the plot area so that the chart is much taller than it is wide, then the lines slope much

more and the change from period to period is much more pronounced. Resize the chart too much in either direction and you will draw negative attention to the shape. To a lesser extent, you can also do this with bar and column charts to get the effects you want. Sometimes, you'll resize the plot area for artistic reasons.

Another reason to resize the plot area is to place the legend on the plot area, thereby freeing the open space at the legend's former location. For monitor display presentations, this would maximize the plot area portion of the screen.

TAKE NOTE

FORMATTING FROM THE CHART AREA

When the chart area is selected and you use either the Formatting toolbar buttons or the Format Selected Chart Area command, the choices you make affect the entire chart, not just the area outside of the plot area.

ADJUST THE PLOT AREA'S SIZE INDIRECTLY

Adjust the font size of the various axes titles and values and the plot area of column, line, and bar charts will change accordingly. Adjust the font size of the Chart title and the size of the plot area will also change.

CROSS-REFERENCE

Learn about annotating a cell with a comment in Chapter 6.

FIND IT ONLINE

If you're interested in the plot of planets, check out http://www.lhs.berkeley.edu/SII/SII-FindPlanets/plot.html.

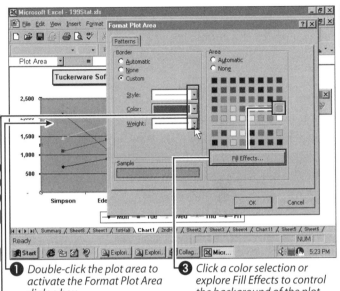

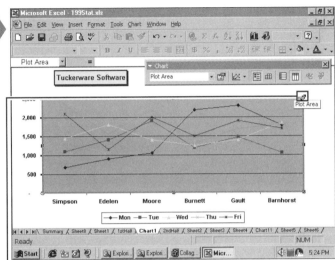

① Double-click the plot area to activate the Format Plot Area dialog box.

② Click here to adjust the perimeter border of the plot area.

③ Click a color selection or explore Fill Effects to control the background of the plot area.

④ Resize the plot area by dragging one of the eight handles in any direction.

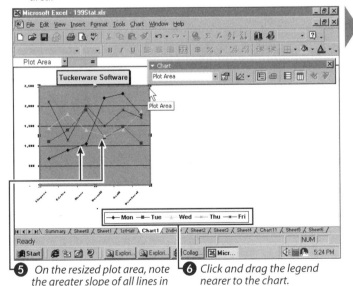

⑤ On the resized plot area, note the greater slope of all lines in the chart compared with the previous image.

⑥ Click and drag the legend nearer to the chart.

⑦ Select Chart Area from the drop-down list box in the Chart toolbar.

⑧ Click various font buttons in the Formatting toolbar to change all fonts throughout the chart.

Manipulating Three-Dimensional Charts

When used properly, three-dimensional charts make bold, colorful statements, enhancing any presentation or worksheet that contains one. The depth effect is emphasized by the contrast between the sides of the chart in bright light and the parts in shadow. Sometimes, three-dimensional charts are misused because it's so easy to mistake their visual appeal for meaningful content. Many three-dimensional charts are unreadable because they're too crowded. Often, the way to clean up such a chart is by converting it to the corresponding two-dimensional version. But don't reject the idea that you can manipulate three-dimensional charts in a variety of interesting ways — special menu commands and mouse techniques are available to manipulate your charts.

Three-dimensional pie charts, which are limited to displaying a row or column of data, can be altered from their default appearance as a giant pill, to look like a thin pizza or like a cylinder. If you're in the oil business, it might make sense to use the cylinder to evoke the look of oil barrels. If you're in the land management business, maybe a flatter look is more appropriate. Infinite variations exist between these extremes. You also have complete control over the extraction of wedges in three-dimensional pie charts.

The most common kind of quick manipulation that you'll do with 3-D column and bar charts is to rotate them. It's not uncommon for these kinds of charts to show taller elements in front of smaller ones so that some columns or bars are hidden. You can rotate the chart quickly and easily, either with the mouse or using the commands. Also, a 3-D view dialog box enables you to rotate, tilt, and change the elevation of the chart. Another change that's worth considering is the ratio of the height of the columns to the width of the chart. Change the ratio setting and the perspective setting in tandem to get a variety of other appearances for your chart.

TAKE NOTE

▶ ROTATE CHARTS WITHOUT THE BLINDERS ON

On many three-dimensional charts, particularly bar and column charts, when you click and drag a corner to rotate them, you lose sight of how the chart is likely to appear because you only see the imaginary rectangular solid that contains the chart. Hold down the Ctrl key as you rotate and you get a much better view of where you're headed.

▶ RESTORING THE DEFAULT VIEW

When you rotate a 3-D chart manually with the mouse, and you let go of the mouse at an inopportune time, you might create a chart that's barely decipherable. To recover, select Chart ⇨ 3-D View and click the Default button.

CROSS-REFERENCE

Review the 3-D effects available for graphic objects in Chapter 11.

FIND IT ONLINE

If you're interested in 3-D images in other media, look at **http://www.3dglasses.com/3dmovie.htm.**

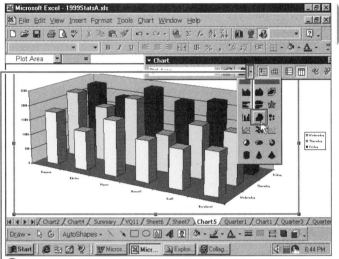

1 To convert a chart to a 3-D chart quickly, click the chart type arrow on the Chart toolbar and make a selection.

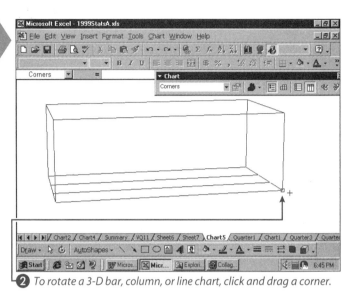

2 To rotate a 3-D bar, column, or line chart, click and drag a corner.

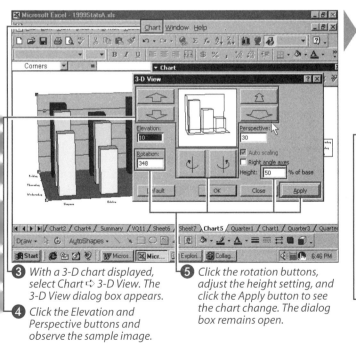

3 With a 3-D chart displayed, select Chart ➪ 3-D View. The 3-D View dialog box appears.

4 Click the Elevation and Perspective buttons and observe the sample image.

5 Click the rotation buttons, adjust the height setting, and click the Apply button to see the chart change. The dialog box remains open.

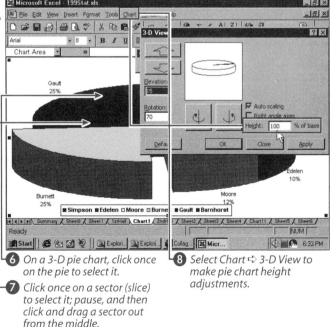

6 On a 3-D pie chart, click once on the pie to select it.

7 Click once on a sector (slice) to select it; pause, and then click and drag a sector out from the middle.

8 Select Chart ➪ 3-D View to make pie chart height adjustments.

Personal Workbook

Q&A

1 True or False: A button on your Formatting toolbar enables you to adjust the angle of values on the Y-axis of a chart.

_____

_____

_____

2 If you adjust the number of decimal places on the Y-axis values in a column chart, will the size of the plot area change?

_____

_____

_____

3 Can you create a multiline title in a chart using the Chart Wizard?

_____

_____

_____

_____

_____

4 When rotating a 3-D chart, how do you get to see the columns, bars, etc., instead of just the outline of the chart's shape?

_____

_____

_____

5 True or False: The Y-axis always starts at zero.

_____

_____

_____

6 How do you resize the main title of a chart?

_____

_____

_____

7 Can you show two rows of data in a pie chart?

_____

_____

_____

_____

ANSWERS: PAGE 328

EXTRA PRACTICE

1 Change a 3-D pie chart to be as tall as it can be; make it as flat as it can be.

2 Create a column chart and change the color of a series of columns.

3 Move a legend from the right side of the chart onto the face of the chart and resize it.

4 Create a two-line title for a chart.

5 Change the font size of all entries in a legend; change the font size of just one of the entries.

REAL-WORLD APPLICATIONS

✔ You need to accentuate the amount of change in your line chart that depicts monthly sales for the last two years. You resize the chart so that it's tall rather than wide.

✔ The names that appear across the X-axis are too crowded. You double-click them, and then click the Alignment tab and rotate the text 90 degrees.

✔ All of the values in your line chart are between 80 and 190. You double-click the Y-axis, click Scale and set the minimum value to 75.

✔ Your Y-axis values have decimals and currency symbols, using up lots of horizontal display space. You click a value, and then click the comma button in the Formatting toolbar and click the decrease decimal button twice.

Visual Quiz

In the screen shown to the right, what's the fastest way to set all of the various text entries to the same size font?

_____

_____

_____

_____

_____

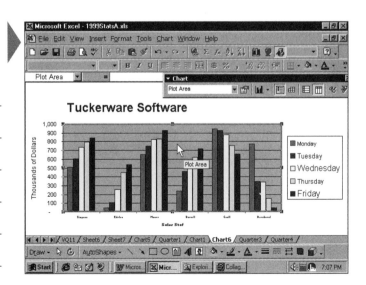

CHAPTER **14**

MASTER
THESE
SKILLS

▶ **Adding and Removing Data**

▶ **Changing the Order of Plot Series**

▶ **Adding Trendlines and Error Bars**

▶ **Adjusting the Chart to Affect Worksheet Data**

Manipulating Chart Data

In the previous two chapters, the focus was on the creation and alteration of your charts — how to create and then how to modify your charts. Because your charts are an accurate reflection of underlying values, you need to think about how those values might change, how they might be better represented in your chart, and how you might need to add or remove data from your chart.

Excel makes it easy to add data to your charts, whether they're on a separate sheet or embedded in your worksheet. Sometimes this is necessary because there's new data on your worksheet, but at other times, you may simply change your mind about what data you're trying to show on a chart. You can use standard copy and paste techniques or you can actually drag data onto an embedded chart. Deleting data from a chart is a simple matter also.

Although you're encouraged to arrange data in your worksheet in a sensible order before using it as the basis for a chart, you can create a chart and make adjustments to the order of data there, if you prefer, without affecting the order of the data in the worksheet. You can rearrange the order of columns, bars, and lines, and, in pie charts, the order of sectors. Often, you'll choose to order your data alphabetically or numerically, but you can also organize data practically. When you have many entries in a series, say more than ten, rearranging the order can be tedious.

Your chart is not just a visual reflection of worksheet data. You can also think of it analytically and add trendlines (based on regression techniques or a moving average) that actually create new information that's not on your worksheet. Excel also has a feature called Error Bars, whereby you can add data on either side of a series of plotted values. This enables you to show contrasting values that are a specific percent, a specific value, or a standard deviation removed from your original data.

Additionally, this chapter shows you how to change the value of data in your chart and cause worksheet data to change accordingly. You're most likely to use this capability when dealing with planning worksheets as you try to adjust a value to smooth a trend.

Adding and Removing Data

Before actually creating a chart, you must select worksheet cells. Normally, those cells consist mostly of values and an accompanying row and column that serve to provide you with a legend and your X-axis and Y-axis labels. As with many other activities in Excel, you might change your mind about what data is being portrayed in your chart. Whether your chart is on a separate sheet or embedded in a worksheet, you need methods to make adjustments so that you can add a row or column of information, or, when necessary, to remove data from your chart.

Occasionally, these kinds of changes are necessary for visual reasons — your chart is too crowded and you need to remove some data to make it more readable. More likely, though, is the idea that your worksheet has grown — you've added new information in a row or column adjacent to your original data.

Adding data works best when what you want to add to the chart represents one of these two situations:

▶ The new data is part of a row that's just as wide as your original chart data and the far-left cell contains text.

▶ The new data is part of a column that's just as tall as your original chart data and the top cell contains text.

For most other situations, you may be better off creating a new chart, an action that you will come to recognize as being fast and easy.

Removing data from your chart, like adding data, proceeds smoothly and logically when you're deleting one of the series entries (equivalent to all columns in a column chart that are the same color) or one of the category entries (equivalent to a cluster of columns in a column chart).

TAKE NOTE

▶ **ERASING OR DELETING WORKSHEET DATA**

If you erase data (that's represented in a chart) from your worksheet, your chart will either have a gaping hole in it or an empty spot at one end or another. If you delete (instead of erase) data from your worksheet, your chart shows no indication that the data was ever there. Deleting data on your chart has no effect on your worksheet.

▶ **DELETE QUICKLY BY REORIENTING YOUR CHART**

The fastest way to delete a series of data from a worksheet is to click one of the points (a bar, column, or point) and press the Delete (Del) key. If what you want to delete is not part of a series but is in a category, click whichever of the By Row or By Column buttons (in the Chart toolbar) is not currently selected. You should be able to click a column (bar, point, etc.) and press the Delete key.

CROSS-REFERENCE

Review "Erasing and Deleting Columns and Rows" in Chapter 6.

SHORTCUT

Use your keyboard arrow keys to select a series that you want to delete; next, press the Delete (Del) key.

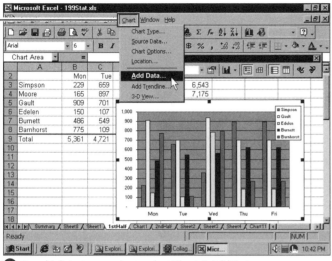

❶ To add data to your chart, select Chart ➪ Add Data.

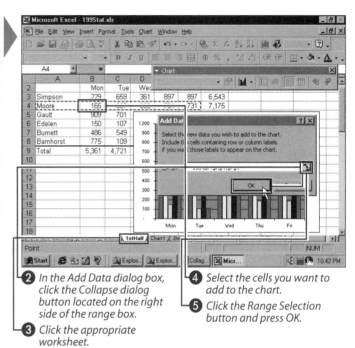

❷ In the Add Data dialog box, click the Collapse dialog button located on the right side of the range box.

❸ Click the appropriate worksheet.

❹ Select the cells you want to add to the chart.

❺ Click the Range Selection button and press OK.

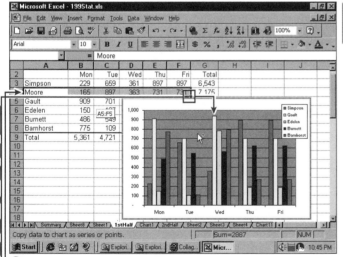
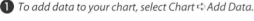

❻ To add data to your embedded chart, select the cells to be added.

❼ Drag the edge of the selected range onto the chart.

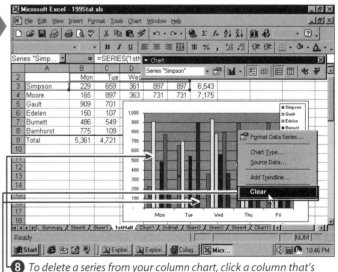

❽ To delete a series from your column chart, click a column that's part of the series.

❾ Press the Delete key or right-click the column and select Clear from the shortcut menu.

Changing the Order of Plot Series

When you've got your chart looking the way you want it to and you're ready to print it, you might find that the names of your sales people, marked in the legend, aren't in the order you want them to be. In another chart, you notice that the names across the X-axis are not in alphabetical order, as you need them to be. Remember, when you create a chart, the order of columns, rows, lines, pie sectors, and so on, is directly analogous to the order of the corresponding data in your worksheet. But what's best in the worksheet isn't always best in your chart.

In both of the situations above, your concerns are about the order of the plot. In the first example, it's about the series order; in the second, it's about the category order. You can adjust the order of the plot series using Excel commands that are available when a chart is selected.

The legend corresponds to the series — the series data in the columns of a column chart, for example, are in the same order left to right as the legend is from top to bottom (unless you've rearranged the legend to be multicolumn). For instance, a red bar in each column cluster is identified by a red box in the legend.

The order of labels across the horizontal axis is referred to as the Category (X) axis. In a column chart, each label corresponds to the cluster of columns located just above it. To change the order along the X-axis and the order of the clusters on a column chart, you need to rearrange data in your worksheet to cause the chart to respond.

There are many reasons for wanting to change the order of a series, some of them visual. For example, if two of your series values have lower or higher values than the rest, it might make sense to move those ranges to the left or to the right of other ranges. Or, if you delete a series from your chart and later decide to bring the data back, the data will end up in a different order and you will probably want to rearrange the series order.

TAKE NOTE

▶ SORTING WORKSHEET DATA AFFECTS PLOT ORDER

If you rearrange your worksheet rows by sorting them, the chart data based on these rows will also be rearranged.

▶ ADJUST SERIES FOR 3-D CHARTS

On 3-D charts, the height of columns in the foreground may block columns behind them. If rotating the chart doesn't seem to improve the view, change the order of the series to range from low to high values and the problem is alleviated.

▶ REORDERING CHART DATA DOES NOT AFFECT THE WORKSHEET

You can change the order of your plot data, but it has no effect on the arrangement of data in your worksheet.

CROSS-REFERENCE

Learn about sorting in Chapter 15, "Using Excel for Database Applications."

SHORTCUT

Hide a row or column in your worksheet to quickly omit the corresponding data in your chart.

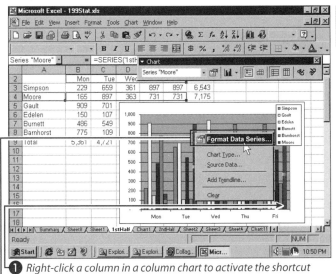

1 Right-click a column in a column chart to activate the shortcut menu.

2 Select the Format Data Series shortcut.

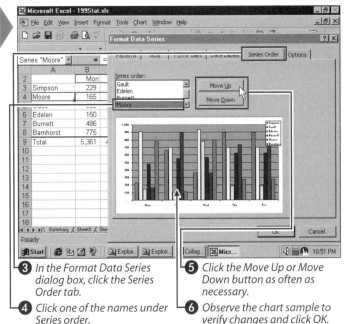

3 In the Format Data Series dialog box, click the Series Order tab.

4 Click one of the names under Series order.

5 Click the Move Up or Move Down button as often as necessary.

6 Observe the chart sample to verify changes and click OK.

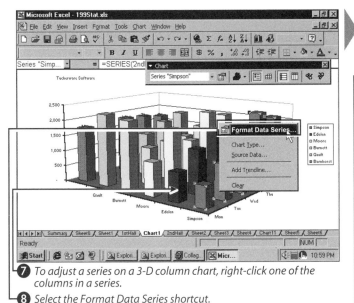

7 To adjust a series on a 3-D column chart, right-click one of the columns in a series.

8 Select the Format Data Series shortcut.

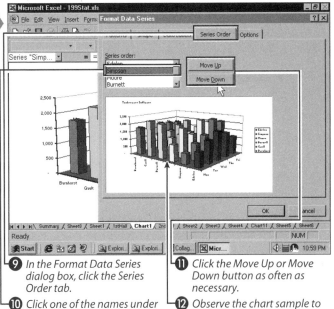

9 In the Format Data Series dialog box, click the Series Order tab.

10 Click one of the names under Series order.

11 Click the Move Up or Move Down button as often as necessary.

12 Observe the chart sample to verify changes and click OK.

Adding Trendlines and Error Bars

Excel has tons of built-in statistical capability, the most obvious being the 75 statistical functions and the Add-in Analysis ToolPak that provides analytical tools for numerous statistical measures. In charting, Excel gives you two features that enhance this already impressive array of statistical features. Using the Trendline feature, you can augment existing data with additional lines based on mathematical analysis of a series of chart data. Using the Error Bars feature, you can add to the existing display of data points by showing bars that extend above and below these points based on a variation (by amount, percent, or standard deviation).

You can't create trendlines on 3-D charts, and although you can use them on column, bubble, and bar charts, you will probably only use them on line charts. Because adding lines to a chart that already has lines produces a visual disaster, you need to be cautious about how many readable lines can exist on a chart. You may consider removing a series or two from the chart before deciding to add trendlines. A legend will also appear on your chart with an appropriately named entry referring to the trendline you added.

Trendlines take one of these forms: Linear, Logarithmic, Polynomial, Power, Exponential, and Moving average. Your statistical familiarity with the first five (all of which are regression lines) will lead you to try them. A moving average is more widely used, and works best, when you have ten or more time periods covered in your chart. Although it's possible to create all six different trendlines to depict a single range, this creates a crowded chart. The more series you show in your chart, the fewer trendlines you should use for each. When you use one of the regression-based trendlines, you can extend them over a number of time periods, into the future or into the past.

You're also more likely to use error bars on line charts, but you can use them on area, column, bar, and XY charts, but not on 3-D charts. As with trendlines, you may want to consider eliminating a series or two so that your chart doesn't become too crowded. In nearly all cases, except when using XY charts, error bars are vertical lines that either overlap, or extend downward or upward (or both) from a series of data points on your chart.

TAKE NOTE

▶ THINK POSITIVELY ABOUT ERROR BARS

The term error bar is often a misnomer. For example, if you use the Error Bars feature to add a contrasting set of points that is ten percent larger than the points in a series, you are not necessarily thinking of them as errors. You add them to your chart to provide useful information.

▶ SMOOTHER LINES

With a moving average, you decide how many periods each average point covers. The longer the time frame, the smoother the moving average line will be.

CROSS-REFERENCE

See the task "Adding and Removing Data" earlier in this chapter for information on how to delete chart entries.

FIND IT ONLINE

For current information on commodity trendlines, go to http://www.telenium.ca/comtrend/.

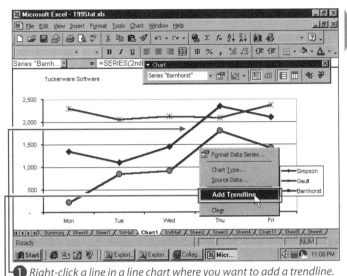

① Right-click a line in a line chart where you want to add a trendline.

② Select Add Trendline from the shortcut menu.

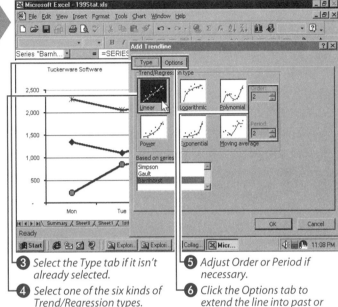

③ Select the Type tab if it isn't already selected.

④ Select one of the six kinds of Trend/Regression types.

⑤ Adjust Order or Period if necessary.

⑥ Click the Options tab to extend the line into past or future time periods.

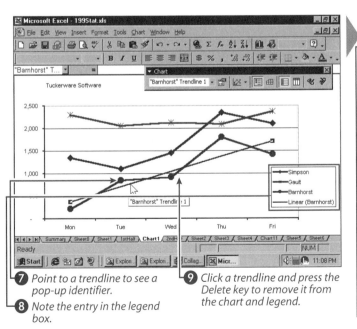

⑦ Point to a trendline to see a pop-up identifier.

⑧ Note the entry in the legend box.

⑨ Click a trendline and press the Delete key to remove it from the chart and legend.

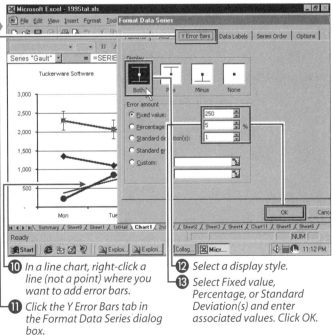

⑩ In a line chart, right-click a line (not a point) where you want to add error bars.

⑪ Click the Y Error Bars tab in the Format Data Series dialog box.

⑫ Select a display style.

⑬ Select Fixed value, Percentage, or Standard Deviation(s) and enter associated values. Click OK.

Adjusting the Chart to Affect Worksheet Data

After working with charts for a while, you'll soon come to terms with the fact that as you make changes to cells in your worksheet, any charts based on those cells change immediately. You see this clearly on embedded charts; less so on charts that are on separate sheets (unless you display your worksheet and chart sheet together). Learning that you can alter the content of a chart and cause the data in your worksheet to be changed, may seem strange at first. This is in contrast to the observation in previous tasks, that changing chart plot order and deleting chart content did nothing to affect the worksheet's content.

One likely scenario for needing to change data in a chart is when you're dealing with a speculative or planning worksheet, and you'd like to see the effect of moving a line or column point in an attempt to create greater smoothness between time periods. If your worksheet has statistics that show the percentage of change month to month, for each quarter, and for the year, you may want to vary the value of a given month and see what some of these percentages would have been. This kind of "what-if" capability is only available in two-dimensional charts and only in bar, column, XY, and line charts.

You can select a single bar, column, or point in a series and drag it upward or downward with onscreen indicators to inform you what the value is at any time. After releasing the mouse, you will have altered your chart's appearance and at the same time changed the content of your worksheet. You can make these kinds of changes to a chart that's on a separate sheet or to one that's embedded in your worksheet. In the latter case, you can see the worksheet results immediately, so you get a more vivid display of what's actually happening. Remember, you can use the Undo button or command to reverse the action.

TAKE NOTE

CHANGING CHART VALUES THAT ARE BASED ON FORMULAS

More often than not, your chart displays data that represents pure values instead of formulas. But Excel charts can, and do, reflect data in cells with formulas. So what happens when you alter the height of a column that's based on a cell that has a formula? Excel relies upon a feature called Goal Seek which asks you the question, "Which of the cells that contributes to the formula is the one that you want to change in order to make the formula calculate the result you just gave." This question appears in a dialog box and you need to confront it before your action of changing the chart can be completed.

CROSS-REFERENCE
Review Chapter 9 to find out how to display different sheets from the same workbook on the screen at once.

FIND IT ONLINE
Check out WHAT-IF, the magazine of the modern philospher, at http://members.tripod.com/~MdrnPhil/WhatIfMag.html.

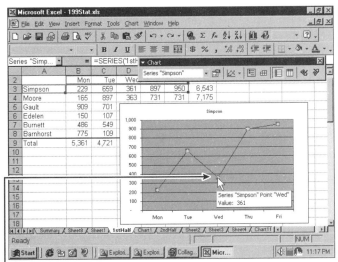

1 Click a line chart point with a value you want to change. Pause, and then click again (don't double-click).

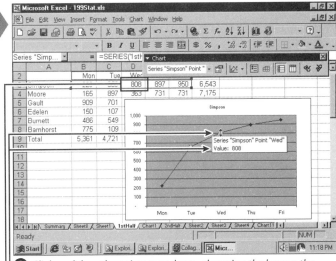

2 Click and drag the point up or down, observing the box on the chart that shows the value changing.

3 Release the mouse to view the changed chart and the changed value in the worksheet.

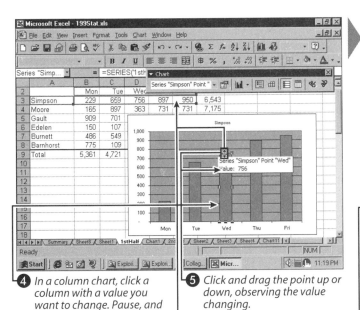

4 In a column chart, click a column with a value you want to change. Pause, and then click again (don't double-click).

5 Click and drag the point up or down, observing the value changing.

6 Release the mouse to view the changed chart and the changed value in the worksheet.

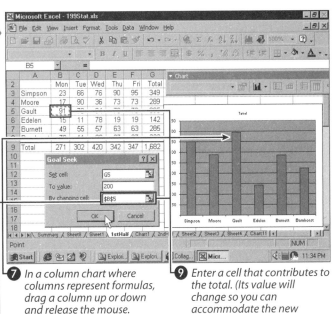

7 In a column chart where columns represent formulas, drag a column up or down and release the mouse.

8 Click in the field next to By changing cell.

9 Enter a cell that contributes to the total. (Its value will change so you can accommodate the new column height). Click OK.

Personal Workbook

Q&A

1. True or False: If you erase a chart's source data in a worksheet, nothing changes in the chart.

   _____

   _____

2. Does a moving average applied to 50 points look smoother if it averages the last five periods or the last two periods?

   _____

   _____

3. Can you change the order of labels on the X-axis (horizontal) through a chart command?

   _____

   _____

4. When you rearrange the order of a series on your chart, what effect does it have on the data in your worksheet?

   _____

   _____

   _____

5. True or False: You can adjust the height of a single column in a 3-D column chart.

   _____

   _____

   _____

   _____

6. What happens to your chart when you delete cells from your worksheet that had been used as category (X-axis) data?

   _____

   _____

   _____

7. If you rearrange the rows in your worksheet that are the source for your chart series, what happens to your chart?

   _____

   _____

   _____

   _____

ANSWERS: PAGE 329

EXTRA PRACTICE

1 In a column chart, change the order of the series to alphabetical.

2 On a chart embedded in your worksheet, delete a series. From your worksheet, select the data for the series and drag it onto the embedded chart.

3 Create a linear trendline for a line in a line chart. Using the same line, create an exponential trendline also. Alter the original worksheet data to better understand how data changes affect the two trendlines differently.

4 Adjust the series order in a 3-D column chart so that you can see the columns better.

REAL-WORLD APPLICATIONS

✔ You need to analyze 12 months of sales data with exponential regression. To make a measured prediction of future sales, you extend your chart four months into the future.

✔ Compare the effect of erasing (Edit ➪ Clear) and deleting (Edit ➪ Delete) cells in your worksheet that are used for chart data.

✔ Rather than creating a new row in your worksheet that shows values 10 percent greater than an existing row, you create a line chart and add error bars with a percentage difference of +10.

Visual Quiz

In the screen shown to the right, what kind of trendline is Trendline 3? Why doesn't it begin at the left side of the chart? What kind of trendline is the straight line that extends across the chart? What's missing from the chart that would help identify all of the line types? How do you delete a trendline?

_____

_____

_____

_____

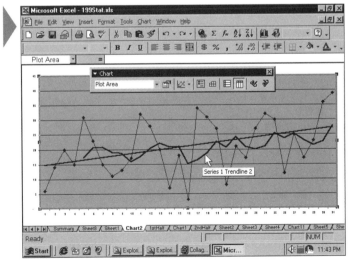

PART

IV

Database Applications

Although Excel is not generally classified as a database software package, its database features are formidable and often more than capable of handling many users' data collection, data organization, and data analysis requirements.

Excel meets your database needs during data entry (Data ➡ Form command), when organizing your data (Data ➡ Sort command), when searching (Data ➡ Filter command), and when consolidating (Data ➡ Subtotals command). But most of all, the database features give you tremendous analytical capability, not just through the aforementioned commands, but through special database functions and array formulas.

Bringing most of these together in one grand operation is the Pivot Table feature, which also offers a charting component. Pivot tables give you a new twist on your data by offering exciting analytical possibilities ranging from very basic to highly sophisticated. Also, pivot charts give you analytical and presentation possibilities that go beyond standard Excel charting capabilities.

Many of Excel's database commands are surprisingly easy to learn and use, and some of them, particularly sorting and array formulas, are useful in nondatabase situations also.

CHAPTER **15**

MASTER
THESE
SKILLS

▶ **Building a Database with Data Form**

▶ **Using Data Validation for Accurate Database Creation**

▶ **Using the Auditing Toolbar to Check Data After Entry**

▶ **Sorting**

▶ **Creating Subtotals on Sorted Lists**

▶ **Using Filters to View Selected Data**

▶ **Using Data Analysis Formulas**

Using Excel for Database Applications

Excel is not generally referred to as a database software package, but since its inception in the late 1980s, Excel has had features (and added to them since) that serve many of the basic needs of building and maintaining a database. These include a mechanism for entering data (Data ➪ Form), a way to validate data entry (Data ➪ Validation), a method to review data accuracy after entry (the Auditing toolbar), and a way to rearrange database records (Data ➪ Sort). In addition, it offers a technique for creating subtotals (Data ➪ Subtotals), a method for extracting selected data on the basis of criteria (Data ➪ Filter), and functions to analyze data (the SUMIF, COUNTIF, and array functions).

However, Excel lacks the ability to set up and handle what is called a relational database (using multiple interrelated tables of data) and has a theoretical limit of 65,536 records. Database packages such as Microsoft Access or Microsoft Visual FoxPro, are capable of handling tables with hundreds of thousands, even millions, of records. As an Excel user, you have all of the tools to handle a sizable database, and can use the wealth of features mentioned above and covered in this chapter.

None of the commands in this chapter uses the word database and, in fact, you won't find much information in the Excel Help system if you look for the word database. Most of the tasks in this chapter and most of the Excel commands that begin with the Data menu rely upon the idea of a list of information.

A list is a contiguous group of cells bounded by empty columns or worksheet boundaries on the left and right, and empty rows or worksheet boundaries on the top and bottom. The top one or two rows should contain title information formatted differently from the rest of the data, and every entry in a specific column should contain the same kind of data — all values, all text, all dates, and so on. If you select a single cell and use a command from the Data menu, Excel automatically selects the list that includes the active cell and surrounding cells.

Building a Database with Data ⇨ Form

You can build a database in a variety of ways, but if you need to make a lot of manual entries, you should use the Data ⇨ Form command. The Data ⇨ Form command gives you a tidy way of viewing a record (actually a row) at a time inside a dialog box instead of merely in a row across the screen.

If you set up column headings and put in a single record, using formulas where necessary, Excel is essentially ready for you to use the Data ⇨ Form command. Using this command means that you can focus on one record at a time, and not be distracted by any others. It will make your data entry much faster. You can also use this feature at a later time when you need to add more records. When using this feature, cells in columns that have formulas are not selectable, so you can zip right by them and not worry about accidentally putting data there.

Managing your database involves not only the creation of new records but also the review of existing records. Although primarily a data entry feature, it's also used for editing and updating. Built into the Data Form dialog box is a feature very much like the Edit ⇨ Find command that allows you to find the next record in your database that meets criteria that you select.

Since deletion is as much a part of database maintenance as adding new records or editing existing ones, the Data Form dialog box lets you do this while going through your records. By deleting records while in the context of data management, you're less likely to make mistakes. In addition, you'll get a confirmation box before the actual deletion can occur.

TAKE NOTE

▶ NAMING YOUR DATABASE

After you create a title row and enter one row of data below it, select both rows and assign the range name Database. If you use the Data ⇨ Form command on this range, as you add new records, the range name Database always refers to the expanding contiguous range.

▶ ADDING NEW RECORDS DOESN'T AFFECT WHAT FOLLOWS

When you use the Data Form dialog box to add new records, the new information appears in the next available row after the last record. Information in rows below your data doesn't get affected in any way. If you attempt to add a record but data exists in the row that follows your current database, you'll be prevented from doing so and get the message, "Cannot extend list or database." Periodically, check the rows below your database to insure that it can grow.

CROSS-REFERENCE
Learn how to name ranges in Chapter 2.

FIND IT ONLINE
For database building tips, check out http://www.trs.com/dbbuild.htm.

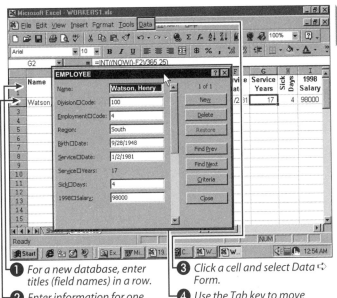

① For a new database, enter titles (field names) in a row.

② Enter information for one record in the next row.

③ Click a cell and select Data ⇨ Form.

④ Use the Tab key to move around. Press enter to go to the next record or to enter a new record.

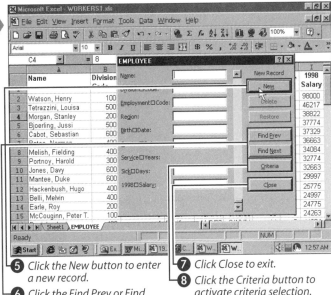

⑤ Click the New button to enter a new record.

⑥ Click the Find Prev or Find Next button to go to the previous record or the next record.

⑦ Click Close to exit.

⑧ Click the Criteria button to activate criteria selection.

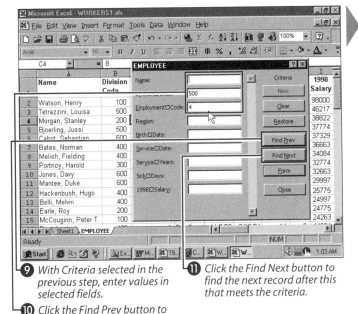

⑨ With Criteria selected in the previous step, enter values in selected fields.

⑩ Click the Find Prev button to find the most recent record before this that meets the criteria.

⑪ Click the Find Next button to find the next record after this that meets the criteria.

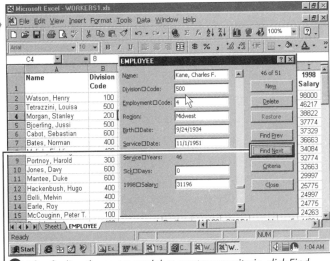

⑫ After finding the next record that meets your criteria, click Find Next again to continue.

Using Data Validation for Accurate Database Creation

Opportunities for introducing errors into your database occur frequently during data entry. Although it's best to gather data from other sources, if possible, when building your data, it's really helpful to be able to scan data as it's being entered and confront errors as they occur. The Data Validation dialog box provides an array of techniques for creating data entry lists and setting limits, complete with warnings before and error messages after entry, all designed to let you catch errors before they corrupt your database.

With data validation, you can control the kinds of entries (whole number, decimal, date, time, etc.), the range of entries (between a range of values, dates, times), and the length of entries. You can use this feature in different locations in a worksheet, with each range having a different set of validation criteria.

If all of the entries in a given column of your personnel database are hire dates, you want to make sure that no hire date is in the future or is before your company existed. You can imagine other kinds of limits put on a column of birth dates or limitations on shipping dates (weekdays only in your company). With the Data Validation commands, you can restrict entries to only those found in a list. You can also base limitations on formulas and functions if necessary.

Along with these restrictions, it's also useful to have a pop-up message appear whenever a cell is selected. This can inform you of limits or preferred styles before you even type an entry. In addition, you might also want a message to pop up when an incorrect entry has been made — something like: "This value must be greater than 59 and less than 100."

TAKE NOTE

▶ DATA VALIDATION AND DATA FORM

Data validation doesn't always work as you might expect it when you use the Data ⇨ Form command (covered in the previous task). When using the Data ⇨ Form command, your data validation constraints don't get recognized until you attempt to advance to the next record or you try to close the Data Form dialog box.

▶ DATA VALIDATION AND AUTOFILL

If you use the AutoFill feature on cells that are subject to data validation constraints, you can enter data that violates those constraints and you'll get no error messages. If you edit one of these cells, however, and fail to adjust the content to satisfy the data validation rule, you'll get an error message.

▶ WEEKDAYS ONLY

If you'd like to restrict a range of cells to date entries that are weekdays only, activate the Data Validation dialog box, select Custom, and enter this formula, substituting the cell address of the first cell for cell D1 in the formula: **=AND(WEEKDAY (D1)>1,WEEKDAY(D1)<7).**

CROSS-REFERENCE
Review the WEEKDAY function in Chapter 8.

FIND IT ONLINE
If you're interested in an HTML validation site that checks for Web site syntax errors, check out **http://www.netmechanic.com/html_check.htm.**

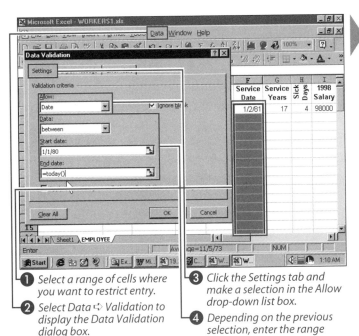

1 Select a range of cells where you want to restrict entry.

2 Select Data ➪ Validation to display the Data Validation dialog box.

3 Click the Settings tab and make a selection in the Allow drop-down list box.

4 Depending on the previous selection, enter the range allowed.

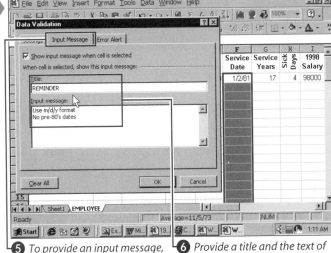

5 To provide an input message, click the Input Message tab.

6 Provide a title and the text of an input message to guide the user during data entry.

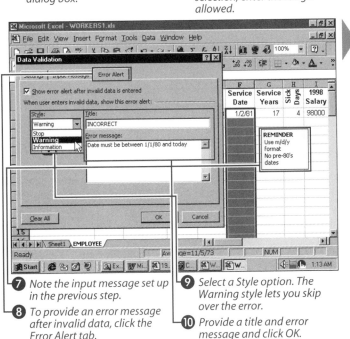

7 Note the input message set up in the previous step.

8 To provide an error message after invalid data, click the Error Alert tab.

9 Select a Style option. The Warning style lets you skip over the error.

10 Provide a title and error message and click OK.

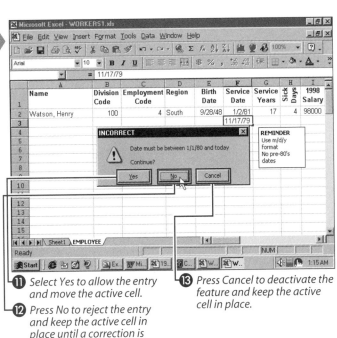

11 Select Yes to allow the entry and move the active cell.

12 Press No to reject the entry and keep the active cell in place until a correction is made.

13 Press Cancel to deactivate the feature and keep the active cell in place.

Using the Auditing Toolbar to Check Data After Entry

While the Data Validation feature is a great tool to prevent bad data from creeping into your worksheets, you also need tools to clean up data that was entered incorrectly without doing a validity check. You may also need to scan data that was imported from another worksheet, workbook, or outside source, such as a table from a database software package. You should also be vigilant about the fact that even when you do have data validation rules in effect for a range of cells, you can copy invalid data to these cells and receive no warning or error message.

The Auditing toolbar, which was introduced in Chapter 6 as a vehicle for tracking those cells (dependents) that are dependent upon a cell or for those cells (precedents) that contribute to a cell's content, can also be used with the Data Validation feature. Using these two features together lets you screen the contents of cells and encircle those that are out of range. When you use the Auditing toolbar, all data validation settings in the worksheet are checked. You get a good visual display — bright red ovals encircle those cells with invalid data — and it makes for a vivid printout also.

The Data Validation feature and the Auditing toolbar are both needed in validity checking, but note these differences:

▶ To limit the kind of information going into your worksheet, use the Data Validation feature

to set up rules before you enter data; the Auditing toolbar has no role in this process.

▶ To review existing data, you need to use the Data Validation feature to set up rules as to what's acceptable data. But this step alone has no effect — you need the Auditing toolbar to locate the unacceptable data.

CROSS-REFERENCE

See Chapter 17 for information on importing data into Excel from other sources.

FIND IT ONLINE

Learn about quality auditing at **http://www.quality. co.uk/quality/qaudadv/qaudint.htm.**

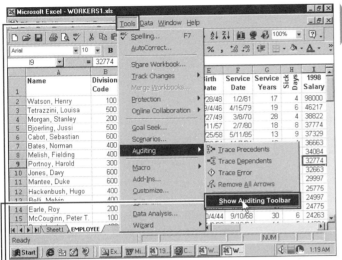

❶ To activate the Auditing toolbar, select Tools ⇨ Auditing.

❷ Slide to the Show Auditing Toolbar shortcut.

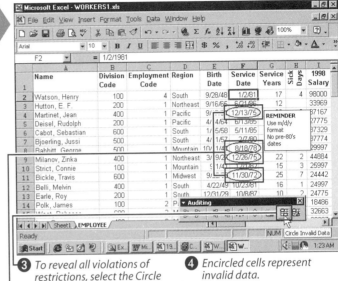

❸ To reveal all violations of restrictions, select the Circle Invalid Data button on the Auditing toolbar.

❹ Encircled cells represent invalid data.

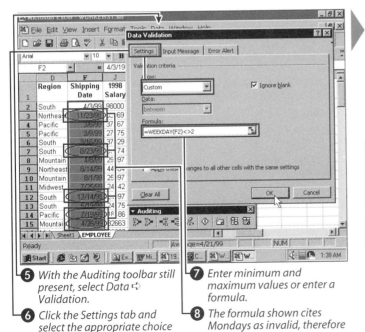

❺ With the Auditing toolbar still present, select Data ⇨ Validation.

❻ Click the Settings tab and select the appropriate choice in the Allow drop-down list box.

❼ Enter minimum and maximum values or enter a formula.

❽ The formula shown cites Mondays as invalid, therefore Mondays get circled.

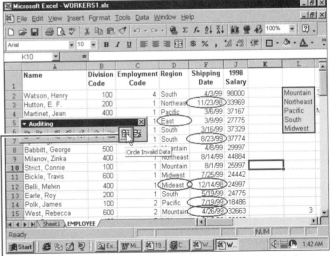

❾ Select Data ⇨ Validation to display the Data Validation dialog box and define additional limits as needed. In Column D, the only entries allowed come from the list in cells L2:L6.

253

Sorting

When done by a computer, sorting is extremely fast, accurate, and error-free. But more important than its speed, accuracy, and efficiency is the fact that it's something you need to do all the time, particularly in database situations.

Your inventory list needs to be printed out in alphabetical order by name; after that you need your list rearranged by birth date; after that by reorder point; then by price; and so on. Your sorting needs are by no means restricted to database situations. You might want to sort spreadsheet entries also. Sorting is nearly always done by column, meaning that you select the content of one or more columns to determine the order of rows. If you visualize your database as a series of horizontal strips of paper, then sorting is simply a way to rearrange those strips of paper based on what you find in the selected columns.

In Excel, there are both toolbar and command methods that are quick and easy. It's also fairly straightforward to introduce your own sorting lists. You can, for example, create a list of all the departments in your company in order of importance, by size, or by some other criteria that's not alphabetical. Sorting can then occur according to this list, not alphabetically. Excel has some built-in lists also. If days of the week are entered in a column as text, you can sort on that column chronologically, not alphabetically.

An important concept to grasp about sorting is that it is cumulative in nature. With toolbar sorting, you sort one column at a time, moving from the least important to the most important. If you sort your database by a column containing salary and then you sort by a column containing regions, your worksheet is in order by region, but for those rows where the region is the same, those rows are in order by salary, since that was the key used for your previous sort.

TAKE NOTE

► SELECTION BEFORE SORTING

Whether you're going to sort by using the buttons in the Standard toolbar or the Data ⇨ Sort command, remember to select either a single cell or the entire sort range. When you sort, Excel will sort only what you select, unless you select just a single cell, in which case it determines the entire list to sort.

► USING THE TAB KEY

If you want to quickly sort a selected range from the toolbar, Excel sorts by the column where the active cell is located. To move the active cell into another column and not disrupt your selection, press the tab key until the active cell is in the correct column.

CROSS-REFERENCE
Review the basics of entering data in Chapter 2.

FIND IT ONLINE
If you're interested in sorting methodology, watch a demo of various sorting techniques at http://www.ludat.lth.se/~dat93tka/javaindex.html.

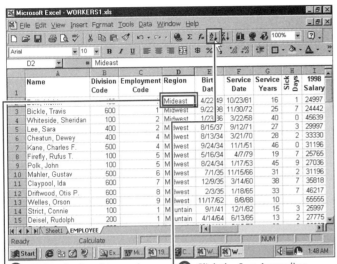

1️⃣ Click a single cell in a column of a database that you want to sort by.

2️⃣ Click the Sort Ascending button in the Standard toolbar to sort the records in the database in alphabetical order.

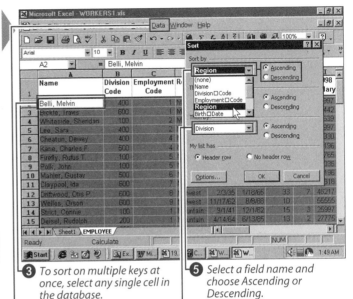

3️⃣ To sort on multiple keys at once, select any single cell in the database.

4️⃣ Select Data ➪ Sort.

5️⃣ Select a field name and choose Ascending or Descending.

6️⃣ Select additional field names, then click OK.

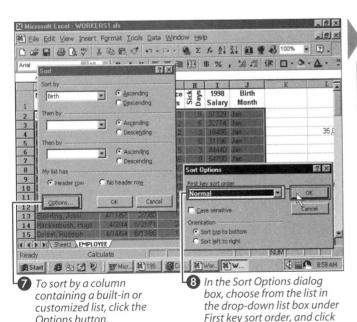

7️⃣ To sort by a column containing a built-in or customized list, click the Options button.

8️⃣ In the Sort Options dialog box, choose from the list in the drop-down list box under First key sort order, and click OK.

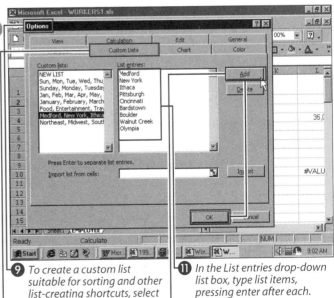

9️⃣ To create a custom list suitable for sorting and other list-creating shortcuts, select Tools ➪ Options to display the Options dialog box.

🔟 Click the Custom Lists tab.

⓫ In the List entries drop-down list box, type list items, pressing enter after each.

⓬ Click the Add button, then click OK.

Creating Subtotals on Sorted Lists

As you become proficient with sorting, it is only a matter of time before you wonder about putting in subtotals after your data is neatly arranged, say, by department, job code, state, and so on. Excel's subtotaling capability seems to follow logically from any discussion on sorting. In fact, if your data is not sorted, the idea of inserting subtotals is practically useless.

There are variations on subtotaling that you need to be aware of also. Subtotaling can be multilevel. If your customer database is sorted by state and within state by county, and then by city, you might want a state subtotal for all states in the country, a county subtotal for all counties in the state, and a city total for all cities in each county.

Excel also gives you outlining symbols so that after you have subtotals, you can collapse your display of subtotals to see certain subtotal levels without the detail. At a glance, therefore, you could see state totals only, or state and county totals while the city totals and detail entries are hidden. Another variation lets you look at the detail for one group while looking only at the aggregate totals for the others. When your data is collapsed and you see only aggregate totals, you have the ability to sort on the subtotals. You could therefore, when seeing a list of state totals, sort them so that the states with the highest values appear first.

Most of the time, you'll use the Subtotals feature to calculate sums, but you can also calculate average, count, min, max, standard deviation, and other statistical functions as well. You get a grand total along with your subtotals and you have the choice of placing it at the top or bottom of your totals.

TAKE NOTE

MAKE THOSE SUBTOTALS REALLY STAND OUT

Although you can apply your own formatting, Excel's AutoFormat command, available from the Format menu, goes a long way toward presenting your subtotals report as attractively as possible. Click any cell inside your subtotals report, then activate the command and pick one of the 16 available choices. If you disable the Subtotals feature, the formatting remains.

MULTIPLE ROW SUBTOTALS

Suppose you need to see a subtotal row containing totals (sums) for certain columns and averages for other columns. You can't do this on a single line, but you can on two separate lines. First, create a subtotal line using Sum for those columns you need added. Return to the Subtotal dialog box, select a different function, uncheck the box next to Replace current subtotals and click OK.

CROSS-REFERENCE
Review sorting in the previous task.

SHORTCUT
Press Ctrl+* before selecting Data ⇨ Subtotals to verify the range that Excel will operate on to create subtotals.

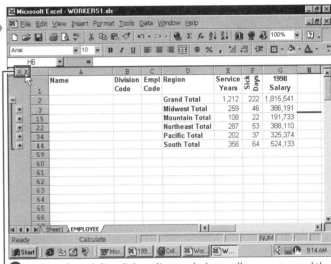

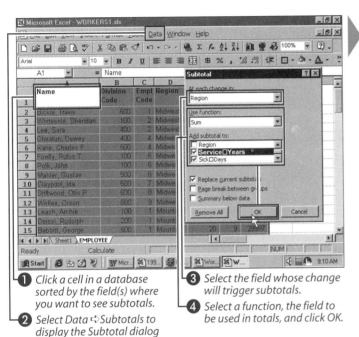

1 Click a cell in a database sorted by the field(s) where you want to see subtotals.

2 Select Data ⇨ Subtotals to display the Subtotal dialog box.

3 Select the field whose change will trigger subtotals.

4 Select a function, the field to be used in totals, and click OK.

5 In the subtotals list, click outline symbols to collapse or expand the detail shown.

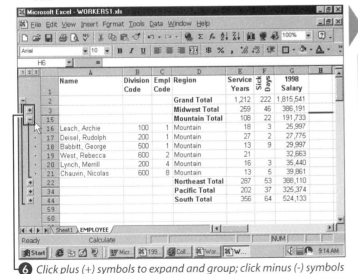

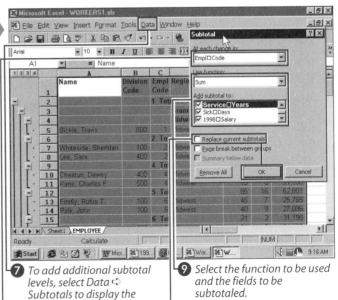

6 Click plus (+) symbols to expand and group; click minus (-) symbols to collapse the detail of any group.

7 To add additional subtotal levels, select Data ⇨ Subtotals to display the Subtotal dialog box.

8 Select an additional field.

9 Select the function to be used and the fields to be subtotaled.

10 Uncheck the box next to Replace current subtotals and click OK.

Using Filters to View Selected Data

atabases have a habit of growing faster than you'd like them to. Invariably, you need to see less of your data at certain times, not to reduce the volume as much as wanting to see only those records that meet certain guidelines. The idea of filtering is that you'd like to see only those records that meet certain criteria. For example, you want to see just those customers that live in Ohio, or just those records of people hired before 1990 whose sales exceed 50,000, or only those records for people in the Ssales or marketing departments.

In a sense, filtering is like extracting, except that you don't really move any data anywhere. Instead, you hide all the records that don't match your request. Filtering offers many opportunities for using multiple criteria and operates on text, date, and numeric data equally well. With filtering, you also get the ability to sort and print the results or copy the filtered results to another location. Filtering does not in any way disrupt or alter the content of your original data. Although not normally described as an editing and validation tool, filtering also lets you find blank entries or values above, below, or within a range of values. With those possibilities in mind, you could very well use them as a complement to the data validation features covered earlier in this chapter.

When you use multicolumn filtering, you can structure a search like this: Show all records where the region is Midwest, the department is not sales or marketing, and the hire date is before 1/1/95.

TAKE NOTE

AND THE TOP TEN ENTRIES ARE...

When filtering, you can choose Excel's so-called Top 10 option, but don't take the terms literally. The default setting is to choose the Top 10 Items. Substitute the 10 with any number you want, substitute the word Bottom for Top, or substitute the word Percent for Items. Looking for all records in the upper quartile? Change 10 to 25 and Items to Percent and you'll get your data.

WILD CARDS

The well-known wild card symbols, the asterisk (*) and the question mark (?), which seem to turn up everywhere in Windows software packages, are available for text searches in filtering also. After you select the drop-down arrow to set the filter, choose Custom and make an entry such as M* to find all of those names beginning with the letter M. Need to find all of those products where the second digit of the product code is an E? Enter E?*.

YOU CAN'T REMOVE FILTERS

When you apply a filter, but your results aren't really what you want, you can't rely on the Undo button or command to return your screen to its previous look. Either remove all filters and start over or rework the filter in question.

CROSS-REFERENCE

Review the Undo command in Chapter 6.

FIND IT ONLINE

Learn more about coffee filters at **http://www.arabica. com/fp1.htm#issue03**.

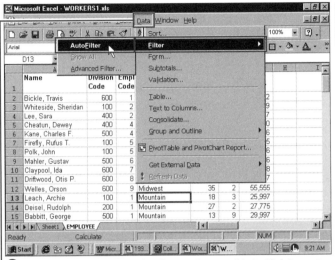

1 To apply filtering to your database, select a cell in it. Click Data ⇨ Filter ⇨ AutoFilter.

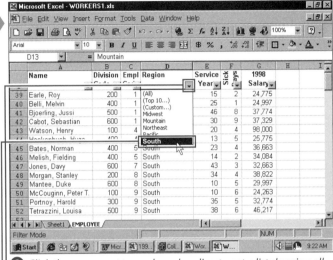

2 Click the arrow next to a column heading to get a list showing all current entries in the column, preceded by special choices.

3 Click an entry to see only those records with that value in the column.

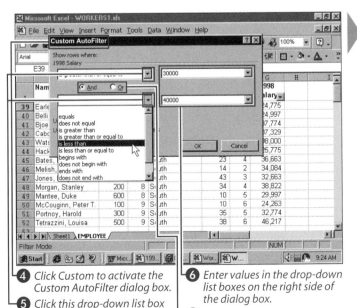

4 Click Custom to activate the Custom AutoFilter dialog box.

5 Click this drop-down list box to expose lists of logical selectors.

6 Enter values in the drop-down list boxes on the right side of the dialog box.

7 For compound criteria, press the And/Or radio buttons to complete the compound condition.

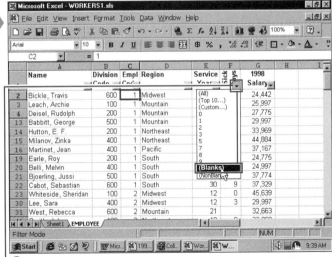

8 Repeat steps 1 and 2 to select additional column criteria. For columns where at least one blank cell exists, click the arrow and select (Blanks).

Using Data Analysis Formulas

Both the filtering and subtotaling capabilities of Excel go a long way in helping you understand and analyze your database. But there are two specific functions and a formula style which greatly augment those features and provide useful statistical information.

As their names suggest, both the SUMIF and COUNTIF functions combine the features of two widely used functions. Use the SUMIF function when you want to say something along the lines of: "If they're part of the Midwest region, I'd like to know the sum of all of their salaries." Expressed in a more formal way, you might say, "If any entry in Column B is Midwest, give me the total of all of the corresponding salaries in Column K."

The COUNTIF function, less expansive in nature, helps you get the answer to a question such as, "How many of the cells in Column D only contain the word Midwest?"

If your database is sorted and you insert subtotals, perhaps some of these kinds of questions are already answered. But SUMIF and COUNTIF can be used anywhere, and you don't need to sort your data.

With array formulas, you can expand the functionality of SUMIF and COUNTIF to include other statistical functions such as AVERAGE, MIN, MAX, MEDIAN, MODE, and so on. With an array formula, you can handle a more complex questions, such as: "What's the second lowest sales amount (from Column Q) of all the people in the Pacific region (from Column D)?" You can also use array formulas in more sophisticated ways, such as having multiple nested IFs as part of the formula construction.

TAKE NOTE

ARRAY FORMULAS AND THE REQUIRED CTRL+SHIFT+ENTER

Array formulas can be frustrating for a while because you'll forget to press Ctrl+Shift+Enter to complete them. You're more likely to forget this when you're editing a cell with an array formula in it than when you're entering it for the first time. When you neglect to use this keystroke combination, you can get a credible (but incorrect) answer, an obvious error, or a zero. If the active cell contains an array formula, it appears in the formula surrounded with curly braces { } but you never type these symbols. They emerge after you press Ctrl+Shift+Enter but they disappear during editing.

ARRAY FORMULA EXAMPLE

Type an array formula like this: =MEDIAN(IF(D2: D52="South",K2:K52)) to find the median salary (from Column K) for all records where the entry in Column D = South.

Type an array formula like this: =AVERAGE(IF (D2:D52="South",IF(H2:H52>4,K2:K52))) to find the average salary for all records where the entry in Column D = South and the entry in Column H is greater than 4.

In both examples, don't forget to press Ctrl+Shift+Enter to complete the entry.

CROSS-REFERENCE

See Chapter 7 to recall how the IF function can be used.

FIND IT ONLINE

Find out more about memorizing using image arrays at http://www.knowhow-kompakt.com/dm/memory/dmme002e.htm.

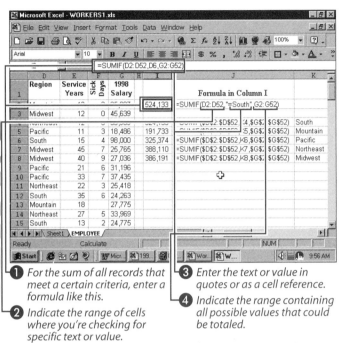

① For the sum of all records that meet a certain criteria, enter a formula like this.

② Indicate the range of cells where you're checking for specific text or value.

③ Enter the text or value in quotes or as a cell reference.

④ Indicate the range containing all possible values that could be totaled.

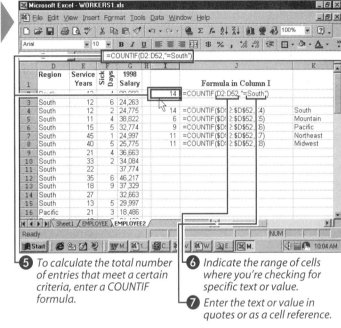

⑤ To calculate the total number of entries that meet a certain criteria, enter a COUNTIF formula.

⑥ Indicate the range of cells where you're checking for specific text or value.

⑦ Enter the text or value in quotes or as a cell reference.

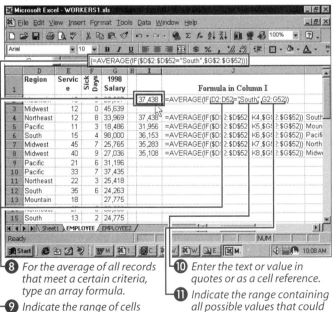

⑧ For the average of all records that meet a certain criteria, type an array formula.

⑨ Indicate the range of cells where you're checking for specific text or value.

⑩ Enter the text or value in quotes or as a cell reference.

⑪ Indicate the range containing all possible values that could be totaled, then press Ctrl+Shift+Enter.

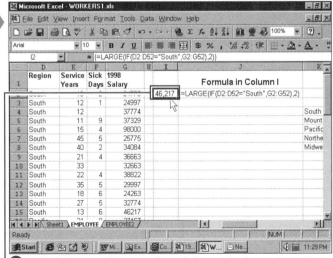

⑫ To find the second largest salary of all records where column D contains the word South, type the formula shown. Press Ctrl+Shift+Enter.

261

Personal Workbook

ANSWERS: 330

Q&A

1 True or False: With data validation, you can restrict entries in a range to dates only.

_____

_____

_____

2 Do you need to sort your database before using the Subtotals feature?

_____

_____

_____

3 When you add a new record using the Data Form dialog box, where is the new record placed?

_____

_____

_____

4 What keystroke combination do you use to properly complete an array formula?

_____

_____

5 True or False: When you sort, you nearly always rearrange the order of columns.

_____

_____

_____

_____

6 Which command sequence lets you set up a special list of items that you can sort by?

_____

_____

_____

_____

7 Do you need to sort your database before using the Data ➪ Filter command?

_____

_____

_____

_____

EXTRA PRACTICE

1. In an existing database, use the Data ⇨ Form command and enter a new record.

2. Sort a database on a column of dates. Do this once ascending and once descending to note the difference.

3. Using the Data ⇨ Filter command on your database, find those records that have a blank in a column where you know there's at least one blank cell.

4. Use the Data ⇨ Subtotals command on a database and apply an AutoFormat.

5. Using the Data ⇨ Filter command on a database, select a column and find all entries that are either less than one value or greater than another. Example: Show all records where sales are less than 10,000 or greater than 30,000.

REAL-WORLD APPLICATIONS

✔ A column in your database is to be filled with one of six department names. You select the entire column, and use the Data Validation dialog box to make a list appear every time you click a cell in that column. The list has the names of the six departments, so you can click the appropriate one without ever needing to type a department name in this column.

✔ You need a quick printout of all the Marketing people. You use Data ⇨ Filter to find them and print your report immediately from the filtered list.

✔ You're ready to print your Subtotal report but it's rather dull-looking. You use the Format ⇨ AutoFormat command and pick one of the 16 colorful alternatives.

Visual Quiz

In the screen shown to the right, four successive sorts were done from the Sort button in the Standard toolbar. On which column was the database sorted last? Which column was the previous sort based on? The one before that? Which column was the first of the four sorts based on? Were any of these sorts descending?

_____

_____

_____

_____

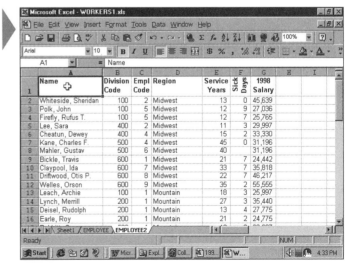

CHAPTER **16**

MASTER
THESE
SKILLS

▶ **Creating a Pivot Table**

▶ **Changing the Layout of a Pivot Table**

▶ **Hiding and Showing Details**

▶ **Grouping and Ungrouping Data**

▶ **Adding or Removing Fields**

▶ **Displaying Pivot Table Data in a Pivot Chart**

Using Pivot Tables

Despite all the useful features in Excel that help you build, maintain, and analyze data, nothing is as powerful or as flexible as a pivot table. It's a tremendous organizational and analytical tool, filled with tricks and shortcuts, and integrated with a complementary charting capability that's new in this version of Excel.

In its simplest form, a pivot table is a summary, or condensed version, of a database or list. Data commands, particularly Sort, Filter, Validation, and Subtotals (all covered in the previous chapter), give you a repertoire of tools with which to manage a list of data efficiently. But a pivot table report brings all of these features together into one powerful and concise capability and also contributes some new and exciting features. At its most sophisticated, a pivot table is a collection of analytical tools that lets you quickly create summary information with the ability to sort, filter, group, and rearrange data using drag-and-drop techniques.

Using the list concept that serves as a basis for most of the database commands, you can create a pivot table quickly without a great deal of planning. A significant aspect of pivot table usage is its flexibility — you can change results simply by dragging fields back and forth between what are called row, column, and page axes.

Adding fields or removing them from your pivot table is very simple. You can do the kind of grouping reminiscent of the Subtotals feature, but you do it faster and can quickly group and ungroup field data without rerunning a command sequence.

Hiding and revealing detail is a standard tool in your pivot table collection and there are numerous ways to hide selected details to simplify the look of your report. There are powerful grouping possibilities for handling dates that are available nowhere else in Excel.

As if all of these features were not impressive enough, the new Pivot Chart tool is a lot more than a mere stepchild of Excel's charting capability. Relying on one of the pivot table's most salient features — redesign by dragging fields — you can quickly alter the chart in the same way.

One final note about pivot tables is that you will not appreciate their power until you try creating a few of them. You'll soon begin to enter a new realm of creativity and analytical thinking.

Creating a Pivot Table

Although you can create a pivot table that does not summarize numerical information, most pivot tables are focused on numbers. You can still, however, create pivot tables that merely provide counts of entries. For example, a human resources database without numerical fields still might warrant a report showing the number of people with a specific job title by division. A more common situation is when you have multiple columns that act as criteria and one or more columns has values that you want to see summarized (using any of the statistical functions — SUM, AVERAGE, and so on).

Imagine a database with columns named Region, Job Code, Empl Status, and Salary. Using two other Data commands, you can sort this database and apply subtotals to create an informative report. You could also use the Data ⇨ Filter command to extract useful, concise information. But neither of these methods is as fast, easy, or as capable as using a pivot table applied to the same data. Upon creation, you can see at a glance what the average salary is for each region, for each job code, and for each kind of employment status. Furthermore, you'll see the average salary for each job code within each region and the average salary per employment status within each job code, and so on.

In most cases, when you create a pivot table, you'll be getting data from an Excel worksheet, even though the table creation process lets you get data from external files. Like many Data commands, Excel uses the idea of a list to include all surrounding cells.

As with a number of other Excel features, you create a pivot table using a wizard, an assistant that leads you through steps, with help and hints along the way. You may have a tendency to think that you're in unknown territory when you create a pivot table, but just as you have a tremendous amount of flexibility when you create a chart and are able to adjust it endlessly, the same is true of pivot tables.

TAKE NOTE

WITH WHAT KIND OF DATABASE WILL A PIVOT TABLE BE MOST EFFECTIVE?

If you have a number of fields in your database where many of the entries are the same and yet there is some variation, a pivot table is more likely to be useful. A field with about 10 to 20 different entries seems about ideal. In a pivot table, that will translate into 10 to 20 columns across the top of the report (a little crowded) or 10 to 20 rows down the side of the report (not so crowded). If each entry in a column is different, the pivot table's aggregate capability is of little use, although the pivot table's grouping capability, addressed later in this chapter, will help.

CROSS-REFERENCE

Learn about getting data from external sources in Chapter 17.

SHORTCUT

Learn how an Excel user created a pesticide record-keeping application using a pivot table at http://www.maine.com/apples/software.htm.

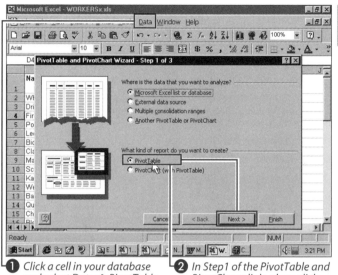

① Click a cell in your database and select Data ⇨ PivotTable ⇨ PivotChart Report.

② In Step1 of the PivotTable and PivotChart dialog box, click the PivotTable radio button and click the Next button.

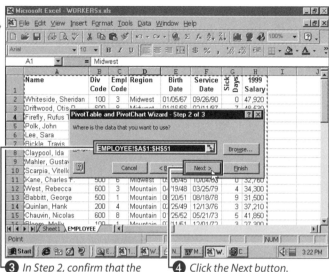

③ In Step 2, confirm that the range selected is the one you want for the pivot table's source or select another range.

④ Click the Next button.

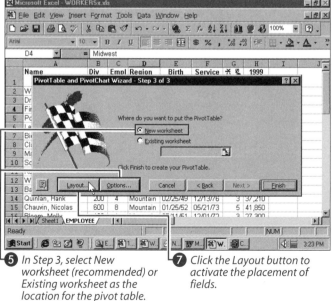

⑤ In Step 3, select New worksheet (recommended) or Existing worksheet as the location for the pivot table.

⑥ Click the Options button to make formatting and data selections.

⑦ Click the Layout button to activate the placement of fields.

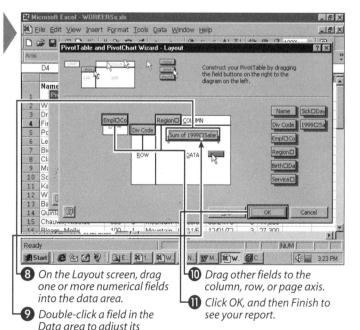

⑧ On the Layout screen, drag one or more numerical fields into the data area.

⑨ Double-click a field in the Data area to adjust its summarization choice and formats.

⑩ Drag other fields to the column, row, or page axis.

⑪ Click OK, and then Finish to see your report.

Changing the Layout of a Pivot Table

The single most impressive feature about pivot tables is the way that you can manipulate them so easily. Drag a field from one axis to another and immediately you get a completely different, and often more illuminating, view of your data. This ability to change fields is at the heart of why we use the word pivot — it's as if we pivot the report to switch column displays into row displays and vice versa. You also have a page axis in the report to provide further creativity in rearranging your data.

As you make some of the changes suggested above, don't worry about disrupting your original data. Furthermore, since your pivot table is dependent on that data, you can choose to update the pivot table to reflect any changes in your database. As with charting, you must not be timid in your approach to changing the layout of your report. Don't be afraid of the consequences — the worst that can happen is that you create something useless or unattractive. Just delete the sheet, go back to your database and create another report. Unfortunately, no textbook example is going to be as pertinent to you as when you're working with the data that you know best, so dive in and start moving fields around your pivot table to see what emerges.

Most pivot table examples show one or more fields on the row axis and on the column axis, but you'll see that some situations lend themselves to having two or more fields on the row axis and no fields on the column axis. Later in this chapter you learn how easy it is to add and remove fields from your pivot table.

Since every field displayed in the row and column axes has a drop-down arrow next to it, you can selectively use filtering. You might decide to compare each region on a column axis with each division code on a row axis, but you'd like to leave out one region for the moment. At another time you may want just one region in your report.

TAKE NOTE

NO DETAIL IN THE PAGE AXIS

If you use a page axis, you'll see a drop-down arrow that lets you pick one of the entries included in that field. For example, if you have a Region field on the page axis, you can't see on the screen a breakout for each region, but you can see one region at a time if you use that drop-down arrow. If you want a detail breakout of page axis entries on your screen at once, drag that field to the row or column axis.

REFRESH YOUR TABLE

If you make frequent changes to the database that's the source of your pivot table, don't assume automatic updating occurs in the table — it doesn't. Click the Refresh Data button on the PivotTable toolbar.

CROSS-REFERENCE

Review the capabilities of Data Filters in Chapter 15.

FIND IT ONLINE

To get all the details about a really flexible pivot table, go to http://www.comforthouse.com/comfort/pertab.html.

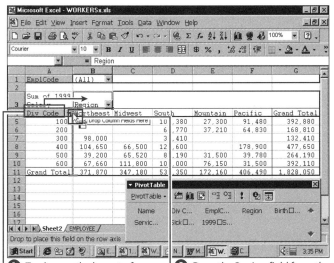

1 To change the layout of a pivot table, click and drag a field from one axis to another.

2 Drag the Region field from the column axis to the row axis.

3 The Region field is now on the row axis.

4 Drag DivCode field from the row axis to the column axis.

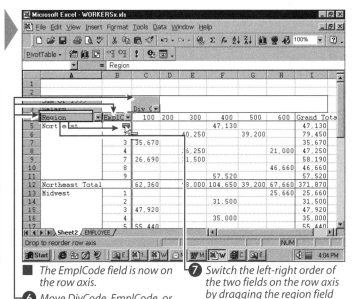

■ DivCode field is now on the column axis.

5 Drag the EmplCode field from the page axis to the row axis.

■ The EmplCode field is now on the row axis.

6 Move DivCode, EmplCode, or Region fields to a different axis as desired.

7 Switch the left-right order of the two fields on the row axis by dragging the region field to the right of the EmplCode field.

Hiding and Showing Details

Despite all of its value as a tool for analysis, there are times when a pivot table shows you more data than you need. In most of these cases, you don't really want to remove a field from your table.

Fortunately, the pivot table capabilities include ways to hide detailed data that you can easily restore later. Imagine a pivot table that has data displaying all four quarters for the year and you want to shorten the report to focus only on the first two quarters. You also want to see this data with subtotals that get adjusted to reflect only the visible quarters. Once again, with a minimum of difficulty, you can obtain these results.

If a field can have different entries in it and the field is not time-based, you can be selective about the entries for which you'd like to see details. Say, for example, that you've got up to six kinds of job titles in each region of your company and have already created a pivot table showing the total number of people who have each job title in each region. What you really want to see, is a list showing just salespersons and marketing managers for each region. Selectively, you can pick those titles only and modify your report.

A similar, yet indirect way to hide data is to limit entries to the top values in a field. For example, in each region, there are many job codes and your current pivot table shows both fields on the row axis, with region to the left of job code. Your pivot table takes up many rows because there are ten or more rows for each region. You would like to see only two rows per region, one showing the job code held by the most people in the region and another showing the job code that's second highest.

TAKE NOTE

▶ HIDING INNER AND OUTER FIELDS

If you have two or more fields side by side on either the row or column axis, the field to the left is the outer field. The other fields are called inner fields. If you select an outer field and click the Hide Detail button on the Pivot Table toolbar, the detail of the inner fields becomes hidden also. If you hide an inner field, you can't bring it back unless you select the outer field and click the Show Detail button on the Pivot Table toolbar.

▶ SORTING RESULTS

Don't be timid about trying to sort the results when you hide or reveal data. Click a field name or a field result, even if it's part of an abbreviated list. Next, click either sort button in the Standard toolbar.

▶ SUBTOTALS GETTING YOU DOWN?

Bedeviled by too many subtotal lines cluttering your report? Double-click the field name and click the None button under Subtotals. Return here if you need to restore subtotals.

CROSS-REFERENCE
See Chapter 17 for information on importing data into Excel from other sources.

FIND IT ONLINE
Read about one person's search for hidden details on the Web at **http://www.webpointers.com/imf.html.**

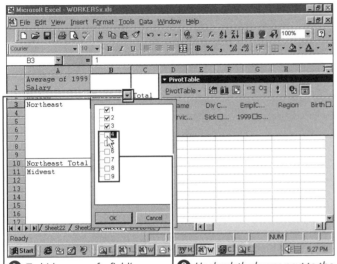

① To hide some of a field's entries, click the drop-down arrow to the right of the field name.

② Uncheck the boxes next to the field entries that you do not want to see and click OK.

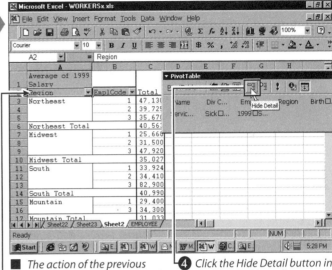

■ The action of the previous step is shown — just values 1, 2, and 3 for EmplCode are shown.

③ To collapse all details of a field, select the field name.

④ Click the Hide Detail button in the Pivot Table toolbar.

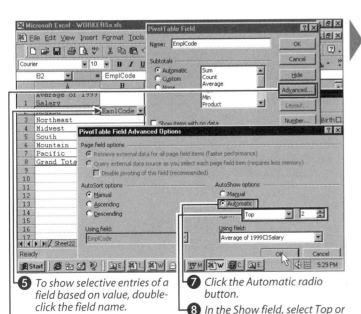

⑤ To show selective entries of a field based on value, double-click the field name.

⑥ In the Pivot Table Field dialog box, click the advanced button.

⑦ Click the Automatic radio button.

⑧ In the Show field, select Top or Bottom, enter a number indicating how many entries, click OK in each dialog box.

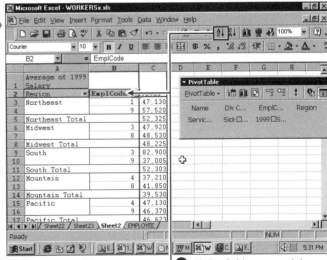

■ The action of the previous step is shown — the top 2 values for average salary are shown for each region.

⑨ Click a field name and then a sort button to sort the fields in ascending or descending order.

Grouping and Ungrouping Data

The grouping and ungrouping capability of the pivot table has some similarities with the previous task of hiding and showing detail. But with grouping, you want to rethink the nature of your data and think of certain fields as being broken into subfields.

If your company has operations in 12 different states, you will frequently want to see the detail data from each in your various pivot table reports. It's also convenient to see some of these reports in more concise form — instead of a 12-column report showing a column for each state, a 4-column report with each column showing a region. Best of all is the idea that you can have both needs met at once. You can create a report that groups data by regions. You can then ungroup your report to show detail by states.

Another benefit to grouping is its aggregate capabilities when handling date fields. It's not uncommon to have date fields filled with specific dates. Your database of 500 records that shows invoice activity for the year could turn into a visual nightmare if you think of a column for every separate date in the year when an invoice was processed. You can imagine the shortcomings with the Data ➪ Subtotals and Data ➪ Filter commands in handling this kind of information.

But with a pivot table's grouping capability, you can group dates by days, months, quarters, or years, and you can use multiple groupings, for example, quarters and months together. On the same table you can see the month-by-month totals and the totals by quarter, and you could easily hide the quarterly subtotals without destroying the grouping. If your data has a field associated with times of the day, there is a similar grouping of field entries by hours, minutes, and seconds.

If a pivot table field contains numbers and you attempt to group that field, you'll get a dialog box that displays the highest and lowest values and lets you pick an interval value for grouping. An ideal use for this is when you've got a field filled with salaries and you'd like to see this information in your pivot table grouped in columns like 20-29,999, 30-39,999, and so on.

TAKE NOTE

▶ **MOVING FIELDS BEFORE GROUPING**

If you're about to group field entries in a way that has nothing to do with alphabetical, data, or numerical order, arrange the field items first. If for example, you have six state names across the column axis and you want to group them into East and West, but the first, third, and sixth states belong in the East, click a field entry name and drag its bottom border and you'll drag all the data for that field entry with it to the new location.

CROSS-REFERENCE

Review "Entering Text, Numbers, and Dates" in Chapter 2 for information on moving cells.

SHORTCUT

Use Alt+Shift+right arrow to group selected pivot table cells.

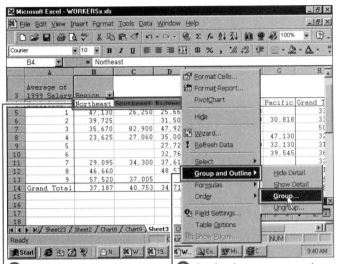

❶ Select field entries that you want to group (three of the six regions shown) and right-click.

❷ On the shortcut menu, select Group and Outline and then Group.

❸ After the group name appears, click in the formula bar and give it a name (East) you prefer. Repeat steps 1 and 2 for additional grouping as needed.

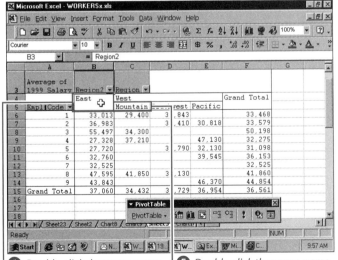

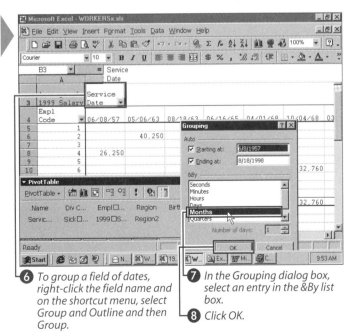

❹ Double-click the group name to hide the detail (East detail is hidden).

❺ Double-click the group name to reveal the detail (West detail is shown).

❻ To group a field of dates, right-click the field name and on the shortcut menu, select Group and Outline and then Group.

❼ In the Grouping dialog box, select an entry in the &By list box.

❽ Click OK.

Adding or Removing Fields

As you gain confidence in redesigning the layout of your pivot table, you will no doubt decide to remove a field to make your table clearer. At other times, it's just as necessary to add fields that you forgot or ones that you mistakenly removed. In any case, these capabilities will become part of your basic vocabulary as you become a proficient user of pivot tables.

Whenever the active cell is in your pivot table, the Pivot Table toolbar is on your screen. A Show/Hide button lets you see the field names in your database whenever you wish. You can drag a field name to your table at any time. If you attempt to drag a field name to your table and the field is already there on the column, row, or page axis, the axis that you drag the field to becomes the location of the field. Any existing occurrence of the field on another axis is eliminated. An exception to this is when you drag a numerical field to a column or row axis and it's already in the data area. In this case, it remains in both locations.

Usually, the numerical information that comprises most of your pivot table, located in the data area below the column axis and to the right of the row axis, is of one type, say, the total of one of your numerical fields. But you can also add additional fields there. In a database with fields for sales and quota, you might want to see the average sales and the average quota so that you can compare the two totals for each region.

TAKE NOTE

▶ ADDING DATA TO YOUR DATABSE

If you alter an entry in your database, it may have structural consequences in any pivot table based on it. After you make a change in the database, be sure to return to the pivot table and refresh your table. If the information you enter in a field is the first time that information has occurred there, updating your pivot table will cause new row(s) or column(s) to appear. A warning box will remind you that there are changes in the pivot table. Ironically, you don't get the warning if your change to the database is not a totally new entry.

▶ USING THE PAGE AXIS AS A HOLDING POINT

If you're about to remove a field from your pivot table report, but think that you might bring it back, you can drag it to the page axis. It won't affect the body of your report unless you select a detail from it. With the field parked there on the page axis, you can easily drag it back on to the table at any time.

CROSS-REFERENCE
Review the first task in this chapter for information on using the Layout screen to add and remove fields from a pivot table.

SHORTCUT
Press Alt+down arrow to display the field list of a selected field cell.

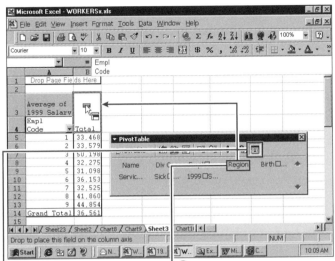

1 Click the Show/Hide fields button on the Pivot Table toolbar to reveal field names if they're not present.

2 To add a field to the pivot table, drag a field name to the row axis, column axis (shown), or page axis.

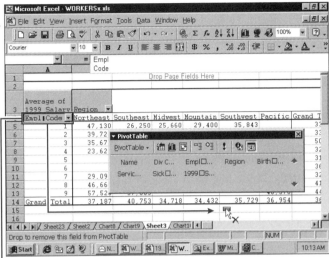

3 To remove a field from a pivot table report, drag the field name outside of the pivot table boundary. Release the mouse when the X appears.

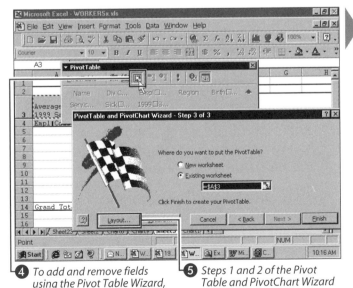

4 To add and remove fields using the Pivot Table Wizard, click the Pivot Table Wizard button in the Pivot Table toolbar.

5 Steps 1 and 2 of the Pivot Table and PivotChart Wizard are automatically skipped. In Step 3, click the Layout button.

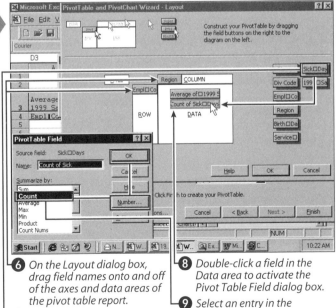

6 On the Layout dialog box, drag field names onto and off of the axes and data areas of the pivot table report.

7 Drag additional numerical fields to the Data area if desired.

8 Double-click a field in the Data area to activate the Pivot Table Field dialog box.

9 Select an entry in the Summarize by box; click the Number button to adjust numeric format; click OK.

275

Displaying Pivot Table Data in a Pivot Chart

After you have created a useful pivot table and refined its appearance, you may want to display its information as a chart. Some of the same techniques you may have learned about charting worksheet data will apply when you create a chart from a pivot table. A new aspect of charting, available for the first time in this version of Excel, is that pivot table charting springs from the Pivot Table command and toolbar, not from standard Excel usage. This is an interesting development because it builds on one of the basic operational methods of pivot tables — dragging fields — and applies it to the building of charts.

An intriguing aspect of pivot table charting is that you can create a pivot chart without creating the pivot table first, but pivot charts must be linked to a pivot table. So you can actually start creating a chart without necessarily seeing that you have a pivot table report being created simultaneously. The pivot table chart and the pivot table remain in sync with each other at all times. If you focus on your report and move fields back and forth to different axes, the corresponding action will occur on the pivot chart simultaneously. Switch to your pivot chart and move data there and your pivot table report reacts immediately. This is quite different from standard Excel chart usage, where changes to your chart do not affect the source worksheet data unless you're moving data points or column edges. If you favor analyzing information visually, rather than numerically, creating the pivot chart directly from your database may be more appealing than creating the pivot table report first and the pivot chart later.

If you have created your pivot table and need to create a chart, the familiar Chart Wizard button is available, but there's no interaction with it. You will automatically get a pivot chart that's a stacked column chart of the data currently in your pivot table report, no questions asked.

TAKE NOTE

A CHART SERIES IS A REPORT COLUMN AXIS

When you move a database field to the column axis in your pivot table report, the corresponding action on the chart is that each of the entries in the field becomes a series in the pivot chart and an item in the chart's legend. If you move a field to the row axis in your pivot table, the corresponding action on the chart is that each of the entries in the field becomes a point on the category (X) axis in the pivot chart.

GROUPING DATA ON A CHART

To group field items on a chart, right-click a field name in the pivot chart and select Group and Outline and then select Group. This is identical to the action you take in the pivot table report.

CROSS-REFERENCE

Review charting capabilities in Chapters 12.

SHORTCUT

Create a pivot chart instantly by simply selecting a cell in your pivot table and pressing the F11 key.

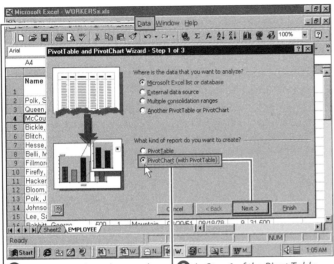

1 To create a pivot chart and pivot table together, select Data ⇨ Pivot Table ⇨ Pivot Chart Report.

2 In Step 1 of the Pivot Table and Pivot Chart Wizard dialog box, click the PivotChart radio button and then click the Next button.

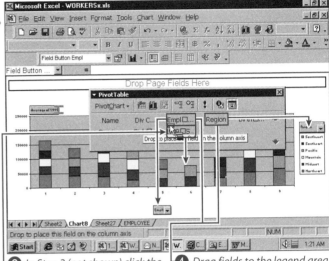

3 In Step 2 (not shown) click the Next button and in Step 3 (not shown) click the Finish button. In the PivotTable Window, drag a numerical field onto the plot area.

4 Drag fields to the legend area to create series data and to the box below the category (X) axis to create category data.

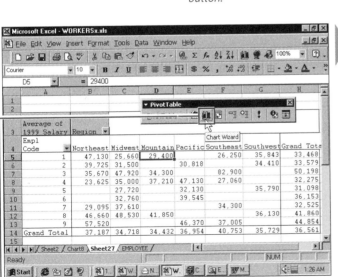

5 To create a pivot chart from a previously started pivot table, click the Chart Wizard button in the Pivot Table toolbar.

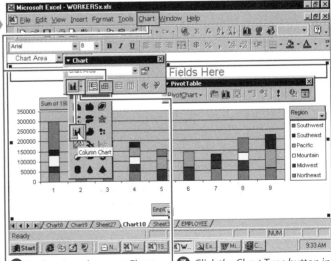

6 In the pivot chart, use Chart commands and Chart toolbar buttons as needed.

7 Click the Chart Type button in the Chart toolbar to choose a style different to the default stacked column chart.

Personal Workbook

Q&A

1 True or False: When you make a change to a pivot table's source data, the pivot table reacts automatically.

_____

_____

2 Do you need to sort your database before you create a pivot table report from it?

_____

_____

_____

3 When you attempt to group some of a numerical field's entries in a pivot table, what onscreen help do you get?

_____

_____

_____

4 What happens when you double-click a group name?

_____

_____

_____

_____

5 True or False: If you drag a field onto a pivot chart, the underlying pivot table does not change.

_____

_____

_____

6 If a field's entries in a pivot table are not in alphabetical or numerical order, how do you sort them?

_____

_____

_____

_____

7 How do you leave out some of a field's entries on a pivot table?

_____

_____

_____

_____

_____

_____

ANSWERS: PAGE 330

EXTRA PRACTICE

① In an existing pivot table, drag a column axis field to the row axis. Drag a row axis field to the column axis.

② Drag a data field onto a pivot table's row or column axis, then group it by months.

③ Follow the previous step by grouping the dates by quarters also.

④ Format your pivot table with the Format Report button on the Pivot Table toolbar.

⑤ In a pivot table report, jump to Step 3 of the Pivot Table Wizard, choose Layout and remove, add, and move fields there.

REAL-WORLD APPLICATIONS

✔ Rather that creating a new column in your database to show months from an adjacent column of full dates, you create a pivot table report, add the date field to a column or row axis, and group the dates by month.

✔ The Data Filter command doesn't let you quickly see just three of your six regions, so you create a pivot table report and pick just these three regions to appear in the region field.

✔ You just assumed responsibility for a 2000 record database. To help understand it faster, you create a pivot table report from it and manipulate fields to analyze its content.

✔ Since most of your presentation needs are for charts, you routinely create a pivot chart and pivot table together.

Visual Quiz

In the screen shown to the right, which button do you click to select only Div Codes 400, 500, and 600 to be shown? Which button do you click to select only the Southeast and Southwest regions to be shown? How do you move the Mountain column to the right of the Southwest column?

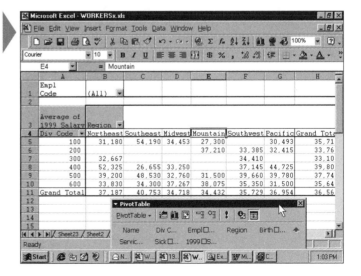

Contents of 'Desktop'

Name

My Computer

Network Neigh

Internet Explore

Microsoft Outloo

Recycle Bin

My Briefcase

3252-9

3259-6

3261-8

3262-6

3281-2

3286-3

DE Phone List

Device Manager

In

Iomega Tools

PART

V

Advanced Excel Skills

For more sophisticated use of Excel, you need to recognize its relationship with other software packages, its ability to mesh with Internet resources, and how you can write Visual Basic routines to take some actions not available through your regular use of Excel's menus and toolbar buttons.

It is no longer unusual to share and link information between two kinds of software that serve different purposes. A report you're writing in Word may be concerned with the quarterly report you're preparing in Excel, so you need an accurate image of your worksheet in your report. Either by copying or linking, you associate the two kinds of software in a productive way.

With Internet and intranet usage expanding rapidly, you should know how to set up links to Web sites, how to create Web pages from inside Excel, and ways to download data into your worksheets.

As a time-saver and as a provider of new programming-like capabilities, you may well want to explore the possibility of using Excel macros. Macros can reduce the amount of time spent repeating common command sequences and creating procedures that cannot be done through regular Excel features.

CHAPTER 17

MASTER
THESE
SKILLS

▶ **Importing Files from Other Software**

▶ **Exporting Files to Other File Formats**

▶ **Linking Workbooks**

▶ **Using Cut, Copy, and Paste with Other Applications**

Importing, Exporting, and Linking Files

Any time you get data from another source, or send data to another user, you need to think out the issues of conversion and compatibility. Excel, part of the Microsoft Office suite of packages, has a number of useful features that make the transporting of files relatively smooth. Because Excel is one of the most widely used software packages, many other kinds of software create files that can be read by Excel. As much as possible, you want to avoid the time-consuming and error-prone nature of data entry, even though Excel has techniques to minimize those problems.

Naturally, when you import data from another file that was created with a different spreadsheet software package, you'll have an easier time than when you import from a word processing or database file. Similar observations can be made about exporting your Excel files to other formats. An additional concern here is that when dealing with database software, you may need to go through the conversion process a worksheet at a time.

You need to be concerned not only about files but also about ranges of data, and ways to copy, cut, and paste smaller amounts of information. Whether you're thinking about copying a single worksheet or a just a range of cells, some of the standard copy and paste techniques you've been using will suffice.

A variation on the concept of cut and paste is the idea that you may want to keep a link between two files after you copy information from one and paste it into the other. Maintaining a relationship between the two files requires some vigilance about where the files are stored and whether you decide to rename them. The value in this arrangement is that if you change the source data in one file, the dependent workbook is updated, although, you need to learn the rules about how and when those updates occur.

Linked workbooks can be fairly easy to establish and maintain, but they can be more sophisticated and complex if you deal with multiple links using more than two workbooks. You can also consider the possibility of having multiple levels of linking, whereby, certain workbooks depend on other workbooks for some of their data and these supporting workbooks, in turn, may themselves depend on other workbooks for some of their data.

Importing Files from Other Software

Normally, when you open a file in Excel, the default file type is an Excel workbook (a file with the extension xls), and you rarely need to change that. However, often you will need to get to the data that's inside one of the many other kinds of files that exist.

Excel can open files created in other spreadsheet packages, such as Lotus 1-2-3 and Quattro Pro. Later releases of those software packages may include newer file types that Excel is not able to open. Other file types that Excel can open include SYLK (Symbolic Link) files, DBF (dBASE standard) files, and DIF (Data Interchange Format) files. Excel can also open all the various file standards used in previous versions of Excel, extending back into the 1980s.

The use of database software is on an increase, so you may need to open files created in Microsoft Access or another database package. Although Excel does not have the ability to handle some of the huge tables that exist in, say, an Access file, Excel has superior analytical tools. Therefore, it might make sense, if you're in an environment where both packages are used, to become familiar with the ways you can share the data.

In addition, many files from different sources are created in Text format. This format has been around many years, but it's still widely used and nearly every software package has some way to save files in that format. You can open text files using the File ⇨ Open command or by selecting Data ⇨ Get External Data ⇨ Import Text File. In either case, you get the Text Import Wizard. The wizard guides you through a series of steps, which structure and format the data so that it becomes a functional worksheet in a file that you can then save as an Excel workbook.

TAKE NOTE

▶ EXPORTING AN ACCESS TABLE TO AN EXCEL FILE

In Access, you can export a table (which is data in columns and rows and looks like a database in Excel) to an Excel file. From there, it's a simple matter to open that Excel file, make changes and additions to it, and save it again. A feature in Access called Analyze it with MS Excel is even better (and faster). It creates an Excel file from an Access table and opens Excel with the newly created file.

▶ SINGLE-COLUMN DATA

Occasionally, you may import a text file that's not delimited — all data ends up in column A but needs to be parsed into multiple columns. In this situation, you may need to rely on the Data Text to Columns command, which leads you through a process similar to the Text Import Wizard. If you're adept at Excel's text functions, use them to parse your data.

CROSS-REFERENCE
Review "Finding and Opening Workbooks" in Chapter 4.

FIND IT ONLINE
Learn all about importing (from the US Customs perspective) at **http://sys1.tpusa.com/dir01/imprtgui/.**

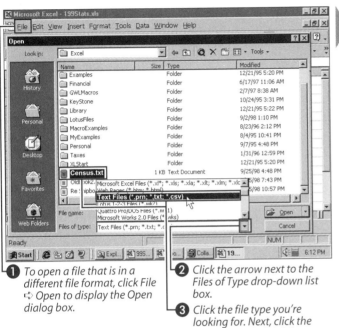

1 To open a file that is in a different file format, click File ⇨ Open to display the Open dialog box.

2 Click the arrow next to the Files of Type drop-down list box.

3 Click the file type you're looking for. Next, click the filename and click OK.

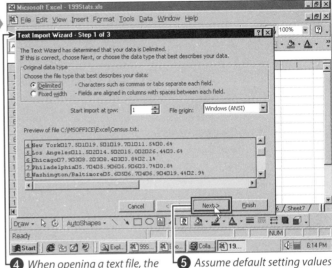

4 When opening a text file, the three-step Text Import Wizard appears.

5 Assume default setting values are correct unless you know otherwise. Click the Next button and proceed through the next two wizard steps.

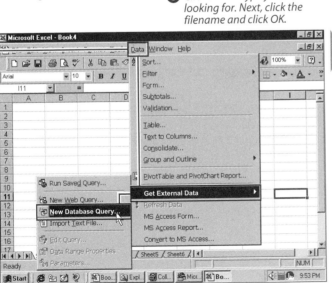

6 To import an Access table to an Excel worksheet, select Data ⇨ Get External Data.

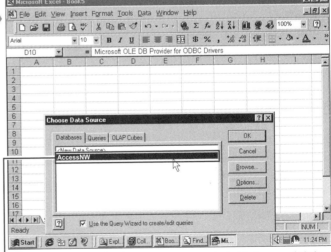

7 Click the Access database you want to get a table from and click OK. Subsequent steps will give you a choice of tables and fields to import.

Exporting Files to Other File Formats

Whenever you need to save your Excel workbook in a format that other software packages can handle, you have a wealth of options. The very first point to consider, though, is the fact that many other software packages can read Excel files, so, you may not need to save your Excel file in another format.

You will have some conversion problems with numeric formats because certain Excel formats have no corresponding format. Similar problems will exist with functions. Additionally, there is not a one-to-one relationship between every Excel function and every function in Lotus 1-2-3 and Quattro Pro. You may want to simplify some functions, where possible. Excel does convert some functions into values during the conversion process. Range names that refer to values in Excel are converted to pure values in most conversions.

Other potential problems that may arise when attempting to save your workbook in other file types are that macros are ignored, pivot tables become pure values, and large worksheets may get truncated if they exceed the row limit of the destination file type. When you save an Excel file as a DBF file, only the data from one worksheet is saved.

You should have little difficulty saving files to older versions of Excel, but you will get warnings about which features will not be translated. Converting to Macintosh files involves few problems, but be aware of the 1904 date standard, commonly used in Mac Excel files, in contrast to the 1900 standard used in Windows Excel files. When comparing dates on two files using different date standards, be aware of the potential inaccuracy. You should also check to see whether or not two-digit years get treated as twentieth or twenty-first century years.

TAKE NOTE

SENDING A WORKSHEET TO ACCESS

If you're an Access user, or need to save an Excel workbook in that format, you have a special command and wizard procedure available to ease the conversion. To use this feature, you must first install Access Links. Do this by clicking the Tools menu, selecting Add-ins, checking the Access Links box, and clicking OK. Thereafter, you can select Data ⇨ Convert to MS Access.

CONVERSION DOESN'T THROW AWAY THE ORIGINAL

When you convert a file into another file type, you don't throw away the original. At this point you have two files. One is an Excel file and the other is a version of the same file in a different file type.

CROSS-REFERENCE
Review the File ⇨ Save As command in Chapter 4.

SHORTCUT
Activate the File ⇨ Save As command with the F12 key.

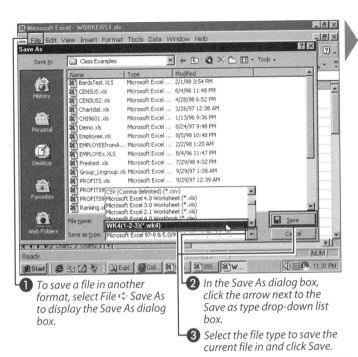

❶ To save a file in another format, select File ⇨ Save As to display the Save As dialog box.

❷ In the Save As dialog box, click the arrow next to the Save as type drop-down list box.

❸ Select the file type to save the current file in and click Save.

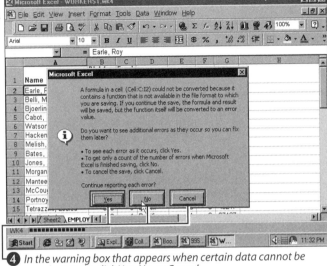

❹ In the warning box that appears when certain data cannot be saved properly, click Yes, No, or Cancel.

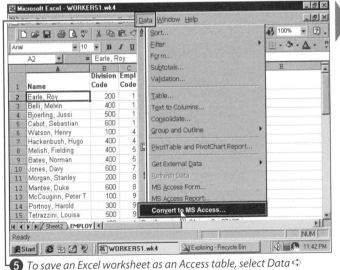

❺ To save an Excel worksheet as an Access table, select Data ⇨ Convert to MS Access.

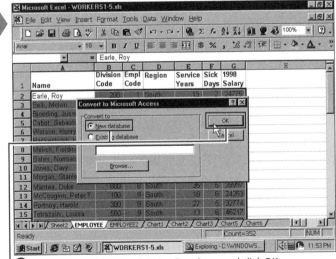

❻ Click New Database or Existing Database and click OK.

Linking Workbooks

If you've got related data in different workbooks, you probably gave some thought to consolidating the workbooks into fewer files or even one file. However, there can be good reasons for keeping data segregated. Sometimes you need to keep files from getting too large — large files can become inefficient users of system memory and sluggish as you use them. If you're in an environment where different people may be responsible for regional files and a master workbook needs information from each of them, you should set up links between these workbooks.

A link is nothing more than a formula with one or more external references. You can set up links in a number of different ways, but the most important aspect of this concept is that all relevant files should be stored either in a common or stable place. Although Excel has a way for you to redirect links to a different workbook or location when necessary, it's an action you should take sparingly because of the opportunity for error. See the Take Note section for further information regarding the renaming of linked files.

To establish links between workbooks, you need to open all of the relevant files, but once those links are set up, you need only open the dependent workbook — the one that gets data from one or more other workbooks. A workbook that serves as a source of data in this kind of arrangement is called a source or supporting workbook. When you open a dependent file, you are given the opportunity to update the links then or to do it later. Whenever you do the updating, Excel needs to find the supporting file(s), so it's critical that source file(s) be available, but they don't need to be open. When updating occurs, Excel does not open supporting workbooks. It's not uncommon to update source workbooks at an earlier session, rather than when you open and update a dependent workbook.

TAKE NOTE

▶ UPDATING LINKS WITH WORKBOOKS CLOSED

To update the links to a dependent workbook that you're currently using, select Edit ⇨ Links. Even though you're most likely to do updating when you open a dependent workbook, if, say, another user on your network is updating one of your source workbooks, using the Link command will insure that your file is as current as the last saved version of the source file.

▶ REDIRECTING A LINK

If you have a dependent file and source file both open, and you save the source file under a new name, the dependent workbook immediately changes its references to the new source filename. But, if you change the name of a source file when the dependent workbook is not open, you've severed the link. You need to use the Edit ⇨ Links command to reestablish the link to the new filename.

CROSS-REFERENCE

Find out about the pivot table's grouping capability in "Grouping and Ungrouping Data" in chapter 6.

SHORTCUT

Check out **http://www.roolfreebielinks.com/cfl/ freebies.htm** and find links to free stuff on the Internet.

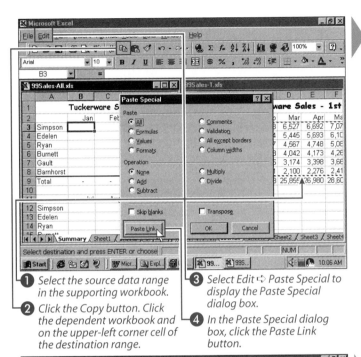

1 Select the source data range in the supporting workbook.

2 Click the Copy button. Click the dependent workbook and on the upper-left corner cell of the destination range.

3 Select Edit ⇨ Paste Special to display the Paste Special dialog box.

4 In the Paste Special dialog box, click the Paste Link button.

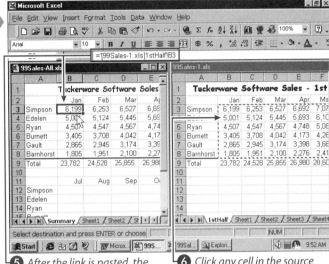

5 After the link is pasted, the active cell shows the linkage formula.

6 Click any cell in the source workbook and change it. The dependent workbook responds immediately.

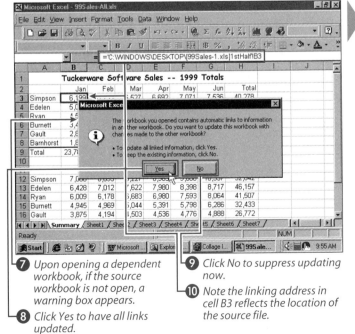

7 Upon opening a dependent workbook, if the source workbook is not open, a warning box appears.

8 Click Yes to have all links updated.

9 Click No to suppress updating now.

10 Note the linking address in cell B3 reflects the location of the source file.

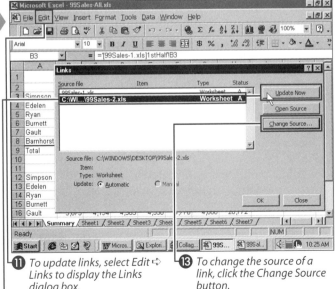

11 To update links, select Edit ⇨ Links to display the Links dialog box.

12 In the Links dialog box, select a link and click the Update Now button.

13 To change the source of a link, click the Change Source button.

Using Cut, Copy, and Paste with Other Applications

One of the best time-saving features available in the Windows environment is the ease with which you can transport data across applications. Whether you're simply copying and pasting information from one workbook to another, or creating a link between workbooks, as was shown in the previous task, the benefits are immediately apparent in the saved retyping effort and the improved accuracy.

But don't limit these activities to Excel only. If you're using Word to write a narrative about your latest marketing effort, you may want to have part of an Excel worksheet, showing monthly projections, in your report. You can copy and paste the range of cells into your Word file and effectively get either an image or a copy of the information.

You should address two other considerations when you're about to copy data into another application. First, you can set up a link between the two files so that if you change any of the cells in the copied range in your Excel workbook, your Word file will reflect the change. It's almost the same as linking workbooks. It's your responsibility to make sure that you don't move or rename your Excel workbook without updating the link in Word. Second, is to copy information from Excel and embed it into the other software. Using this technique, the pasted data is not linked to the source, but if you double-click the data, Excel commands and toolbars help you to manipulate the data.

You can also use copy and paste to bring information into Excel, choosing merely to paste information, to maintain a link (when you change information in the other file, it will change in Excel also), or to embed the information in Excel. In the latter, you can double-click the pasted information and activate the other software's commands and toolbars.

TAKE NOTE

▶ EDITING LINKS

In Word, you edit links in virtually exactly the same way as you do in Excel. If your Word file is dependent on data from Excel workbooks and you need to update the links using the Word commands, click the Edit menu and select Links. Click the Update Now button; also go to this command when you either move the source Excel workbook or rename it. Otherwise, Word's link to the Excel data is lost.

▶ MAINTAINING CURRENT PRESENTATIONS

If you use PowerPoint, previous descriptions about Word also apply. It means that if you choose to have links to your Excel workbooks, your presentations can have information in them that's current at all times. If you embed the Excel data in PowerPoint, you won't have the link but you can double-click the Excel data and make data and formatting changes.

CROSS-REFERENCE
Review Chapter 6 for cut, copy, and paste techniques.

SHORTCUT
With two workbooks displayed on your screen, you can drag data from one workbook to another. Use the Ctrl key to ensure that it's a copy; otherwise, it's a move.

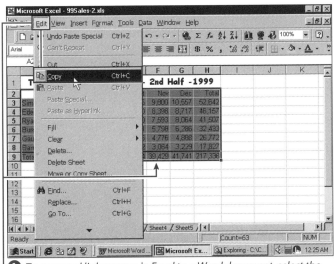

❶ To copy and link a range in Excel to a Word document, select the range, next, choose the Edit ⇨ Copy command.

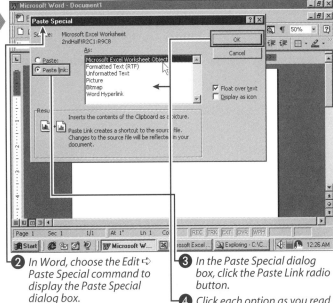

❷ In Word, choose the Edit ⇨ Paste Special command to display the Paste Special dialog box.

❸ In the Paste Special dialog box, click the Paste Link radio button.

❹ Click each option as you read the description; select one and click OK.

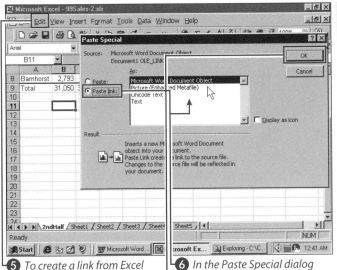

❺ To create a link from Excel into Word, select the text in Word, and choose the Edit ⇨ Copy command. Next, in Excel, choose the Edit ⇨ Paste Special command.

❻ In the Paste Special dialog box, click the Paste Link radio button.

❼ Click each selection and read the description; select one and click OK.

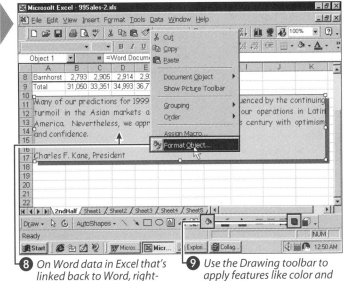

❽ On Word data in Excel that's linked back to Word, right-click the Word data and select Format Object from the shortcut menu.

❾ Use the Drawing toolbar to apply features like color and shadows.

Personal Workbook

Q&A

1 True or False: You can open a text file without using the File ⇨ Open command.

_____

_____

_____

_____

2 If you open a workbook that is dependent on a second workbook, does the second workbook need to be open also for data updating to occur?

_____

_____

_____

_____

3 When you change a cell in a supporting workbook does the dependent workbook get updated immediately?

_____

_____

_____

_____

4 Do formulas in an Excel file get saved when you save the file as a DBF file?

_____

_____

_____

_____

5 True or False: When you save your current Excel workbook as Lotus 1-2-3 file, you lose your Excel version of the file.

_____

_____

_____

_____

6 Which command do you use to reestablish a severed link?

_____

_____

_____

_____

ANSWERS: PAGE 331

EXTRA PRACTICE

1. Save an Excel file as a Lotus WK4 file and then close it. Open the WK4 file in Excel.

2. With two separate workbooks open, copy data from one, and paste a link in the other using the Edit ⇨ Paste Special command.

3. Change the name of a workbook that's a supporting file. Open the dependent file and observe the error message. Reestablish the link by using the Edit ⇨ Links command in the dependent workbook.

4. In a dependent workbook, use the Edit ⇨ Find command to locate all occurrences of the exclamation point (!) to find all cells with links.

REAL-WORLD APPLICATIONS

✔ You need to convert a group of Lotus 1-2-3 files to Excel files, so you open each Lotus file in Excel and save it as an Excel file.

✔ Three people on your staff maintain three regional workbooks. You're responsible for the company-wide consolidation file that's dependent on the regional files. Updates are done when needed. When you open the consolidation file, you see the latest data from all regions. All files are stored on the same server.

✔ Although you use Excel's Text Import Wizard to handle text files coming into Excel, you also use the text functions to parse data.

Visual Quiz

In the screen shown at the right, name the source workbook for the dependent workbook shown. Name the source worksheet. Where is the source file located?

_____

_____

_____

_____

_____

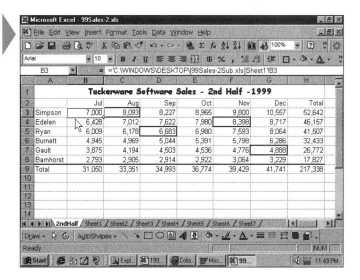

CHAPTER 18

MASTER
THESE
SKILLS

▶ **Creating an Internet Document**

▶ **Creating Hyperlinks to Web Sites**

▶ **Viewing the Web from Excel**

▶ **Getting Data from the Web**

Hyperlinks and the Internet

The Internet has been with us for many years but it's only been since the mid-1990s that a groundswell of interest and subsequent usage has had its impact on software such as Excel and other office productivity tools.

The World Wide Web (the Web) has rapidly become one of the most popular features on the Internet. It's a system of finding and using Internet files and programs. With the Web, you can follow links from documents on one computer to documents on others. The Web uses HTML (Hypertext Markup Language), which lets you view files in a graphical format. A Web site, which typically refers to a home page and other linked pages, has become the centerpiece of many companies' operations. Many older businesses are finding that they are considered out of the mainstream if they don't have a Web site for marketing their products and services and handling orders and deliveries.

Within companies, an intranet serves a similar purpose. A company's intranet serves as the conduit for e-mail, and increasingly, as a giant billboard for posting items of interest to employees.

Using Excel and the other software components in Office 2000, you can convert your workbooks, documents, and presentations into HTML format, making them suitable for display as Web pages. When you save a workbook as an HTML file, you have the opportunity to create static or interactive pages. A challenge for many users is creating appealing pages that retain their informative content yet don't overload the screen with too much detail.

You can embed links to Web sites in your Excel workbook, making it possible to view important information and quickly return to your workbook. These hyperlinks open the door to new ways of using Excel because the links to the Internet can just as easily be links to your company's intranet or to other files on your network. Using a function called Hyperlink, you can set up variable links, perhaps using the IF or VLOOKUP function to jump to different Web sites based on the result of a formula or some other worksheet condition.

Creating an Internet Document

If you have an Excel workbook that others need access to — either to view or to make contributions to — you can publish the workbook on a Web page. To do this, you need to convert it into an HTML document and make it available on your company's intranet or on the World Wide Web.

If your worksheet is being prepared primarily for others to view and not alter, you can save it in a way that prohibits interaction; viewers will be able to copy it or download it to their computers as a picture. This kind of status is referred to as static.

If you save your file in HTML format with interactivity allowed, you will have some choices regarding the level of interactivity. You can allow interactivity at a high level, called Spreadsheet functionality, wherein users can actually change cell content, sort, use the filter commands, enter new calculations, adjust formatting, and alter formulas. With Pivot Table functionality, you give users the ability to manipulate pivot tables but not to alter the original data. Chart functionality enables viewers to change the underlying data that the chart is based on.

If you create an HTML document in Word or PowerPoint (using procedures nearly identical to those in Excel), you can add data from Excel into that document.

Prior to actually uploading your HTML document to the Web site or intranet site, you may want to see how it will appear in those environments. You can do this by opening your Web browser and viewing it as it would appear as a Web page, or by using the Web Page Preview directly in Excel. However, slight differences do exist between browsers in terms of the appearance of your HTML document.

TAKE NOTE

WORKBOOKS, WORKSHEETS, AND INTERACTIVITY

If you put an entire workbook on a Web page, you cannot save it with interactive functionality — viewers cannot make changes to the workbook. If you want interactivity, you need to save either cell ranges or worksheets separately. If you attempt to save a worksheet that has an embedded chart on it, the chart does not get included when you save the file as a Web page. Save a chart separately if you want to put it on a Web page.

WHAT IS HTML?

Literally, HTML is Hypertext Markup Language, the programming format that's the standard for all Web pages. As with macros, you can be quite productive without learning the elements of this language, although, it's considered rather easy to learn. Web browsers, such as Microsoft Internet Explorer and Netscape Navigator, can read files created in the HTML format. In Explorer, you can view the HTML code if you click View and select Source.

CROSS-REFERENCE
Review saving files in Chapter 4.

FIND IT ONLINE
Learn how to create your own Web site at **http://www. geocities.com/sotto/9272/webomat.htm**.

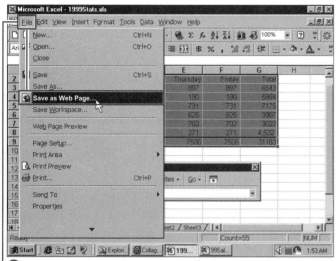

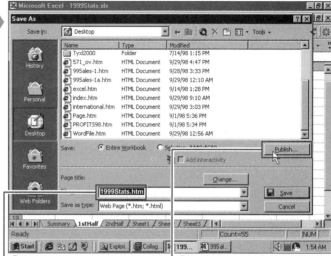

1 To save the current workbook as a Web page, select File ⇨ Save as Web Page.

2 In the Save As dialog box, accept or alter the filename as needed (keeping the htm file extension).

3 Click the Publish button if you need to add interactivity.

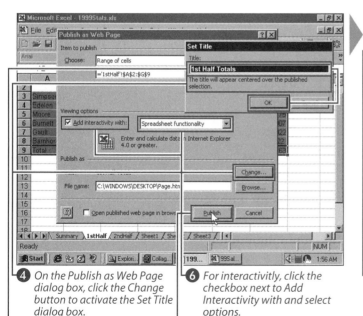

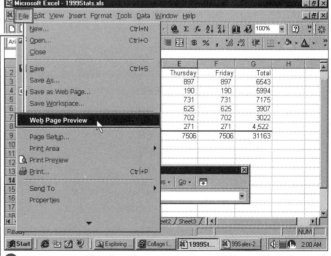

4 On the Publish as Web Page dialog box, click the Change button to activate the Set Title dialog box.

5 Enter a title in the Set Title dialog box and click OK.

6 For interactivily, click the checkbox next to Add Interactivity with and select options.

7 Click the Publish button to complete the save operation.

8 To view a workbook as if it were a Web page, choose the File ⇨ Web Page Preview command.

Creating Hyperlinks to Web Sites

If you want to provide a rapid connection between your Excel workbook and an Internet or intranet site, you need to establish a hyperlink to the external site. In effect, what you do is list the address of the Internet or intranet location in a worksheet cell so that anytime you point and click it, you jump to the site. A hyperlink is not really a way to transmit information to a Web page, it's really a navigation tool, a way to jump to a different location.

When using an Excel workbook, I'm sure you can imagine a lot of situations where it would be appropriate to be able to jump to an internal or external Web site to view some related information. You could then copy and paste information from one of these sites into your Excel workbook or into a Word document. If the information that you copy contains links to other sites, you can click them to jump to their locations.

A hyperlink is not restricted to external sites alone. You can also use it to link to a document on your company's intranet, to an Excel file on your hard drive or shared network location, to a location in the current workbook, or even to an address on the current worksheet. However, it's different from linking files via formulas. A hyperlink in an Excel workbook is merely a pointer to another location. If that location is another Excel workbook or a Word document, when you point and click the cell containing the link, you open the file.

Reflecting the increasing importance of hyperlinks among Excel users, Excel offers you four ways to create a hyperlink. The four ways are: the Insert ⇨ Hyperlink command, the Hyperlink command on the shortcut menu (available when you right-click a cell), the Ctrl+k keystroke shortcut, and a function named Hyperlink.

In addition to creating a hyperlink from a cell, you can also associate a hyperlink with Excel objects, such as WordArt, Clip Art, pictures, and drawing objects from the Drawing toolbar.

TAKE NOTE

▶ EDITING A HYPERLINK

Point to a hyperlink and the mouse pointer looks like an index finger pointer. Click to jump to the link, but if you want to edit the cell display, use the keyboard to position the active cell at the hyperlink and click the formula bar. Now you can edit the cell display. If you point to the cell, a pop-up address appears showing you the hyperlink unchanged.

▶ THE HYPERLINK FUNCTION

With your knowledge of other Excel functions such as IF and VLOOKUP, you can create nested functions with the Hyperlink function and create a variable jump to a link. For example, you could use: =Hyperlink(If(J1>L1,N7,P7),"Higher Score") to jump to a link that's listed in cell N7 or P7.

CROSS-REFERENCE

For more information about linking through formulas, see Chapter 10.

FIND IT ONLINE

Looking for hyperlinks to employment sites on the Web? Check out **http://www.ceweekly.com/ helpful/joblinks.html**.

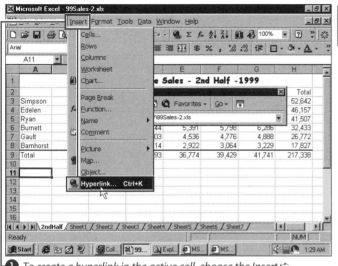

1 To create a hyperlink in the active cell, choose the Insert ⇨ Hyperlink command.

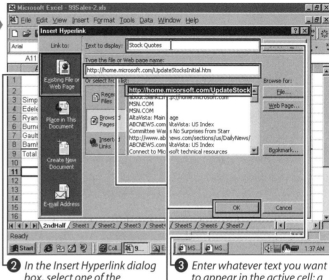

2 In the Insert Hyperlink dialog box, select one of the destination categories in the Link to section.

3 Enter whatever text you want to appear in the active cell; a Web address, for example.

4 Type the destination file or Web page name or select from the list and click OK.

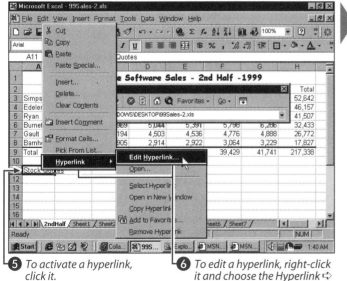

5 To activate a hyperlink, click it.

6 To edit a hyperlink, right-click it and choose the Hyperlink ⇨ Edit Hyperlink command. A dialog box like the one shown in step 2 appears.

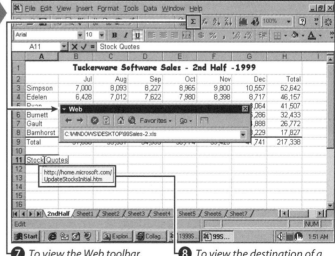

7 To view the Web toolbar, right-click any toolbar button and select Web from the list of choices.

8 To view the destination of a hyperlink without activating it, point to the hyperlink and observe the pop-up indicator.

Viewing the Web from Excel

Y ou can't help but notice the plethora of articles in the popular press about the Internet and its endless supply of information. With the increasing awareness of the unlimited resources available on the World Wide Web, the desire to see some of these treasures has turned into a need for many users. The Web gives you access to a ton of data, whatever kind of business you're involved in.

Rather than stepping outside of Excel to get to these resources, you can access Web sites while using Excel. The ability to move freely from Excel to intranet and Internet sites offers new possibilities for viewing and gathering information from thousands (soon to be millions) of sites. As you gain proficiency in moving from site to site, and absorb the concept of readily available information in diverse locations, you can apply some of the same principles to your own local area network or server.

One of the many toolbars available in Excel is the Web toolbar, which can be activated at any time. Although its name and buttons suggest its primary use — to navigate to and from the Web — you can use it also for jumping back and forth through your exploration of Web pages, intranet sites, and Excel workbooks.

One of the most useful aspects of Internet use is the way in which you can search for information. If you've used the Web toolbar to get your Web startup page, you can access a number of popular search sites to begin looking. Each has its particular strengths. One might be more comprehensive in one subject area over the others. Some are faster at finding what you need, whereas others might return more possible sites. For the most part, you use the same kind of logical statement to structure your requests and they each have onscreen tips and help screens.

TAKE NOTE

JUMPING BACK

When you click a hyperlink and you jump to the new location, you can later return to the previous site by clicking the left arrow in the Web toolbar.

OPENING EXCEL FILES WHILE BROWSING

If you become a regular Internet or intranet user, you can open an Excel workbook (saved in HTML format) using the File ⇨ Open command of Microsoft Internet Explorer or Netscape Navigator. The file opens without switching you back to Excel and Excel need not be open for this to work. Excel toolbars and the Excel menu enable you to work with your workbook, make changes, and save it as an Excel file, all the time within the Explorer environment.

CROSS-REFERENCE
See Chapter 10 to review how worksheets in a workbook are linked.

FIND IT ONLINE
Check out Browser Tips for Best Viewing the Web at http://www.netphoria.com/browsers.htm.

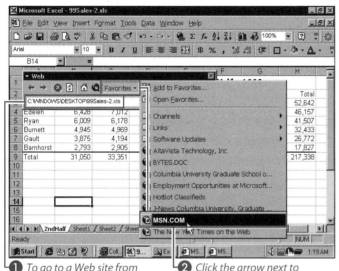

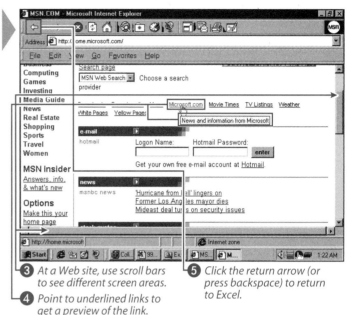

1 To go to a Web site from Excel, type a Web address in the toolbar and press enter.

2 Click the arrow next to Favorites on the Web toolbar and select one of the sites you visit frequently.

3 At a Web site, use scroll bars to see different screen areas.

4 Point to underlined links to get a preview of the link.

5 Click the return arrow (or press backspace) to return to Excel.

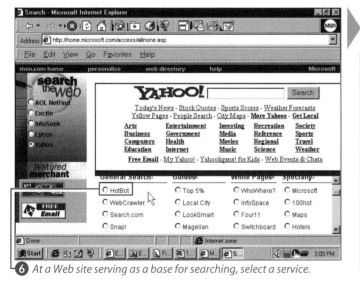

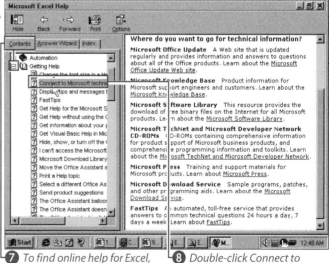

6 At a Web site serving as a base for searching, select a service.

7 To find online help for Excel, choose the Help ⮕ Microsoft Excel Help command. Click the Contents tab and then click the plus (+) sign next to Getting Help.

8 Double-click Connect to Microsoft technical resources. To go directly to online help from Excel, select the Help ⮕ Office on the Web command.

301

Getting Data from the Web

In the 80s, software packages tended to be stand-alone creatures, with each devoted to one general kind of activity. It was difficult to copy information created in one type of software into another type. Efforts to create all-purpose software just didn't pan out too smoothly. By the early 90s and the evolution of Windows usage, software was increasingly designed with the idea that information should be more easily shared amongst the components of a suite of packages.

The trend toward the free-flow of data has accelerated with the burgeoning use of the Internet and company intranets. Today, information can be gathered from a Web site, copied into an Excel workbook, and perhaps then pasted as a link into a Word document, which could have hyperlinks to a different Web site.

After you've become adept at exploring the World Wide Web (and it doesn't take much time), you will become more than just interested in viewing what's out there. You'll find information pertinent to your business, hobby, or pastime that you'll want to download into a Word document or an Excel workbook.

Downloading information from the Web is straightforward and uncomplicated. In fact, sometimes just a simple copy using keystroke shortcuts or menu commands (that you may have been using for some time anyway) will get you the Web data you need so that you can paste it into your Excel workbook.

You can also download Web information to an HTML file and, at a later time perhaps, open that HTML file in Excel as if you were opening a workbook.

TAKE NOTE

▶ ONLINE HELP

Need more help but can't find what you want in the Help menu? From the Help menu select Office on the Web. This leads to Microsoft's help site on the Web that has tons of tips not built in to Excel's help menu. Since this is an online dynamic site, a good deal of the help is recent and may reflect the latest techniques for solving the problems you need help on. It will also keep you informed on new problems and fixes related to the most recent version of the software.

▶ NEED MORE CLIP ART?

No matter how many clip art images you have, it seems as if you always need more. When you click the Clip Art image in the Drawing toolbar, the Insert Clip Art dialog box appears. In its Web-like toolbar, is the Clips Online button. Click it to go to the Clip Gallery Live (http://www.microsoft.com/clipgallerylive/default.asp?ea=1) where you will find thousands of clip art images and the instructions on how to download the ones you want.

CROSS-REFERENCE
Review Chapter 6 for cut, copy, and paste techniques.

FIND IT ONLINE
For more information on downloading from the Web, see: **http://webnovice.com.**

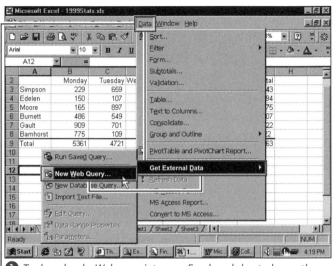

❶ To download a Web page into your Excel worksheet, choose the Data ➪ Get External Data ➪ New Web Query command.

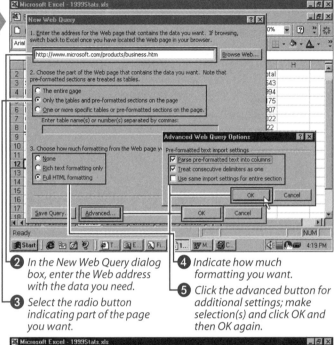

❷ In the New Web Query dialog box, enter the Web address with the data you need.

❸ Select the radio button indicating part of the page you want.

❹ Indicate how much formatting you want.

❺ Click the advanced button for additional settings; make selection(s) and click OK and then OK again.

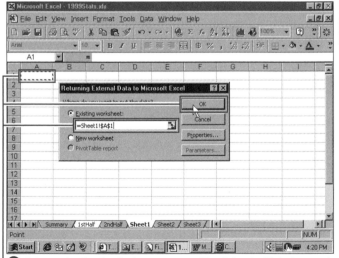

❻ Select a destination in the current workbook for the Web data and click OK.

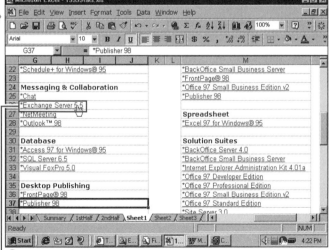

❼ In the downloaded example in Excel, click a link to jump to that site.

Personal Workbook

Q&A

1 True or False: A hyperlink is used only for access to Internet or intranet sites.

_____

_____

_____

2 How do you get online help for Excel?

_____

_____

_____

3 How do you find additional downloadable clip art images?

_____

_____

_____

4 How do you save your workbook as an HTML file?

_____

_____

_____

5 True or False: From Excel you can set up a Web page that's interactive.

_____

_____

_____

6 Can you assign a hyperlink to an object or picture?

_____

_____

_____

_____

ANSWERS: PAGE 322

EXTRA PRACTICE

① Create a hyperlink to another workbook.

② Jump to a Web site from the Web toolbar by typing in a Web site address.

③ Create an object on your worksheet. Enter text in it describing a link and then assign a hyperlink to it.

④ Create a hyperlink to a search engine (Altavista, Infoseek, Excite, Hotbot, etc.).

⑤ Compare these two ways of editing what's displayed in the cell where a hyperlink is located:

▶ Using the arrow keys, position the active cell on a hyperlink and click in the formula bar.
▶ Right-click a Hyperlink and select Hyperlink ➪ Edit Hyperlink.

REAL-WORLD APPLICATIONS

✔ Your worksheet includes some analysis of stock prices. You create a hyperlink to a Web site with current stock quotes.

✔ You set up four hyperlinks to four separate workbooks on your hard drive. When necessary, you click one of the hyperlinks to open one of the files.

✔ Using the VLOOKUP and Hyperlink functions together, you write a formula that jumps to one of a number of links listed in a table, depending on the value of a specified cell.

✔ You've used the same clip art images too often so you download some new images from Microsoft's Clip Gallery Web site.

Visual Quiz

In the screen shown at the right, how can you tell where the hyperlink in cell B13 takes you?

_____

_____

_____

_____

_____

_____

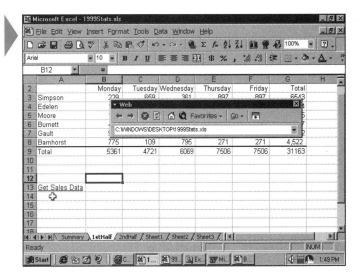

CHAPTER 19

MASTER THESE SKILLS

▶ Recording a Macro

▶ Assigning a Macro to a Keystroke or Toolbar Button

▶ Running a Macro from the Menu

▶ Assigning a Macro to a Worksheet Button or Object

▶ Altering the Macro Code

Creating Macros

Macros can save you time and reduce some of the drudgery of repetitive tasks, yet they involve some procedures that are quite different from standard Excel usage. In a sense, an Excel macro is a computer program — you tell your software to complete a series of actions rather than performing those actions yourself. When you prepare a macro, it's often because the series of tasks you want it to perform is a series that you frequently need to execute.

However, macros go well beyond this simple concept. There are some things that you can't do directly in Excel that you can do through writing macro code. As you get into this kind of macro creation, you're more clearly entering the realm of programming, replete with its own syntax, rules, and procedures.

Does every Excel user need to use macros? Not necessarily. With new features and functions enhancing every Excel release, what used to be achievable only through macros might now be embedded in a new command.

You are likely to create your first macros by turning on the macro recorder. You perform the steps that you want to be stored in your macro so that you can run it in the future whenever you like. When you create a macro this way, you automatically generate macro code, and you should at least observe this code. Later, perhaps, you may want to learn more about it, and possibly to make some changes to it.

After you've created a few macros, you may begin to recognize some of them as being unique to the current workbook, while others may have wider applicability.

You can run a macro in a number of ways; some of these methods — using a new toolbar button or a keystroke combination — are quite fast, whereas other methods — using existing or new menus — take longer. There are good reasons for using the different macro-activating techniques. In this chapter you get exposure to the concept of macros and see an example of a simple yet useful macro that may whet your appetite for more exploration into this highly creative side of Excel usage.

Recording a Macro

If you were a computer programmer and had been told that an Excel macro was like a program, your first thoughts might be: How do I begin to write a program? Show me some commands. How many commands do I need to know? Explain some of the syntax.

As an Excel user, maybe you're not a programmer, and you don't really have enough time to learn all the rules and procedures involved with any programming language. Fortunately, you don't need to know these things in order to create an Excel macro. Perhaps the way you plan to use macros may never necessitate dealing directly with macro code.

You can create many macros simply by turning on a recording feature that tracks your every action through the series of steps that you need to complete to achieve your goal. Once you've recorded the macro, you can use it over and over whenever you need to have those steps performed again. In subsequent tasks in this chapter, I demonstrate many different ways in which to run your macro.

A key concept behind recording a macro is that the recording process keeps track of everything that you do between the moment you activate the recorder and the moment you turn it off. Fortunately, some of your unnecessary forays into a command sequence that you don't complete will be ignored. However, when you record a macro, it's best to stay focused so that you don't introduce useless steps.

When you create a macro, you can choose to place it in the current workbook or store it in the Personal Workbook, which is available for all other workbooks. If you later decide that a macro in one workbook has wider applicability in other workbooks, you can move it to the Personal Workbook. Later in this chapter, you see how you can get to a macro through a new toolbar button that could be available to all workbooks.

TAKE NOTE

▶ YOU'VE BEEN USING MACROS ALL ALONG

In a sense, you've already been using macros — every time you use a toolbar button. When you click the $ button in the Formatting toolbar, for example, the numeric contents of all selected cells become prefaced with a dollar sign and two decimal places appear. What you're really doing is activating a macro that performs the following instructions so you don't have to: Click the Format menu, click Cells, click the Number tab, click the Currency category, adjust the decimal places, and click OK.

▶ YOU CAN'T UNDO A MACRO

Even though you could undo each of the actions in the macro if they were done during regular worksheet manipulation, you can't undo any actions taken by a macro.

CROSS-REFERENCE

Look ahead to the next three tasks in this chapter to see different ways that you can run a macro.

FIND IT ONLINE

To get an in-depth technical view of digital recording, take a look at: **http://www.digital-recordings.com/ publ/pubrec.html.**

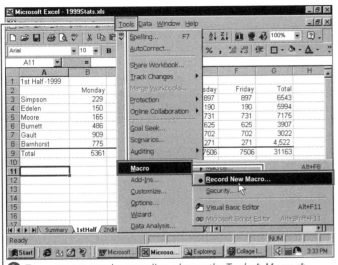

1 To create a macro by recording, choose the Tools ⇨ Macro ⇨ Record New Macro command.

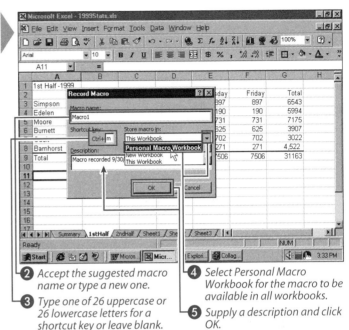

2 Accept the suggested macro name or type a new one.

3 Type one of 26 uppercase or 26 lowercase letters for a shortcut key or leave blank.

4 Select Personal Macro Workbook for the macro to be available in all workbooks.

5 Supply a description and click OK.

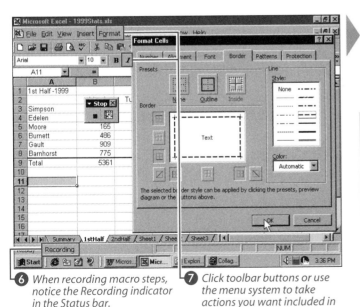

6 When recording macro steps, notice the Recording indicator in the Status bar.

7 Click toolbar buttons or use the menu system to take actions you want included in the macro.

8 Click the Stop button in the Stop toolbar to terminate macro recording.

Assigning a Macro to a Keystroke or Toolbar Button

Among the many ways that you can run your macro are two very quick methods — a keystroke shortcut and a toolbar button. They're quite different from each other but what they have in common is the speed with which you can access them.

At the time you create a macro, you have an opportunity to assign a keystroke shortcut so that you can later run the macro quickly just by hitting that keystroke combination. Any keystroke shortcut you create automatically includes the Ctrl key and either an uppercase or lowercase letter, so you have a maximum of 52 possible shortcuts amongst all the open files, including the Personal Workbook, where you store global macros. If you assign a macro to an uppercase letter, you will need to use the Shift key (along with the Ctrl key) and the letter to activate your macro.

Because you won't be able to remember too many keystroke shortcuts, you should probably assign shortcuts to just a few macros — the most important ones. Another downside to assigning keystroke shortcuts to your macros is that you negate the current meaning, if any, that the shortcut currently has. For example, Ctrl+c is used throughout the Windows environment, including Excel, to mean Edit ➪ Copy. Assign one of your macros to this combination and Ctrl+c will no longer mean copy, it will run your macro instead. If you're not a prolific user of keystroke combinations in general, this may not be an issue with you, but many Excel users find that over time, they become bigger users of the well-known shortcuts and would like to use them for macros. In some cases you may want to eliminate some of your macro shortcuts or change the keystroke combinations.

Assigning a macro to a new toolbar button certainly takes more initial energy than assigning a keystroke shortcut, but its benefits are more apparent. It's a simple matter to run your macro by simply clicking the button you've assigned to the macro. You can create a new toolbar that contains only macro buttons and activate the toolbar at will. You can also see to it that each macro toolbar button has a pop-up tool tip also.

TAKE NOTE

▶ THE CTRL KEY AND COMMONLY USED SHORTCUTS

Avoid using these lowercase letters in your keystroke shortcuts because of their wide use in Excel and other Office 2000 software:

a — Select All	u — Underline
b — Bold	v — Paste
c — Copy	x — Cut
i — Italic	y — Redo, Repeat
p — Print	z — Undo.
s — Save	

▶ REDESIGN YOUR MACRO BUTTON

If the appearance of a macro button doesn't seem related to the macro it represents, right-click the button, choose Customize, right-click the button again and select Edit Button Image. Create your own design by clicking the Colors panel, and then the Picture panel.

CROSS-REFERENCE

See Chapter 9 for details about customizing toolbars.

SHORTCUT

Press Alt+F8 to get to the list of your macros quickly.

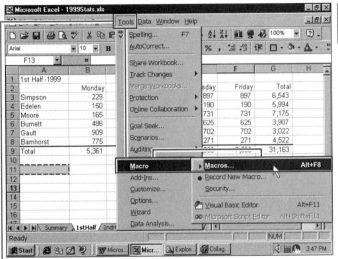

❶ To assign a letter for a shortcut key to run your macro (if you didn't do so when creating the macro), choose the Tools ➪ Macro ➪ Macros command.

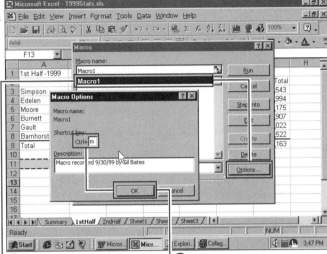

❷ In the Macro dialog box, click the name of the macro, and then click the Options button.

❸ In the Macro Options dialog box, use one of the 26 uppercase or lowercase letters as a shortcut key and click OK.

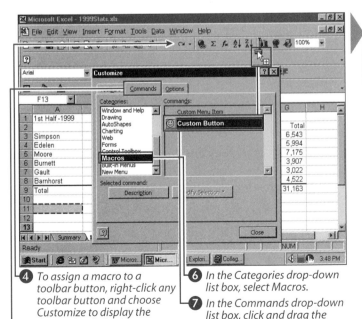

❹ To assign a macro to a toolbar button, right-click any toolbar button and choose Customize to display the Customize dialog box.

❺ Click the Commands tab.

❻ In the Categories drop-down list box, select Macros.

❼ In the Commands drop-down list box, click and drag the Custom Button to a location on an existing toolbar.

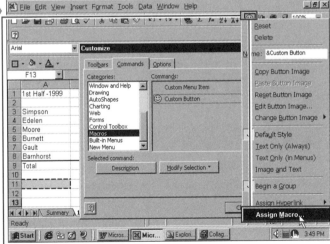

❽ Right-click the Custom button and select Assign Macro. In the Assign Macro dialog box (not shown) click the appropriate macro and click OK.

Running a Macro from the Menu

After you've taken the time to create your macro, you need to consider some of the different ways that you can get to it quickly to run it whenever you need it. For a macro that you won't be using often, there's no special need to create a toolbar button or a use up a keystroke shortcut that might be better used elsewhere. Furthermore, you have a tendency to forget the keystroke shortcut anyway if you don't use the macro frequently.

There are a number of ways to run a macro from the menu. One such way is available even if you don't make a special effort to set it up as a menu item. All of your macros are accessible from the Tools menu, but you sometimes need to look through a list that has grown long and contains names like Macro2, Macro3, and so on, if you didn't take the time to rename them. This is the slowest method of getting to a macro, but it's reliable. You can always track down a macro by starting at the Tools menu.

If the macro you need to access is used enough to warrant a special command on the regular Excel Tools menu, you can do that. However, the potential problem here is that you may want to do that again for the next macro and again for the next, and so on. Eventually it becomes unwieldy to have too many macros listed in the menu. A better approach is to set up an entirely new menu item almost as if you were setting up a new toolbar (see the previous task). This way you have a new menu entry, perhaps named

MACROS and placed to the right of the Help command, that can be a repository for macros that you want relatively quick access to. As with standard Excel menu commands, you can get to the new menu and all of the entries in it by using the Alt key and a single letter.

TAKE NOTE

STANDARD MENU COMMANDS AND YOUR MACRO MENU COMMANDS

If you want the macro command that you put on either the Tools menu or a new menu to look like a standard Excel command, capitalize all words in the macro menu entry except conjunctions (and, or, etc.) and articles (a, an, the). If you'd prefer your macro commands to look different from regular commands, make them all uppercase.

ADD TOOLBAR BUTTONS TO MACRO MENU COMMANDS

Just as many standard menu commands have toolbar equivalents, so can macros. When you set up a menu entry for your macro, you can make its toolbar symbol (which you would have created previously) appear to the left of the menu entry, just like many standard commands.

CROSS-REFERENCE

Review the basics of menu display in Chapter 1.

FIND IT ONLINE

Review some of the menus available at **http://members.aol.com/lorbus/menu.html**.

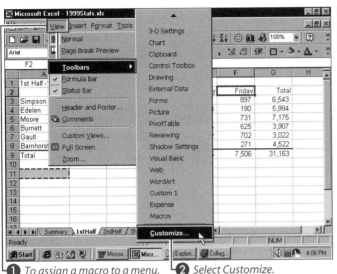

1 To assign a macro to a menu, select the View ➡ Toolbars command.

2 Select Customize.

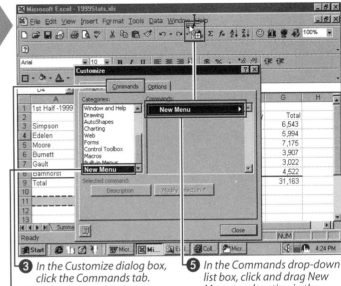

3 In the Customize dialog box, click the Commands tab.

4 In the Categories drop-down list box, select New Menu.

5 In the Commands drop-down list box, click and drag New Menu to a location in the Excel menu.

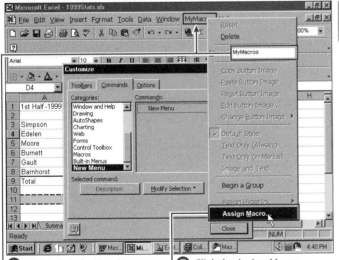

6 Right-click the New Menu entry and type a new name, if desired, in the Name field.

7 Click the Assign Macro shortcut. In the Assign Macro dialog box (not shown), select the macro and click OK.

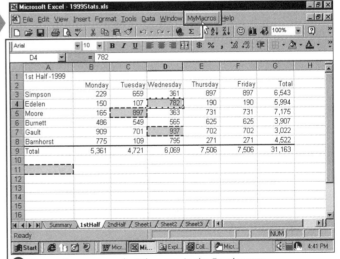

8 To run the macro, select the entry in the Excel menu.

Assigning a Macro to a Worksheet Button or Object

For macros that you create for use in one worksheet only, you may want to be able to run them by clicking a worksheet button or an object, such as a piece of WordArt, a clip art image, or any kind of picture imported into Excel. If it's important that you include some text to either identify or document the object, you can use one of the objects found on the Drawing toolbar. If you create two or three macros to sort and print your database in different ways, you might want to assign each of the three macros to a different object and put a short description on each, such as Sort by City, Sort by Company, and so on.

One of the advantages to setting up a worksheet button to run a macro is that you have a lot of latitude in deciding how to design the button and identify it properly. Remember that potentially, there may be others using the workbook. If you have a number of macros in a specific workbook that you will run frequently, you could have each one assigned to a different colored button and have all buttons arranged in a cluster for easy access.

The number of objects available through the Drawing toolbar is seemingly endless, and no matter which ones you decide to use, you are able to apply shadows, 3-D effects, variable line thickness, and a colored background (including the seemingly endless supply of Fill Effects). You have almost as many variations as this when it comes to formatting the text that you put on the button to explain what effect clicking the button has.

TAKE NOTE

ASSIGN YOUR MACRO TO RUN FROM WORDART TEXT

To get a colorful light-show effect, set up some text in WordArt and then assign a macro to it — right-click the text and select Assign Macro. Whenever you click the WordArt text, your macro will run and the WordArt text will shimmer and go through some color changes for a few seconds. You get a similar effect if you assign a macro to a clip art image, but here, it's more like toggling between the image and an overexposure of the image.

FORMATTING AN OBJECT THAT HAS A MACRO ASSIGNED TO IT

Once you assign a macro to an object on your worksheet, every time you point to the object, the index finger pointer appears. To avoid running the macro when you really want to format the object, right-click it and select Format Object (or Format Picture, Format WordArt, etc.). Also right-click the object and select Edit Text if you want to alter text features.

CROSS-REFERENCE

Review Chapter 11 for information on the Drawing toolbar and creating objects.

FIND IT ONLINE

If you'd like to gather a colorful set of buttons, suitable for use with macros, go to **http://www.cbull.com/ buttons.htm**.

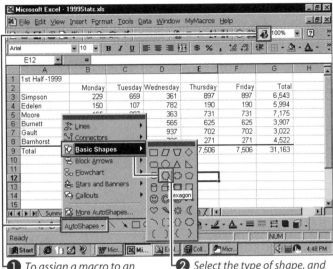

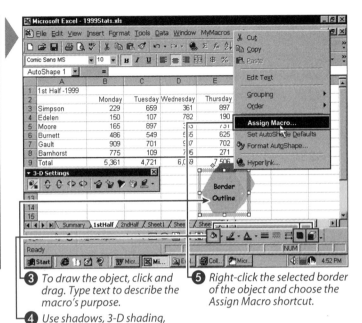

1 To assign a macro to an object, activate the Drawing toolbar and click AutoShapes.

2 Select the type of shape, and then the specific shape you want and click it.

3 To draw the object, click and drag. Type text to describe the macro's purpose.

4 Use shadows, 3-D shading, and other formatting features, as desired.

5 Right-click the selected border of the object and choose the Assign Macro shortcut.

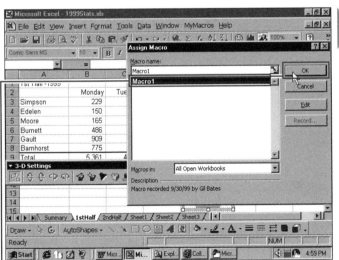

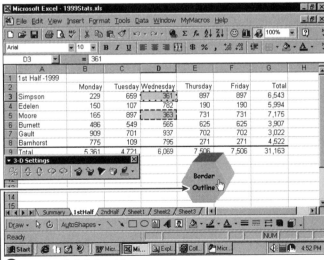

6 In the Assign Macro dialog box, select the appropriate macro and click OK.

7 Point and click the object to run the macro.

Altering the Macro Code

For every macro that you create through the recording method, there is actually code being generated. This code is like a computer program and every command or action that you take is, in effect, translated into one or more lines of code. If you have little or no experience with programming languages, you may find your first encounter with this code to be a bewildering experience.

The code generated from your macro is stored in a module in your worksheet using the programming language Visual Basic. It's certainly not a foreign language but there are some similarities — perhaps you recognize some of the words and since you know what the macro does, you begin to have some sense of how to begin reading the macro. Before long, you'll be more interested in altering the code to make your macro do additional, or different, things.

Keep in mind that if you use macros with more frequency, you will probably need to create one that does things that you cannot record. For example, suppose you want to write a macro than checks a condition that cannot be checked using the IF function, or any function. How do you check, using Excel commands and functions, to see if gridlines are on or off, or if a cell is formatted as bold? Maybe you'd like a macro to quickly remove or restore gridlines to the current worksheet. Maybe you want to prepare a macro that checks the value of all cells in a range that have been formatted as bold.

A sensible approach to understanding code is to begin by looking at the code generated by a macro. Also, check Excel's Help system for useful examples that you can copy and paste into your macro. And don't forget that you can freely copy code from one macro module to another. In the future you may take a more formal approach to macros, but initially you can proceed by writing macros through recording.

TAKE NOTE

A MACRO FOR JUST ONE ACTION?

As an aid in helping you to understand macro code, you might want to turn on the macro recorder, take a single action and then turn off the recorder and examine the code generated. Need to see what kind of code Ctrl+Home generates? Create a quick macro and then use it as a building block in other macros.

THE LOWERCASE LETTER L AND THE NUMBER 1 LOOK IDENTICAL

Since Excel's Visual Basic Editor uses Courier as its default font, lowercase L and the number 1 are nearly identical. To change the font while using the Visual Basic Editor, choose the Tools ⇨ Options command. Next, click the Format tab and in the font panel choose a font, such as Times New Roman, that differentiates the two characters better.

CROSS-REFERENCE
Review Chapter 6 for cut, copy, and paste techniques that will come in handy when altering macro code.

SHORTCUT
Press Alt+F11 to toggle from workbook to the Visual Basic Editor.

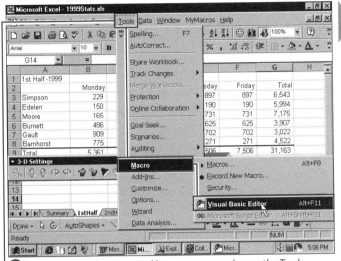

① *To view the code generated by your macro, choose the Tools ⇨ Macro ⇨ Visual Basic Editor command. Alternatively, choose the Tools ⇨ Macro ⇨ Macros command; select the macro and click Edit.*

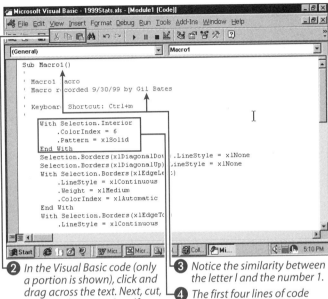

② *In the Visual Basic code (only a portion is shown), click and drag across the text. Next, cut, copy, and/or paste it as if using a word processor.*

③ *Notice the similarity between the letter l and the number 1.*

④ *The first four lines of code assign the color yellow (6), with no pattern, to the selected cells.*

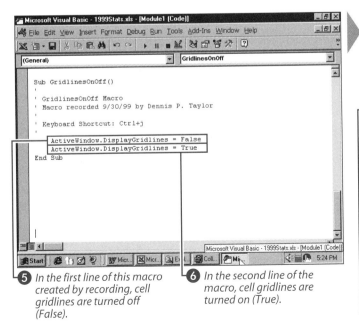

⑤ *In the first line of this macro created by recording, cell gridlines are turned off (False).*

⑥ *In the second line of the macro, cell gridlines are turned on (True).*

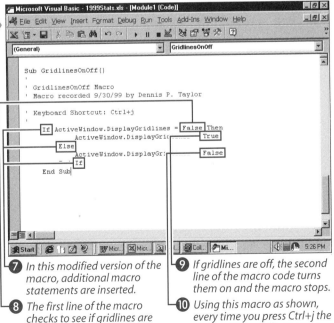

⑦ *In this modified version of the macro, additional macro statements are inserted.*

⑧ *The first line of the macro checks to see if gridlines are off.*

⑨ *If gridlines are off, the second line of the macro code turns them on and the macro stops.*

⑩ *Using this macro as shown, every time you press Ctrl+j the status of the gridlines gets reversed.*

Personal Workbook

Q&A

1 True or False: You can use Ctrl+# as a shortcut to run a macro.

_____

_____

_____

_____

2 How do you stop a macro when it's running?

_____

_____

_____

_____

3 How do you adjust the formatting of an object that you've assigned a macro to?

_____

_____

_____

_____

4 Can you assign your macro to WordArt text?

_____

_____

_____

_____

5 True or False: You can click the Undo button just after you've run a macro if you want to undo all of the steps in the macro.

_____

_____

_____

_____

6 Can you put one of your macros on the Tools menu?

_____

_____

_____

_____

ANSWERS: PAGE 332

EXTRA PRACTICE

① Record a short macro where the only thing you do is press Ctrl+Home. Copy this macro code into another macro that you have written and rerun that macro.

② Assign a keystroke shortcut to a macro that doesn't have one assigned to it.

③ Record a short macro that does the following to selected cells: makes the background light blue, the text red, and the border a thick box border.

④ Enter some WordArt text that describes a macro you have written. Assign that macro to the WordArt text.

REAL-WORLD APPLICATIONS

✔ You frequently need to sort your contact database by name or by company. You record two separate macros and create two AutoShape images on your worksheet identifying the different sorts. You assign each of the macros to the appropriate object so that you can sort your data quickly.

✔ You frequently scour the Help menu seeking guidance on macro code. When you see examples you copy them into existing, or new, macros and try running them.

✔ You often only need to see records in your HR database of full-time employees with selected benefits and high service years. Rather than setting up three separate filters every time you need this list, you record a macro to do these things and run it when needed.

Visual Quiz

In the screen shown at the right, what does this macro do? What happens if you change the item in the fourth line from the end from Copies:=1 to Copies:=3? What happens if you eliminate the line that ends with Collate:=True?

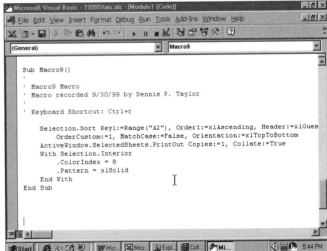

Personal Workbook
Answers

Chapter 1

see page 4

1 If you can't start Excel from the Start button, how can you start the software?

A: Excel might be available as a shortcut on the desktop (double-click it) or you can find the Excel.exe file if you click the Start button and activate the Find feature. When you locate Excel.exe, double-click it to start Excel.

2 True or false: If you don't need all 65,586 rows in a worksheet, you can delete some of them.

A: False. When you delete a row, a new one gets added at the bottom of a worksheet.

3 Will all of your open workbooks be automatically saved when you exit from Excel?

A: No, but you will be prompted to save those that you have changed and did not save.

4 If you've finished using Excel, does it make any difference whether you minimize Excel or exit from it?

A: If you intend to use Excel soon and you don't have many other applications open, it's okay to minimize Excel. When you exit from Excel, you provide more system memory for other open applications to run more efficiently.

5 True or false: Like the menu bar and toolbars, you can customize the appearance of shortcut menus.

A: False. You cannot customize the shortcut menu.

6 True or False: Keystroke shortcuts are next to every command in the menu system.

A: False. Not every command has a keystroke shortcut equivalent.

7 Why (and when) do some toolbar buttons appear sunken?

A: Some toolbar buttons appears sunken when in use. If the active cell is bold, the Bold button in the Formatting toolbar appears sunken.

Visual Quiz

Q: In the screen image shown on the right, the Formatting toolbar is missing. Using the shortcut menu, how do you quickly return the Formatting toolbar to its usual location below the Standard toolbar?

A: Right-click any toolbar button and select Formatting from the pop-up menu.

PERSONAL WORKBOOK ANSWERS

Chapter 2

see page 22

1 Will a date entry typed as 11/31/99 appear left- or right-aligned in a cell?

A: Since 11/31/99 is an impossible date, Excel will align it on the left side of the cell, in contrast with an acceptable date, which appears right-aligned.

2 Describe three ways in which to select a range of cells.

A: Click and drag across a range of cells. Hold down the Shift key as you use arrow keys, PgUp, or PgDn keys. Holding down the Shift key as you click a cell selects all cells between that cell and the active cell.

3 How would you create a series of text entries for each month in the second half of the year?

A: Type Jul or July in a cell, then point to the lower-right corner of that cell and click and drag down or to the right five additional cells.

4 What keystroke combination can you use to make a cell entry when you want to select from a list of previous entries?

A: Alt+down arrow.

5 True or False: When you use the AutoSum tool, you can't edit the function it creates.

A: False.

6 True or False: When you write a formula without parentheses, Excel performs all calculations from left to right.

A: False. Excel follows the rules of precedence.

7 What keystroke combination can you use to display the range names you need when writing a formula?

A: The F3 key.

8 True or False: You can edit a cell that contains text, a number, a formula, a date, or a function.

A: True.

Visual Quiz

Q: In the screen image to the right, you're trying to get a total in cell F5 that sums the cells B5 through E5, but after you clicked the AutoSum tool the function displayed added the cells F2 through F4. What can you do with the mouse to make AutoSum do what you want?

A: Click and drag across the cells B5:E5, then press Enter.

Chapter 3

see page 40

1 Can you select fonts from a toolbar or do you need to use the Font tab in the Format Cells dialog box?

A: You can select fonts from the Formatting toolbar.

2 True or False: Bold print doesn't take up more space, it just looks bigger.

A: For text entries, bold print takes up more horizontal display space.

3 Why does Excel make it difficult to center numbers in a cell?

A: Numbers used arithmetically should always be aligned to the right. If you've formatted cells *numerically*, you can't center their contents.

4 Can you rotate the contents of a cell containing formulas to a 45-degree angle?

A: Yes.

5 True or False: Numeric formatting, unlike other kinds of formatting, can actually alter content.

A: False. Formatting never changes the content of a cell, only its appearance.

6 What's the difference between putting a bottom border on a cell and underlining a cell?

A: A bottom border is unrelated to cell content; underlining underlines the characters in a cell and the line does not coincide with the cell's bottom border.

7 What do you need to do when you see a cell filled with ##### ?

A: Widen the column.

8 Once you use the best-fit technique on a column, will it automatically expand when you type a long entry in one of its cells?

A: No, use the best-fit feature.

Visual Quiz

Q: In the screen shown to the right, can you create this border effect from the Borders palette in the Formatting toolbar? If not, which command can you use?

A: No. You need to use the Format ⇨ Cells command and select the Border tab.

Chapter 4

see page 60

1 What toolbar button can you use to update the changes you've been making to your worksheet?

A: The Save button — third from the left in the Standard toolbar.

2 True or False: Use the File ⇨ New command to open a file you previously created and saved.

A: False. Use the File ⇨ Open command.

3 How do you make Excel display recently opened filenames on the File menu?

A: On the Tools menu select Options and then click the General tab. Adjust the number of recent filenames.

4 How many previously used files can you see on the File menu?

A: Up to nine.

5 True or False: The three-letter .xls file extension appears automatically.

A: True.

6 Does it make any difference if you rename an Excel file and omit the three-letter extension?

A: You should always use the three-letter extension when you rename an Excel file. Otherwise, the file will not appear in the list of Excel files that you see when you perform various file management tasks.

Visual Quiz

Q: In the screen shown, what's the most efficient action you can take to find and open the Lotus 1-2-3 files that you want to convert into Excel files?

A: Click the drop-down arrow on the right side of the Files of Type panel and select Lotus 1-2-3 Files.

Chapter 5

see page 74

1 Is there an expand-to-fit button in Excel's Page Setup command?

A: No.

Personal Workbook Answers

2 **Do hidden columns and rows appear on printed output if they are within the range selected for printing?**

A: No.

3 **How can you start page numbering at a number other than 1?**

A: On the Page tab of the Page Setup dialog box, enter a page number in the box next to First page number.

4 **What button must you use to get total pages in a header or footer, so that you can use a phrase like Page 2 of 5?**

A: When creating a custom header or footer, click the button that has two plus signs on it (third button from the left in the Header or Footer dialog box).

5 **If you include cell gridlines on your printed output, does it take up more space? What about row and column headings?**

A: Gridlines do not take up additional space, but row and column headings do.

6 **If you want to be able to make worksheet changes as you observe page breaks, do you use Print Preview or Page Break Preview?**

A: Page Break Preview.

Visual Quiz

Q: How do you center the output between the left and right side of the paper and between the top and bottom of the paper? Can you expand it to fill out the page better? How would you remove the column letters and row numbers and show gridlines instead?

A: Click the Setup button, then click the Margins tab. In the Center on page section, check the boxes next to Horizontally and Vertically. To make the image fill the page better, click the Page tab and experiment with the number in the box next to the Adjust to panel. To remove the column and row numbers and add gridlines, click the Sheet tab and (un)check the boxes next to Row and column headings and Gridlines.

Chapter 6

see page 94

1 **Can you use the Undo feature to Undo the File ⇨ Save command?**

A: No, you cannot Undo the action of the File ⇨ Save command.

2 **Is deleting a row equivalent to erasing all data in that row?**

A: No, deleting a row causes all data in rows below to move up a row and erasing data simply makes cells blank.

3 **Do you need to adjust any worksheet formulas if you insert a row or column?**

A: No.

4 **True or False: If you don't see the destination on your screen, you can't move a range of cells by dragging it.**

A: False. Although it's best to be able to see where you're going to move cells, you can drag cells to locations that are not currently visible.

5 **Can you copy formulas up or to the left of adjacent cells just as you can copy them down or across to adjacent cells?**

A: Yes.

6 **Can you write formulas that refer to data in hidden columns or rows?**

A: Yes.

7 What's a quick way to display all formulas in your worksheet?

A: Press the keystroke combination Ctrl+~ (that's the key above the Tab key on most keyboards).

Visual Quiz

Q: You want to replace all occurrences of US with USA in Column D. Do you need to select Column D first? How do you activate the dialog box shown? Do you need to check the Match case box? Should you also check the box next to Find entire cells only? What will happen if you leave both boxes unchecked and click the Replace all button?

A: It's not required to select column D first, but your search/replace actions will occur faster if you focus on a smaller range. Activate this dialog box from the Edit menu by selecting Replace. You should check the Match case box or you will replace the lowercase us in words like Russia, Austria, and Cyprus with the letters USA. You should also check the box next to Find entire cells only to avoid replacement in cells where all content is uppercase.

Chapter 7

see page 116

1 Cells B3 through B6 contain these entries: 20, 0, Blank, and 70. If you write this function =AVERAGE(B3:B6) what value is displayed?

A: The result is 30. The blank cell is not part of the average.

2 How should you adjust this function to make the result appear more reasonable?

A: =Average(B3:B4,B6) or =AVERAGE(B3,B4,B6).

3 The range C3:C10 contains these values: 20, 30, 85, 26, 82, 45, 61, and 47. If you type the function =LARGE (C3:C10,2) what value is displayed?

A: The value 82 is the second largest in the group.

4 If you type =RIGHT(A5,3) and cell A5 contains the text string A423B6765, what will you see?

A: The character string 765.

5 If cell B3 contains 100, what does this function display =IF(_B3>100,10%,5%)?

A: The result is 5% since B3 is not greater than 100.

6 If you click the equal sign (=) in the formula bar, what happens?

A: You get a list of recently used functions.

7 True or False: The CHOOSE function, unlike VLOOKUP, doesn't require you to have a table in your worksheet.

A: True.

8 If cell A5 contains the value 27.571, what does the function =ROUND(A5,2) return?

A: The value 27.57.

Visual Quiz

Q: What formula is in cell E11? Why is the result negative? If March or April profits were zero, would this affect the formula in E11 in any unusual way?

A: The formula is either =E6/D6-1 or =(E6-D6)/D6 and the result is negative because profits decreased in April. If March profits are zero, the formula would be in error — division by zero is impossible. If April (but not March) profits are zero, the formula produces the meaningless 100% as an answer.

PERSONAL WORKBOOK ANSWERS

Chapter 8

see page 136

1 True or False: To enter the time 2:30 (afternoon) into a cell, you should type 14:30.

A: True. You can also type 2:30 pm or 2:30 PM or 2:30p.

2 What keystroke combination can you use to enter today's date into a cell?

A: Ctrl+semicolon.

3 What's the difference between using ddd and dddd in a custom date format?

A: The format ddd displays a day with its three-letter abbreviation, such as Tue. The format dddd displays a day with its complete spelling, such as Tuesday.

4 On what date will you be (or were you) 10,000 days old?

A: If your birthday is May 13, 1973, enter 5/13/73 in one cell, say A4. In another cell write a formula =A4+10000 and format your answer as a date to find out your 10,000th day.

5 True or False: If you're not sure about whether a date is going to be recorded as twentieth or twenty-first century, use a 4-digit year during data entry.

A: True.

6 What day of the week is March 17, 2001? (Use the WEEKDAY function.)

A: Saturday.

7 How many days are there between 5/28/99 and 9/13/99?

A: There are 108 days between the two dates.

Visual Quiz

Q: In the screen shown to the right, cell B3 formerly contained a date. You selected the cell and pressed the Delete key to erase it. Later you typed the value 20000 here. Why does the cell contain the date 10/3/54? Is that the date you had typed there before erasing the cell? What's a quick way to adjust the format so that the value 20000 appears there?

A: The Delete key removes content, not formats. Excel displays the number 20000 as 10/3/54 — the 20,000th day in its date numbering system. The previous date in this cell is irrelevant. Click the Comma button in the Formatting toolbar to display the value as 20,000.00 and then adjust the decimals as desired.

Chapter 9

see page 150

1 True or False: If you're viewing more than one workbook, you can't display multiple worksheets for any of the open workbooks.

A: False. You can view multiple worksheets of a workbook even if that workbook is one of many currently in view on your screen.

2 What's the fastest way to eliminate a dual split screen?

A: Double-click the intersection of the panes.

3 The Window drop-down list box shows you the names of open workbooks, but does it show you how many windows are open for the current workbook?

A: Yes. Each window for a worksheet is identified by the workbook name followed by a colon and a sequential number and if one of the intermediate windows is closed, the ones with higher numbers are renumbered downward to plug the gap.

④ What keystroke combination enables you to jump from one open workbook to another or from one window to another?

A: Ctrl+F6.

⑤ If you'd like to see row 13 and row 75 onscreen at the same time, what kind of split would you activate?

A: A horizontal split screen.

⑥ If you mistakenly set up a split screen at the wrong location, can you use Undo to reverse your action?

A: No. Split screens actions can't be undone through the Undo feature.

⑦ What keystroke combination moves an active cell from pane to pane on a split screen?

A: F6 (clockwise) or Shift+F6 (counter-clockwise).

Visual Quiz

Q: In the screen shown to the right, how many workbooks are open?

A: Two workbooks are open: Frestest.xls and 1999Stats.xls. Each file has multiple windows open.

Chapter 10

see page 166

① Can you undo the action you just took to delete a worksheet?

A: No

② How many sheets can you insert at a time?

A: You can insert as many sheets as you can select at a time. If your workbook has five sheets and you select them all, when you use the Insert ⇨ Worksheet command, you will get five new sheets.

③ What's a good reason for using short, rather than long names for worksheets?

A: With short names you can see more worksheet tabs along the bottom of the screen and will need to use the navigation arrows less often.

④ True or False: There's not really any difference between copying a worksheet and using the copy-and-paste technique to copy all the cells of a worksheet to another worksheet.

A: False. When you copy an entire worksheet, column widths and row heights get copied also. When you copy selected cells, you won't get these features copied.

⑤ Can you copy more than one worksheet at a time? Can you move more than one worksheet at a time?

A: Yes, you can copy or move more than one sheet at a time.

⑥ True or False: If you're writing a formula that refers to a cell in another worksheet, you must type the name of that worksheet in your formula.

A: False. Although it's not incorrect to type the name of a worksheet, it's easier to select that worksheet and click the appropriate cell as you prepare your formula.

⑦ In your workbook that has 12 worksheets named after each month and one called Summary, what happens to this formula — =SUM(JANUARY:DECEMBER!B17) — if you delete the sheet named OCTOBER?

A: The formula does not change, but there's no longer any data from the October sheet in the result.

Personal Workbook Answers

Visual Quiz

Q: In the screen shown to the right, can you change the name of the sheets Quarter1, Quarter2, and so on to Q1, Q2, and so on without worrying about formulas working properly?

A: Yes, the formulas will automatically adjust to reflect the new sheet names.

Chapter 11

see page 182

1 True or False? To edit two of many graphical objects on a screen, you can select just those objects by holding down the Shift key as you click each one.

A: True. Use the Shift key while clicking on objects to select those objects.

2 When you want to make changes to a WordArt image on your screen, how do you activate the WordArt toolbar?

A: Click the WordArt image and the WordArt toolbar appears automatically

3 When creating an arrow or line, how can you insure that it's at a 45-degree angle?

A: Hold down the Shift key as you draw the line to set the line at any incremental 15-degree setting.

4 If you use one of the choices in the Connectors palette (found in AutoShapes) to connect two graphical objects, what happens when you move one of the objects?

A: If you move any object that has one of the Connector choices attached, the connector line remains attached as it grows or shrinks.

5 True or False: You can rotate an object from its center or from any of its corners

A: True. Select an object and click the Rotate button in the Drawing toolbar. Drag the object from any corner and you rotate from the center. Hold down the Ctrl key as you rotate and you rotate from the opposite corner.

6 What happens when you click an object and press Ctrl+D?

A: You create a duplicate of the object.

Visual Quiz

Q: In the screen shown at the right, how do you change the selected arrow's text to be bold? Which button in which toolbar do you use to make the arrow's perimeter line thicker? Which button can you use to apply a background color to the arrow?

A: Click the Bold tool in the Formatting toolbar. Click the Line Style button in the Drawing toolbar to select a thicker perimeter line. Click the Fill Color button, either on the Formatting or Drawing toolbars to apply a background color to the arrow.

Chapter 12

see page 200

1 True or False: You can drag a legend anywhere on your chart.

A: True. You can click and drag the Legend anywhere on the chart

2 Which key do you press to create a chart instantly on a new sheet?

A: The F11 key.

3 When resizing a chart on your worksheet, how do you make the chart's edges align with the worksheet's cell boundaries?

A: Hold down the Alt key as you drag an edge. Accelerate the process by dragging a corner and aligning two edges at once.

4 Can you use a pie chart to show negative data?

A: It's not a great idea to show positive and negative data together in a pie chart. Not only is the concept bad, you won't be blocked from doing it and the negative numbers will be treated as positive values in the chart.

5 Is there a way to print a chart that's on a worksheet so that you don't see the worksheet data or gridlines?

A: Yes. Right-click a worksheet chart and select Chart Window. Click the Print Preview button in the Standard toolbar to verify the appearance of the output, then print.

6 If you need to create a chart that shows a trend over time, what would be a good chart type to use?

A: Line charts are generally considered best for showing trends.

7 How do you resize an embedded chart proportionally?

A: Hold down the Shift key as you drag one of the corner handles of the chart.

Visual Quiz

Q: In the screen shown to the right, which cells in the worksheet were selected to create this pie chart?

A: D3:D8.

Chapter 13

see page 216

1 True or False: A button on your Formatting toolbar enables you to adjust the angle of values on the Y-axis of a chart.

A: False. But there are two buttons on the Chart toolbar that let you angle text up or down 45 degrees.

2 If you adjust the number of decimal places on the Y-axis values in a column chart, will the size of the plot area change?

A: Yes. Changing the amount of text and its size has an impact on the plot area.

3 Can you create a multiline title in a chart using the Chart Wizard?

A: No. On a chart that has a title, click it, then click at a line break point and press Enter.

4 When rotating a 3-D chart, how do you get to see the columns, bars, etc., instead of just the outline of the chart's shape?

A: Hold down the Ctrl key as you rotate the chart.

5 True or False: The Y-axis always starts at zero.

A: False. Usually that's where it starts, but if you have negative data, the chart will start below zero.

6 How do you resize the main title of a chart?

A: You can't really resize it unless you add to it by typing additional characters or spaces.

7 Can you show two rows of data in a pie chart?

A: No. Pie charts only show data from a single row or from a single column.

Personal Workbook Answers

Visual Quiz

Q: In the screen shown to the right, what's the fastest way to set all of the various text entries to the same size font?

A: Select the Chart Area and click the Font Size button in the Formatting toolbar and select the size you want. You can select the Chart Area either by clicking on the outer edge of the display area or by repeatedly pressing the up or down arrow keys until the phrase Chart Area appears on the left side of the formula bar.

Chapter 14

see page 232

1 True or False: If you erase a chart's source data in a worksheet, nothing changes in the chart.

A: False. You will see missing columns, bars, points, etc, depending on the chart type.

2 Does a moving average applied to 50 points look smoother if it averages the last five periods or the last two periods?

A: Five periods. Moving averages tend to be smoother if they cover longer time periods.

3 Can you change the order of labels on the X-axis (horizontal) through a chart command?

A: No. Rearrange the data in a worksheet to adjust the information.

4 When you rearrange the order of a series on your chart, what effect does it have on the data in your worksheet?

A: No effect at all.

5 True or False: You can adjust the height of a single column in a 3-D column chart by dragging it.

A: False. You can't adjust the values on any 3-D charts by dragging them.

6 What happens to your chart when you delete cells from your worksheet that had been used as category (X-axis) data?

A: The chart no longer shows the category. No holes or missing elements (column, bar, line, etc.) occur. It's as if the category was never there.

7 If you rearrange the rows in your worksheet that are the source for your chart series, what happens to your chart?

A: You change the order of the plot series.

Visual Quiz

Q: In the screen shown to the right, what kind of trendline is Trendline 3? Why doesn't it begin at the left side of the chart? What kind of trendline is the straight line that extends across the chart? What's missing from the chart that would help identify all of the line types? How do you delete a trendline?

A: Trendline 3 is a moving average. This line averages the last five entries, therefore it does not appear until the fifth data point. The straight line extending across the chart is a linear trendline. A legend would help define the lines on the chart. Click a trendline and press the Delete key to remove the trendline.

PERSONAL WORKBOOK ANSWERS

Chapter 15

see page 246

1 True or False: With data validation, you can restrict entries in a range to dates only.

A: True. Date is one of a number of criteria you can use to restrict data entry through the Data Validation feature.

2 Do you need to sort your database before using the Subtotals feature?

A: Yes. If you don't, the feature still works but you might get subtotals on almost every other line.

3 When you add a new record using the Data Form dialog box, where is the new record placed?

A: The record is placed after all of the other records in your database. There is no insertion feature in Data Form.

4 What keystroke combination do you use to properly complete an array formula?

A: Ctrl+Shift+Enter.

5 True or False: When you sort, you nearly always rearrange the order of columns.

A: False. Usually sorting involves the rearrangement of rows, based on column content. There is a way, however, to sort so that you can rearrange the left-right order of columns.

6 Which command sequence lets you set up a special list of items that you can sort by?

A: You can set up a custom list and use it for sorting by selecting the Tools menu, then Options. Click the Custom Lists tab and create your list in the List entries panel.

7 Do you need to sort your database before using the Data ⇨ Filter command?

A: No. Filtering does not require that your data be sorted first.

Visual Quiz

Q: In the screen shown to the right, four successive sorts were done from the Sort button in the Standard toolbar. On which column was the database sorted last? What column was the previous sort based on? The one before that? What column was the first of the four sorts based on? Were any of these sorts descending?

A: The database was last sorted on the Region field. The previous sort was based on Division Code and the one before that was based on Empl Code. The first field sorted was the 1988 Salary field, in descending order.

Chapter 16

see page 264

1 True or False: When you make a change to a pivot table's source data, the pivot table reacts automatically.

A: False. The pivot table does not react until you press the Refresh button on the Pivot Table toolbar.

2 Do you need to sort your database before you create a pivot table report from it?

A: No.

3 When you attempt to group some of a numerical field's entries in a pivot table, what onscreen help do you get?

A: The Grouping Dialog box appears with suggestions for grouping the information numerically by interval.

Personal Workbook Answers

4 **What happens when you double-click a group name?**

A: The underlying detail of the grouping either gets hidden or revealed.

5 **True or False: If you drag a field onto a pivot chart, the underlying pivot table does not change.**

A: False, the pivot chart and the pivot table are always in sync with one another. Drag a field on the chart and the report gets changed immediately.

6 **If a field's entries in a pivot table are not in alphabetical or numerical order, how do you sort them?**

A: Click a field name, then click either Sort button in the Standard toolbar.

7 **How do you leave out some of a field's entries on a pivot table?**

A: Click the down arrow next to the field name and uncheck those entries you don't want to see.

Visual Quiz

Q: In the screen shown to the right, which button do you click to select only Div Codes 400, 500, and 600 to be shown? Which button do you click to select only the Southeast and Southwest regions to be shown? How do you move the Mountain column to the right of the Southwest column?

A: Click the down arrow just to the right of Div Code to select from a list of division codes. Click the down arrow just to the right of Region to select from a list of region names. To move the Mountain column, point to the bottom edge of the cell containing the word Mountain and when you see the arrow, click and drag the bottom edge of the cell to the right of the Southwest column.

Chapter 17

see page 282

1 **True or False: You can open a text file without using the File ⇨ Open command.**

A: True. You can use the Data menu and choose Get External Data and then Import Text File.

2 **If you open a workbook that is dependent on a second workbook, does the second workbook need to be open also for data updating to occur?**

A: No.

3 **When you change a cell in a supporting workbook does the dependent workbook get updated immediately?**

A: Only if the dependent workbook is open on the same computer at the same time.

4 **Do formulas in an Excel file get saved when you save the file as a DBF file?**

A: No.

5 **True or False: When you save your current Excel workbook as a Lotus 1-2-3 file, you lose your Excel version of the file.**

A: False. You now have at least two versions of the file, one in Excel format, the other in Lotus format.

6 **Which command do you use to re-establish a severed link?**

A: Edit ⇨ Links.

PERSONAL WORKBOOK ANSWERS

Visual Quiz

Q: In the screen shown at the right, name the source workbook for the dependent workbook shown. Name the source worksheet. Where is the source file located?

A: The dependent workbook is 99Sales-2Sub.xls. The source worksheet is Sheet1. The source file is located on the Desktop, which is actually a subfolder of the Windows folder located on the C drive.

Chapter 18

see page 294

1 True or False: A hyperlink is used only for access to Internet or intranet sites.

A: False. You can create a hyperlink to other workbooks and to cells in the current workbook or worksheet.

2 How do you get online help for Excel?

A: Select the Help menu and choose Office on the Web.

3 How do you find additional downloadable clip art images?

A: Click the clip art image in the Drawing toolbar; then in the Insert ClipArt dialog box, click the Clips Online button.

4 How do you save your workbook as an HTML file?

A: Click the File menu and select Save as Web Page.

5 True or False: From Excel you can set up a Web page that's interactive.

A: True. When you save your workbook as a Web Page, you will be able to check a box labeled Add interactivity with.

6 Can you assign a hyperlink to an object or picture?

A: Yes. Right-click the object or picture and select Hyperlink.

Visual Quiz:

Q: In the screen shown at the right, how can you tell where the hyperlink in cell A13 takes you?

A: To find where the hyperlink in cell A13 points, right-click cell A13 and select Hyperlink, then Edit Hyperlink.

Chapter 19

see page 306

1 True or False: You can use Ctrl+# as a shortcut to run a macro.

A: False. Only uppercase and lowercase letters can be used as shortcut keys to run macros.

2 How do you stop a macro when it's running?

A: Press the Esc key.

3 How do you adjust the formatting of an object that you've assigned a macro to?

A: Right-click it and select Format ➪ Object.

4 Can you assign your macro to WordArt text?

A: Yes. Right-click it and select Assign Macro.

5 True or False: You can click the Undo button just after you've run a macro if you want to undo all of the steps in the macro.

A: False. You can't use the Undo button to undo the actions of a macro.

6 Can you put one of your macros on the Tools menu?

A: Yes, although it's a better idea to put it in a new menu.

Personal Workbook Answers

Visual Quiz

Q: In the screen shown at the right, what does this macro do? What happens if you change the item in the line fourth from the bottom from Copies:=1 to Copies:=3? What happens if you change the statement Collate:=True to Collate:=False?

A: This macro sorts the selected data based on the contents of column A in ascending order and prints the results. Copies:=3 means that three versions of the output will be printed. If you change the phrase Collate:=True to Collate:=False while printing three copies, you will get three copies of page one, then three copies of page two, and so on.

Glossary

A

absolute references When copying formulas, the cell references remain the same. Access these sheets by clicking a notebook-like tab. The sheets can be worksheets or chart sheets.

AutoFill The AutoFill handle (the small box at the lower left of the active cell) can be dragged to copy the cell automatically or to complete a series.

AutoFormat Excel will automatically format your table according to the style you choose. Select Format ➪ AutoFormat.

Average A function that will provide the arithmetic mean of a range of values.

B

boolean settings A VBA code setting that is identified as either on or off (true or false).

bin range A range of values that specifies the limits for each column of the histogram. If you omit the bin range, Excel creates ten equal-interval bins for you.

C

cell The intersection of each row and column. A cell can hold a number, a text string, or a formula that performs a calculation by using one or more other cells.

cell address Every worksheet consists of numbered rows and lettered columns. The cell address is determined by the row number and the column letter that intersect in that particular cell.

chart An Excel interpretation of your data into a visual format. You can choose from many different styles.

chart sheet A page within a workbook for charts, which does not contain worksheet cells.

clipboard An area of memory that stores information that has been cut or copied from a Windows program.

concatenate A function to combine the text of two labels.

D

data tables Display the data inside a chart with the use of data tables.

depreciation The devaluation of an asset over time.

GLOSSARY

F

filtering The process of hiding all rows in the list except those that meet certain criteria that you specify.

formulas Performing actions on numbers, such as multiplying, dividing, adding and subtracting within a cell.

functions Built-in formulas that can be included to simplify calculations. Custom functions can also be created. The following table summarizes some of the main Excel functions.

FUNCTION	WHAT IT DOES
ADDRESS	Returns a reference as text to a single cell in a worksheet
AREAS	Returns the number of areas in a reference
CELL	Returns information about the formatting, location, or content of a cell
CHOOSE	Chooses a value from a list of values
COLUMN	Returns the column number of a reference
COLUMNS	Returns the number of columns in a reference
COUNTBLANK	Counts the number of blank cells within a range
DATE	Returns the serial number of a particular date
DATEVALUE	Converts a date in the form of text to a serial number
DAVERAGE	Returns the average of selected database entries
DAY	Converts a serial number to a day of the month
DAYS360	Calculates the number of days between two dates, based on a 360-day year
DCOUNT	Counts the cells containing numbers from a specified database and criteria
DCOUNTA	Counts nonblank cells from a specified database and criteria
DGET	Extracts from a database a single record that matches the specified criteria
DMAX	Returns the maximum value from selected database entries
DMIN	Returns the minimum value from selected database entries
DPRODUCT	Multiplies the values in a particular field of records that match the criteria in a database
DSTDEV	Estimates the standard deviation based on a sample of selected database entries
DSTDEVP	Calculates the standard deviation based on the entire population of selected database entries
DSUM	Adds the numbers in the field column of records in the database that match the criteria
DVAR	Estimates variance based on a sample from selected database entries
DVARP	Calculates variance based on the entire population of selected database entries
EDATE	Returns the serial number of the date that is the indicated number of months before or after the start date
EOMONTH	Returns the serial number of the last day of the month before or after a specified number of months
ERROR.TYPE	Returns a number corresponding to an error type
GETPIVOTDATA	Returns data stored in a PivotTable

FUNCTION	WHAT IT DOES
HLOOKUP	Looks in the top row of an array and returns the value of the indicated cell
HOUR	Converts a serial number to an hour
HYPERLINK	Creates a shortcut that opens a document on your hard drive, a server, or the Internet
INDEX	Uses an index to choose a value from a reference or array
INDIRECT	Returns a reference indicated by a text value
INFO	Returns information about the current operating environment
ISBLANK	Returns TRUE if the value is blank
ISERR	Returns TRUE if the value is any error value except #N/A
ISERROR	Returns TRUE if the value is any error value
ISEVEN*	Returns TRUE if the number is even
ISLOGICAL	Returns TRUE if the value is a logical value
ISNA	Returns TRUE if the value is the #N/A error value
ISNONTEXT	Returns TRUE if the value is not text
ISNUMBER	Returns TRUE if the value is a number
ISODD*	Returns TRUE if the number is odd
ISREF	Returns TRUE if the value is a reference
ISTEXT	Returns TRUE if the value is text
LOOKUP	Looks up values in a vector or array
MATCH	Looks up values in a reference or array
MINUTE	Converts a serial number to a minute
MONTH	Converts a serial number to a month
N	Returns a value converted to a number
NA	Returns the error value #N/A
NETWORKDAYS	Returns the number of whole workdays between two dates
NOW	Returns the serial number of the current date and time
OFFSET	Returns a reference offset from a given reference
QUERYGETDATA	Gets external data using Microsoft Query
QUERYGETDATADIALOG	Displays a dialog box to get data using Microsoft Query
QUERYREFRESH	Updates a data range using Microsoft Query
ROW	Returns the row number of a reference
ROWS	Returns the number of rows in a reference
SECOND	Converts a serial number to a second
SQL.BIND	Specifies where to place SQL.EXEC.QUERY results
SQL.CLOSE	Terminates a SQL.OPEN connection
SQL.ERROR	Returns error information on SQL functions
SQL.EXEC.QUERY	Executes a SQL statement on a SQL.OPEN connection
SQL.GET.SCHEMA	Returns information on a SQL.OPEN connection

GLOSSARY

FUNCTION	WHAT IT DOES
SQL.OPEN	Makes a connection to a data source via ODBC
SQL.REQUEST	Requests a connection and executes a SQL query
SQL.RETRIEVE	Retrieves SQL.EXEC.QUERY results
SQL.RETRIEVE.TO.FILE	Retrieves SQL.EXEC.QUERY results to a file
TIME	Returns the serial number of a particular time
TIMEVALUE	Converts a time in the form of text to a serial number
TODAY	Returns the serial number of today's date
TRANSPOSE	Returns the transpose of an array
TYPE	Returns a number indicating the data type of a value
VLOOKUP	Looks in the first column of an array and moves across the row to return the value of a cell
WEEKDAY	Converts a serial number to a day of the week
WEEKNUM	Returns the week number in the year
WORKDAY	Returns the serial number of the date before or after a specified number of workdays
YEAR	Converts a serial number to a year
YEARFRAC	Returns the year fraction representing the number of whole days between start date and end date

G

goal seeking Determines the value that is required in a single input cell to produce a result that you want in a dependent (formula) cell. *See Solver.*

graphs *See Charts.*

H

histogram A procedure for producing data distributions and histogram charts. It accepts an input range and a bin range. *See Bin Range.*

hyperlinks A clickable object (or text) that opens another document.

I

input messages Messages inserted into a worksheet to let other users know what kind of data is expected to be input in a specific cell.

intentional circular references A *resolvable* circular reference in which Excel uses iteration to keep calculating until the formula results don't change anymore. In other words, the result gets increasingly accurate until it converges on the final solution.

K

keyboard shortcuts Also called shortcut keys. Keys pre-programmed on your keyboard to do the same things as equivalent menu commands. Usually displayed next to the menu item.

L

legends An explanatory list relating to the chart elements. Legends consist of text and a key. The key corresponds to the chart's series.

M

merging cells Creating a larger cell from any number of other cells, enabling the new cell to contain a single value.

N

name box This displays the name of the active cell in the current workbook.

P

passwords Passwords can be applied to worksheets in the Protect Sheet dialog box.

R

relative references When copying formulas, the cell references in the original change to keep their relative relationships with the new location.

S

Scroll Bar A bar along either the side or the bottom of the worksheet that enables you to use your mouse to view other parts of the worksheet not currently in the screen.

solver Determines the values that are required in multiple input cells to produce a result that you want. Moreover, because you can specify certain constraints to the problem, you gain significant problem-solving ability.

sorting Arranging the order of the rows in a list.

spreadsheet A collection of rows and columns displayed onscreen in a scrollable window.

syntax The way Excel requires a formula to be stated so that the program clearly understands.

T

templates Custom spreadsheets which are preconfigured shells that include text, row, and column headings, as well as formats, column widths, macros, and so on. You can use these templates to help create similar spreadsheets.

toolbars Groups of buttons representing commands.

Glossary

V

values Numbers used to represent a quantity of some type, dates, or times.

W

WYSIWYG (What You See Is What You Get) Used to describe software that enables the reader to see their document as it will appear in its final form, and that enables the user to edit within this view.

Index

INDEX

INDEX

Index

INDEX

H

handles, 224
- around objects, 186
- basic description of, 186

Header/Footer tab, 84

headers
- advantages of, 75
- alignment of, 84
- allowing more room for, 84
- controlling, 84–85
- custom, 84
- margin settings and, 82
- selecting, 84

help
- function descriptions provided by, 120

Help command, 312

Help menu, 302
- basic description of, 16–17

help screens, 300

Help system, 247

Hide command, 174

hiding
- columns, 78, 86, 108–109
- comments, 112
- details, 270–271
- fields, 270
- rows, 78, 86, 108–109
- toolbars, 184
- worksheets, 174

hierarchical conditions, 130

HLOOKUP function, 132

Home key, 34

home pages. *See* Web sites

horizontal alignment, 48

horizontal scroll bar, 12

horizontal split screens
- basic description of, 156–157
- setting up, 156–157

horizontal title panes
- basic description of, 158–159
- setting up, 158–159

HTML (HyperText Markup Language)
- basic description of, 295, 296
- files, downloading Web information to, 302
- format, saving files in, 61

- saving workbooks in, 295, 296
- source code, viewing, 296

human resources databases, 266

Hyperlink command, 298

Hyperlink function, 298

hyperlinks
- basic description of, 295–305
- creating, 298–299
- editing, 298
- increasing importance of, 298
- to Web sites, 298–299

I

identical data, in charts, 206

IF function, 130, 132, 137, 298, 316

illegal references, 102

images
- in charts, 212
- creating, 183–197
- inserting, 194–195

Import Text File command, 284

importing
- basic description of, 282–293
- files, from other software, 284–285

Increase Decimal button, 50

Increase Indent button, 46

indent button, 220

indenting, 46

Index tab, 16

Insert Clip Art dialog box, 302

Insert drop-down list, 162

Insert menu, 88, 298

inserting
- columns, 100–101
- graphics, 194–195
- rows, 100–101
- worksheets, 168–169

INT function, 126

integer values, 126

integration, of the Excel package, 217

intensity, of light effects, 188

interactivity, 296

interest rates, 124

internal clock, 146

Index

logical operators, 130
logos, 183, 190–191
longevity, performance, 130
lookup functions
    basic description of, 132
    using, 132
lookup tables, 132, 167
Lotus 1-2-3, 284, 286
lowercase letters, 310, 316

M

Macintosh, 286
macros, 296
    assigning, to buttons or objects, 314–315
    basic description of, 307–319
    code, altering, 316
    commands, 312
    creating, 308, 307–319
    placing, in workbooks, 308
    recording, 307, 308–309
    running, from a menu, 312–313
    undo action and, 308
mailing charges, 132
manipulating
    chart data, 233–243
    chart elements, 218–219
    objects, 186–187
margins
    measurement of, in inches, 82
    printing and, 75, 82–83
Margins tab, 82
marketing managers, 270
mathematical analysis, 238
mathematical functions
    basic description of, 126–127
    using, 126–127
MAX function, 122, 260
MEDIAN function, 260
memorization, 218
memory
    closing files and, 68
    empty worksheets and, 168
    linking workbooks and, 288

workbook displays and, 154
menu bar, 162
    location of, 8
menus
    assigning, to keystrokes or toolbar buttons, 310–311
    items, setting macros up as, 312
    running macros from, 312–313
Merge button, 46
Merge cells option, 46
Microsoft Office Update Web site, 16
Microsoft Web site, 302
MID function, 128
MIN function, 122, 260
minimizing windows, 6
minus sign (-), 24, 32
MODE function, 260
monitor, 54
    resolution, 160
    Zoom control and, 160
MONTH function, 146
mouse
    copying worksheets with, 172
    dragging data between worksheets with, 152
    manipulating date series with, 144
    selecting a range of cells with, 26
moving
    active cells, 254
    charts, 208–209
    data within or across worksheets, 102–103
    fields, 268
    legends, 224
    titles, 224
    toolbars, 162
    worksheets, 174–175
moving averages, 233, 238
multiple-sheet workbooks
    basic description of, 167
    copying worksheets in, 172–173
    creating formulas for, 176–177
    deleting worksheets in, 168–169
    grouping worksheets in, 178–179
    inserting worksheets in, 168–169
    moving worksheets in, 174–175
    renaming worksheets in, 170–171
    working with, 167–181

INDEX

INDEX

INDEX

Continued

INDEX

my2cents.idgbooks.com

Register This Book — And Win!

Visit **http://my2cents.idgbooks.com** to register this book and we'll automatically enter you in our fantastic monthly prize giveaway. It's also your opportunity to give us feedback: let us know what you thought of this book and how you would like to see other topics covered.

Discover IDG Books Online!

The IDG Books Online Web site is your online resource for tackling technology — at home and at the office. Frequently updated, the IDG Books Online Web site features exclusive software, insider information, online books, and live events!

10 Productive & Career-Enhancing Things You Can Do at www.idgbooks.com

- Nab source code for your own programming projects.

- Download software.

- Read Web exclusives: special articles and book excerpts by IDG Books Worldwide authors.

- Take advantage of resources to help you advance your career as a Novell or Microsoft professional.

- Buy IDG Books Worldwide titles or find a convenient bookstore that carries them.

- Register your book and win a prize.

- Chat live online with authors.

- Sign up for regular e-mail updates about our latest books.

- Suggest a book you'd like to read or write.

- Give us your 2¢ about our books and about our Web site.

You say you're not on the Web yet? It's easy to get started with IDG Books' *Discover the Internet,* available at local retailers everywhere.

DATE DUE

DEMCO 38-296